Daily De
Faith

365 inspiring stori

MW01235828

Sherry Hoppe

Your unfailing love, O Lord, is as vast as the heavens; your faithfulness reaches beyond the clouds. —*Psalm 36:5 (NLT)*

DAILY DEVOTIONS FOR FINDING FAITH BEHIND CLOUDS
365 inspiring stories and more with post-it-meditations

Copyright © 2012 by Sherry Hoppe

For information or permissions:

Pine Rose Press, L.L.C.
admin@pinerosepress.com
http://www.pinerosepress.com

ISBN-13: 978-0615687865
ISBN-10: 0615687865

Cover design by Kacie Yates,
Creative Citizens Premium Graphic and Web Design

Printed in the United States of America

Dedicated to the memory of my parents, whose
faith never dimmed under cloudy skies

May 28, 2016

Dear Crystal,

Happy Mother's Day!

You are a very Special Person and we are happy to have you in our lives.

I really enjoy reading this book along with other devotionals and sincerely I hope you do as well!

Love you,
Eddie

Other Books By

Sherry Lee Hoppe

HOOKED BUT NOT HOPELESS:
Escaping the Lure of Addiction
Co-author, Sylvia F. Yates
(Pine Rose Press, 2011)

FACES OF GRIEF:
Stories of Surviving Loss and Finding Hope
(Wakestone Press, 2011)

SIPS OF SUSTENANCE:
Grieving the Loss of Your Spouse
(Wakestone Press, 2010)

A MATTER OF CONSCIENCE:
Redemption of a hometown hero, Bobby Hoppe,
with Dennie B. Burke
(Wakestone Press, 2010)

MAXINE SMITH'S UNWILLING PUPILS:
Lessons Learned in Memphis's Civil Rights Classroom
Co-author, Bruce W. Speck
(University of Tennessee Press/Knoxville, 2007)

Acknowledgments

Inspirational stories have been used throughout history to teach, encourage, and stimulate—to motivate people to build better, more fulfilling lives. Recognizing this, while serving as a college/university president over a long number of years, I collected emotionally stirring stories for use in speeches and other communications. Because others knew I loved using stories to illuminate topics, they often sent me their own favorites. Many of those stories appear in this book.

The Internet provided another source for illustrations used to bring life to the daily meditations in *Finding Faith Behind Clouds*. While the capacity to research almost any subject and find information, quotes, or stories reveals abundant results, unfortunately, many of the web sites do not provide the source for the quote or story. When an internet search or emails from friends and colleagues had a link to a story, I have searched diligently to find the original source. When available, the original source or author is indicated on the page where the story appears. However, if the story was located on multiple web sites, the sites are not listed on the devotional page but are included in the list below.

Internet sites which provided a number of the stories include:
http://www.precious-testimonies.com
http://www.creativebiblestudy.com
http://lordsgrace.com
http://www.inspire21.com
http://www.values.com
http://www.websites-host.com
http://www.agiftofinspiration.com
http://www.thestorytelling-resource-centre.com
http://www.inspirationalarchive.com
http://inspirationalstories.com
http://www.cleanandsobernotdead.com
http://www.motivateus.com
http://www.helpothers.org
http://www.rogerknapp.com
http://www.turnbacktogod.com
http://godslittleacre.net
http://www.motivational-inspirational-corner.com
http://www.lectionary.org/hymnstories.htm

http://www.inspirationpeak.com
http://www.wow4u.com
http://www.slideshare.net
http://www.goal-setting-for-success.com
http://www.storiesaboutgod.org
http://academictips.org/blog
http://www.emmitsburg.net
http://www.frtommylane.com
http://www.thoughts-about-god.com

Should a reader know the source of any story used without credit, please contact me and I will ensure that the appropriate attribution is provided in the next edition of the book.

Love and special thanks go to my sisters, Flavia Fleming and Sylvia Yates, who carefully read a draft of the book and provided comments and insights that enhanced the final product.

Grey skies are just clouds passing over.

Introduction

Hope smiles from the threshold of the year
to come, whispering, "It will be happier...."
~Alfred Lord Tennyson, English poet

Another year begins—a fresh start, new resolutions, hope for a better tomorrow.

Something about January 1 urges us toward optimism, even though it is separated from the ending of December 31 with a single second of time. It is as if our contentment clock wants to be re-set, as if our spirit seeks renewal. What better way to recalibrate our lives than with stories that inspire us to...relish life...re-order our priorities...see beyond obstacles...show compassion...forgive others...let go of guilt...trust God with our problems...have a thankful heart...look for hidden treasures...and claim God's promises for security and strength.

This book of devotions, which covers all of these topics and more, is based on faith that all parts of our lives—those producing both joy and heartache—work together for good even when we cannot see how that can possibly be true (Romans 8:28). The stories and meditations turn us to the essence of faith—being sure of what we hope for and certain of what we do not see (Hebrews 11:1). That hope and certainty come from God's manifestation in our lives. As Arthur Foote wrote, "If God is, he is everywhere present. He is not an occasional visitor, nor ever more truly present than at this very instant. He is always ready to flow into our heart; indeed, he is there now—it is we who are absent."

Right now, why not make a pledge to be present with God every moment of every day this year? With his presence, God will hold you close when you feel weak and vulnerable, and he will show you how to find blue skies and sunshine behind dark clouds. My prayer is that the devotions in this book will lift you up with God's power and grace and that the post-it meditations for each day will keep you grounded in his love and care.

POST-IT MEDITATION

I will not waste the inspirational stories in this book. I will use them to encourage, motivate, and teach valuable life lessons. I will think about them, smile about them, and occasionally cry about them. Most of all, I will ask God to help me use the stories and devotions to motivate me to act in ways pleasing to him, to trust him, to believe in myself, and to change my life in positive ways for his glory.

January 1

Therefore do not be foolish, but understand what the will of the Lord is.
~*Ephesians 5:17 (ESV)*

Successful leaders often ask their top people, "What questions do I need to ask you so that I will have the information I need to make the best decisions for our organization?" Christians make similar queries, probing for answers about how to make choices that will help our lives be fulfilling and pleasing to God. Asking the right questions is the only way to get the right answers. But how do we know what to ask?

As we seek answers for our lives, especially at the dawning of a new year, we pray for guidance. Wouldn't it be wonderful if we could talk to God and hear an audible response? Are there questions you would like to ask him and hear his response with your ears—not just in your heart? One lady had a dream that she had just such an opportunity. In the dream, she asked God if she could interview him—if he had time to talk with her.

GOD smiled. "My time is eternity...what questions do you have in mind for me?"

"What surprises you the most about humankind?"

GOD answered, "That they get bored with childhood, that they rush to grow up, and then long to be children again. That they lose their health to make money...and then lose their money to restore their health. That by thinking anxiously about the future, they forget the present, such that they live in neither the present nor the future. That they live as if they would never die, and die as though they had never lived."

GOD's hand took the lady's hand...and both were silent for a while.

And then the lady asked, "As a parent, what are some of life's lessons you want your children to learn?"

GOD replied, "To learn they cannot make anyone love them. All they can do is let themselves be loved. To learn it is not good to compare themselves to others. To learn to forgive by practicing forgiveness. To learn it only takes a few seconds to open profound wounds in those they love, and it can take many years to heal them. To learn a rich person is not one who has the most but is one who needs the least. To learn there are people who love them dearly but simply do not yet know how to express or show their feelings. To learn two people can look at the same thing and see it differently. To learn it is not enough that they forgive one another, but they must also forgive themselves."

"Thank you for your time," the lady said humbly. "Is there anything else you would like your children to know?"

GOD smiled and said, "Just know that I am here. Always."

God is always there—you can turn to him, you can depend on him, and you can trust him whether the sky is azure blue or gloomy grey.

January 2

Time and tides wait on no one.
~14th century proverb

We sometimes feel as if we are in limbo. We want to accomplish something with our lives, take action that will help others, or even change the world in some way. The goals may be small: We want to go back to school, lose weight, learn to dance, or play golf or whatever. But we wait…

- ✓ *Until the kids are older*
- ✓ *Until we have more money*
- ✓ *Until the house is paid off*
- ✓ *Until we retire*
- ✓ *Until we have more energy*
- ✓ *Until our parents die…*
- ✓ *Or until countless other events happen*

Sometimes we forget life is a journey, not a destination. If we are always waiting for the right time to make a difference in our lives or in the lives of others, we may die before we begin. Each moment provides an opportunity. A situation—a call to action—is presented…

A mouse looked through the crack in the wall to see the farmer and his wife open a package.

"What food might this contain?" the mouse wondered. But soon he was devastated to discover it was a mousetrap. Retreating to the farmyard, the mouse proclaimed the warning: ""There is a mousetrap in the house!"

The chicken clucked and scratched, raised her head and said, "Mr. Mouse, I can tell this is a grave concern to you, but it is of no consequence to me. I cannot be bothered by it."

The mouse turned to the pig and told him, "There is a mousetrap in the house!"

The pig sympathized but said, "I am so very sorry, Mr. Mouse, but there is nothing I can do about it but pray. Be assured you are in my prayers."

The mouse turned to the cow and said, "There is a mousetrap in the house!"

The cow said, "Wow, Mr. Mouse. I'm sorry for you, but it's no skin off my nose."

The mouse returned to the house, head down and dejected, to face the farmer's mousetrap alone.

That very night a sound was heard throughout the house—like the sound of a mousetrap snaring its prey. The farmer's wife rushed to see what was caught. In the darkness, she did not see it was a venomous snake whose tail had been trapped. The snake bit the farmer's wife. Soon she had a high fever. Everyone knows you treat a fever with fresh chicken soup, so the farmer took his hatchet to the farmyard for the soup's main ingredient. But his wife's sickness continued, so friends and neighbors came to sit with her around the clock. To feed them, the farmer butchered the pig. Sadly, the farmer's wife did not get well and died. Many people came for her funeral, and the farmer slaughtered the cow to provide enough meat for everyone.

The mouse looked upon it all from his crack in the wall with great sadness.

The next time you hear someone is facing a problem and think it doesn't concern you, remember, when one of us is threatened, we are all at risk. We are all involved in this journey called life. We must keep an eye out for one another and make an extra effort to encourage and help each other.

Every person is a vital thread in another person's tapestry; our lives are woven together for a reason. When we need to take action for ourselves or others, we should do it then, not postpone it until later. Just as the tides come in every 12 hours without fail, time doesn't wait on us. Three simple "do's" to guide us:

DO IT NOW

DO IT WITH LOVE

DO IT REGARDLESS OF THE SACRIFICE

POST-IT MEDITATION FOR JANUARY 2

I can call a friend, write a letter or send a card,
visit someone in the hospital, or perform some other act of
love and kindness to brighten the spirits of others.
And, I can act on my own dreams as well.

January 3

God's voice thunders in marvelous ways; he does great things beyond our understanding.
~Job 37:5 (NIV)

Years ago in Scotland, the Clark family had a dream. Clark and his wife worked and saved, making plans to bring their children to the United States. It had taken years, but they had finally accumulated enough money and had gotten passports and reservations for the family on a new liner to the United States.

The entire family was full of anticipation and excitement about their new life. However, seven days before their departure, the youngest son was bitten by a dog. The doctor sewed up the boy but hung a yellow sheet on the Clarks' front door. Because of the possibility of rabies, they were being quarantined for fourteen days.

The family's dreams were dashed. They would not be able to make the trip to America as they had planned. The father, filled with frustration and anger, stomped to the dock to watch the ship leave–without the Clark family. Shedding tears of disappointment, the father cursed both his son and God for their misfortune.

Five days later, the tragic news spread throughout Scotland: The mighty Titanic had been hit by an iceberg. The unsinkable ship had sunk, taking hundreds of lives with it. The Clark family was to have been on that ship, but because the son had been bitten by a dog, they were left behind in Scotland.

When Mr. Clark heard the news, he hugged his son and thanked him for saving the family. He praised God for preserving their lives and turning what he had felt was a tragedy into a blessing.

With our limited human minds, we cannot fathom why icebergs sink ships or why shadowy skies bring problems into our lives, but we know rainbows can follow storms. And, we have witnessed God work great wonders, beyond our understanding, in lives today just as he did for the Clark family. We see only disappointment or despair in dark clouds, but God sees the silver lining he paints there for our lives. Why not rest secure in our faith, even when storm clouds gather and thunder rolls?

POST-IT MEDITATION FOR JANUARY 3
Thank you, God, for life, for faith, and for love—and especially for the assurance that you paint the sky behind the clouds.

January 4

...Those who are wise will find a time and a way to do what is right.
~Ecclesiastes 8:5 (NLT)

Too many people put off something that brings them joy just because they haven't thought about it, don't have it on their schedule, didn't know it was coming, or are too rigid to depart from their routine.

Have you ever thought about all those women on the Titanic who passed up dessert at dinner that fateful night in an effort to cut back?

How many women out there eat at home because their husbands suggest going out to dinner after something had been thawed? How often have your kids sat in silence while you looked at pictures on Facebook or Instagram? How many times when your child asks you to play with him do you say, "In a minute...."

One lady recalls, "I cannot count the times I called my sister and said, 'How about going to lunch in a half hour?' She would stammer one of these lines, 'I can't... I have clothes on the line... My hair is dirty... I wish I had known yesterday... I had a late breakfast... It looks like rain.' And the best one: 'It's Monday....' She died a few years ago. We never did have lunch together."

Because we cram so much into our lives, we live on a sparse diet of promises we make to ourselves when all the conditions are perfect! We'll go back and visit the grandparents when we get Stevie toilet-trained. We'll entertain when we replace the living-room carpet. We'll go on a second honeymoon when we get two more kids out of college.

Life has a way of accelerating as we get older. The days get shorter, and the list of promises to ourselves gets longer. One morning, we awaken, and all we have to show for our lives is a litany of "I'm going to," "I plan on," and "Someday, when things settle down a bit."

"I have a 'seize the moment' friend. When someone calls, she is open to adventure and available for trips. She keeps an open mind on new ideas. Her enthusiasm for life is contagious. You talk with her for five minutes, and you're ready to trade your bad feet for a pair of rollerblades and skip an elevator for a bungee cord."

The anonymous writer who wrote the above words added, *"My lips have not touched ice cream in 10 years. I love ice cream. It's just that I might as well apply it directly to my stomach with a spatula and eliminate the digestive process. The other day, I stopped the car and bought a triple-decker. If my car had hit an iceberg on the way home, I would have died happy."*

Not every day, but every now and then, we should all splurge on ice cream or something else that will bring us joy. And, we should stop long enough to call a loved one or spend time with a friend.

Forget what you SHOULD do for a moment and do what you would do if you knew you were going to die soon.

First, make sure you are ready to meet the Son of God, who "will come at an hour when you do not expect him" (Luke 12:40, NIV). When your soul is secure, then enjoy life—every day in every season of the year.

Walk in the snow, feeling the fresh invigoration of tingling icicles on your face. Make snow angels with your kids. Watch children playing on a merry-go-round or listen to rain drops dancing on the ground. Follow a butterfly's erratic flight or gaze at the sun fading into the night. Sit by a quiet lake, watching a mother duck herding her ducklings. Sleep late if you always arise at the break of dawn. Get up early and savor a sunrise if you routinely sleep late. Stroll barefooted in dew-laden grass. Take a stroll through the woods and behold the fall colors.

*Do you run through each day on the fly? When you ask "How are you?" do
you hear the reply?*

*When the day is done, do you lie in your bed with the next hundred chores
running through your head? Ever told your child, "We'll do it tomorrow," and
in your haste, not see his sorrow? Ever lost touch? Let a good friendship die? Just
call to say "Hi"?*

When you worry and hurry through your day, it is like an unopened
gift...thrown away. Life is not a race. Take it slower. Hear the music
before the song is over. The year is young and life is short—do something special today.

POST-IT MEDITATION FOR JANUARY 4
I will slow down and savor special moments of life.

January 5

Launch out into the deep and let down your nets for a catch.
~Luke 5:4 (NKJV)

When life is uncertain, we must still take action. Undoubtedly, failure
is possible, but is that really worse than doing nothing? How can we
ever make our lives better, more fulfilling, if we aren't willing to take a
chance—on God and on ourselves? Risk is scary, but it can also fill us
with anticipation and hope of success. Will we triumph, reach our goal?
Perhaps, but if not, to have tried and failed brings honor, not shame.

Are we satisfied with our lives, our jobs, our family relationships? Do
we seek deeper understanding, a more fulfilling career, stronger family ties? Do we have unmet goals that linger from our past? A new year
has just begun. Twelve months from now it will draw to a close. Will
we be bored, discontented, unhappy, or sad? Or will we be filled with
satisfaction and excitement about our accomplishments? The choice
is ours. The call to action rings in our head, but we have to answer it
with decisive deeds if we want the 31st of December to be dramatically
different from today.

When the disciples told Jesus they had fished all night and caught
nothing, he told them to go out in the deep and throw in their nets.
Amazingly, they pulled in more fish than their nets could carry. One
lesson from this story is that we can look for peace and contentment
on the surface of life, or we can go out in the deep, having faith that
when we cast our nets, they will come up full.

Each day is a new adventure into the unknown. God wants us to
think big. He wants us to pull in great catches. Our job is to follow his

guidance and not limit our expectations. If we surrender our complacency and qualms to him, we can advance with boldness toward a new and more satisfying life.

I've never been a fan of reality shows, but I became one after seeing *Extreme Makeover: Home Edition* produced in Clarksville, Tenn. As president of Austin Peay State University, I had been asked to award a college scholarship to a wounded Ft. Campbell soldier whose home was to be totally rebuilt to accommodate his injury. I was thus invited to witness the building of the home. From that day, I became a fan of Ty Pennington and the show he hosts. It was only later, though, that I learned how Ty was inspired to begin his popular television series.

Ty says he took to the fast-paced building environment easily. Not only has he been good with a hammer since his youth, he is also "Mr. Energy." His mom says he has always been that way. As a kid, he was constantly in trouble at school because he couldn't concentrate on anything—today, his behavior problems would have been quickly diagnosed as ADHD (attention-deficit/hyperactivity disorder). Back then, all his mother knew to do was pray.

One day, sent to the back yard after starting to pry off the leg of a piano so he could use it to build something, Ty decided to turn a big idea that had been growing in his head into reality. He had been collecting old planks and two-by-fours to build a tree house—"not a wimpy Dennis the Menace tree house, but a deluxe three-story one." After he got underway, a few friends came by and pitched in. By the end of the day, he "stepped back and stared upward like [the structure] was the Empire State Building." His mom's jaw dropped when she saw the tree house. At that moment, Ty says, he realized he had found something he could do—something both he and his mom could be proud of despite what anyone else, especially his teachers, thought about him. "There was a plan for me. I held on to that.... I wasn't stupid. God had given me skills that didn't show up on an SAT exam." His mother's prayers had been answered—she had hope for her problem kid.

Later, as an adult, Ty continued to use his talents. "I'd seen how God could use my gifts and turn them into something." He began to wonder if he could "turn it up a notch" and use his talents to really help people. Not too far in the future, he instituted Extreme Makeover: Home Edition. Today he says he would never have guessed having such a show would be his career. "But then all along I think I've been part of a larger plan." Making impossible dreams and hopes come true for people who have lost jobs, faced catastrophic illnesses, and suffered war injuries, Ty says, "is one of the most amazing things you can do for an individual, a gift not just for the recipient but also for the giver."

God can give us the courage to think big when faced with disappointment and discouragement—this is true for Ty Pennington, for the recipients of the houses he builds, and for you.

TY PENNINGTON story adapted from Guideposts

When I am tempted to sit idle, accepting life as it is, I will remember
unknown possibilities may come from waters so deep I can't see the bottom.
With faith, I will cast my net and seek opportunities to renew my life.

January 6

Trust in the Lord with all your heart and lean not on your own
understanding.
~ Proverbs 3:5 (NIV)

A ship from the Orient became lost on its journey to South America, and because it had underestimated its water supply, its crew and passengers faced a certain death. Suddenly, a ship appeared in the distance, and the weak crew flashed a message, asking it to share its water. The other vessel responded, "Dip where you are." The captain thought this was insane—they were on the ocean and the salty water would make the situation worse, not better. He personally signaled the frantic request for water again, but the same response came back: "Dip where you are." Exasperated, but without any other help available, the captain lowered a rope and bucket. When the bucket was lifted, the captain touched his finger to the liquid and then to his tongue—shocked, he tasted pure water. Later, he learned his ship had been in the center of a mile-wide current where the Amazon River was still making its surging thrust into the ocean.

Just as Christ knew where the fish were swimming, the passing vessel's captain knew where the fresh water was gushing. The lesson is simple: Solutions to life's problems may be right in front of us. The disciples dropped their nets in deep water because they trusted Jesus. The ship's captain dipped his bucket because it was the only hope he had. If we reach out in faith, we, too, may find the fresh water we so desperately need for our souls. We may not be able to see the clear current—it may be invisible in the sea of life—but it is there waiting for us to dip and find. And remember, looking isn't the same as seeing.

God deals with impossibilities effortlessly. Whether it is a masterful design that puts the flow of pure Amazon water into the midst of a salty sea, or his plan that holds the solutions for all our needs, nothing is too hard for him. Moreover, he "is able to do immeasurably more than all we ask or imagine." The one caveat is that what is done must be "according to his power that is at work within us" (Ephesians 3:20, NIV). To allow God to do more than we ask or think, we must allow him into our hearts so he can work within our innermost being.

POST-IT MEDITATION FOR JANUARY 6
*When I am struggling and life seems hopeless,
I will not fail to look for the possibilities
that may be hidden all around me.*

January 7

Be kind and compassionate to one another….
~Ephesians 4:32 (NIV)

It was a bitterly cold evening in northern Virginia many years ago. Winter's frost glazed the old man's beard while he waited for a ride across the river. The wait seemed endless. His body became numb and stiff from the frigid north wind.

The chilled man heard the faint, steady rhythm of approaching hooves galloping along the frozen path. Anxiously, he watched as several horsemen rounded the bend. He let the first one pass by without an effort to get his attention. Then another passed by, and another. Finally, the last rider neared the spot where the old man sat like a snow statue. As this one drew near, the old man caught the rider's eye and said, "Sir, would you mind giving an old man a ride to the other side? There doesn't appear to be a passageway by foot."

Reining his horse, the rider replied, "Sure thing. Hop aboard." Seeing the old man was unable to lift his half-frozen body from the ground, the horseman dismounted and helped him onto the horse. The horseman took the old man not just across the river, but to his destination, which was a few miles away.

As they neared the tiny but cozy cottage, the horseman's curiosity caused him to inquire, "Sir, I noticed you let several other riders pass by without making an effort to secure a ride. Then I came up and you immediately asked me for a ride. I'm curious why, on such a bitter winter night, you would wait and ask the last rider. What if I had refused and left you there?"

The old man lowered himself slowly down from the horse, looked the rider straight in the eyes, and replied, "I've been around these here parts for some time. I reckon I know people pretty good." The old-timer continued, "I looked into the eyes of the other riders and immediately saw there was no concern for my situation. It would have been useless to ask them for a ride. But when I looked into your eyes, kindness and compassion were evident. I knew, then and there, your gentle spirit would welcome the opportunity to give me assistance in my time of need."

Those heartwarming comments touched the horseman deeply. "I'm most grateful for what you have said," he told the old man. "May I never get too busy in my own affairs that I fail to respond to the needs of others with kindness and compassion."

With that, Thomas Jefferson turned his horse around and made his way back to the White House.

We all send messages without words. When you pass by someone in need, what do they see in your face? Is your expression inviting or dismissive? What kind of spirit from your heart is reflected in your eyes?

POST-IT MEDITATION FOR JANUARY 7
*Help me, God, to be tender-hearted
enough to help those in need.*

January 8

What we do for ourselves dies with us. What we do for others and the world remains and is immortal.
~Albert Pike, attorney, Confederate officer, and writer

Too many times, people in the 21st century look the other way, not wanting to spend time or effort helping someone else. Too often, no one wants to sacrifice for another.

It hasn't always been that way. In a prison camp during World War II, a man named Ernest Gordon witnessed the ultimate sacrifice:

Life in the prison camp had reached a desperate state. There was so little food and so little water and such a severe lack of medical help that there was continual "warfare" among the prisoners, each one trying to get enough of what he needed to survive— and get it any way he could. Everyone was for himself against the others.

Then one day I was out on a work detail of twelve men, out about two miles from the camp.

We were digging a trench. At the end of the day, the guards instructed us to turn in our shovels. We threw them all in a pile, and when the guards counted the shovels in preparation for heading back to camp, they found there were only eleven.

One, they assumed, had been hidden for a weapon or escape tool to be used later. The prisoners were lined up and told that the guilty man must confess. No one spoke out.

And then we heard the frightening words: "If the one who hid his shovel does not come forward now, you will all be shot."

We knew the guard's threat was not just talk. As we stood there, fearful for our lives, one man stepped forward and said, "I did it." He was shot immediately and thrown into the trench, and the other eleven were marched back to camp.

When we arrived there, the shovels were recounted, and there were twelve. In the earlier count, there had been a mistake.

A remarkable change occurred in the prison camp as the story of that one man's death circulated. People started helping one another, sharing scraps of food, tending to those who were ill.

As 1 John 3:16 (NIV) tells us, "This is how we know what real love is: Christ laid down his life for us. And we ought to lay down our lives for our brother." Sacrificing should be contagious.

POST-IT MEDITATION FOR JANUARY 8
I will strive to be more self-sacrificing
in my relationships with others.

January 9

The grace of God operates at a profound level in the life of a loving person.
~Brennan Manning, Episcopal priest, recovering alcoholic, and author

Many years ago, a minister shared a sermon anecdote (original source unknown) that was later repeated in Brennan Manning's book titled *The Ragamuffin Gospel:*

One icy, bone-chilling night in January, 1935, during the depths of the Great Depression, Mayor Fiorello LaGuardia arrived at night court in one of the poorest areas in the city. He told the judge to take the night off and stepped to the bench to preside over the court himself. A short time later, an old woman dressed in threadbare clothing stood before him, charged with stealing a loaf of bread.

"Did you steal the bread?" LaGuardia asked. Confessing, the old woman explained that her daughter's husband had run out on the family, her daughter was sick, and her two grandchildren had nothing to eat. Turning to the shopkeeper, the mayor asked if given these circumstances, he really wanted to press charges. The shopkeeper felt sorry for the woman but said it was a bad neighborhood, and she needed to be punished as an example for everyone else.

LaGuardia had a dilemma. Under the law, the woman was guilty and would have to be punished. Turning to the old woman, he said, "I've got to punish you. The law makes no exceptions—ten dollars or ten days in jail." But even as he pronounced sentence, the mayor was already reaching into his pocket. He extracted a bill and tossed it into his famous sombrero, saying, "Here is the ten dollar fine which I now remit; and furthermore, I am going to fine everyone in this courtroom fifty cents for living in a town where a person has to steal bread so her grandchildren can eat. Mr. Bailiff, collect the fines and give them to the defendant."

Moments later, the old lady stood bewildered as the bailiff turned $47.50 over to her—money collected from the red-faced grocery store owner, almost seventy petty criminals, people with traffic violations, and New York City policemen. Then, each person who just paid fifty cents gave the mayor a standing ovation.

After concluding the story, Manning wrote, "What an extraordinary moment of grace for anyone present in that courtroom!"

POST-IT MEDITATION FOR JANUARY 9
God, may I have grace to help,
rather than condemn, others.

January 10

Those who stand firm during testing are blessed. They are tried and true. They will receive the life God has promised to those who love him as their reward.
~James 1:12 (CEB)

Many years ago, Indian youths went away in solitude to prepare for manhood. One of these youths hiked into a peaceful valley, shadowed by green trees, laden with smiling flowers. After fasting for two days, he looked up at the tall rugged peak, capped with silvery snow, at the highest point of the mountains surrounding the valley. It came to him that he should test himself against the mountain, so he put on his buffalo-hide shirt, threw his blanket over his shoulders, and set off to climb to the top of the peak.

When he arrived at the top, the youth stood on the rim, thinking, "I can see the whole world." Filled with pride, he heard a slight noise at his feet and looked down, where he saw a snake. Before he could move, the snake spoke:

"I am about to die. It is too cold for me up here, and I am freezing. I have no food and will starve to death. Put me under your shirt and take me down to the valley. Please."

But the youth had been forewarned about snakes. "I know your kind," he said. "You are a rattlesnake. If I pick you up, you will bite, and it will kill me."

"Oh, no," responded the snake. "I will not hurt you if you save me."

Although he resisted for a while, the youth finally gave in to the snake's persuasive words. Tucking the snake under his shirt, he carried it down to the valley, where he laid it gently on the green grass. Suddenly, the snake coiled, shook its rattles, and bit him on the leg.

"But you promised," cried the youth.

"You knew what I was when you picked me up," said the snake as it slithered away.

Helping a snake or playing with fire is dangerous. So is associating with people whose values differ from ours or involving ourselves in materials or substances that lead to destructive behavior. When we reach for a beer, a *Playboy* magazine, a joint, a narcotic pain pill, or just something as simple as a new car magazine, we need to know what we are picking up. The beer, pain pill, or joint may lead to addiction, the *Playboy* magazine to pornography, or the new car magazine to a purchase we can't afford.

Alone, many of the above items will not lead to sin. But without caution and moderation in all we do, paths sometimes lead where we never intended to go. As long as we know what we are picking up and stand firm if we are tested, we can stay in God's will, receiving the life God has promised us.

POST-IT MEDITATION FOR JANUARY 10
I can avoid temptation more easily if I don't pick up a snake.

January 11

I will not keep silent but will pay back in full; I will pay it back into their laps.
~Isaiah 65:6 (NIV)

One day a man saw an old lady stranded on the side of the road. Even in the dim light of day, he could see she needed help. So he pulled up in front of her Mercedes and got out. His Pontiac was still sputtering when he approached her.

Despite the smile on his face, she was worried. No one had stopped to help for the last hour or so. Was he going to hurt her? He didn't look safe; he looked poor and hungry. He could see she was frightened, standing out there in the cold, so he said, "I'm here to help you, ma'am. Why don't you wait in your car where it's warm? By the way, my name is Bryan Anderson."

Bryan quickly changed the tire. As he was tightening the lug nuts, the lady rolled down the window and began to talk to him. She couldn't thank him enough for coming to her aid.

Bryan just smiled as he closed her trunk. The lady asked how much she owed him. Any amount would have been all right with her. Bryan never thought twice about being paid. This was not a job to him. This was helping someone in need, and God knows there were many who had given him a hand in the past. He told her if she really wanted to pay him back, the next time she saw someone who needed help, she could give that person the assistance needed, adding, "And think of me."

He waited until the lady started her car and drove off. It had been a cold and depressing day, but he felt good as he headed home, disappearing into the twilight.

A few miles down the road the lady saw a small cafe. She went in to grab a bite to eat and take the chill off before she made the last leg of her trip home. The waitress, about eight-months pregnant, came over with a smile on her face, cheerful and helpful. The old lady wondered how the tired employee could be so warm and welcoming to a stranger. Then she remembered Bryan.

After the lady finished her meal, she paid with a hundred dollar bill. The waitress quickly went to get change, but the old lady slipped out the door before she returned. *Back at the table, the waitress noticed something written on the napkin. There were tears in her eyes when she read what the lady wrote: "Somebody helped me out today, the way I'm helping you. If you really want to pay me back, here is what you do: Do not let this chain of love end with you." Under the napkin were four more $100 bills.*

That night when the waitress got home from work and climbed into bed, she was thinking about the money and what the lady had written. How could the lady have known how much she and her husband needed it? With the baby due next month, it was going to be hard....

She knew how worried her husband was, and as he lay sleeping next to her, she gave him a soft kiss and whispered soft and low, "Everything's going to be all right. I love you, Bryan Anderson."

God works in mysterious ways, his good deeds coming in and out of our lives on angels' wings—or from men and women who heed his instructions to care for others as he would.

POST-IT MEDITATION FOR JANUARY 11
God, give me a heart of love and caring for those less fortunate, asking nothing in return.

January 12

If the skies fall, one may hope to catch larks.
~Francois Rabelais, French Renaissance writer, doctor, monk, and Greek scholar

Chicken Little screamed that the sky is falling; and, sadly, we sometimes succumb to such hysterical wisdom. *In the original version of the story, found in Buddhist scriptures, a hare is hit on the head by falling fruit and starts a stampede among the other animals because he thinks the world is coming to an end. A lion, wiser than the other animals, halts the panic, investigates what dropped on the hare, and restores calm.*

In western forms of the tale, an acorn falls on a chicken's head, and he becomes unreasonably afraid. As he races to tell the king the sky is falling, he convinces other animals of his doomsday warning by telling them, "I saw it with my eyes, I heard it with my ears, and a bit of it fell on my head." Some versions of the story have happy endings, providing a lesson that we should have courage instead of assuming the worst. In less positive versions, the chicken and his companions are duped, usually by a fox, who takes advantage of their irrational alarm.

The moral in all of the adaptations of the story: Don't believe everything you are told.

Daily, we are faced with possibilities that something bad may happen to us. But the odds of our fears becoming reality are usually quite slim. Even so, we worry and fret, fearful our worst imaginings may come true. How can we fight back against our fright?

Second Timothy 1:7 (KJV) tells us, "God has not given us a spirit of fear, but of power and of love and of a sound mind." We must use our sound mind to claim the power within us, surrendering our fears to God. Then, as Rabelais suggests, if the sky falls, perhaps God will send us larks to catch.

POST-IT MEDITATION FOR JANUARY 12
When I am tempted to panic about my future, I will submit my worries to God in prayer, assured he will be there to guide me through good and bad times.

January 13

The Good Lord knows what He's doing. And, as the years pass, he's busy using the dry spells, and the stormy seasons, to do a job of beautifying our souls....
~Unknown Author

A stranger, clearly a "city type," stopped by a farmer's house one day and wanted to buy an old barn sitting by the road. The farmer, shocked that the man thought the barn was beautiful, told him he had a funny idea of beauty. The barn had been a handsome building in its day, but lots of winters had passed, with snow, ice, and howling winds weathering the structure. And the summer's scorching sun added its damage, bleaching the barn silver.

The man said he was going to use the lumber from the old barn to line the walls of his den in a new country home he was building down the road, adding you couldn't buy new wood that beautiful.

Standing in the field staring silently at the old barn, the farmer grasped that humans are a lot like the worn structure. Days of sunshine and stormy seasons of our lives have turned us silver gray, but our souls have been beautified in a way that wouldn't have been possible with balmy weather.

The day the old barn was taken down and hauled away, the farmer reckoned we humans will likewise be hauled off to heaven to take on whatever new purpose the Lord has for us in the great ranch in the sky. "And," he added, "I suspect we'll be more beautiful then for the seasons we've been through here...and just maybe even add a bit of beauty to our Father's house."

Proverbs 16:31 (NIV) reminds us, "Gray hair is a crown of splendor; it is attained by a righteous life." Whether your hair is gray or still untouched by years, you can work toward growing more beautiful with time. Weathered barn wood or hair refined to silver—both can come from living a good life, doing what we were made to do. When our task is finished, we will move on to a higher purpose.

POST-IT MEDITATION FOR JANUARY 13
When I am weathering the seasons of life, I will remember the storms and sunshine come from God to refine and beautify me for his kingdom.

January 14

At the end of the day, a loving family should find everything forgivable.
~Mark V. Olsen and Will Sheffer, Big Love, "Easter"

Aesop tells the story of a farmer who had a quarrelsome family:

Attempting to reconcile the differences disrupting family life, the farmer told his sons to stack a bunch of sticks before him. Then, after laying the sticks parallel to one another and binding them, he challenged his sons, one after the other, to pick up the bundle and break it. Despite their best efforts, none of the sons succeeded. Not surprised, the farmer then untied the bundle and gave his sons the sticks to break one by one, which they were able to do easily. When they had finished, the farmer said, "Thus, my sons, as long as you remain united, you are a match for anything, but differ and separate, you are undone."

And so it is with our families. If we stick together, we can conquer any problem and any adversary. Sure, families are like fudge, sweet with a few nuts. Others may even be tart like persimmons. But we love them all—or should. Family ties are sometimes stretched by disagreements, and major ones threaten the ties that bind us together, but they should never be severed.

F. Scott Fitzgerald reminded us, "Family quarrels are bitter things. They don't go by any rules. They're not like aches or wounds; they're more like splits in the skin that won't heal because there's not enough material." Central to strong family relationships is the lack of such bitterness. We can simply agree to disagree, without resorting to dog fights, which drag everyone down and often cause deep injuries.

As David wrote in Psalm 133:1 (NIV), "… how good and pleasant it is when people live together in unity!" We should never let the sun set on harsh words or disagreements within our family. Clear the air with an apology or an acknowledgment of wrong, and sleep will be pure and deep. And, the morrow will be peaceful and pleasant.

January 15

For I know the plans I have for you…plans to prosper you and not to harm you; plans to give you hope and a future.
~Jeremiah 29:11 (NIV)

Many years ago a king had a servant who was a faithful believer in the goodness of God. He often told his master God was never wrong, that in all circumstances God had a purpose and a plan. One day when the king and his servant were out hunting, a wild animal attacked the king. The servant fought off the animal but not before the king had lost a finger. Furious, the king didn't thank the slave for saving his life, instead berating him because his "good" God had allowed such a catastrophe to happen. Still fervent in his beliefs, the servant told the king, "I don't know why God let this happen, but I am convinced he has a purpose. He is perfect, and he does not make mistakes." Incensed the slave would not acknowledge God was wrong in allowing him to lose a finger, the king had him thrown in jail.

Sometime later the king and another servant went on a hunt. This time, they fell into a band of man-eating savages. Soon, the king was strapped to an altar where a knife was raised above his head. Just before the knife was lowered toward his chest, the attacker noticed the king was missing a finger. He was thus imperfect and not suitable for eating. The savages let him go but kept his servant.

When the king returned to his castle, he sent for the first slave and told him he was right—God was good. The lack of a finger had saved his life. But the king had one question, "If God is always right, then why did he let me throw you into prison?"

The servant smiled, saying, "If I had been with you, I would have been sacrificed in your place since I have all my fingers."

When we wonder why God lets us experience trouble and sorrow, the story of the king and his slave can be a reminder God's plan is not always evident to us when we are suffering. If we trust that he cares for us and if we believe that his will is perfect, it will help us endure the days when clouds overhang our lives.

POST-IT MEDITATION FOR JANUARY 15
When I doubt God's goodness, I will remember nothing that happens to me is random—each circumstance and event is part of God's plan for my life.

January 16

But if any of you lack wisdom, you should pray to God, who will give it to you because God gives generously and graciously to all. But when you pray, you must believe and not doubt at all. Whoever doubts is like a wave in the sea that is driven and blown about by the wind. If you are like that, unable to make up your mind and undecided in all you do, you must not think that you will receive anything from the Lord.
~James 1:5-8 (GNT)

In June of 1859, Frenchman Charles Blondin became the first person to cross a tightrope stretched over a quarter of a mile across the mighty Niagara Falls. Amazingly, he walked across the 160 feet above the roaring falls not just once but several times, each time daring a different feat. Once he crossed in a sack, once on stilts, once on a bicycle. He even crossed in the dark. Unbelievably, one time he carried a stove and cooked an omelet.

Another time, Blondin walked blindfolded while pushing a wheelbarrow. Spectators held their breaths and then broke into resounding applause and loud cheers as he reached the other side safely. Turning to the crowd, Blondin asked, "Do you believe I can carry a person across in this wheelbarrow?"

The enthusiastic crowd shouted, "Yes, yes, yes! You are the greatest tightrope walker in the world. You can do anything."

"Okay, then," Blondin began, asking, "Which one of you wants to get in the wheelbarrow?"

The crowd suddenly grew silent. No one stepped forward.

Espousing belief in Blondin was blatantly different from trusting him with their lives.

Blondin's story illuminates a contrast between spoken faith and true faith. We sometimes say we believe, but our actions prove we truly don't. It is easy to say we believe in God, his love, and his protection, but when we are asked to ride across a tightrope with him, doubts descend and we are driven and tossed by the wind. If we truly trust God, we can get in the wheelbarrow and know he will carry us safely across the tumultuous ravines of our lives to heaven's shore.

POST-IT MEDITATION FOR JANUARY 16
I will pray for faith to walk tightropes with God.

January 17

I believe in the sun even if it isn't shining.
I believe in love even when I am alone.

I believe in God even when he is silent.
~World War II refugee

Believing in God when all is well with our lives is easy. Although we sometimes forget him when clear blue skies hang overhead, he is there watching over and blessing us even if we become submerged in the busyness of our lives. Our faith moves to front and center, though, when dark clouds cover the sun and the stars. We fall to our knees, pleading for mercy and grace—heal our loved one, help us find a job, save a family member from the abyss of addiction, or intervene in whatever peril threatens our lives.

If God answers "yes," we praise him for his goodness. If he seems deaf to our pleas, we pray harder. And if he shuts the door in our face, allowing the unthinkable to happen, we are faced with two choices: accept the bad as part of God's will for our lives, or turn away, tempted to fear God is not good, that he is uncaring or even malicious.

We stand staring at the closed door, slammed and bolted. To let our faith die, or to look for strength to hang on to our beliefs, those are the questions.

When a section of river is impossible to navigate, locks are built to lift boats, enabling them to float upward until the lock opens, freeing them to sail on in the higher body of water. Without the lock, the boat would be stuck, unable to continue. Faith does the same maneuver for our hearts and minds, enabling us to rise above whatever is holding us back. When the sun isn't shining, when we are alone, and when God appears silent, faith empowers us to believe anyway, just as the lock enables a boat to rise above impassable waters.

Like any good mother, when Karen discovered another baby was on the way, she did what she could to help her three-year-old son, Michael, prepare for a new sibling. They found out the new baby was going to be a girl, and day after day, night after night, Michael sang to his sister in Mommy's tummy. The pregnancy progressed normally for Karen, but complications arose during delivery.

Finally, Michael's little sister was born, but she was in serious condition. With sirens howling in the night, the ambulance rushed the infant to a distant neonatal intensive care unit. As the days inched by, the little girl became worse. The pediatric specialist told the parents to prepare for the worst.

Karen and her husband contacted a local cemetery about a burial plot. They had fixed up a special room in their home for the new baby; now they planned a funeral.

Michael kept begging his parents to let him see his sister, "I want to sing to her," he said, but kids are not allowed in intensive care. Karen made up her mind. She decided to take Michael whether they liked it or not. If he didn't see his sister now, he might never see her.

As Karen held Michael up to the tiny infant who was losing the battle for life, in the pure voice of a three-year-old, the little boy began to sing, "You are my sunshine, my only sunshine. You make me happy when skies are grey."

As the mother watched in amazement, the tiny infant responded, her pulse rate calming. "Keep singing, Michael," the mother urged.

"You'll never know, dear, how much I love you. Please don't take my sunshine away."

By now, the ragged breathing had become steady and strong. Michael's little sister relaxed as healing rest seemed to sweep over her. The love of her younger brother had lifted the baby above her illness. Like a boat in a lock, the baby had been raised to sail on into life. The very next day she was well enough to go home. A miracle of a brother's love and the power of God.

John 20:31 (NIV) reminds us, "By believing you may have life in his name." Belief isn't always answered with a miracle, but how marvelous when it is!

POST-IT MEDITATION FOR JANUARY 17
*When dark clouds hover, I will trust God
to help me rise above the conditions of my life.*

January 18

Every child is an artist. The problem is how to remain an artist once he grows up.
~Pablo Picasso, Spanish artist

A little boy, enthusiastically drawing an Indian teepee, had his excitement squashed by his first grade teacher. Walking by his desk, she criticized him for not being more realistic. In a belittling tone, she asked, "Don't you know there were no purple teepees?" Crestfallen, the little boy hung his head in embarrassment as his classmates chuckled.

In the second grade, the child's teacher told her class they could draw anything they wanted. Remembering the rejection from the previous year, the little boy sat staring at the blank piece of paper in front of him. As the teacher walked around the room, the boy's heart pounded like a tom-tom in his chest. But his fears vanished when the teacher stopped by his desk, gently touched his head, and in a quiet voice said, "Snowfall. How clean and white and beautiful."

How often do we close down creativity by our "superiority"? And, it's not just children we put down, however unintentionally. We imply others aren't worthy or acceptable if they don't fall in line with how we believe they should behave or act. Instead of encouraging their efforts, we dampen their feelings and self-image by critical remarks or sometimes just the disapproving look on our faces. Each of us has the capacity to lift others up or put them down—we need to be thoughtful and careful in our words, looks, and actions.

Christ treated all people the same—the prostitute was as acceptable to him as Mary Magdalene. If we are trying to walk in his footsteps, why, then, do we not respect people who are unattractive, who dress differently, who speak in unfamiliar ways, or whose skin, religion, or ideas are diverse? As Christians, we should understand and value others, treating them kindly.

Children don't see rich or poor, colored or white, Baptist or Buddhist, superior or inferior—they see a potential friend. If only we could hold onto the innocence and unconditional love of a child…. Instead, we sometimes squeeze the goodness and creativity out of them with our thoughtless ways.

Living a Christ-like life often requires adjusting our attitude and our views—toward a parent, a child, a spouse, a friend, or someone else in our community. We should praise people for blank pages, purple teepees, and any other attempt to be creative or helpful.

POST-IT MEDITATION FOR JANUARY 18
I will resist sending out sparks of negativity. Instead, I will light fires of encouragement and support by seeing the beauty of a blank page and coloring it with love and acceptance.

January 19

The Lord will guard you; he is by your side to protect you.
~Psalm 121:5 (GNT)

A man who worked for a company that did maintenance work at remote sites was working in an isolated area of central Pennsylvania prone to heavy rainstorms with an extraordinary amount of lightning. The property was surrounded by a 10-foot high cyclone fence for security, with gates to allow access to a road running through the center of the property.

Around 1:30 p.m., the man noticed heavy rain clouds coming over the nearby hills and knew a storm was approaching. When the sky started to darken and the wind picked up and the first few heavy raindrops began falling, he locked one of the gates. Then, as the first burst of lightning lit up the sky and the first crash of thunder shook the air, he got back into his truck and pulled inside the second gate. The latch was broken on this gate, and he had to wrap a short length of chain around the gatepost and through the edge of the panel.

By then the lightning was closer, and the rain was starting to get a little heavier. The worker shoved the thick chain around the post and threaded it through the diamond-shaped openings in the fence on the gate and held both ends in one hand. Next, with his other hand, he took the open lock off the fence, where it had been hanging. Just when he was about to put the lock on the chain, a gnat flew into his open right eye. It stung so much he instantly dropped the lock and the chain to put his hands to his eye, taking one step back at the same time.

Not a second later, lightning struck somewhere close by, and he saw the whole fence in front of him light up and glow bright blue. That beautiful but lethal shade of light blue from high-voltage radiation nearly filled in all those little diamond-shaped openings in the fence.

Awestruck, he realized what had just happened. He was standing, wet, in rain, holding onto a chain threaded through a metal fence that was just about to be struck by lightning, when an insignificant insect, an annoying pest, a bug, flew into his eye and saved his life. He was completely unharmed, not even a tingle was felt.

When he tells the story, the man always closes with, "Now, I've always believed the Lord watches over us, but I don't know for sure just how he protects us. At night when I lie down to go to sleep, I thank the Lord for his protection. Who knows how many times he has saved my life, and I don't even know about it."

POST-IT MEDITATION FOR JANUARY 19
Thank you, God, for looking out for me,
even when I don't know it.

January 20

So I tell you to be free in giving to your brother, to those in need, and to the poor in your land.
~Deuteronomy 15:11 (NLV)

A nurse took the tired, anxious serviceman to the bedside.

"Your son is here," she said to the old man. She had to repeat the words several times before the patient's eyes opened.

Heavily sedated because of the pain from his heart attack, the man dimly saw the young uniformed Marine standing outside the oxygen tent. He reached out his hand. The Marine wrapped his toughened fingers around the elderly man's limp ones, squeezing a message of love and encouragement.

The nurse brought a chair so the Marine could sit beside the bed. All through the night the young Marine sat in the poorly lighted ward, holding the old man's hand and offering him words of love and strength. Occasionally, the nurse suggested the Marine move away and rest awhile. He refused. Whenever the nurse came into the ward, the Marine was oblivious of her and of the night noises of the hospital—the clanking of the oxygen tank, the laughter of the night staff members exchanging greetings, the cries and moans of the other patients. Now and then she heard him say a few gentle words. The dying man said nothing, only holding tightly to his son all through the night.

Along toward dawn, the old man died. The Marine released the now lifeless hand he had been holding and went to tell the nurse. While she did what she had to do, he waited.

Finally, she returned. She started to offer words of sympathy, but the Marine interrupted her.

"Who was that man?" he asked.

Startled, the nurse responded, "He was your father."

"No, he wasn't," the Marine replied. "I never saw him before in my life."

"Then why didn't you say something when I took you to him?"

"I knew right away there had been a mistake, but I also knew he needed his son, and his son just wasn't here. When I realized he was too sick to tell whether I was his son, knowing how much he needed me, I stayed."

All around us people are in need—people without families close by. How blessed they might be by a small effort on our part.

POST-IT MEDITATION FOR JANUARY 20
*Help me, God, to care about those in need
as much as the young Marine did.*

January 21

Love the Lord your God with all your heart and with all your soul and with all your strength.
~Deuteronomy 6:5 (CEB)

How we spend our time reflects our priorities. Often, we say our families are the most important part of our lives. And, not infrequently, we put God at the top of our list. But, if we take the 24 hours of each day and list what we do, we may find what we say doesn't match what we do.

In recent years, Facebook, Twitter, Instagram, and other social media sites absorb increasing amounts of time. If we sit in front of a notebook or tablet computer or a smart phone and connect with friends, spending hours going through their pictures or uploading our own, posting and reading messages, it has to take time away from something: spending time with our children, cooking or cleaning, taking care of our yard, managing our finances, reading our Bible, or even going to church, and on and on. It happens so slowly we may not realize our priorities have shifted.

Social media networking is not all bad. It can reconnect old friends and help us make new ones. But the downside may outweigh the good. If it dominates our time or if we have withdrawal symptoms when we are not online for a day or more, then it has become a problem.

While at the park one day, a woman sat down next to a man on a bench near a play-ground. "That's my son over there," she said, pointing to a little boy in a red sweater who was gliding down the slide.

"He's a fine looking boy," the man said. "That's my son on the swing in the blue sweater." Then, looking at his watch, he called to his son. "What do you say we go, Todd?"

Todd pleaded, "Just five more minutes, Dad. Please? Just five more minutes." The man nodded and Todd continued to swing to his heart's content.

Minutes passed and the father stood and called again to his son. "Time to go now?" Again Todd pleaded, "Five more minutes, Dad. Just five more minutes." The man smiled and said, "OK."

"My, you certainly are a patient father," the woman responded.

The man smiled and then said, "My older son Tommy was killed by a drunk driver last year while he was riding his bike near here. I never spent much time with Tommy, and now I'd give anything for just five more minutes with him. I've vowed not to make the same mistake with Todd. He thinks he has five more minutes to swing. The truth is, I get five more minutes to watch him play."

Keeping our priorities in order is easier if we are centered in God's love. When we focus on the big picture—how this life is temporary, leading to another world—we will spend our time on important tasks and not "sweat the small stuff." And, as Richard Carlson notes in his book, "it's all small stuff." When placed in the perspective of eternity, all that matters is our faith. The trifles and trauma we get caught up in are all "small stuff."

POST-IT MEDITATION FOR JANUARY 21
I will center my thoughts on God, asking him to help me keep my focus on the single-most important purpose in life.

January 22

If you are angry, be sure that it is not out of wounded pride or bad temper. Never go to bed angry—don't give the devil that sort of foothold.
~Ephesians 4:26 (PNT)

A man was on his way back home from market with his camel and, since he had enjoyed a good day, he decided to stop at a church along the road and offer his thanks to God.

He left his camel outside and spent several hours offering thanks to God, praying and promising to be a good and righteous person in the future, helping the poor, holding his temper, and loving his neighbor.

When he emerged it was already dark and behold – his camel was gone!

He immediately flew into a violent temper and shook his fist at the sky, yelling: "God! How could you do this to me? I put all my trust in you and then you have done this to me!"

A passing believer heard the man yelling and chuckled to himself. "Listen," he said, "Trust God but, you know, tie up your camel."

This little story has two lessons: Take care of what you can take care of yourself. And, we are never so deserving as to be free from problems. None of us is righteous on our own merit. Getting angry at God is not fair or wise.

Have you ever been angry at God? If so, you are not alone. When we lose a loved one, especially at a young age, we may be tempted to blame God for cutting the life short. When we see others who are seemingly more blessed by God than we, it is easy to be resentful, especially if they are not Christians or are not serving God and we are. Or, if God says "no" to a request when we think we deserve or need what we are asking for, we may rage against him.

Our God is a loving God, and he is slow to anger, but there are numerous incidences in the Bible where his wrath boils over. While he loves us and is patient with us, he is as capable of rage as we are, so we need to be cautious about letting our anger go unchecked. The Israelites, God's chosen people, invoked and incurred the wrath of God numerous times. In the 16th chapter of Numbers, God's fury is poured out on Korah, Dathan, Abiram and some 250 others who rebelled against Moses as God's appointed leader. These men and their followers were first burned to death and then the ground opened, swallowed them, and subsequently closed over them. God's righteous anger was justified because these sinful men had rebelled against Moses and later Aaron.

Other examples of God's ire, among myriad ones in the Bible, include flooding the earth, destroying all except those in the ark he had instructed Noah to build (Genesis 6-9); the destruction of Sodom and Gomorrah (Genesis 19); in Deuteronomy 32, where he tells us vengeance is his; and in Nehemiah 9, when his people refused to obey him. Jesus, too, displayed his temper on occasion, including when he threw the moneychangers out of the temple (John 2). The hard hearts of the Pharisees brought anger, and he chastised Peter for talking about his sacrificial death (Matthew 16).

Righteous anger can be good, but directing it toward God may not be the right target. Even against others or ourselves, we must be sure our hearts are pure before we display anger. Still, we would be wise to let our rage dissipate before the sun goes down.

POST-IT MEDITATION FOR JANUARY 22
I will remember God is all-powerful and all-knowing.
Anger against him, the one who created me
and controls the universe, is unmerited.

January 23

Do not worry about tomorrow; it will have enough worries of its own.
~Matthew 6:34 (GNB)

When we read the verses preceding Matthew 6:34, we are heartened. If God clothes the wild grass—grass that is here today and gone tomorrow—then why should we not believe he can clothe us, provide our food, and indeed, fill our every need? But then we look around us and see godly people who don't have enough food to feed their children or put clothes on their backs. We see parents who have lost their jobs, leaving them unable to pay their mortgages. Do those people take heart that they shouldn't worry about tomorrow? While they know the days ahead will have worries of their own, with today so dismal, how can they not be concerned about tomorrow? How can we offer encouragement to people who feel hopeless? How can they rebuild after so many setbacks?

Songbirds offer us a lesson in perseverance. Some time ago, a friend sent me a slide presentation with scenes of the most extraordinary songbirds I have ever glimpsed. The message on each slide was even more inspiring:

Have you ever observed the behavior of birds in the face of adversity?

For days and days they make their nests, sometimes gathering materials brought from far away.

And when they have completed the nest and are ready to lay eggs, the weather, or the work of humans or some animal destroys it, and it falls to the ground; all they have done with so much effort scattered in the grass and leaves.

Do the birds stop? Bewildered? Leave the work? No way. They start over, building again and again until they have eggs in the nest.

Sometimes, and very often before the chicks are hatched, an animal, a child, or a storm destroys the nest once again, but this time with all of its valuable contents.

It hurts to go back to begin again…even so, the birds never stop; they continue to sing and build, and keep singing and building….

Do you sometimes get the feeling your life, your work, your family are not what you dreamed? Do you sometimes want to say, "Enough, the effort is not worthwhile? It is all too much for me?"

Are you tired of it all? Do you feel the daily struggle is a waste of time, your trust has been betrayed, your goals not reached just as they were within sight?

Life strikes you down sometimes, but do you go on, say a prayer, and put your hope in faith, not darkness?

Do not worry if you get injured in the battle; that is to be expected. Gather yourself together and rebuild your life, so that it runs well again.

No matter what happens, do not shrink back, but move forward. Life is a constant challenge, but it is advisable to accept most of what happens to us with resolve. And never stop singing.

POST-IT MEDITATION FOR JANUARY 23
When I am discouraged, not knowing how I will get through tomorrow, I will remember the lesson of perseverance taught by the songbirds.

January 24

For everything that is hidden will eventually be brought into the open, and every secret will be brought to light.
~Mark 4:22 (NLT)

Life is full of bumps and lumps, and too often we fear the worst when we encounter them. With cancer rampant, feeling a lump under the skin sends panic into our hearts and heads. Even a lump under the carpet can send imagination into overtime.

A professional carpet-layer finished his job in a house undergoing remodeling and stepped back to survey the newly installed carpet. Reaching into his shirt pocket for a cigarette, he realized the pack was missing. At the same time, he noticed a lump under the carpet in the middle of the room, about the size of the misplaced cigarette package.

His heart thudding, he knew there was no way to retrieve his cigarette pack from under the carpet, firmly attached to the floor, without ripping everything up and starting over. But he also knew he couldn't leave the job with a lump in the middle of the floor. Finally, he beat the object flat, destroying any evidence of his mistake. With a few good whacks, the lump disappeared.

Picking up his tools, the carpet-layer walked out to his truck. As he started to get inside, he saw the mislaid pack of cigarettes on the seat. About that time, the homeowner hurried out of the house and asked, "Hey, have you seen my son's hamster?"

We can learn a couple of lessons from the carpet-layer's experience:

1 – Don't jump to conclusions. Make sure to have sound information before taking action. What seems to be a lump may be something

totally different from what we expect. As we look down a path, we may see what appears to be the end of a road; but upon closer examination, it may be a big bend in the lane. Who knows what will happen or be discovered around the sharp curve?

2 – Don't cover up mistakes. It may work for the moment, but sooner or later, the truth will come out. Re-doing a job we've botched is better in the long run than hiding our mistakes. If what we do doesn't come out right the first time, we should begin again, whether it is a carpet job or a conversation with a non-believer about Christ. While God holds us accountable for our mistakes, he created us with imperfections and stands ready to forgive us when we fail. It takes faith to admit we are wrong, to acknowledge our shortcomings; but hypocrisy—pretending we are perfect—is a horrible Christian witness.

POST-IT MEDITATION FOR JANUARY 24
I will dare to be honest and open about
my mistakes and imperfections.

January 25

But we have this treasure in jars of clay to show that this all-surpassing power is from God and not from us.
~2 Corinthians 4:7 (NIV)

An elderly Chinese woman had two large pots, each hung on the ends of a pole which she carried across her neck. One of the pots had a crack in it while the other pot was perfect and always delivered a full portion of water. At the end of the long walks from the stream to the house, the cracked pot arrived only half full.

This went on daily, with the woman bringing home only one and a half pots of water. Of course, the perfect pot was proud of its accomplishments. But the poor cracked pot was ashamed of its imperfection, miserable that it could only do half of what it had been made to do.

After two years of what it perceived to be bitter failure, the damaged pot spoke to the woman one day by the stream. "I am ashamed of myself, because this crack in my side causes water to leak out all the way back to your house."

The old woman smiled, "Did you notice there are flowers on your side of the path, but not on the other pot's side? That's because I have always known about your flaw, so I planted flower seeds on your side of the path, and every day while we walk back, you water them.

"For two years I have been able to pick these beautiful flowers to decorate the table. Without your being just the way you are, there would not be this beauty to grace the house."

We humans are like the cracked pot—ashamed because we are flawed. We are all imperfect, and few of us are saints, so we might as well give up trying to look and act like we are. Instead, we should accept, in author Brennan Manning's words, that we are "earthen vessels who shuffle along on feet of clay." Manning recognizes we are "bent and bruised...feel[ing] our lives are a grave disappointment to God." Something in our lives has left us cracked. But God can use us, just as the old Chinese woman used the fissured pot and its spilled water, to create beauty.

POST-IT MEDITATION FOR JANUARY 25
From this day forward, I will believe
God can use my imperfections for his glory.

January 26

...Their strength is to sit still.
~Isaiah 30:7 (KJV)

When troubles swirl all around us, we work ourselves into a frenzy, looking for a way out. If only we could enter the eye of the storm, we would find stillness and quiet even as massive and dangerous winds prevail all about us. In that inner stillness, if we call his name, we can hear the voice of God, saying, "Peace, be still."

An old song tells us the winds and the waves obey God's will, so why should we worry and fret? If he lives within our lives and we walk with him daily, he can calm the overpowering storm. No matter how desperate the situation, how harsh the hurt, or how deep the pain, God's grace and strength are sufficient.

The reason we sometimes don't find relief rests with us, not God. Even when we give him our problems, if he doesn't handle them as quickly as we think he should, we get discouraged. It is like tying our troubles up in a trash bag and attaching a piece of rope. We toss the bag as far as we can into the ocean, emphatically declaring, "Okay, God. I've tried and I cannot handle the garbage of my life. I'm giving it to you to wash away and make me a better person." A little later, if our problems still threaten to engulf us, we give up on God and pull the trash bag back to shore, again running around trying to tackle the issues ourselves. We are back at the outer edge of the tornado, when we should have stayed still in its eye. We have to trust God, not for just a few moments or only part of our lives, but always and in everything.

Jesus came one day and knocked at the door to the entrance of a two-story mansion. The owner opened the door for Jesus and welcomed him. He showed him around and before long gave him the best room in the 2nd story and said, "Please stay here with me." The man now felt secure with Jesus having taken possession of his favorite upstairs room.

Before long the man heard another knock and went to open the door. His new guest was Satan, who made a mess of every other room in the building except the one in which Jesus stayed. Frightened, the man ran to Jesus and asked, "Why did you not come to help?" Pointing to the room in which he stayed, Jesus said, "Son, you gave me only this room, how do you expect me to interfere with what is happening in the other rooms?"

The man realized his mistake and promptly gave Jesus the whole upstairs. The next morning he heard a knock on the door. It was Satan again, who started playing havoc in the rooms on the ground floor. The man tried his best to rid Satan but could not. After a while he lost his patience and stormed upstairs. Everything was calm and quiet upstairs.

"Lord, how could Satan come in with you upstairs?" quizzed the man.

Jesus smiled and answered, "Son, you only surrendered the rooms upstairs to me. As for the rooms downstairs, I have already told you I never interfere in anything that is not surrendered to me." The man now realized what Jesus wanted him to do and promptly gave Jesus the keys to the entire building. Satan fled and never troubled the man again.

Giving God complete control of our lives isn't easy. Part of our tendency to pull back from God may be fear that what he thinks is best for us is not what we want. If we turn our lives over to him to straighten out, we might not like how he does it. So, instead of sitting still and feeling his peace, we go in circles trying to "fix" the issue, or we only give him the part for which we are willing to surrender control. If we let go and let God be in charge, we will find peace and inner stillness.

POST-IT MEDITATION FOR JANUARY 26
Christ is in the eye of every storm.

January 27

Watch out! Guard yourself against all kinds of greed. After all, one's life isn't determined by one's possessions, even when someone is very wealthy.
~Luke 12:15 (CEB)

As a fisherman sat near a seashore in South Florida, under the shadow of a palm tree, a rich businessman passing by approached him and asked why he was in the shade smoking and not working. The fisherman replied simply: "I've caught enough fish for today."

Hearing this, the rich man was mystified and said, "Why don't you catch more fish instead of sitting in the shadows wasting your time?"

"Why would I want to catch more fish?"

Trying to explain, the businessman answered, "You could sell them, earn more money, and buy a bigger boat."

"What would I do then?" the fisherman queried, although he didn't seem too interested.

"You could go fishing in deep waters and catch even more fish and earn even more money," the businessman said enthusiastically.

"What would I do then?" the fisherman wondered aloud.

"You could buy many boats and employ many people to work for you and earn even more money," the other man responded, his excitement growing that he might be inspiring the lazy fisherman.

"What would I do then?" the fisherman asked, his curiosity piqued.

"You could become a rich businessman like me."

Again, the fisherman asked, "What would I do then?"

"You could then enjoy your life peacefully."

With more wisdom than the businessman, the fisherman said with a grin, "But that's what I'm doing right now."

How many of us are like the businessman, believing the good life is always in the future—that we must have more and more to be happy, that money and possessions hold the key to success?

We don't need to wait for tomorrow to be happy and enjoy life. We don't even need more money or power to savor life. Life is what is happening now, at this moment. Instead of just hanging on to have more in the future, we need to relish life right now.

POST-IT MEDITATION FOR JANUARY 27
Thank you God, for all that you have given me. It's enough.

January 28

...[God] knows who trusts in him.
~Nahum 1:7 (NCV)

When you see a penny on the street, do you stop to pick it up or do you pass it by, thinking it isn't worth bending over for?

A husband and wife were invited to spend the weekend at the husband's employer's home. They were a bit nervous, because the boss was very wealthy, with a fine home on a waterway, and cars costing more than their home.

The first day and evening went well, and the couple was delighted to have this rare glimpse into how the very wealthy live. The husband's employer was quite generous as a host, and the wife knew she would never have the opportunity to indulge in this kind of extravagance again, so was enjoying herself immensely.

As the three of them were about to enter an exclusive restaurant one evening, the boss was walking slightly ahead of the lady and her husband. He stopped suddenly, looking down on the pavement for a long, silent moment. There was nothing on the ground except a single darkened penny that someone had dropped and a few cigarette butts. Still silent, the man reached down and picked up the penny. He held it up and smiled, then put it in his pocket as if he had found a great treasure. How strange…what need did this man have for a single penny? Why would he even take the time to stop and pick it up?

Throughout dinner, the entire scene nagged at the lady. Finally, she could stand it no longer. She casually mentioned that her daughter once had a coin collection and asked if the penny he had found had been of some value.

A smile crept across the man's face as he reached into his pocket for the penny and held it out for her to see. She had seen many pennies before! What was the point of this?

"Look at it," he said. "Read what it says."

She read the words "United States of America."

"No, not that; read further."

"One cent?"

"No, keep reading."

"In God We Trust?"

"Yes! And if I trust in God, the name of God is holy, even on a coin. Whenever I find a coin I see that inscription. It is written on every single United States coin, but we never seem to notice it! God drops a message right in front of me telling me to trust Him—who am I to pass it by? When I see a coin, I stop to see if my trust IS in God at that moment. I pick the coin up as a response to God; that I do trust in Him. For a short time, at least, I cherish it as if it were gold. I think it is God's way of starting a conversation with me. Lucky for me, God is patient and pennies are plentiful!"

POST-IT MEDITATION FOR JANUARY 28
Whenever I see a penny on the ground, I will
pick it up and be reminded to trust in God.

January 29

For where your treasure is, there your heart will be also.
~Luke 12:34 (NIV)

A philosophy professor stood before his class with some items on the table in front of him. When the class began, wordlessly he picked up a very large and empty mayonnaise jar and proceeded to fill it with rocks, about 2 inches in diameter.

He then asked the students if the jar was full. They agreed that it was.

So the professor then picked up a box of pebbles and poured them into the jar. He shook the jar lightly. The pebbles, of course, rolled into the open areas between the rocks.

He then asked the students again if the jar was full. They agreed it was.

The professor picked up a box of sand and poured it into the jar. Of course, the sand filled up the remaining space.

He then asked once more if the jar was full. The students responded with a unanimous "Yes."

"Now," said the professor, "I want you to recognize that this jar represents your life. The rocks are the important parts—your family, your partner, your health, your children—things that if everything else was lost and only they remained, your life would still be full. The pebbles are the other things that matter— like your job, your house, your car. The sand is everything else. The small stuff. If you put the sand into the jar first," he continued, "there is no room for the pebbles or the rocks. The same goes for your life."

If we spend all of our time and energy on small stuff, the most important parts of our lives will be shut out. Work is important, having an expensive car makes us feel good, and living in a grand house makes us proud. But none of those—or smaller pieces of activity like mowing the lawn, dusting the furniture, doing paperwork, going shopping, surfing the Internet, or playing games on an I-Pad—is important in the larger scheme of life. Instead of busying our lives with inconsequential pursuits, we should spend time with family, read our Bibles, pray for guidance, and stay in touch with those we love.

POST-IT MEDITATION FOR JANUARY 29
God, help me take care of the rocks in my life first, making them my highest priority.

January 30

Get rid of all bitterness, rage and anger, brawling and slander, along with every form of malice. Be kind and compassionate to one another, forgiving each other, just as in Christ God forgave you.
~Ephesians 4:31-32 (NIV)

Sand and stone come from some of the same materials, but they have far different properties in terms of permanence. One can last for centuries, but the other can be blown far away with the wind.

One day when two friends were walking through the desert, they started arguing. In the heat of the moment, one slapped the other. With his face stinging from the slap, the man stopped and without saying anything, began to write in the sand: "Today my best friend slapped me in the face."

Still silent, the man arose and started walking with his friend again. Finally, they came upon an oasis and decided to get in the water to cool their parched bodies. The water was deeper than anticipated, and the friend who had been slapped got stuck in the mire and fell in the water. Seeing he was about to drown, the other man saved him.

After he recovered, the man who almost drowned carved these words on a stone: "Today my best friend saved my life."

Again, he remained silent, but the friend who had first slapped and then saved him asked, "After I hurt you, you wrote in the sand and now, you write on a stone. Why?"

With a smile, the friend replied, "When someone hurts us we should write it down in sand, where winds of forgiveness can erase it away. But, when someone does something good for us, we must engrave it in stone, where no wind can ever erase it."

Instead of doing what the wise man in the story did, we often harbor our hurts and soon forget the good someone does for us. We need to learn to write our hurts in sand and carve our blessings in stone.

POST-IT MEDITATION FOR JANUARY 30
Today I will take a few minutes to find a special friend or family member and tell them I am thankful for the blessings they bring to my life. And in my heart, I will scratch off bad memories from the stones where I wrote them and let forgiveness take their place.

January 31

May today there be peace within you; may you trust God that you are exactly where you are meant to be.
~Unknown

An old legend relates that long ago God had a great many burdens, which he wished to have carried from one place to another on earth, so he asked the animals to lend a hand. But all of them began to make excuses for not helping: the elephant was too dignified; the lion, too proud; and so on.

Finally the birds came to God and said, "If you will tie the burdens into small bundles, we'll be glad to carry them for you. We are small, but we would like to help."

So God fastened upon the back of each one a small bundle, and they all set out walking across the plains to their destination. They sang as they went, seeming not to feel the weight of their burdens at all. Every day the burdens seemed lighter and lighter, until the loads seems to be lifting the birds, instead of the birds carrying the burdens.

When they arrived at their destination, they discovered that when they removed their burdens, there were wings in their place, wings which enabled them to fly to the sky and the tree tops. They had learned how to carry their burdens, and their loads had become wings to carry them nearer to God.

Our burdens may be heavy, and we may not be where we want to be; but, if we have turned our lives over to God, we are where he planned for us to be. Content in that place, we can say, "Hallelujah anyway!"

How do we move from being disappointed with our problems and our lives to praising God anyway? It starts with the realization that God blesses us continually even though we can't see the blessing because our human eyes have only earthly vision.

When God created the heavens and the earth, he had a master design and plan. Everything has a season and a reason. The purpose may not be fulfilled on earth, but we have the assurance from Romans 8:28 that all things do work together for those who love the Lord. It is as true for us as it was for the birds.

Thankfully, sometimes we don't have to wait until we get to heaven to see how things work together. We are especially blessed when we see God turn a bad or tragic event in our lives into a triumph. Those times make it easy to be thankful. On the other hand, when circumstances turn against us and we see no possibility for better days, it is difficult to accept that a good God would leave us in such distress. In those times, we struggle to rise above our discouragement to do as Ephesians 5:20 (ASV) commands: "Giving thanks always for all things to God the Father in the name of our Lord Jesus Christ."

In a steel mill, the metal is tested to the limit and marked to show its breaking point. Twisted, stretched, and compressed, it doesn't break because the master of the steel mill knows exactly how much strain each piece can withstand. The testing room reveals how much the steel can bear if placed in a great ship, a gigantic building, or a long bridge span. So it is with us—God wants to be sure we are tough enough to withstand the pressures of life, so sometimes he tests us through struggles and suffering.

Hallelujah anyway? It's not easy, but it is possible if we believe God cares, that he has a magnificent plan for this earth and the heavens beyond. With this assurance, we can slowly move to acceptance that we can survive bad times. More importantly, we will find we grow stronger in our faith during difficulty than in more peaceful times in our lives.

POST-IT MEDITATION FOR JANUARY 31
*God, give me the faith to believe you are in
control and have a plan for my life.*

February 1

I will be glad and rejoice in your love, because you saw my suffering; you knew my troubles.
~Psalm 31:7 (NCV)

A soldier, finally coming home after having fought in Vietnam, called his parents from San Francisco.

"Mom and Dad, I'm coming home, but I've a favor to ask. I have a friend I'd like to bring home with me."

"Sure," they replied. "We'd love to meet him."

"There's something you should know; he was hurt pretty badly in the fighting. He stepped on a land mine and lost an arm and a leg. He has nowhere else to go, and I want him to come live with us."

"I'm sorry to hear that, son. Maybe we can help him find somewhere to live."

"No, mom and dad. I want him to live with us."

"Son, you don't know what you're asking. Someone with such a handicap would be a terrible burden to us. We have our own lives to live, and we can't let something like this interfere. Just come on home and forget about this guy. He'll find a way to live on his own."

At that point, the son hung up the phone. The parents heard nothing more from him. A few days later, however, they received a call from the San Francisco police. Their son died after falling from a building, they were told. The police said it was suicide.

The grief-stricken parents flew to San Francisco and were taken to the city morgue to identify the body of their son. They recognized him, but to their horror, they also discovered he had only one arm and one leg. Shocked and shaken, they realized their son had been talking about himself. In their selfishness, they had made him feel the weight of caring for him would have been more than they wanted to bear.

How many of us would have responded any differently than the parents? Of course, if we knew the disabled person was our own son, we would welcome him home. But would our true feelings be revealed if we thought the person was a stranger?

POST-IT MEDITATION FOR FEBRUARY 1
God, help me treat others as you treat
me—loving me in spite of how I am.

February 2

It is not enough to be busy; so are the ants. The question is: what are we busy about?
~Henry David Thoreau, American author, poet, and philosopher

At times, the purpose in our lives has been crystal clear. But sporadically, we may have felt like Alice in Wonderland as she stopped to ask which road to take and the Cheshire cat asked her where she was going. When Alice responded that she really didn't know, the cat sagely stated, "Then it doesn't really matter which road you take."

Like Alice, many people don't know which road to take, because we don't know where we want to go. Notions of a new life, a better one, bounce through our heads, but we are seemingly incapable of capturing them as tangible goals or opportunities.

Occasionally, it's probably normal to be in limbo, empty of desire and drive. But it can be ruinous if we get lodged long-term in such a purposeless life. If we don't have a clear image of where we are going, not only will we likely not get there, but we might not even recognize it if we arrive.

Henry, a painter, had spent his entire life working for others. He had often dreamed of owning his own painting business someday, but he just didn't have the drive or energy to make it happen. Then one day, his boss was sick and couldn't come to the job site. Henry had worked for him a long time, and the boss thought it would be fine for Henry to continue the paint job without him.

Late in the afternoon, the boss began feeling better and decided to check on Henry. He was astounded to find Henry propped up against a tree, watching a couple of young teenagers on ladders, painting the house. When he asked Henry what was going on, Henry replied, "I'm paying each of these guys $3 an hour to paint for me."

Henry's boss responded in disbelief, "But I'm only paying you $5 an hour."

"I know," said Henry, "but it's worth it to be the boss once in my life."

Henry's story illustrates that having an ill-conceived purpose can be as hapless as having no purpose at all. His failure to act on his dream—to have a realistic, action-driven goal—left him with an incredibly stupid, half-baked way to get where he wanted to be. Unlike Alice, he knew where he wanted to go—he just took a dead-end street. We should have a plan for our lives that will take us where both we and God want us to be.

POST-IT MEDITATION FOR FEBRUARY 2
God, help me recognize and avoid dead-end streets in my life.

February 3

Make money your god and it will plague you like the devil.
~Henry Fielding, 16th century English novelist and dramatist

In her heartrending novel, *A Prologue to Love*, Taylor Caldwell told the story of a woman, rich beyond belief, whose sole purpose in life was to hold onto and increase her wealth.

From Caroline Ames' youngest days, her father instilled in her a horror of poverty and a conviction that only through money would she be respected. Set in the late 19th and early 20th centuries, Caldwell's story depicts the tragic result of Ames' fears: She was unable to give or receive love. Despite her millions, she lived a reclusive life in a cold, deteriorating house. Compelled to hoard her money, refusing to hire adequate help or pay for coal and wood to have warmth, Ames lived in two rooms of her 15-room house among thick layers of dust.

Ames' purpose, like that of Henry in the story for February 2, was ill-founded. At a profoundly deeper level, though, Ames works her way through her desperate obsession to a realization that her father's teachings were not only wrong but also catastrophic. Too late, she recognized her fixation on wealth had cost her the love of her husband and children. But it was not too late for redemption; in the end she overcame the evil that had possessed her and found a way to undo at least a degree of the destruction she had created. Late in life, she sat on an ocean-side boulder at dawn and cast her evil purpose aside. Simultaneously, she found she was not beyond God's forgiveness and love.

Caldwell's story, tragic and tumultuous through almost 600 pages, ended with a peace that most readers never suspect will arrive until late in the novel. How sad it took so long—almost her entire life—for Ames to recognize and acknowledge the wretchedness to which she had subjected herself and her loved ones.

Both Alice and Henry have lessons for us. First, a purpose is essential to give our lives direction and meaning. Second, the purpose must be, in simplest terms, right and good.

POST-IT MEDITATION FOR FEBRUARY 3
Today I will ask God to help me find a purpose for my life that is worthwhile and pleasing to him.

February 4

Learn to get in touch with the silence within yourself, and know that everything in life has purpose. There are no mistakes, no coincidences; all events are blessings given to us to learn from.
~Elizabeth Kubler-Ross, Swedish-America psychiatrist

In the busyness of daily existence and in the midst of television and web images of the "good" life, we sometimes succumb to thinking that we don't have as much as others and that our own lives don't measure up. In such times, we would be wise to pull apart from the world for a while and look deep inside ourselves. In the light of our spiritual being, we need to examine those events and circumstances seeming to diminish our lives. Along with Kubler-Ross, we will then know: All that happens to us has a good purpose. Both joyous and sad times bring blessings and lessons if we open our minds and hearts.

A legend cited in *On Learning and Teaching* illustrates what can happen if we are receptive to possibilities:

A great light suddenly surrounded some nomads one night, and they knew they were in the midst of a heavenly being. A voice spoke, telling the men, "Gather as many pebbles as you can. Put them in your saddle bags. Travel a day's journey and tomorrow night will find you glad and it will find you sad."

The nomads were disappointed; they had expected some divine revelation, perhaps one that would lead them to wealth and a purpose for the world—or at least for their lives. The menial task they were given made no sense at all. Even so, the light was so unusual and so powerful that they each picked up a few pebbles and with a bit of grousing, put them in their saddlebags. Soon, they found the little pebbles didn't make for a comfortable ride as they poked against their legs, so they grumbled even more.

The next day, after their travels, they stopped to make camp. As they unloaded their saddlebags, they were astounded to discover every pebble they had gathered had become a diamond. As the celestial voice had predicted, they were glad and they were sad—glad they had diamonds but sad they had not gathered more pebbles.

POST-IT MEDITATION FOR FEBRUARY 4
Today I will be open to blessings in disguise.

February 5

Who has woe? Who has sorrow? Who has strife? Who has complaining?
Who has wounds without cause? Who has redness of eyes?
~Proverbs 3:29 (ESV)

Life is full of hilltops and valleys; sometimes we are glad and some-times sad. Regretfully, when we are down, we sometimes pull others down with our gripes and groans. Have you ever known people who seemed to look for something to complain about? Have you wondered if they declare, like English dramatist W.S. Gilbert, "Oh, wouldn't this world seem dull and flat with nothing whatever to grumble about?" Thankfully, we also know folks who seem to take life in stride and don't burden others with their problems.

How can we avoid the pitfalls of a complaining life?

Isaiah 40:31 answers by telling us we can simply "wait" on the Lord—but that doesn't mean literally, "wait." The *Good News Bible* translation of the verse tells us we should trust the Lord for help; and when we do, we can run and not get weary; walk and not grow weak.

Can trust alone really enable us to rise above our problems? Sounds too easy to be true, doesn't it? And anything that sounds that way usu-ally is that way.

God not only expects us to trust him, but he also expects us to work with him. We are required to put our hand to the plow, do whatever we can to address our difficulties, and then trust God to take the work of our hands and finish the job. Even when we don't know what to do, God is there to guide us in our part of his plan to help us through the race of life. We should not fear failing. That could keep us from starting.

So we work on our troubles and trust God...but we may sometimes still be tempted to grouse about our problems. One man found a way to avoid that temptation:

A carpenter I hired to help me restore an old farm house has just finished a rough day on the job. A flat tire made him lose an hour of work, his electric saw stopped working, and now his ancient truck refused to start. While I drove him home, he sat in stony silence. On arriving, he invited me in to meet his family.

As we walked toward the front door, he paused briefly at a small tree, touching the tips of the branches with both hands.

Opening the door, he underwent an amazing transformation. His tanned face was wreathed in smiles as he hugged his two small children and gave his wife a kiss. Afterward, he walked me to the car. We passed the tree, and my curiosity made me ask about what I had seen him do earlier.

"Oh, that's my trouble tree," he replied. "I know I can't help having troubles on the job, but one thing for sure, troubles don't belong at home with my wife and the children. So I just hang them up on the tree every night when I come home. Then in the morning I pick them up again."

"Funny thing is," he smiled, "when I come out in the morning to pick them up, there aren't nearly as many as I remember hanging up the night before."

Could it be that God worked on those troubles during the night, changing their shape and complexion?

POST-IT MEDITATION FOR FEBRUARY 5
*God, help me to hang my troubles on a
tree for you to deal with overnight.*

February 6

Let each of you look not only at his own interests, but also at the interests of others.
~Philippians 2:4 (ESV)

Sometimes God sends simple opportunities to make a difference; how we respond can make them extraordinary.

In Phoenix, Arizona, a 26-year-old mother stared at her 6-year-old son, who was dying of terminal leukemia. Although her heart was filled with sadness, she also had a strong feeling of determination. Like any parent, she wanted her son to grow up and fulfill his dreams. Now, the leukemia would ensure that was not possible. But she still wanted her son's dreams to come true.

She took her son's hand and asked, "Billy, did you ever think about what you wanted to be once you grew up? Did you ever dream and wish what you would do with your life?"

"Mommy, I always wanted to be a fireman when I grew up."

Mom smiled back, saying, "Let's see if we can make your wish come true." Later that day she went to her local fire department in Phoenix, Arizona, where she met Fireman Bob, who had a heart as big as Phoenix. She explained her son's final wish and asked if it might be possible to give him a ride around the block on a fire engine.

Fireman Bob said, "We can do better than that. If you'll have your son ready at seven o'clock Wednesday morning, we'll make him an honorary fireman for the whole day. He can come down to the fire station, eat with us, go out on all the fire calls, the whole nine yards! And if you'll give us his sizes, we'll get a real fire uniform for him, with a real fire hat, a yellow slicker like we wear, and rubber boots. They're all manufactured right here in Phoenix, so we can get them fast."

Three days later Fireman Bob picked up Billy, dressed him in his fire uniform, and escorted him from his hospital bed to the waiting hook and ladder truck.

Billy got to sit on the back of the truck and help steer it to the fire station. He was in an earthly heaven. There were three fire calls in Phoenix that day, and Billy got to go out on all three calls.

Having his dream come true, with all the love and attention lavished on him, so deeply touched Billy that he lived three months longer than any doctor thought possible. Finally, one night all of his vital signs began to drop dramatically, and the head nurse began to call family members to the hospital. Remembering the day Billy had spent as a fireman, she also called the fire chief and asked if it would be possible to send a fireman in uniform to the hospital to be with Billy as he made his transition.

The chief replied, "We can do better than that. We'll be there in five minutes. Will you please do me a favor? When you hear the sirens screaming and see the lights flashing, will you announce over the PA system that there is not a fire? It's just the fire department coming to see one of its finest members one more time. And will you open the window to his room?"

Five minutes later a hook and ladder truck arrived and extended its ladder up to Billy's third-floor open window. Sixteen firefighters climbed the ladder into Billy's room. With his mother's permission, they hugged him and held him and told him how much they loved him. With his dying breath, Billy looked up at the fire chief and said, "Chief, am I really a fireman now?"

"Billy, you are, and the Head Chief, Jesus, is holding your hand," the chief said.

With those words, Billy smiled and said, "I know, he's been holding my hand all day, and the angels have been singing...."

He closed his eyes one last time.

POST-IT MEDITATION FOR FEBRUARY 6
I will be inspired by the fire chief to give
of myself to brighten the days of others.

February 7

The righteous care for the needs of animals....
~Proverbs 12:10 (NIV)

A family had gathered at a lakeside cabin in the Catskill Mountains of New York for skating and ice fishing one winter and found the lake covered by only a thin layer of ice—not enough for their planned activities. Still, the scenery was stunning and became even more picturesque when someone spotted a deer. But to the horror of those watching, the young doe ran onto the ice, her hoofs going out from under her on the slippery surface. The doe scrambled up, only to slide down again, a struggle she repeated over and over. By the time she reached the middle of the lake, the ice *gave way and within seconds, only her head was visible. She didn't give up, but her frantic thrashing did no good.*

Family members ran to the edge of the lake but could see no way to help the terrified deer. Although they returned to the cabin, feeling helpless, they couldn't bear listening to the sounds of the struggle outside. Back at the shore of the lake, they tried throwing huge rocks into the ice. When that didn't work, they tried to push a canoe—and then a sturdier rowboat—through the ice to make a path for the deer. With the sun setting, they watched in sadness as the deer stopped fighting her unbeatable foe. Unwilling to give up, the men found a sledgehammer and started making a path for the rowboat. They discovered if two of the men got in the rowboat, their weight caused it to crash through whole yards at a time, bringing them closer.

Knowing the panic-stricken animal would never let them put a rope around her neck, the men got behind her and with a canoe paddle herded her into the channel they had opened from the shore. She moved so slowly it was excruciating, but she made it! When she was on solid ground, though, she collapsed, her face drooping. Exhausted, the family knew the deer would freeze to death, her wet coat dooming her, but again they felt helpless. As they mourned, within minutes they were astounded to see the doe rise from the shore and in three large leaps disappear into the trees. With a few moments of rest, the deer had miraculously revived.

This story, written by Elizabeth Sherrill, appeared first in *Guideposts* and later in *Reader's Digest*, and ended with the author's introspective thoughts: "I thought of how we'd set out with no clear plan in mind. Nor could we see ahead now. The deer had escaped to face fresh problems. A hunter could shoot her the next day. She could starve over the winter. It's a complicated world, and we don't have all the answers. But that should not stop us from doing all we can."

POST-IT MEDITATION FOR FEBRUARY 7
In the same way one family did, I will thank God for giving me "some small part to play in this complex world."

February 8

...The crooked places shall be made straight, and the rough places smooth.
~Isaiah 40:4 (NKJV)

The Chinese symbols for "crisis" and "opportunity" are identical. If we can accept that each predicament in our lives brings an opportunity, we will find adapting to the crisis possible.

Denis Waitley, in <u>Seeds of Greatness</u>, *shares the story of a German immigrant in Philadelphia who was trying to make a living in the 1930's selling* knockwurst and sauerkraut in his small restaurant. He couldn't afford plates and silverware, so he used inexpensive cotton gloves for his customers to hold the knockwurst, covered in sauerkraut, while they ate it. Unfortunately, his patrons often took the gloves home to use in their gardens, so he constantly had to replace them, creating more expense. To solve the problem, he came up with the idea of splitting a German roll down the center and placing the knockwurst and sauerkraut in the opening. On the first day he substituted the rolls for the gloves, a customer saw one of the owner's dachshunds snoozing in a corner and quipped, "Now we know why you're trying to cover up your knockwurst in that fancy roll. What happened to the other dog you used to have around here?" In that moment, the hot dog was born.

No problem is insurmountable. We should not shy away from challenges and difficulties. As poet Gail Brook Burket wrote, we should say, "I do not ask to walk smooth paths nor bear an easy load. I pray for strength and fortitude to climb the rock-strewn road. Give me such courage, and I can scale the hardest peaks alone and transform every stumbling block into a stepping stone."

The people who most often expect a breakthrough in the midst of a problem are those who have faith. Their belief that God will help make a rough place smooth provides strength to hold on until a difficulty is resolved. They pray about the obstacle, work to find a way out, and wait for God to come through—maybe only with an idea, but always with the essence needed to see the way ahead.

It takes faith to hang in there when the road is crooked, but if we are patient, God will provide the direction we need. And, just as the German restaurant owner had the solution in front of him all of the time, we need to be mindful that the answer to our own quandaries may lie within our sight and grasp.

POST-IT MEDITATION FOR FEBRUARY 8
I will seek creative ways to solve my problems.

February 9

Be glad of life because it gives you the chance to love, to work, to play, and to look up at the stars.
~Henry Van Dyke, American author, educator, and clergyman

A man tells of being frustrated at repeated delays on the closing of the aircraft doors so his flight could take off. He became even more irritated when the attendant announced a further delay because "we are holding the aircraft for some very special people."

"Why should we wait for some celebrities, sports figures, or rich people?" he grumbled to himself. When several U.S. Marines walked on board, on their way home from Iraq, his attitude changed in a flash and he joined the whistles, cheering, and occasional "Oorrahh" that erupted across the plane. His spirit ashamed yet uplifted, minutes before the plane landed, the man suggested to the attendant that she announce for everyone to remain in their seats until the heroes were allowed to gather their gear and be the first off the plane. As the Marines departed, applause again swelled the air.

Undeniably proud to be home and thankful for the cheers, the Marines still carried a heavy burden: some of their fellow Marines would never come back.

Sometimes we fail to remember: Life itself is a gift and a blessing. Before the end of 2012, more than 6600 U.S. service members had lost their lives in Operation Iraqi Freedom and Operation Enduring Freedom. Each of these protectors of *our* freedom left behind family members—parents, spouses, children, and others—who no longer have the joy of that person in their lives. And each person who died lost the future that was waiting for him or her.

Every day, people die from wars, accidents, illnesses, or violence. And, although some of them had lived a long, full life, many had only begun to realize their potential before their lives were cut short. When we are tempted to grumble and complain about life's unfairness, we need to be reminded that, if we don't think every day is a great day, we should try going without one. Faced with the choice of a life with problems or giving up our lives, most of us would choose life.

Sadly, we tend to forget joy doesn't come from the absence of unfairness or from having all of our needs (and even wants) met. Instead, happiness comes from recognizing and appreciating what we do have.

When we realize the totally free parts of our lives—the love of family, friends, and God—are more important than any worldly possession, we will appreciate our existence. We may never be millionaires, live in mansions, or travel to exotic places, but we can enjoy a home-cooked meal, a kid's hug, a warm fire on a snowy night, a kiss from a loved one, and thousands of other wonderful pleasures.

How can we move from wanting more to appreciating what we have? It may be as simple as thinking about what happens when we receive a gift. If we fail to express our thanks to the giver, will that person be as generous or thoughtful in the future? On a broader scale, the same lesson applies to our lives. We will be given more blessings if we show a deep appreciation to God for those we already have. "Give thanks to the Lord, for he is good. His love endures forever" (Psalm 136:1, NIV). A thankful heart generates more love—and more gifts.

POST-IT MEDITATION FOR FEBRUARY 9
*I will pause today and be thankful for both
small and large blessings in my life.*

February 10

You obey the law of Christ when you offer each other a helping hand.
~*Galatians 6:2 (CEV)*

None of us ever knows when a small act of kindness strikes a chord that resonates in another's life.

Mark was walking home from school one day when he noticed the boy ahead of him had tripped and dropped all of the books he was carrying, along with two sweaters, a baseball bat, a glove, and a small tape recorder. Mark knelt down and helped the boy pick up the scattered articles. Since they were going the same way, he helped carry part of the burden. As they walked, Mark discovered the boy's name was Bill, that he loved video games, baseball, and history, and that he was having lots of trouble with his other subjects and had just broken up with his girlfriend.

They arrived at Bill's home first, and Mark was invited in for a Coke and to watch some television. The afternoon passed pleasantly with a few laughs and some shared small talk, then Mark went home. They continued to see each other around school, had lunch together once or twice, then both graduated from junior high school. They ended up in the same high school where they had brief contacts over the years. Finally the long awaited senior year came and three weeks before graduation, Bill asked Mark if they could talk.

Bill reminded him of the day years ago when they had first met. "Did you ever wonder why I was carrying so many things home that day?" asked Bill. "You see, I cleaned out my locker because I didn't want to leave a mess for anyone else. I had stored away some of my mother's sleeping pills, and I was going home to commit suicide. But after we spent some time together talking and laughing, I realized if I had killed myself, I would have missed that time and so many others that might follow. So you see, Mark, when you picked up those books that day, you did a lot more. You saved my life."

Suicides of adolescents most often take others by surprise. We are shocked because we can't understand how anything at that age could be bad enough for a young person to give up the rest of his earthly life. What may seem trivial and inconsequential to us, such as the break-up of young love, may be earthshattering to a youth who can't envision ever finding someone else to cherish. Irrational thoughts take over, and if the teenager feels totally alone, suicide can result. The scenario isn't that different for adults. Suicide is the 11th ranking cause of death in the United States—a person takes his own life every 16 minutes. More than 30,000 people a year give up on life.

As Christians, even when we don't suspect irrational thinking, we can help save others from suicide if we consistently offer help to those whose paths we cross. We should never miss an opportunity to show someone we care—we may never know what a difference it may make.

POST-IT MEDITATION FOR FEBRUARY 10
I will seek to raise the spirits of others by showing them I care.

February 11

He also told this parable to some who trusted in themselves that they were righteous, and treated others with contempt: "Two men went up into the temple to pray, one a Pharisee and the other a tax collector. The Pharisee, standing by himself, prayed thus: 'God, I thank you that I am not like other men, extortionists, unjust, adulterers, or even like this tax collector. I fast twice a week; I give tithes of all that I get.' But the tax collector, standing far off, would not even lift up his eyes to heaven, but beat his breast, saying, 'God, be merciful to me, a sinner!'"
~Luke 18:9-14 (ESV)

A little girl on the way home from church turned to her mother and said, "Mommy, the preacher's sermon this morning confused me."
The mother said, "Oh! Why is that?"
The girl replied, "Well, he said God is bigger than we are. Is that true?"
"Yes, that's true," the mother answered.
"He also said God lives within us. Is that true, too?"
Again the mother replied, "Yes."
"Well," said the girl, "if God is bigger than us and he lives in us, wouldn't he show through?"

A YouTube video making the rounds on Facebook (FB) in early 2012 featured a poem designed to highlight the difference between false religion and Christianity. Some consider the statements made by spoken-word artist Jefferson Bethke to be controversial, but a core of truth underlies his message. One salient point he makes is that a problem exists if people only know you are a Christian by your FB page. (Bethke compares this to declaring you play for the Lakers because you wear their jersey.) Many people make FB their personal billboard of testimony. There are a couple of problems with that:

First, constantly posting messages about their good deeds or prayer life sets people up to expectations that their lives will reflect what they post. No one is perfect, so inevitably someone watching will be disillusioned when the person falls short in his or her Christian life. Regrettably, this can turn people away from God.

Second, while proclaiming their faith publicly (and there is good in that), people sometimes create a "holier than thou" attitude. Bethke believes, "At its core, Jesus' gospel and the good news of the Cross is in pure opposition to self-righteousness/self-justification." He notes, "The son of God never supports self-righteousness."

Even with the above cautionary notes, Christians should not refrain from telling others about their personal belief in God, whatever the vehicle or venue. We should never deny our faith—but we should always attempt to live what we espouse.

While not agreeing with everything Bethke says, we can be reminded that just saying we are Christians doesn't make it so. Our lives need to reflect the principles taught by Christ. Bethke is careful to note that following rules doesn't make us Christians. That makes us a good person (and sometimes gives us false pride that we are better than others), but it doesn't make us a Christian. If we call ourselves by that name, how we act and what we do is a reflection on God and his son; even so, the core of our Christianity comes not from actions but from the feelings that reside within our hearts.

AUTHOR'S NOTE: Bethke's YouTube video can be found at http://www.youtube.com/ watch?v=1IAhDGYlpqY&feature=g-

POST-IT MEDITATION FOR FEBRUARY 11
Before I boast about my Christian works and prayer,
I will pause and examine if my life matches my words.

February 12

Clouds come floating into my life, no longer to carry rain or usher storm, but to add color to my sunset sky.
~Rabindranath Tagore, Indian poet

The "Touch of the Master's Hand," by Myra Brooks Welch, is one of the most well-known and heart-warming poems of the 20th century. It tells the story of an auctioneer who bought a battered and scarred violin, not expecting to get very much for it at his next public auction. And, indeed, after he started the bidding at only a dollar, the highest bid was a mere three bucks. Surprisingly, as he was saying, "Going once, going twice," a gray-haired man walked to the front of the room, picked up the violin, and wiped off the dust. After tightening the strings, "he played a melody pure and sweet—as sweet as the angels sing."

When the music stopped, the auctioneer asked in a quiet voice, "What now am I bid for the old violin?"

"One thousand, one thousand. Do I hear two?"

"Two thousand. Who makes it three?"

"Three thousand once, three thousand twice, going and gone," said he.

People cheered, and amid the clamor, someone expressed what others were feeling—"What changed the worth of the old violin?"

A soft voice quickly replied, "The touch of the master's hand."

Although the poem doesn't end there, the message is already clear. We often cannot tell the worth of a person or an object by its exterior. And so it is that we can't always discern whether the clouds in our lives are white and fluffy or dark and dangerous, good or bad. In a full life, both come and go. But the real evidence of the cloud's worth comes when the master's hand paints its colors of burnt orange, scarlet red, and blushing pink at day's end, creating a stunning sunset.

So it is with our lives. Welch ends her poem by comparing a life that is dark and sullied to the old violin. Until the human being—like the violin—is touched by the master's hand, it is out of tune. It is cheap and has little value to others. But the same God who can transform a muted, cloud-filled sky into a glorious sunset knows "the worth of a soul" and uses his touch to tune a battered and scarred man into one of his precious children.

AUTHOR'S NOTE: Although Welch's poem is widely acclaimed, many do not know that she created her masterpiece with hands badly scarred from severe arthritis. When she had to give up playing her organ, she turned to poetry, using the eraser end of two pencils to slowly type. Her talent as a writer lay undiscovered until she, too, was touched by the Master's hand.

POST-IT MEDITATION FOR FEBRUARY 12
When I see someone whose life appears sinful, dirty, or distasteful, I will look beyond the exterior, remembering God sees the soul. I should not judge until that life has been touched by the Master's hand.

February 13

Blessed be the Lord, my rock, who trains my hands for war, and my fingers for battle....
~Psalm 144:1 (ESV)

Harriet Ross Tubman, born a Maryland slave around 1820, is one of the most well-known of the "conductors" in the Underground Railroad during the Civil War. Her courage came forth early in life. As a young teen, she suffered a terrible injury when she blocked a doorway to protect a fellow field hand from an angry overseer. The two-pound weight he threw at her struck her head, leaving her with spells in which she would fall into a deep sleep.

Not too many years later, after marrying a free black named John Tubman, she became fearful she and other slaves on the plantation would be sold. Resolved to run away, she set out alone. Following the North Star by night, she eventually made her way to Philadelphia, where she found a job. There, she saved her money and returned to Maryland to help her sister and her sister's two children to freedom. But she didn't stop there, going back to the South to rescue her brother and two other men. Sadly, when she returned again to get her husband, he had taken another wife. That didn't deter her; her goal never wavered. Over a 10-year period in 19 trips through the south, often at great peril, through the Underground Railway she rescued more than 300 slaves, including her elderly parents. She herself once proudly pointed out that "she never lost a single passenger" in all of her journeys.

How did she do it?

"Trust me, 'twas the Lord. I always told him, 'I trust you. I don't know what to do, but I expect you to lead me,' and he always did." Quite cleverly, she devised techniques such as using a white slave owner's horse and buggy for the first part of the journey, starting the escapes on Saturday nights because runaway notices couldn't be placed in newspapers until Monday morning, and drugging babies so they wouldn't cry when slave hunters were nearby.

But the question of how Harriet Tubman found the courage to face hardships, as well as the possibility of capture and punishment, is much larger than her ability to outwit slave owners. It came from her commitment to free enslaved people, and more significantly, from her belief that God would guide her even when she didn't know how she would get herself out of tight situations. As the psalmist said in 56:3-4 (NLT), when she was afraid, she put her trust in God, asking, "What can mere mortals do to me?"

POST-IT MEDITATION FOR FEBRUARY 13
When my courage wavers, I will remember Tubman and know that the same God who helped her will help me if I will just trust him.

February 14

'Tis better to have loved and lost than never to have loved at all.
~Alfred Lord Tennyson, English poet

Winter doldrums sometimes set in by mid-February. Overcast skies, sub-zero temperatures, and in some parts of the country, mountains of snow trigger boredom and sluggishness. Sure, the first snowfalls earlier in the winter were welcomed as white wonderlands, energizing us to throw snowballs, make snow angels, or build snowmen. But when the white powdery stuff hangs around too long, or even without snow when we are so cold we don't think we will ever thaw out, winter skies leave us lethargic. Valentine's Day offers a welcome break, reminding us love trumps weather any time.

Celebrating affections brightens any day, cloudy or fair. Memories of candlelight dinners with violins playing in the background, a romantic walk holding hands, or a cozy night cuddling by the fire with the love of your life all conjure up feelings of delight—or sadness. For those whose loved one is by their side, Valentine's Day represents a time to pause and reflect on love shared and treasured. For those whose soul mate is serving the country on foreign land, it is a time to pray especially hard for a safe return. For those whose marriage has been ripped apart, it can be a time of regret and remorse. And, for those whose spouses have left their earthly home, it can be a reminder of what was….

For all, it should be a time to be thankful for the gift of love. As Tennyson wrote, regardless of what befalls our beloved, the worst sorrow of all is never to have experienced love. Although Valentine's Day has historically celebrated the love between man and woman, love can be cherished from parents, children, teachers, special friends, and on and on. While most have the wonderful blessing, at some time in their lives, of the traditional "in love" feeling, it doesn't mean those who never find their true love have to miss out on affection. The world is full of people needing love. Regardless of the other kinds of love we have or do not have in our lives, we can spread warm feelings among those around us. The old hymn, "Somebody Needs Your Love" says it well: "Many are helpless, and wait for your call, longing for courage and strength for the fight…somebody needs your love" *(B.B. McKinney)*. Give it to them, and you may receive a gift in return. And even if you don't, like the little boy in the story below, your heart will glow from the gift of giving.

Little Chad was a shy, quiet child. One day he came home and told his mother he'd like to make a valentine for everyone in his class. Her heart sank. She thought, "I wish he wouldn't do that!" because she had watched the children when they walked home from school. Her Chad was always behind them. They laughed and hung on to each other and talked to each other. But Chad was never included. Nevertheless, she decided she would go along with her son. So she purchased the paper and glue and crayons. For three weeks, night after night, Chad painstakingly made 35 valentines.

Valentine's Day dawned, and Chad was beside himself with excitement. He carefully stacked the valentines up, put them in a bag, and bolted out the door. His mother decided to bake his favorite cookies and serve them nice and warm with a cool glass of milk when he came home from school. She just knew he would be disappointed and maybe that would ease the pain a little. It hurt her to think he wouldn't get many valentines—maybe none at all.

That afternoon she had the cookies and milk on the table. When she heard the children outside, she looked out the window. Sure enough, there they came, laughing and having the best time. And, as always, there was Chad in the rear. He walked a little faster than usual. She fully expected him to burst into tears as soon as he got inside. His arms were empty, she noticed, and when the door opened she choked back tears.

"Mommy has some cookies and milk for you," she said.

But he hardly heard her words. He just marched right on by, his face aglow, and all he could say was: "Not a one. Not a one."

Her heart sank.

And then he added, "I didn't forget a one, not a single one!"

POST-IT MEDITATION FOR FEBRUARY 14
If I can hold my soul mate close today, I will be thankful; but if I can't, I will find someone who needs my love and offer it freely.

February 15

For if they fall, one will lift up his fellow. But woe to him who is alone when he falls and has not another to lift him up.
~Ecclesiastes 4:10 (ASV)

When we hear the word *sacrifice*, thoughts typically turn to completely selfless acts in which someone does something for another purely for the other's benefit, not his own. This calls to mind a soldier who sacrificed his life for his comrade:

Horror gripped the heart of the World War I soldier as he saw his lifelong friend fall in battle. Caught in a trench with continuous gunfire whizzing over his head, the soldier asked his lieutenant if he might go out into the "no man's land" between the trenches to bring his fallen comrade back.

"I won't stop you if that's what you feel compelled to do," said the lieutenant, "but I don't think it will be worth it. Your friend is probably dead, and you may throw your life away." The lieutenant's advice didn't matter, and the soldier went anyway. Miraculously, he managed to reach his friend, hoist him onto his shoulder, and bring him back to their company's trench. As the two tumbled together to the bottom of the trench, the officer checked the wounded soldier and then looked kindly at his friend.

"I told you it wouldn't be worth it," he said. "Your friend is dead, and you are mortally wounded."

"It was worth it, sir," said the soldier.

"What do you mean, worth it?" queried the lieutenant. "Your friend is dead."

"Yes, sir" the private answered. "But it was worth it because when I got to him, he was still alive and I had the satisfaction of hearing him say, 'Jim..., I knew you'd come.'"

Sacrifice isn't necessarily altruistic. It can simply be giving up something for a value you believe is greater than the loss you will feel. The soldier cherished his comrade (and his comrade's respect) more than he prized his own life.

Many times in life, whether a thing is worth doing really depends on how we look at it in light of our value system. As Christians, we should take all our courage and do something our heart tells us to do so we won't regret not doing it later in our lives.

A true friend is one who walks in when the rest of the world walks out. As John 15:13 (ASV) asserts, "Greater love has no one than this, that someone lay down his life for his friends."

POST-IT MEDITATION FOR FEBRUARY 15
God, grant me the grace to be a loyal, courageous friend.

February 16

In His time, God makes all things beautiful.
~Diane Ball, songwriter

My mother, her body ravaged by Parkinson's disease, prayed continuously for healing. At some point, she felt God had given her the specific day on which she would be healed. My sisters and I huddled a few days before the appointed date, concerned how it would affect her if she awakened that morning and was still hopelessly bedridden. And then, I discovered the little contemporary song quoted above. "In His Time" had a powerful message: Not only does God make all things beautiful in his time, but he will show us, every day, as he teaches us his way, that he does just what he says, in his time.

On the day Mother believed she would be healed, my sisters and I played "In His Time" for her, trying to help her (and us) understand God's time is not always the time we pray for and want so desperately. Truth be known, our mother's faith was stronger than ours, and the song may have been needed more by us than by her. Perhaps that's why, when she died in the wee hours of a cold December morning several years later, out of the blue my sisters and I heard "In His Time" on the radio as we drove home.

Sometimes God tells us "no"; sometimes he tells us "later." That "later" may be in another dimension after our weak and ill human bodies have died to this life, but we have the assurance from God that he will keep his promises in *his* time. While we wait, our prayer can be for courage and strength to live through life's burdens, illnesses, and sorrows. This is a prayer God answers over and over—all that is required is for us to believe in his goodness and power.

We should never forget our human understanding is limited; our earthly vision is like looking through a foggy glass. As 1 Corinthians 13:12 (NLT) reminds us, "Now we see things imperfectly, like puzzling reflections in a mirror, but then we will see everything with perfect clarity. All that [we] know now is partial and incomplete, but then [we] will know everything completely, just as God now knows [us] completely."

In his time, God not only makes all things beautiful and does exactly what he says he will do; in his time, he will also allow us to understand the "why's" we cannot comprehend in this life.

POST-IT MEDITATION FOR FEBRUARY 16
I will pray for God to help me accept his answers to my prayers, even when they may not be what I want to hear, knowing in time, I will see my earthly life with new eyes of wisdom.

February 17

Adopt the attitude that was in Christ Jesus....
~Philippians 2:5 (CEB)

Chuck Swindoll, Christian pastor and author, wrote extensively on positive attitudes. Among his most remembered lines are these:

"The longer I live, the more I realize the impact of attitude on life. Attitude, to me, is more important than facts. It is more important than the past, education, money, circumstance, failure, success, and what other people think or say or do. It is more important than appearance, giftedness, or skill. It will make or break a company...a church...a home. The remarkable thing is we have a choice every day regarding the attitude we will embrace for that day. We cannot change our past... we cannot change the fact that people will act in a certain way. We cannot change the inevitable. The only thing we can do is play on the one string we have, and that is our attitude. I am convinced that life is 10% what happens to me and 90% how I react to it. And so it is with you...we are in charge of our attitudes."

A 92-year-old, petite, poised, and proud woman lived Swindoll's words:

She is fully dressed each morning by eight o'clock, with her hair fashionably coifed, and her makeup perfectly applied, in spite of the fact she is legally blind. Today she has moved to a nursing home. Her husband of 70 years recently passed away, making this move necessary.

After many hours of waiting patiently in the lobby of the nursing home, she smiled sweetly at the attendant when told her room was ready. As she maneuvered her walker to the elevator, the employee provided a visual description of her tiny room, including the eyelet curtains that had been hung on her one window.

"I love it," Mrs. Jones stated with the enthusiasm of an eight-year-old having just been presented with a new puppy.

"Mrs. Jones, you haven't seen the room....just wait," the attendant said.

"That does not have anything to do with it," she gently replied. "Happiness is something you decide on ahead of time. Whether I like the room does not depend on how the furniture is arranged. It is how I arrange my mind. I have already decided to love it. It is a decision I make every morning when I wake up. I have a choice. I can spend the day in bed recounting the difficulty I have with the parts of my body that no longer work, or I can get out of bed and be thankful for the ones that do work. Each day is a gift, and as long as my eyes open, I will focus on the new day and all of the happy memories I have stored away...just for this time in my life."

POST-IT MEDITATION FOR FEBRUARY 17
I will pray for the wisdom to see each day as a gift.

February 18

He chose to give birth to us by giving us his true word. And we, out of all creation, became his prized possession.
~James 1:18 (NLT)

Many years ago, my husband and I visited Taiwan. While there, we toured Chaung Tai, a Buddhist monastery, and were amazed at the number and size of Buddha idols (some as high as a three-story building) made of gold, ivory, and other precious materials. But the most lasting memory came from a nun-in-training, with whom we talked about her faith and her commitment to give her life in service. While our beliefs radically differed from hers, we were impressed with her sincerity and especially her insights about life. For several years following our visit, we exchanged emails with Jian Hong Shi, and often those emails back and forth contained inspirational stories. The story that follows was one she sent us:

One day the father of a very wealthy family took his son on a trip to the country with the firm purpose of showing him how poor people live. They spent a couple of nights on the farm of a family of modest means.

As they returned home, the father asked his son what he learned from the trip. The son answered: "I saw we have one dog, and they have four. We have a huge pool, and they have a creek that has no end. We have imported paper lanterns in our garden, and they have stars at night. Our patio reaches to the front door, and they have the whole horizon. We have a small piece of land to live on, and they have fields that go beyond our sight. We have servants who serve us, but they serve others. We buy our food, but they grow theirs. We have walls around our property to protect us; they have friends to protect them." Then his son added, "Thanks, Dad, for showing me how poor we are."

The father was speechless.

As our friend the nun added at the end of the story, "What is one person's worthless object is another's prized possession. Too many times, we forget what we have and concentrate on what we don't have. It is all based on one's perspective. Makes you wonder what would happen if we all gave thanks for the bounty we have instead of worrying about wanting more." After all, we are God's most prized possession.

POST-IT MEDITATION FOR FEBRUARY 18
Today I will appreciate the simple aspects of life.

February 19

The beginning of strife is like letting out water, so quit before the quarrel breaks out.
~Proverbs 17:14 (ESVUK)

Max Lucado, American author and preacher, avowed, "Conflict is inevitable, but combat is optional." Conflicts occur between friends, among family members, and even with strangers. How can we minimize the damage? First, we should not fight every battle. Some simply aren't worth it. Before we engage in conflict, we need to decide if this is a "fall on your sword" issue. If not, we may want to pull back and sidestep the fray. In short, we should choose our battles.

Second, as Martin Luther King advised, we should reject revenge, retaliation, and aggression. Those motivations and attitudes are not based on love, and they should be shunned.

Third, we need to realize differing opinions are acceptable, but how we express them is critical. When conflicts escalate because we have expressed how we feel in a condescending or hateful manner, we have passed the line of "disagreeing agreeably."

After choosing our battles, rejecting negative attitudes, and recognizing differences of opinion will always exist, we are ready for the next step: managing the conflict. Making a decision to control the conflict rather than letting it hold sway over our emotions and actions gives us the power to avoid destructive behaviors. The goal is not to win the battle, but to survive the war. When we engage in hurtful words, we take the risk of damaging relationships we may need in the future. We should heed the wisdom in Proverbs 15:1, which advises that a soft answer will diminish conflict while harsh words stir up anger. Unfortunately, many times we respond too quickly to a perceived insult. At other times, we become self-righteous and defend our position based on the faulty premise that we are always correct.

If we control our temper, we can avoid clashes with colleagues or others. By holding our words, or by responding in a tempered way, we can dodge disagreements. Then, the conflict can be resolved reasonably. Battle-hardened Ulysses S. Grant expressed this lesson well: "It has been my misfortune to be engaged in more battles than any other general on the other side of the Atlantic, but there was never a time during my command when I would not have chosen some settlement by reason rather than the sword."

A mother of four heeds Grant's approach to solving conflicts. A dinner table story serves as an example:

One night the seven-year-old asked for two forks, one for his potatoes and one for his meatloaf. The father of the young brood of four children was about to say, "No," believing his kid should learn to adapt since everyone else was functioning with one fork. The mother, wanting to avoid a tantrum that would spoil dinner for everyone, opened a calm, pro and con discussion with her husband and the children. After a few minutes, it seemed clear (even to the seven-year-old) that two forks weren't necessary. That wasn't the most important outcome. The kids experienced firsthand the value of considering all sides of a conflict and listening to others respectfully. In the future, the kids used negotiation instead of simply demanding what they wanted.

As John F. Kennedy once said, "We should never negotiate out of fear, but we should never fear to negotiate."

POST-IT MEDITATION FOR FEBRUARY 19
When others offend me or differ with
my opinions, I will defuse the conflict
by responding in a non-inflammatory way.

February 20

What a person deserves is unfailing love.
~Proverbs 19:22 (NIV)

Sally was suffering from a rare disease from which her younger brother had miraculously recovered two years previously. The doctors decided Sally's only chance to live was a blood transfusion from her five-year-old brother. One of the doctors explained the situation to Tommy and asked if he would be willing to give his blood to his sister. Tommy hesitated for only a moment and then drew himself up and said, "Yes, I'll do it if it will save Sally."

The next day Sally and Tommy lay side by side in the sterile operating room. As the transfusion progressed, Tommy smiled at his sister, watching the color returning to her cheeks. Then, with trembling lips, his own face turning pale, the little boy turned to the doctor and asked, "Will I begin to die right away?"

Immediately, the doctor realized Tommy had not understood, explaining his slight hesitation. In giving his blood to his sister, Tommy had thought he was giving up his life—he thought he would have to give his sister all of his blood to save her.

In the one brief moment when he had hesitated, Tommy had called up more courage than most of us can muster in a lifetime. He was willing to give his life so his sister might live.

Most of us aren't asked to give transfusions or donate organs while we are alive. The sacrifices we are asked to make are usually much smaller. A single parent on welfare eats less so her children can have more; two people job share so neither one is laid off; a husband works double shifts so his wife can go to college, and on and on.

Each day we see others in need, but how often do we respond and help? Helping a family member or close friend usually comes easily, but giving money or food or shelter to a stranger makes us hesitate.

Self-sacrifice is a symbol of the Christian life, and we can begin by reciprocating to those who sacrifice for us. Then we should turn to those who can do nothing for us in return. That is the essence of true Christianity. Every human being deserves unfailing love.

POST-IT MEDITATION FOR FEBRUARY 20
*God, please give me a heart of enduring
love for family, friends, and strangers.*

February 21

Know also that wisdom is sweet to your soul; if you find it, there is a future hope for you.
~Proverbs 24:14 (NIV)

American writer/physician Oliver Wendell Holmes wrote, "Pretty much all of the truth-telling there in the world is done by children." So it is that kids can teach us more about life than any source other than the Bible. Three stories illustrate the truth of this fact:

When we are disappointed about something in our lives, we should stop and think about a child who had his heart set on being in a school play. *Like the other kids, the little boy bravely tried out. On the day the kids were chosen for roles in the play, the little boy's mother was relieved when he walked up from the bus stop with a big smile on his face. "Guess what, Mom?" he shouted. And then the words that are a lesson to all: "I've been chosen to clap and cheer."* (Teachers are among those who can learn from this—they should help kids feel good about events or decisions that could make them feel disappointed or inferior.)

When we are unable to find words to speak to someone in sorrow, we can learn from a four-year-old whose elderly neighbor had recently lost his wife. *Seeing the man sitting on his front porch crying, the little boy crossed the yard and walked up on the porch. Then he climbed into the old man's lap and just sat there. When his mother asked him what he had said to the neighbor, the little boy responded, "Nothing. I just helped him cry."* Sometimes when we are at a loss for words, it can be helpful to just "be there."

When it appears we are not successful, we may find encouragement from the little boy whose Little League baseball team was behind 14-0. *Looking at the lopsided score, a father who had arrived late at the game walked up to his son during a timeout and said, "You don't look too discouraged considering the score." The little boy looked up at his dad with a puzzled look on his face. "Why should we be discouraged? We haven't been up to bat yet."*

It has been said that while we try to teach our children all about life, our children teach us what life is all about.

POST-IT MEDITATION FOR FEBRUARY 21
*When I am confused about life, I will listen
for lessons I can learn from children.*

February 22

The light died in the low clouds. Falling snow drank in the dusk. Shrouded in silence, the branches wrapped me in their peace. When the boundaries were erased, once again the wonder that I exist.
~Dag Hammarskjold, Swedish diplomat and Secretary General of the United Nations

If we ever doubt the existence of God, all that is necessary to restore our faith is to look at nature. Low clouds covering the light of day, snow descending at dusk, leaf-laden trees surrounding us in a forest—all speak to a divine design. And then *man*—what a wondrous creature man is—how could anyone other than God have envisioned a body so intricate and complex? Only a supreme being could have created every human as a matchless being. Likewise, no cloud is ever the same as another. No snowflake is ever replicated. Every leaf has its own shade of color. The wonder and uniqueness of human existence erases our boundaries with nature—words can't describe and science can't explain the details of every facet of God's creation.

When God created the amazing universe in which we live, the earth was desolate and shapeless. The raging ocean that covered everything was engulfed in total darkness, and God's power moved over the water. And then God created light. What a sight that must have been—for darkness to be overcome with light! He separated the light and darkness to create day and night. The next day God created a dome and divided the water above and below it, calling the dome, "sky." On the third day, he commanded the water below the sky to move to one place so land could appear—that land became our earth, and the water surrounding the land became the seas. From there, God created all kinds of plants.

God had already created light and separated it from darkness, but he added a sun to rule over day and the moon to rule over the night. And then, he molded the glorious stars that shine in the heavens above us. As the days evolved, he formed living beings in the water and air—what an imagination he must have had: sharks, catfish, eels, shrimp, bluebirds, penguins, flamingos, eagles, and on and on, magnificent creatures of the air and water, so many we will never see all of them. When God got to animals and insects—large and small, domestic and wild—his creativity went wild—bears, cows, dogs, elephants, rhinos, giraffes, rats, butterflies, centipedes, fireflies, and roaches (we sometimes wonder why God created some organisms, but no doubt he had a plan for them).

And then came man, formed in the image of God. And woman, created from the rib of the first man. The most stunning part of God's creation may well be the distinctive and delightful way he designed the body of a man and woman to fit together to produce new life. And, of course, many animals share a similar procreation design.

The vision and imagination of God is mind-boggling. Awesome is an overused word—perhaps we should reserve it to describe God's creations.

POST-IT MEDITATION FOR FEBRUARY 22
If I ever doubt the existence of God, I can renew my faith by opening my eyes to the world he created and all that is in it.

February 23

The Indian elephant is said sometimes to weep.
~*Charles Darwin, English naturalist*

Years ago my husband introduced me to a book called *When Elephants Weep,* and I found its message compelling. Not only do the authors remind us that no one who has ever had an animal doubts that non-humans feel, they also show (through field studies) how deeply animals love and suffer, how they show curiosity and disappointment, how they can be lonely or joyful, and how they reveal compassion and shame. The authors warn readers they "may be surprised by the unexpected emotional level of some of the animals: an elephant who keeps a pet mouse, a chimpanzee awaiting the return of her dead baby, a bear lost in rhapsody as it watches a sunset, an ice-skating buffalo, a parrot who means what it says, a dolphin inventing her own games...." And most incredibly of all, they tell how animals form lasting friendships and even willingly give their lives for the humans they love. Undeniably, God gave animals the ability to live emotional lives.

Two stories in the book illustrate the depth of love animals can live. One will be told here, and one will be shared February 24.

The first, whether fact or legend, is told by Jan Harold Brunvand in *The Choking Doberman*:

A prince came home and found his faithful hunting hound bloodied and gasping in the hall of his home. When he saw an overturned crib through the open doorway, the prince panicked. Jumping to the conclusion the dog had killed the baby it had been left to guard, the prince instantly slayed the dog. As he walked through the house to find his dead baby, the prince was shocked to find a huge wolf lying dead and just beyond, his unharmed baby. The prince felt deep sorrow that he had killed his loyal hound who had fought the huge wolf to save his baby, berating himself for not thinking before killing the dog who had been his friend.

We can find two lessons from this story. The first is that we should understand and honor the fierce loyalty of animals. The second is that we humans are often too quick to judge.

POST-IT MEDITATION FOR FEBRUARY 23
I will understand and cherish the capacity of animals to love, and I will emulate their loyalty—both with them and with humans. It is what God would want me to do with his precious creatures.

February 24

…Every day elephants are slaughtered for their tusks, rhinos for their horns, gorillas for their hands. My hope is that as it begins to dawn on people what feeling creatures these animals are, it will be difficult to justify these cruel acts.
~Jeffrey Mousasieff Masson, American author

The authors of *When Elephants Weep* suggest the most famous account of the bond of gratitude, friendship, and compassion between a person and an animal is likely in an ancient account of Androcles and the lion, told by someone who claimed to have witnessed the event.

In the tradition of the time, exhibitions of battles between wild beasts and humans created spectacles of sports beyond what we can probably imagine. Of all of the animals, lions excited the most wonder, and on a particular day, one was particularly impressive because of its huge size. When a slave named Androcles was brought into the arena, the crowd awaited with anticipation the lion's attack. But, as they watched in amazement, the ferocious animal simply stopped and stared at the man, and then slowly and quietly approached him. As the crowd held its collective breath, the king of the lions wagged its tail like a dog happy to see its master and then started licking his feet and hands.

The emperor Caligula, who was watching, immediately called Androcles to him and asked why the lion had spared the man. Timidly, Androcles told how he had run away from his master and was hiding in a remote cave when the lion limped into the cave, bleeding and moaning. Holding out its injured paw to Androcles, it was clear he wanted help. Androcles removed a huge splinter and cared for the foot, after which the lion put his paw in the man's hand, lay down, and went to sleep. Androcles continued that for three years he and the lion had shared the cave, and for that entire time, the lion had hunted food for both of them. At the end of the three years, Androcles was recaptured, returned to Rome, and condemned to death in the arena. After hearing the story, the emperor freed the man and the lion, and for years afterward the two walked the streets together.

Every person who saw them pointed to them and said, "This is the lion who was a man's friend; this is the man who was physician to a lion."

What better testimony might be found of the innate longing God installed in both man and beast to love and be loved by another?

POST-IT MEDITATION FOR FEBRUARY 24
I will do my part to help and protect innocent animals, knowing they depend on me—and often I depend on them— never forgetting they were created by God.

February 25

You did not choose me, but I chose you. I gave you a big work to do. That work is to go out and do good things and to make the good things that you do remain strong....
~John 15:16 (WE)

Our human nature pushes us to hide the dark sides of our lives. We don't want others to know anything about us that might cause them to look down on us. So, most of us don't talk about certain subjects unless someone else forces the issue. A son is arrested for DUI—if it doesn't make the local newspaper, the parents keep quiet about it with other family members. A husband is physically abusive, but his wife suffers in silence. A granddaughter endures sexual abuse from her stepfather, but her mother cannot admit it, sometimes not even to herself. A daughter loses her home to foreclosure, but mom and dad don't want their friends to know. The examples are endless. Shameful events and circumstances are kept hidden, locked deep inside.

After almost two decades of prescription drug abuse, one of my sisters found her way out of the abyss of addiction and now lives a drug-free life. For a long time, she was embarrassed about the awful actions she engaged in to support her drug needs, but after prayerful consideration, she decided to tell her story in a book called <u>HOOKED BUT NOT HOPELESS: Escaping the Lure of Addiction (2011)</u>. Like Elie Wiesel, Romanian-born Holocaust survivor, she believed that "Whoever survives a test, whatever it may be, must tell the story." The response has been amazing. Friends and strangers alike have contacted her not only to express admiration for her courage, but also to say how much it has helped to know that someone who seemingly had a wonderful, normal life had been through the horrors of addiction, often revealing they have an addict in their own family.

In one of the closing chapters of the book, Sylvia tells how difficult it was to share her story and explains why she was willing to open the darkest days of her life not only to her friends but also to the world: "I sobbed uncontrollably as I wrote the sordid story of my addiction. Reliving the mistakes I made, the decisions I regret, and the wrongs I've done hurt deeply—maybe more than when I was living through them. Then, my feelings were numbed by drugs. As I wrote my saga for this book, I was stone sober—not one pill to soften the remembrances or the remorse I felt. But I wanted to tell my story—if it will help just one person and give hope when that person feels hopeless, then dredging the dirt of my life back up will have been worth the pain."

We never know when a stranger or someone we know needs a message we carry hidden in our heart.

POST-IT MEDITATION FOR FEBRUARY 25
*I will pray for courage to share dark experiences
if they will bring light into another person's life.*

February 26

In my trouble I called to the Lord; I called to my God for help. In his temple he heard my voice; he listened to my cry for help.
~Psalm 18:6 (GNT)

When America and other parts of the world plunged into a deep recession in 2008, the stock market took a nose dive and millions saw their retirement savings plummet. Banks failed and businesses went bankrupt. Some were saved by the infusion of government money, but others went under. Banks foreclosed on thousands and thousands of homes, and the housing market collapsed. Unemployment soared above 10 percent in some areas as companies—large and small—cut back or closed their doors.

When the financial foundations of our country are shaken, when many Christians lose everything, our faith can hold us firm. As the psalmist knew, in our distress we can cry out to God and pray for help, and he will hear our plea. Nothing that happens can take away our belief that he will see us through hard times.

Sometimes the troubles we face are not just financial. Natural disasters strike, sometimes taking family members and destroying homes, including precious photographs and other cherished items that can never be replaced. No one is immune from calamity—earthquakes, hurricanes, floods, fires, avalanches, volcanic eruptions, tsunamis, and tornados hit indiscriminately. But even when disasters strike in record numbers, as tornados did in America in 2011, followed by a hurricane in 2012 that created massive destruction along northeastern coastal areas, Psalm 46:1-3 (NLT) provides the underpinning of our survival:

"God is our refuge and strength, always ready to help in times of trouble. So we will not fear, even if earthquakes come and the mountains crumble into the sea. Let the oceans roar and foam. Let the mountains tremble as the waters surge!"

Whether the storm is economic, physical, emotional, or even religious suppression, the refuge never changes: God is always there in times of difficulty or disaster, ready to give us strength. No matter what happens in the economy or with our personal possessions—or even our health or freedom—God wants us to turn to him. He is in control and will make a way for us through the storms of our lives. He is the only sure security. According to a true story told by one of the first missionaries to enter Russia, a handful of Russians believed that enough to risk their lives:

In Russia before the Berlin Wall came down and freedom to worship freely was against the law, many Christians were forced to get together in secret to worship. One group of Christians were gathered together in a simple house studying the Bible when suddenly the door was thrown open violently and three Russian soldiers burst in with rifles. One of the soldiers bellowed out that anyone who wasn't a Christian could leave immediately but anyone who had come to worship God should stay.

After a moment of silence, many of the people filed out of the house leaving a few people behind. One of the soldiers closed the door behind them and locked it; then, the soldiers all put down the rifles and explained to the remaining few that they also were Christians and wanted to worship with true believers.

Could we pass such a test of our faith?

POST-IT MEDITATION FOR FEBRUARY 26
Help me, God, to depend on you in times of turmoil.

February 27

Now as they went on their way, Jesus entered a village. And a woman named Martha welcomed him into her house. And she had a sister called Mary, who sat at the Lord's feet and listened to his teaching. But Martha was distracted with much serving. And she went up to him and said, "Lord, do you not care that my sister has left me to serve alone? Tell her then to help me." But the Lord answered her, "Martha, Martha, you are anxious and troubled about many things, but one thing is necessary. Mary has chosen the good portion, which will not be taken away from her."
~Luke 10:38-42 (ESV)

A woman named Ann Wells shared this story in the *Los Angeles Times*:
My brother-in-law opened the bottom drawer of my sister's bureau and lifted out a tissue-wrapped package. "This," he said, "is not a slip. It is lingerie." He discarded

the tissue and handed me the slip. It was exquisite: silk, handmade, and trimmed with a cobweb of lace. The price tag, with an astronomical figure on it, was still attached. "Jan bought this the first time we went to New York, at least eight or nine years ago. She never wore it. She was saving it for a special occasion. Well, I guess this is the occasion." He took the slip from me and put it on the bed with the other clothes we were taking to the mortician. His hands lingered on the soft material for a moment, then he slammed the drawer shut and turned to me. "Don't ever save anything for a special occasion. Every day is a special occasion."

Holding possessions for special occasions deprives us of pleasure we can experience today. But possessions are such a small and insignificant part of our lives. The lingerie symbolizes much more. It not only represents how we delay simple pleasures waiting for a "special occasion," but it also embodies how we brush aside opportunities to spend time with our family and friends because of the mundane chores and events that make up our daily lives.

I'm a list maker, and I never feel comfortable "wasting" time until I have checked off everything on my "to do" list. I would not want to count how many times in my life I put off doing something with my husband or son because I was too busy. Now, my husband is dead, and my son is grown, and it is too late. I wish I had realized the truth in poet Patricia Clafford's words many years ago: "The world will wait while you show the child the rainbow. But the rainbow won't wait while you finish the work."

The days of our lives are as transitory as a rainbow. And each day— each rainbow of our lives—is a special occasion. We should never fail to pause to enjoy a game with a child or grandchild. We should never brush aside a request to go for a walk with a loved one.

Each day is a special occasion. How we spend each hour of those days reflects what is important to us. Simply saying our family and friends— and our God—are valued above all else doesn't make it so. Taking time with another person to enjoy a rainbow, a starlit sky, or a jonquil raising its head from the earth does.

POST-IT MEDITATION FOR FEBRUARY 27
Beginning today, I am going to work hard not to hold back or save special times that will add joy to my life and others.

February 28

If you then, though you are evil, know how to give good gifts unto your children: how much more will your father in heaven give the Holy Spirit to them that ask him?
~Luke 11:13 (NIV)

The Mississippi River was flooding its banks, and waters had risen around Clem's house to the level of the front porch where he was standing. A man in a rowboat came by and called to Clem, "Hop in and I'll take you to high ground."

Clem replied, "No, my God will save me!"

The river continued to rise until it reached the second story windows and Clem, looking out, saw a powerboat come up. The man in the powerboat called to Clem, "Hop in and I'll take you to high ground."

Clem replied, "No, my God will save me!"

The river had now risen to the roof of the house. Clem was sitting on the ridge at the top of the house, with the waters swirling around his feet. A helicopter flew over and the people inside yelled over a bull horn, "Grab the rope and climb in and we'll take you to high ground."

Clem replied, "No, my God will save me!"

The river continued to rise, and finally it engulfed the house—Clem was drowned. The next thing he knew, he was standing before his creator. In anger, he attacked God, "I put my trust in you. Why have you forsaken me?"

God replied, "What do you want from me? I sent you a rowboat, a powerboat, and a helicopter!"

Like Clem, when we pray to God for help, we sometimes fail to see his answer. We have a preconceived idea about the solution we think we need, and that image gets in the way of our ability to see a different way out of our situation. God's promise is not a blank contract to give us our every whim or exactly what we want when we want it. Clem had unwavering faith, but it was blind faith. While we should be bold in our faith, we should also be open to believing God knows best about how to answer our prayers.

POST-IT MEDITATION FOR FEBRUARY 28
I will be open to God's plan for answering my prayers in a way that fulfills his purpose, knowing he cares for me.

February 29

(LEAP YEAR)
Keep your lives free from the love of money and be content with what you have....
~Hebrews 13:5a (NIV)

The story is told of a farmer who lived in Africa. Through a visitor, the man heard diamonds had been discovered on the African continent and became excited about the possibility of finding diamonds himself. Dreaming of the millions of dollars he could make, the farmer sold his farm and headed out to discover diamond mines. For years, he wandered over the continent, constantly searching, but he never uncovered a new cache of precious stones. Eventually, he became discouraged, totally broke, and threw himself into a river and drowned.

Back at the old farm, the new owner found an unusual rock about the size of a hen egg and put it in the center of his mantle as a sort of curiosity. One day, a visitor stopped by and gasped when he saw the stone. When his shock wore off, he told the farmer the funny-looking rock on his mantle was bigger than any diamond he had ever seen. "Heck," the new owner said, "the whole farm is covered with rocks like this one." And it was. The farm, later renamed the Kimberly Diamond Mine, became the richest mine the world has ever known. The original farmer had been standing on a fortune when he took off to search for diamonds in other parts of Africa.

Like the farmer, we sometimes stand on acres of diamonds but don't realize it. We whine and complain, seeking wealth or happiness any place except the present. What we fail to grasp is that real contentment may be exactly where we are right now. Unfortunately, only when we lose what we have can we truly appreciate the magnitude of our blessings. When tragedy and sorrow come, we look back on the times in our lives when we lived in a diamond mine but couldn't see its sparkle.

If we have family members who love us, good health to enjoy life, adequate resources for food and shelter, and a God who cares for us, why are we tempted to find greener pastures? For most of us, most of the time, "our cup runneth over." We should take what God gives with a thankful heart, praising him for what we have instead of worrying about what we don't have. As Isaiah 52: 12 advises, we need not make haste to leave where we are. We need to wait for God to go before us, knowing he will also be our rear guard. Satisfaction, full and deep, can fill our soul if we develop the ground where we stand.

POST-IT MEDITATION FOR FEBRUARY 29
To be content, I simply have to appreciate what I have.

March 1

Each person will be judged according to what he has done.
~Revelations 20:13 (NIV)

Beginning with the fall of man in Genesis, the Bible teaches that earthly beings were created with the capacity to make choices. Moreover, we will be held accountable for those decisions. Adam and Eve could have chosen to be obedient and been blessed with life in a beautiful garden, but they elected disobedience and were thrown out of the Garden of Eden, cursed. They were not victims of fate or an uncaring God—they knew what the consequences were when they made their decision to eat the forbidden fruit.

Like Adam and Eve, we sin because we choose to—not because someone else (or God) tempts us or because we are predestined to sin within God's plan for our lives. James 1:13-14 (NIV) says, "When tempted, no one should say, 'God is tempting me.' For God cannot be tempted by evil, nor does he tempt anyone, but each one is tempted when, by his own evil desire, he is dragged away and enticed."

Yet, when we foolishly wreck our lives, rather than accept responsibility, we blame others for our mistakes and failures. This is folly, accomplishing nothing. We are responsible for our own lives, and only when we accept accountability will we grow and develop into the persons God wants us to be.

Louis L'Amour, an American novelist, addressed man's responsibility with these words:

"Up to a point a man's life is shaped by environment, heredity, and movement and changes in the world about him; then there comes a time when it lies within his grasp to shape the clay of his life into the sort of thing he wishes to be. Only the weak blame parents, their race, their times, lack of good fortune, or the quirks of fate. Everyone has it within his power to say, 'This I am today, that I shall be tomorrow.' The wish, however, must be implemented by deeds."

The date: Friday, January 11, 2002. The setting: a packed gymnasium just prior to the start of the varsity game. Five girls (four of them starters), members of the Danville High School basketball team, weren't in uniform to play that night and wouldn't be for the remainder of the season. They were there to explain they had been kicked off the team because they had admitted a serious infraction of team rules. Voluntarily, they were there to support their coach's decision to take them off the team. And they did it with regret rather than defensiveness.

On New Year's Eve, the girls had gone to a party with several friends. Alcohol was served, and all five girls drank some.

The coach had a zero-tolerance rule on drugs and alcohol, and every kid who played for her knew that rule. She didn't have to confront the five, for they got together and decided to go to her with the full story.

The coach said she couldn't back down on her policy, and the two juniors and three seniors agreed. That Friday night in the gym was part of their public support of the coach's decision.

One of the seniors spoke last. "We hope you will understand we are not bad kids. We made a mistake....What we did was definitely not worth it. We hope this event will make everyone open their eyes and realize there is a big drug and alcohol problem in our community," she said. "And if you work with us to try to solve this problem, you will help us feel we have not been thrown off our basketball team for nothing." The five left the floor to deafening applause.

I don't know if the team won another game that year, but every player and all who heard the girls' contrition learned something about personal responsibility. They also internalized the effect of one's actions on others. No doubt, they said as L'Amour did, "This I am today, that I shall be tomorrow."

POST-IT MEDITATION FOR MARCH 1
I will not blame others for my shortcomings, failures, or what I don't have. I will accept responsibility for where I am in life and take positive action to move forward.

March 2

For I have given you an example, that you also should do just as I have done unto you.
~John 13:15 (ESVUK)

A veterinarian had been called to examine a ten-year-old Irish wolfhound named Belker. The dog's owners, Ron, his wife Lisa, and their little boy Shane, were all very attached to Belker, and they were hoping for a miracle. It was not to be. An examination revealed Belker was dying of cancer. The vet told the family nothing could be done for Belker and offered to perform the euthanasia procedure for the old dog in their home. As they made arrangements, Ron and Lisa decided it would be good for six-year-old Shane to observe the procedure—that it might help him to see the dog die peacefully.

The next day, with a familiar catch in his throat as Belker's family surrounded him, the vet noticed Shane seemed calm as he petted the old dog for the last time. He wondered if Shane understood what was going on. Within a few minutes, Belker slipped peacefully away.

The little boy seemed to accept Belker's transition without any difficulty or confusion. The vet sat with the family for a while after Belker's death, wondering aloud about the sad fact that animal lives are shorter than human lives. Shane, who had been listening quietly, piped up, "I know why."

Startled, everyone turned to him. What came out of his mouth next stunned the vet, who said he had never heard a more comforting explanation.

Shane said, "People are born so they can learn how to live a good life—like loving everybody all the time and being nice, right?" The six-year-old continued, "Well, dogs already know how to do that, so they don't have to stay as long."

So live like a dog:

…Live simply…Love generously…Care deeply…Speak kindly.

Remember, if a dog was the teacher you would learn things like:

➢ When loved ones come home, always run to greet them.
➢ Never pass up the opportunity to go for a joyride.
➢ Allow the experience of fresh air and the wind in your face to be pure ecstasy.
➢ Take naps. Stretch before rising.
➢ Run, romp, and play daily.
➢ Thrive on attention and let people touch you.
➢ Avoid biting when a simple growl will do.
➢ On warm days, stop to lie on your back on the grass.
➢ On hot days, drink lots of water and lie under a shady tree.
➢ When you're happy, dance around and wag your entire body.
➢ Delight in the simple joy of a long walk.
➢ Be loyal.
➢ Never pretend to be something you're not.
➢ If what you want lies buried, dig until you find it.
➢ When someone is having a bad day, be silent, sit close by, and nuzzle him gently.
➢ ENJOY EVERY MOMENT OF EVERY DAY!

SOURCE OF BELKER STORY: http://www.upgradereality. com/a-dogs-purpose-from-a-6-year-old/

POST-IT MEDITATION FOR MARCH 2
Thank you, God, for dogs who teach me how to live and love.

March 3

Just a closer walk with Thee, grant it Jesus is my plea.
~Unknown

The old hymn "Just a Closer Walk with Thee" carries a simple yet powerful message. The songwriter reminds us we are weak and God is strong. Recognizing we are born with sinful natures, he knows we need Jesus to keep us from all wrong. On our own, we can't resist temptation, but with God's help we can stand firm against evil that threatens to seduce us. We merely have to be willing to ask for strength and accept it.

The song's second verse takes us to the end of our earthly life, when "time for [us] will be no more." Assured that "God will guide [us] gently to that shore," we can be at peace. But what do we want to look back upon as we travel to the next dimension? How will we view our lives in hindsight and how will we be judged?

The first test, the Bible instructs, is simply whether we believed in God's son and accepted his promise of eternal life. We may expect the next test to be, "What have you done?" But, instead, the second examination may be, "How have you loved?" The test of what we believe is not through works alone, if at all. It is not what we have achieved—how many sermons we have preached, how many choirs we have sung in, how many casseroles we have taken to shut-ins. All those are good and important and contribute to the spreading of God's message. What matters most is how we loved. Did we love with a pure heart or because we had no choice? Did we give of ourselves— our time and our possessions—willingly or grudgingly? Did we give because we wanted praise or did we give from a heart of love? Did we help strangers or only those we liked or cherished?

Faith should be lived moment by moment. In a closer walk with God, as paraplegic Joni Eareckson Tada reminds us, "Details count: passing thoughts, small sacrifices, a few encouraging words, little acts of kindness." In short, a closer walk with God demands compassion that is pure and constant—love that emulates the love God has for all his children. Sometimes the sacrifice for genuinely deep love is great, as illustrated by the following story:

There was a blind girl who hated herself because of her blindness. She hated everyone, except her loving boyfriend. He was always there for her. She told her boyfriend, "If I could only see the world, I would marry you."

One day, someone donated a pair of eyes to her. When the bandages came off, she was able to see everything, including her boyfriend.

He asked her, "Now that you can see the world, will you marry me?" The girl looked at her boyfriend and saw he was blind. The sight of his closed eyelids shocked her. She hadn't expected that. The thought of looking at them the rest of her life led her to refuse to marry him.

Her boyfriend left in tears and days later wrote a note to her saying, "Take good care of my eyes, dear. I'll always love you."

That's the kind of unfathomable love Christ had for us when he died for our sins. If we pray for a closer walk with him, we can love friends, family, and strangers equally and fully.

POST-IT MEDITATION FOR MARCH 3
I will not boast about what I do for others; and I will show love not only to those who can love me back but also to those who may have nothing to offer me in return.

March 4

…Tomorrow the Lord will do wonders among you.
~Joshua 3:5 (ESV)

In the Broadway musical Annie, *set in 1933 in the depth of the depression, a little orphan girl escapes from a New York City orphanage run by a cruel, embittered woman to look for her parents, who abandoned her eleven years previously. Although she finds a mongrel dog that she adopts, she is unsuccessful in locating her parents. Returned by police officers to the orphanage just before Christmas, she barely escapes being beaten by the heartless headmaster when she is chosen by a wealthy man's assistant to come to his home for the holidays. With the same charm and cheerfulness that lit the dreary rooms of the orphanage, Annie wins Mr. Warbucks over, even though he had wanted a boy for the holidays. He institutes a search for her parents, attracting a number of shyster couples, one of whom comes close to claiming Annie, but the plot is foiled. When it is finally determined Annie's parents are dead, Warbucks declares he will adopt Annie himself. That year becomes the most wonderful Christmas ever for Annie, capped off by opening a big box containing the dog she had found and then lost. It's the beginning of a whole new life for Annie, whose cheery buoyancy has finally turned a dire situation into an unbelievable home filled with love.*

Do you remember the song "Tomorrow" from the musical? With the forward-looking optimism of a kid, Annie sings, "The sun'll come out, tomorrow; bet your bottom dollar, that tomorrow, there'll be sun!"

Fortunately, "tomorrow" isn't tied to a specific day of the week. So, if the sun doesn't shine today, we can look forward to it shining tomorrow. And if not, the next tomorrow, or the next. Just thinking about tomorrow, Annie sings, clears away cobwebs and sorrow until there are none. So when she gets stuck in a lonely, grey day, she just sticks out her chin, and with a grin, sings, "…you gotta hang on 'til tomorrow come what may…[because] tomorrow is always a day away."

Like Annie, we should love tomorrow. When we are down and out, depressed or in despair, we should say with Joshua: "Tomorrow the Lord will do powerful works among [us]" (Joshua 3:5, NLV). We can wait with hope and trust that God will bring sunshine again—he will not leave us in darkness. In his master design, he has plans for all of our tomorrows. His blueprint may not be what we expected or wanted, but his plan is perfect and as it unfolds, it may be better than we could have hoped or imagined. Through it all, we learn to trust in our creator. Wherever we go, whatever we are faced with, God will be with us. We can trust him no matter what comes our way. He is always there for us. As the psalmist professed, "If I go up to the heavens, you are there. If I lie down in the deepest parts of the earth, you are also there." (Psalm 139:8, NIRV).

"Tomorrow, tomorrow…." Oftentimes, tomorrow is unknown. But God is always known, and he will be in all our tomorrows. If today is bad, we can look forward to tomorrow. If we fear tomorrow, we can claim God's promises and rest assured, "Surely goodness and mercy will follow [us] all the days of [our lives]…" Psalm 23:6 (KJV).

March 5

So then, confess your sins to one another and pray for one another, so that you will be healed. The prayer of a good person has a powerful effect.
~James 5:16 (GNT)

A little Texas boy was outside playing with his dog one day while his mom was inside cooking. Soon, he bounced into the house, dripping excitement.

"Mom, there's a lion in the back yard."

Grabbing a gun, the mother ran outside, but no lion was visible.

"Johnny, there's no lion—just old Spot."

"But mother, there IS a lion!"

"Johnny, there is no lion. Now I want you to go upstairs and don't come down until you've talked to the Lord about your lying."

A little while later the boy returned.

"Well, did you talk to the Lord about the lion, Johnny?"

"Yes, mom, and the Lord thought it was a lion, too."

Former President Lyndon Johnson told this story as he was leaving office, disappointed he had not accomplished all he set out to do—from the Vietnam War to Civil Rights. He concluded by telling his audience he hoped they would see poverty, unemployment, and civil rights as lions.

Like Johnson, God sees lions everywhere. The lions among us threaten to scar our lives or even kill us, and God wants us to defend ourselves—with his help. Johnny ran to his mom for help when he envisioned a lion in his backyard. We need to run to God when the lions of the 21st century—greed, lust, envy, addiction, adultery, homosexuality, divorce, wrath, sloth, pride, gluttony, cursing, pornography, and countless other sins—invade the backyards of our lives. Others may not see the sins as lions, but God does and he stands ready to help us defend against them.

POST-IT MEDITATION FOR MARCH 5
*I will turn to God for insight to recognize
sin and for power to fight it.*

March 6

Why am I discouraged? Why am I restless? I trust you! And I will praise you again because you help me, and you are my God.
~Psalm 43:5 (CEV)

There is an old saying that you can't kill a frog by dropping him into hot water. That's because as you drop the frog into the hot water, he reacts so quickly he immediately jumps out unharmed. But if you put him in cold water and gradually warm it up until it is scalding hot, he will be cooked before he realizes what is happening to him. The progression of bad habits in our lives is very much like this. Similarly, the encroachment of wrong thinking takes its hold on our lives so slowly we are unaware it controls the temperature of our spirit. When that happens, we are lulled into asking God for what we think we need—not what he knows is of most value.

I asked God to take away my habit.
God said, "No. It is not for me to take away, but for you to give it up."
I asked God to make my handicapped child whole.
God said, "No. His spirit is whole, his body is only temporary."
I asked God to grant me patience.
God said, "No. Patience is a byproduct of tribulations;
it isn't granted, it is learned."
I asked God to give me happiness.
God said, "No. I give you blessings; happiness is up to you."
I asked God to spare me pain.
God said, "No. Suffering draws you apart from worldly
cares and brings you closer to me."
I asked God to make my spirit grow.
God said, "No. You must grow on your own,
but I will prune you to make you fruitful."
I asked God for all things that I might enjoy life.
God said, "No. I will give you life,
so that you may enjoy all things."
I asked God to help me love others, as much as he loves me.
God said..."Ahhhh, finally you have the idea."

How much more richly blessed our lives would be if we realized that loving others as God loves us is the beginning and end of life's blessings, the answer to all our problems, and the source of our growth and development as Christians. Walking the journey of faith requires confidence—we may not see the reasons for what happens to us, but we can have assurance that God's plan is infallible. He knows what is best for us, and when we believe that, we can praise him regardless of our circumstances.

POST-IT MEDITATION FOR MARCH 6
I will find the secret to a life of
contentment through unconditional love.

March 7

My command is this: "Love each other as I have loved you."
~John 15:12 (NIV)

Charles Plumb, a U.S. Navy jet pilot in Vietnam, flew 75 combat missions before his plane was brought down by a surface-to-air missile. After ejecting and parachuting into enemy hands, he spent six years in a communist prison in Vietnam. He survived and later lectured on lessons learned from that experience.

One day, while Plumb was sitting in a restaurant, a man recognized him. "You're Plumb! You flew jet fighters in Vietnam from the aircraft carrier Kitty Hawk...you were shot down."

Plumb, mystified because he didn't recognize the man, asked him how on earth he knew that. "I packed your parachute," the man replied, adding, "I guess it worked."

Plumb couldn't sleep that night, thinking about the man, wondering how many times he might have walked by the sailor without even speaking. After all, Plumb was a fighter pilot and the other man was just a sailor. But now Plumb thought about how many hours the sailor had spent at a long wooden table in the bowels of the ship, carefully weaving the shrouds and folding the pieces of each chute, holding in his hands each time the fate of someone he didn't know.

After that day, Plumb's speeches always started by asking his audiences, "Who packs your parachute?"

Everyone has someone who provides what it needed to make it through the day. Not only family or friends, but someone who stood at bottling machinery and made sure orange juice was poured into sanitary containers. Someone who installed the brakes on our cars. Someone who worked all night because a tree had hit a power line. A researcher who toiled for years in a lab to develop a new cancer treatment. On a smaller scale, the elderly man who bags our groceries. The volunteer at the hospital. The custodian who cleans our office building.

Somewhere along the way we let our lives get so busy and our egos so big that we sometimes fail to notice people. Or, we think they get paid for what they do, so why should we acknowledge their service? We may neglect to say "hello," "please," or "thank you," or congratulate someone on something positive that has happened to him or her. We don't pause to give a compliment or simply do something nice for no reason.

Christ commanded us to love one another as he loved us; we should remember that he loved a leper, a prostitute, and others who were looked down on by the society of the day. His command requires we follow his example.

POST-IT MEDITATION FOR MARCH 7
*I will remember that every person I pass by
each day may be packing my parachute.*

March 8

We know not what we ought to pray for.
~Romans 8:26 (NIV)

When we search the Bible for answers, we sometimes find conflicting guidance. It becomes difficult to know how specific our prayers should be. Do we simply pray, "Thy will be done," or do we ask what we really want—healing, a new job, a companion, or countless other desires? If we pray for patience, do we suddenly become afraid God will answer that prayer? If we pray to trust God, do we fear he will send a tragedy to test our faith? If we pray for strength, and God sends temptation, do we wish we hadn't asked?

In Left to Tell, 22-year-old Immaculee Ilibaugiza shares her story of survival during the 1994 Rwanda genocide. From an idyllic life with her parents, she was thrown into danger and chaos; yet, despite the massacre of her family members, she sought God to sustain her. Along with seven other women, she huddled silently in unspeakable terror in a cramped bathroom in a local pastor's house for 91 days. During those dark days when she was hunted by machete-wielding killers, when nearly one million ethnic Tutsis were slaughtered, she found strength in prayer, forging a powerful relationship with God.

A poem by Annie Johnson Flint could well have expressed Immaculee's feelings, "I prayed for light; the sun went down in clouds." The poem continues that the moon became darkened by misty doubt, and the stars were dimmed by human fears. When even candle flames burned out, the poet says, "While [she] sat in shadow, wrapped in night, the face of Christ made all the darkness bright."

The message is clear: we may be down for a time; we may feel discouraged and without hope, unable to see the light. But the light is always there—behind the clouds, the sun, moon, and stars still shine. And the clouds will sooner or later move on or dissipate, leaving the light to brighten our lives again. Immaculee finally found that light.

Even knowing the clouds won't last forever, how should we pray when our very souls ache? Perhaps surprisingly, we don't need to pray when we are too broken to think or just can't find the words. In the final assurance of Romans 8:26, we find that when *we* don't know how to pray, the Spirit himself intercedes for us through wordless groans. Most of us have, at one time or another, found ourselves in need of this intercession. We can become so soul-sick that, in words penned long ago by Shakespeare, we realize, "My words fly up, my thoughts remain below: Words without thoughts never to heaven go." When we get to this place, the Spirit takes our unspoken and often unformed thoughts and groans on our behalf. We may not know what to pray for, but the Spirit knows our needs and knows God's plan—the words the Spirit utters for us are always the right ones, and they are always heard.

POST-IT MEDITATION FOR MARCH 8
When I can't pray, I can trust the Spirit to see my needs and carry my unspoken pleas to God.

March 9

I am the true vine, and my Father is the gardener. He cuts off every branch in me that bears no fruit, while every branch that does not bear fruit he prunes so that it will be more fruitful.
~John 15:1-2 (NIV)

Today I trimmed the crepe myrtles in my front yard. I cut them deep and low with confidence, knowing they would regrow their height and be filled with vibrant, fragrant blossoms in only a few weeks. I haven't always been that confident. I remember the first time my husband trimmed our crepe myrtles many years ago. I thought he had ruined them for life! What he knew—but I didn't—was that this kind of flowering tree blooms on new wood or new growth. My husband also taught me about "suckers," shoots that form at the very base of the plant near where the trunk meets the soil. Suckers pull life from the plant and also make it look like a bush instead of a tree.

I've often thought are lives are like crepe myrtles—God expects us to prune them. Periodically, we should remove the parts that no longer produce fruit. Do we participate in activities that crowd out the time we could spend studying God's word? Do our lives bloom for God or for others? Do our commitments of time and money bear fruit for God or for ourselves? And, do we have suckers that pull the very lifeblood from our souls—bad habits, sinful pastimes, or wasteful indulgences? If so, it is time to cut dead branches and suckers that bear no fruit for God. Time to trim the tree of our lives so that new growth can sprout.

Success as a Christian requires development—not just when we first believe, but continuously. As with crepe myrtles, that new growth comes from new wood—not old. Titus 2:7 commands us to be a pattern of good works in all that we do. We can start new patterns of Bible reading and prayer as commitments to keep ourselves blooming after the dead wood has been cut from our lives. Granted, sometimes we get off track and don't prune ourselves soon enough. Then, God may decide we are more like a pumpkin than a crepe myrtle and take action:

A lady recently asked her co-worker what it was like to be a Christian.

The lady replied, "It's like being a pumpkin: God picks you from the patch, brings you in, and washes all the dirt off you may have gotten from the other pumpkins. Then he cuts the top off and scoops out all the yucky stuff. He removes the seeds of doubt, hate, greed, etc., then he carves you a new, smiling face and puts his light inside of you to shine for all the world to see."

A walk of faith demands that we spend time with God, studying his word and talking with him. Revitalized patterns of meditation and worship, alone or with others, bear fruit that delights our creator.

POST-IT MEDITATION FOR MARCH 9
I will pray for courage and strength to trim the dead wood from my life, making room for new growth pleasing to God.

March 10

In all things I have shown you that by working hard in this way we must help the weak and remember the words of the Lord Jesus, how he himself said, "It is more blessed to give than to receive.
~*Acts 20:35 (ESV)*

We live in an age of visual images—on our smart phones and tablet computers, on high definition television, and on countless other high technology innovations. These images shape our concepts of life and people. They form expectations of how we and others should appear and act if we are to be viewed as having potential. But sometimes the frame of reference we have developed causes us to miss the very attributes we wish to emulate because they are obscured by a person's physical looks or apparent lack of motivation.

Mildred Hondof, a musician, supplemented her income by teaching piano lessons. Over the years, she taught children with a wide range of talent, and when he started, Robby was at the bottom of the list. Eleven years old, he was too old to begin, Hondof thought, but he persisted. That is, until he just stopped showing up. Months later, when she mailed a copy of a recital flyer to the homes of all her students, Hondof was surprised when Robby called to say he wanted to play in the recital. Despite her reluctance, Robby wore her down and she agreed to let him perform.

The night of the recital, Robby showed up looking like a vagabond—clothes wrinkled, hair uncombed. Hondof thought to herself, "Why didn't his mother at least make him comb his hair for this special night?"

Pulling out the bench and seating himself carefully, Robby began playing Mozart's Concerto #21 in C Major. Amazingly, nimble fingers danced lightly over the ivories, going from pianissimo to fortissimo...from allegro to virtuoso. When he finished to a standing ovation, Hondof ran up on stage and hugged Robby. "I've never heard you play like that Robby. How did you do it?" Through the microphone, Robby explained: "Remember I told you my mother was sick... she died this morning. She was born deaf, so this is the first time she ever heard me play. I wanted to make it special."

Tears flowed across the audience. As social service personnel led Robby from the stage to be placed in foster care, Hondof bowed her head, thankful she had given Robby a chance. More importantly, she acknowledged she had learned more from him than he had learned from her. In her words, "I've never had a protégé but that night I became a protégé...of Robby's. He was the teacher and I was the pupil. For it is he who taught me the meaning of perseverance and love and believing in yourself, maybe even taking a chance on someone and you don't know why." She concluded:

"This is especially meaningful to me since after serving in Desert Storm, Robby was killed in the senseless bombing of the Alfred P. Murrah Federal Building in Oklahoma City in April of 1995, where he was reportedly...playing the piano."

SOURCE OF HONDOF STORY: *www.wsmonline.com*

POST-IT MEDITATION FOR MARCH 10
Help me, God, not to be quick to judge the potential of others.

March 11

Life is real! Life is earnest! And the grave is not its goal. "Dust thou art and to dust thou returneth" was not spoken of the soul.
~Henry Wadsworth Longfellow, American poet and educator

When my mother's Parkinson disease rendered her totally helpless—powerless to raise her head from her pillow and unable to speak the coherent thoughts trapped by the nerve connections between her brain and her tongue—my sisters and I reluctantly made the decision to admit her to a nursing home. It was, at the time, the worst day of my life. My mother didn't object to the admission—in fact, she seemed to welcome it, realizing we could no longer safely move her back and forth from bed to chair (where she had to be propped with pillows to keep from falling over). Even so, I felt guilty we could no longer care for her. I couldn't shake the feeling we had abandoned her, even though we continued to spend several hours with her daily. I went by the nursing home on my way to work every morning to help with breakfast; my sister Sylvia sat with her for hours after she took her children to school, and I went by the nursing home again on my way home to make sure mother had help with dinner. After going home for dinner with my family, I returned to the nursing home to tuck my mother in and make sure her call button was within reach. Still, my heart broke that she was in a foreign environment, and we couldn't be with her every minute.

The experiences at the nursing home over the next seven weeks remain etched in my mind. Two memories stand out. The first was that we discovered our mother could still sing, even though she couldn't speak. When I visited, I often pushed her in a wheelchair to the recreation room and played the piano—hymns she had sung beautifully for so many years. The first time I heard her feeble voice singing along, I was stunned. I later read this is not uncommon, that it is similar to people who stutter but can often sing flawlessly. Another sign of the amazing brain God created....

The second memory stems from the 94-year-old lady who shared my mother's room. Her mind had returned to days long gone, and frequently she called one of Sylvia's children by her own child's name. But when she quoted poetry, she moved back into the classroom where she had taught English many years before. Frequently, as I entered the room, I heard her quoting from Longfellow's *A Psalm of Life*. The poet tells us the grave is not our goal and reminds us that in Genesis, when God told Adam, "You were made from soil, and you will become soil again" (Genesis 3:19 GNT), he was not speaking of our soul. He was explaining that death of our bodies is inevitable—they were created from the earth and eventually, when the flesh decays, will return to the earth. While humans are mortal and all of us will die, our souls will live forever. When God breathed into the nostrils of the man he had created, "...man became a living soul"— a soul that can exist without the body, as seen when Jesus differentiated between the two in Matthew 10:28 (ESV): "...do not fear those who can kill the body but not the soul...."

What an assurance God gives us in facing our own death or the death of loved ones! The body will die, but the soul will live forever.

AUTHOR'S NOTE: Actually, there is a third memory...When I visited the nursing home on Saturdays, I always carried a fresh batch of brownies I had baked that morning and shared them with several patients at the home. After a while, two men began waiting for me on the front porch each Saturday morning. Even after my mother died, I continued to take brownies to the nursing home each week until I moved to another city. One week, I didn't have time to go on Saturday, so I made the brownies but waited until Sunday to deliver them. When I handed them to the two men on the front porch, one of them, after taking his brownies, looked up at me and said, "But they aren't warm!" From then on, I went back to taking the brownies as soon as they came out of the oven.

POST-IT MEDITATION FOR MARCH 11
When I grieve the death of a loved one,
I will remember that the soul did not
die—it awaits a heavenly reunion.

March 12

Lord, please help us learn the secret even little flowers know.
~Danny Lee, songwriter and singer

People who post their feelings on social media pages sometimes offer suggestions worth considering. I particularly liked this one:

Recently it dawned on me I've been complaining a lot. Work woes, weight-gain blues, vague "what-am-I-doing-with-my-life" worries.... And generally my life is pretty groovy, so it's like my brain is hunting for things to be perturbed about. I know you have days—or weeks— like this, too. Nothing seems right. So I've been thinking: What about a day of no complaining?

It's harder than it sounds. That's a full 24 hours of not once whining or grumbling about anyone or anything, no matter how much it's bugging you. It's an exercise in being mindful about what you're projecting.

Now, I believe in venting. I do. Sometimes just gotta let it out. But when you find yourself constantly talking about the same old things that irritate you and make your life difficult, your words have a strange way of bringing you further down.

Danny Lee's song, "Little Flowers," carries a powerful message: Flowers never worry when the wind begins to blow and the rain begins to fall. They know, "Tho' it's wet, and oh, so cold, soon the sun will shine again" and then they'll smile to the world, their beauty brightened, not dampened, by the deluge. In the second stanza, Lee writes that flowers don't complain when the clouds begin to gather and the storm begins to grow, even though they are tossed to and fro, because they've learned the secret: "If it never, never rained, then they'd never, never grow."

Flowers are one of God's grandest gifts to mankind. As we breathe in their sweet fragrance, we can almost feel the breath of God in our nostrils, lifting us with a spiritual high. We gaze on the gorgeous blooms, seeing the strokes of God's paintbrush, the vibrant colors brightening our day. A wonderful creation, the flower was planted by God, but like all living creatures, it must be nourished, so he sends the rain to keep it alive and growing. And the little flowers never complain, because they know the secret.

If only we could be like flowers, singing in the rain, knowing we will grow lovelier and stronger by enduring storms. Learning this lesson, we can chant with the blossoms, "Let it rain, let it rain…let it pour…. Let old trouble keep a knock-in' at my door."

The squalls and suffering we face teach us many lessons, including right from wrong, patience, and persistence. Without hard times, the experiences necessary to grow in faith would be missing from our lives: The downpour that threatens to drown us is the sustenance we need to grow. Within each tribulation is a message and a gift from God; it is up to us to look up after the storm, just as little flowers lift their heads when the tempest is past.

In the same way God can turn the most barren field into a garden of wildflowers with a good soaking, he can transform our lives into a garden of faith.

POST-IT MEDITATION FOR MARCH 12
God, help me learn the secret that
growth can come from misery.

March 13

It takes faith to wade into deep waters—especially when you don't know where the bottom is.
~Robert H. Schuller, American televangelist, pastor, speaker, and author

The clouds dumped gushing spouts of water on the Walmart parking lot as a crowd of shoppers waited for the rain to slack before making a dash to their cars. Some waited patiently, others irritably, aggravated Mother Nature was holding them hostage. And then the sweet voice of a child broke the strained quiet that enveloped the group: "Mom, let's run through the rain."

"No, honey," the mother responded, "We'll wait until it slows down a bit."

But the child persisted, and the mother, about to get exasperated, said, "We'll get soaked!"

"No we won't," the little girl said, tugging on her mother's arm. "Don't you remember what you said this morning? When we were talking to Daddy about his cancer, you said, 'If God can get us through this, he can get us through anything.'"

Everyone under the awning stood still in stark silence, waiting for the mother's response. After a pause, while she thought about laughing it off or even scolding her daughter for being silly, the mother realized she couldn't ignore the teachable moment.

"Honey, you are absolutely right. Let's run through the rain. If God lets us get wet, well maybe we just needed washing." Then off they ran.

As the crowd huddled under the awning watched, the mother and her little girl laughed and smiled as they ran to their car. They got soaked.

A few brave souls followed, making joyful noises as they splashed through the rain. Guess they needed washing, too.

From this little story that circulated over the Internet during 2001, we can learn not only about the joys of acting like a child occasionally but also about how we might face more serious events in our lives. E.B. Pusey, an English Anglican theologian, wrote, "God does not take away trials or carry us over them, but strengthens us *through* them." God didn't keep the little girl dry, and he may not have healed her father, but he taught her how to live her faith a day at a time.

POST-IT MEDITATION FOR MARCH 13
Each time I encounter challenges, I will act in faith more fervent than yesterday. I may even run through the rain.

March 14

Something there is that doesn't love a wall…
~Robert Frost, American poet

Frost's poem, "Mending Wall," uses nature to illustrate how some people build walls between themselves and others. He tells us that the frozen ground swells under a rock wall and spills the boulders, making wide gaps. Hunters also knock down the stone walls when their yelping dogs need a path to their prey. No one sees the gaps made, but they are visible every spring when the two neighbors in the poem walk the wall, one on each side. One man, who has pine trees on his side, works hard to keep the rocks in place, saying, "Good fences make good neighbors." The other man, who has an apple orchard, disagrees, arguing that his apple trees will never go across and eat the pine cones. But the other just repeats again, "Good fences make good neighbors," and continues picking up stones, balancing one on top of the other.

How often do we build fences in our lives? We put them up around swimming pools for safety, but in truth, we are probably glad the law requires a fence; it keeps the neighbor's kids out. We build fences to keep cows in and coyotes out. We build them so our dogs will have a place to run without offending neighbors.

Physical fences can be seen regularly across the landscape, but there are other kinds of fences—invisible ones—that we put up in relationships. Teenagers frequently build barriers to keep their parents out of their "business." Other parts of the family also get walled off—sometimes grandparents aren't made to feel welcome; some husbands and wives let their marriage deteriorate so much that walls become thick and wide. Walls are erected between people on their jobs because of competition, jealousy, or other reasons.

"I'll never forgive him. I told him I would never forgive him." The elderly lady spoke softly, but with resolve, as the nurse brought her nightly medication. The lady's expression was troubled as she turned away, focusing on the drape wrapped around her nursing home bed. This brief exchange revealed a deep, deep hurt.

She told of how her brother had approached her bed, accusing her of taking more than her share of family heirlooms following their mother's death. He spoke of various items, ending with "the berry spoon." He said, "I want the berry spoon." For the forty years since the mother's death he had hidden his feelings, and now they erupted. She was both hurt and angered by his accusation and vowed never to forgive him.

"It's my spoon. Mother gave it to me," she defended herself. "He's wrong and I won't forgive him."

Standing at her bedside, the nurse felt her own spirit soften and grieve. A spoon—a berry spoon! In the bed lay a woman given two months to live—just sixty days—and she would face eternity and never see her brother again in this life. Her mind and spirit were in anguish, and her only remaining family ties were broken over a berry spoon.

As the nurse returned to her station she was drawn deep into thought: "How many berry spoons are there in my life? How many things, as insignificant as a spoon, in light of eternity, separate me from God—and from others? How does a lack of forgiveness keep me separated from my family?" She asked God to search her heart, asking again, "How many berry spoons are there in my life?"

How about you? Are there any berry spoons or fences in your life festering hurt feelings toward another?

When we build walls or other barriers between ourselves and others, we often think we are protecting ourselves—isolating ourselves from harsh words, meddling, or other offenses. But if too many walls exist in our lives, we become insular, which can lead to feelings of loneliness and bitterness. Before building walls, we should do as the poet suggests: ask what it is we are shutting in or shutting out. If it is not wild animals or something else that can do great harm, we might want to leave the spaces open.

POST-IT MEDITATION FOR MARCH 14
When I begin building a wall, I will ask myself,
"Why?" and "Will I likely give
offense or cause myself harm?"

March 15

…but with God all things are possible.
~Matthew 19:26 (KJV)

Frank Leahy, all-time great football coach of Notre Dame, says, "In our locker room, we kept one sentence hanging prominently as long as I was coach: "When the going gets tough, the tough get going." He taught and believed that the tougher the problem or opponent, the tougher his players had to become. Like football players, we must take charge and take control when faced with adversity. We can't let our fear overtake us.

Another famous football coach, Bear Bryant of Alabama, once told a story about his coaching days at Texas A&M:

Bryant's team had arrived in town to play SMU (Southern Methodist University) in a big bowl game, only to find all of the local newspapers were predicting Texas A&M was going to be slaughtered. Knowing his players had read the negative forecasts, Bryant was petrified what it would do to their morale. He admitted he himself was affected. Unable to sleep, early the next morning, he remembered this Bible verse: "If you have faith as a grain of mustard seed, you will say to this mountain, 'Move from here to there,' and it will move; and nothing will be impossible unto you" (Matthew 17:20, NIV).

His heart in his throat, Bryant jumped from the bed and assembled his coaches and team. He started by telling them he knew naysayers had predicted they would be beaten by four, five, or six touchdowns. But then he read what Jesus said. Without another word, he sent the team back to bed. Later that day, his players got tough instead of playing scared. Did they win? No, but they were only three points behind their victorious hosts. They lost the game, but they saved their pride.

We are never failures when we try to the best of our ability. One day, when we stand before God, we will be accountable—even if we have not built great churches, fed masses of hungry people, or served as missionaries on foreign soul, God will be pleased if we dared to try something, however small, for his glory.

POST-IT MEDITATION FOR MARCH 15
When the going gets tough, I will not lose my faith.
I may not win the game of the day, but I will know
I have faced life with courage and have
served God, if only in small ways.

March 16

Behold I am the Lord…Is anything too difficult for me?
~Jeremiah 32:27 (NASB)

Someone once said it's not the size of the mountain; it's the size of the mountain mover. When the all-powerful creator of the mountain is in charge, we know no peak is too high to shove or scale. God is greater than any problem we will ever face. Nothing is too difficult for him. Even so, we are not promised every problem will be solved.

Robert Schuller tells the story of a pastor who felt overwhelmed by an obstacle in his life:

Walking through the countryside, the man of God's head hung low. A farmer in a nearby field noticed the downcast man and asked if anything was wrong. The pastor admitted he was facing a major obstacle in his life and was worried what might happen. Turning toward an enclosure in front of his house, the farmer asked him what the cow in the distance was doing.

"Why, she's just looking over the wall," the pastor replied.

"Do you know why?" the farmer persisted, but the man had no answer.

"She's looking over the wall because she can't see through it," the farmer exclaimed.

Like the cow, we are faced with walls we cannot see through, walls appearing to hold us back from what we want to do, walls imprisoning us with our troubles.

Schuller says he once believed there was a solution to every problem, but he came to realize some difficulties can't be resolved. Instead, he says, we have to find a way to overcome the problem, manipulate it, or mold it. When we can't see a way through an obstruction, we must look beyond it.

The size of the mountain we face may seem insurmountable, but God can help us find a way to tunnel through it, go around it, or even guide our thinking so we no longer want to get to the other side of the mountain. He can help us see that the valley where we are may be sufficient for our needs. We humans have a tendency to think the grass is always greener on the other side. When we get there, we may find the grass scorches in withering sunlight just like the green on the side where we were dissatisfied. The miracle God sends may simply be in helping us find peace and contentment wherever our life leads. Even that is not too difficult for God.

POST-IT MEDITATION FOR MARCH 16
God, help me find your will for
my life through my difficulties.

March 17

How can anyone discover what life means? It is too deep for us, too hard to understand.
~Ecclesiastes 7:24 (GNB)

Most human beings search for meaning in their lives, only to find it is beyond comprehension. Great philosophers like Aristotle, Confucius, and Epicurus spent their lives on this quest for the impossible. They searched and searched, but they ended up with more questions than answers. As Oliver Wendell Holmes said, "Any two philosophers can tell each other all they know in two hours." God's master plan remains elusive, even to wise minds.

Yet, the quest is compelling, and we cannot resist its lure. To know why we exist, to understand our purpose in this life, to perceive our connection to eternity—the pursuit itself is worthy. But sometimes the search for purpose takes us on a different path. We attempt to fill our lives with possessions, unconsciously thinking they will bring meaning. Yet, all we have to do is look at rich people who have no joy and peace to realize that what we own has no relation to our true purpose.

Robert Heilbroneer, writing in *Psychology Today*, said, "...It's great to have two cars and a swimming pool. But there are disappointments; after you've made some money and acquired some things, and after the initial excitement has passed, life goes on, just as bewildering as it always was, and the great problems of life and death once again come to the fore. We reemerge from our love affair with goods and know consumption isn't the answer, and we ask ourselves what is."

The story of a wise woman traveling in the mountains illustrates this point.

On her travels, the woman found a precious stone in a stream. The next day she met another traveler who hadn't had anything to eat that day and was hungry. The woman willingly opened her bag to share her food.

The hungry traveler saw the precious stone and asked the woman to give it to him, never expecting she would, but that is exactly what she did. The man left rejoicing in his good fortune, knowing the stone was worth enough to give him security for a lifetime.

A few days later, the traveler journeyed back to the mountains and looked for the wise woman. When he found her, he took the stone and placed it in her hand. "I've been thinking," he said. "I know how valuable this stone is, but I give it back in the hope you can give me something even more precious. Give me what you have within you that enabled you to give me this stone."

What the wise woman knew—and what the man learned—is that life's meaning and purpose are to be found within our inner being. Within her was a contentment and peace that came from caring more about others than she did about wealth.

POST-IT MEDITATION FOR MARCH 17
I will look for the wonders of life within
myself, not in what the world can give me.

March 18

When you encounter difficulties…, do not try to break them, but bend them with gentleness and time.
~St. Francis de Sales, Roman Catholic saint

A father took his young son into a toy shop to give him a chance to look at some special gifts he would like to receive for his birthday. The father told the boy to wander around on his own for a few minutes to see what he would like. At the back of the shop, his young son found a statue of a man made from lots of colorful balloons. He looked at the balloon man for a minute, and then he drew back his fist and hit him as hard as he could. The balloon man fell back and hit the floor, then rocked backward and forward and after a few seconds he stood upright again. The confused boy backed off and looked at the balloon man and then hit him again, as hard as he could. The balloon man fell back once more and hit the floor but was soon standing upright again.

The father saw his young son hit the balloon man and asked, "Why do you think he comes bouncing back up when you hit him and knock him down?"

The boy thought for a minute and said, "I don't know Dad; I guess it's because he's standing up on the inside."

Bouncing back when we are knocked down isn't easy—but we can stand straight on the inside because God is in our innermost being. The key is not staying down too long.

Today, thinking about the balloon man, I looked outside and saw ice-laden trees, bending beneath the burden of a late-winter storm, bringing to mind Robert Frost's poem, "Birches."

Having grown up swinging on birch trees, Frost knows young boys can bend birches, but they don't stay that way from the weight of a child. Ice storms carry the load that bends them to the point of breaking, holding them down day after day. After they are bowed so low, so long, they never completely right themselves. And so, Frost contends, he had much rather a young boy ride the branches, fleeing the earth for a while but letting go in time for the birch to right itself.

As a swinger of birches, in adulthood Frost contemplates, when he is weary of life's considerations, he would like to escape the bounds of earth once again before coming down to begin his life anew. He's quick to say he doesn't want the fates to think he wants to be snatched away, never to return. He just wants to take flight for a few moments, a temporary diversion from life's problems.

Unfortunately, as adults we cannot find peace of mind from a momentary escape. Starting our lives fresh and clean would be appealing, but the responsibilities we accumulate on earth don't disappear that easily. We can learn from the poem, though, how the birches survive—they bend instead of break. In the same way, we should bow with our problems, slowly and deliberately, until the burden melts. If we don't let problems snap us, we can once again look toward the sky when the coldness of our life gives way to the warmth of the sunshine. Some troubles and tragedies are so heavy we think we will never again stand quite as straight as we once did, but even a cruel bend in our spirit won't forever cover our eyes from the light of God's promises. God has the power to make us totally straight again: "Consider the work of God: for who can make straight what he has made crooked?" (Ecclesiastes 7:13, ESV). He may allow us to bend, but he will be waiting when we look upward, ready to make us straight once again.

POST-IT MEDITATION FOR MARCH 18
I thank God for the reprieves I find in swinging on birches, but I will remember that returning to the world is requisite to recovery and growth.

March 19

Though you have made me see troubles, many and bitter, you will restore my life again...You will increase my honor and comfort me once again.
~Psalm 71:20-21 (NIV)

A couple who liked antiques and pottery, especially teacups, went to England to shop in the beautiful stores on their twenty-fifth wedding anniversary.

One day in a tiny shop they saw an elegant teacup and asked to see it, saying they had never seen one quite as lovely.

As the lady handed it to them, suddenly the cup spoke. "You don't understand," it said. "I haven't always been a teacup. There was a time when I was red clay. My master took me and rolled me and patted me over and over and I yelled out, 'Let me alone,' but he only smiled, 'Not yet.'

"Then I was placed on a spinning wheel," the cup said, "and suddenly I was spun around and around and around. 'Stop it! I'm getting dizzy!' I screamed. But the master only nodded and said, 'Not yet.'

"Then he put me in the oven. I never felt such heat!" the teacup said. "I wondered why he wanted to burn me, and I yelled and knocked at the door. I could see him through the opening, and I could read his lips as he shook his head, 'Not yet.'

"Finally the door opened, he put me on the shelf, and I began to cool. 'There, that's better,' I said. But then he brushed and painted me all over. The fumes were horrible. I thought I would gag. 'Stop it, stop it!' I cried. He only nodded, 'Not yet.'

"Then suddenly he put me back into the oven, not like the first one. This was twice as hot, and I knew I would suffocate. I begged. I pleaded. I screamed. I cried. All the time I could see him through the opening, nodding his head saying, 'Not yet.'

"Then I knew there wasn't any hope. I would never make it. I was ready to give up. But the door opened, and he took me out and placed me on the shelf.

"One hour later he handed me a mirror and said, 'Look at yourself.' And I did. I said, 'That's not me; that couldn't be me. It's beautiful. I'm beautiful.'

"'I want you to remember, then,' he said, 'I know it hurts to be rolled and patted, but if I had left you alone, you would have dried up. I know it made you dizzy to spin around on the wheel, but if I had stopped, you would have crumbled. I know it hurt and was hot and disagreeable in the oven, but if I hadn't put you there, you would have cracked. I know the fumes were bad when I brushed and painted you all over, but if I hadn't done that, you never would have hardened; you would not have had any color in your life. And if I hadn't put you back in that second oven, you wouldn't survive for very long because the hardness would not have held. Now you are a finished product. You are what I had in mind when I first began with you.'"

When we are filled with pain, when we think the fire we are in will kill us, we can have faith we will not only endure our tribulations but will become stronger and lovelier because of the heat and hurt.

POST-IT MEDITATION FOR MARCH 19
I will see myself and God's creative mastery in the story of the teacup.

March 20

They looked…and behold, the glory of the Lord appeared in the cloud.
~Exodus 16:10 (ESV)

Enigmatically, the luminous light of God appeared in a cloud after he tired of the Israelites complaints. They had fussed and fumed, declaring they wished God had left them in Egypt, where at least they had plenty of food, instead of starving them to death in the wilderness. After the dazzling light had departed, in the evening a large flock of quails flew in; and, the next day, when the morning dew evaporated, thin, flaky cakes wrapped in the taste of honey covered the ground. The Israelites ate manna for the next 40 years, until they reached the land of Canaan.

The discouraged Israelites had felt hopeless, even though God had parted the Red Sea for them to escape the Egyptian armies. Despite that awesome evidence of power, they had doubted God's capability (or perhaps desire) to take care of them. But God heard their moaning and grumbling, and in a blaze of light from a cloud, he told Moses to tell his people he would prove that "I, the Lord, am their God."

Mrs. Charles E. Cowman, in *Streams in the Desert*, tells about an autumn day when she saw a tragic sight:

A prairie eagle was mortally wounded by a rifle shot. His eyes still gleaming like a circle of light, the eagle slowly turned its head and gave one more searching and longing look at the sky. The magnificent bird "had often swept those starry spaces with his wonderful wings. The beautiful sky was the home of his heart. It was the eagle's domain. A thousand times he had exploited there his splendid strength. In those faraway heights he had played with the lightning and raced with the winds, and now, so far away from home, the eagle lay dying, done to the death, because for once he forgot and flew too low."

Cowman compares our soul to the eagle. This is not our soul's home, and it must not fly too low, losing its skyward view. Our eyes should always look upward so our soul can behold the glory of the Lord. The light shining through the cloud is there to prove the Lord is our God, and as long as our soul keeps its skyward look, we will never lose hope. As the Israelites received quail and manna for their physical bodies, our soul will be fed with God's love and care.

POST-IT MEDITATION FOR MARCH 20
I will keep looking up, letting the light of God nourish my hungry soul.

March 21

Even the smallest act of caring for another person is like a drop of water; it will make ripples throughout the entire pond....
~Jessy and Bryan Matteo

Rabbi Paysach Krohn, author of *ArtScroll Maggid* short stories, shares a powerful story about his son Shay, who is physically and mentally disabled, to illustrate how true human nature presents itself in the way people treat those who are unlike themselves.

As Shay and his father walked by a group of boys playing ball in a park one day, the boy asked, "Do you think they'll let me play?" Even though he assumed the boys wouldn't want a handicapped child on the team, he couldn't tell his son "No" without at least asking, so he did. One boy took it upon himself to answer: "We're losing by six runs and the game is in the eighth inning. I guess he can be on our team, and we'll try to put him in to bat in the ninth."

Shay struggled to the team's bench, ecstatic, and the boys on the team saw the boy's father smiling broadly, full of joy that his son was doing something "normal." In the bottom of the eighth inning, Shay's team had scored a few runs but was still behind by three. As promised, in the top of the ninth, Shay was given a glove and instructed to go to right field. No balls came his way, but it didn't matter. He was playing!

In the bottom of the ninth, Shay's team scored again. Excitement filled the air—with two outs and the bases loaded, the potential winning run was on base—but Shay was next at bat. Sadly, he didn't even know how to hold the bat. The other boys knew they could substitute—but they didn't. And, in a moment the father will never forget, the pitcher, recognizing the other team had put aside winning for this moment in Shay's life, moved in a few steps to lob the ball so softly Shay could make contact. Two pitches went by with only clumsy swings. Stepping closer, the pitcher put the ball where Shay couldn't miss it—and he hit a slow ground ball right back to the pitcher! As everyone watched in silence, the pitcher intentionally threw the ball right over the head of the first baseman. And then, the magnanimous gesture continued. As Shay ran around the bases, player after player threw the ball away, leaving no possibility Shay would be tagged out. The crowd went wild, yelling "All the way, Shay!" And he did, scoring the winning run.

"That day," the father concludes with tears in his eyes, "the boys from both teams helped bring a piece of true love and humanity into this world. Shay didn't make it to another summer and died that winter, having never forgotten being the hero...."

In today's era of irrationally competitive sports at the Little League level, would this ever happen again? We need to teach children Galatians 5:22-23 (NLT): "But the fruit of the Spirit is love...kindness... goodness...gentleness...."

POST-IT MEDITATION FOR MARCH 21
***God, help me never forget that caring
is more important than winning.***

March 22

Speak, for your servant is listening.
~1 Samuel 3:10 (NIV)

God speaks to us every day, but like the Biblical Samuel, who thought Eli was calling him, we think the voice is from someone else. And, our task of identifying the voice as God's is even more difficult than what Samuel encountered, because the voice is not audible. How many times have we wished God would speak to us so loudly we couldn't mistake his voice? But he speaks with a still, small sound. To hear it, our hearts must be open and waiting in anticipation.

A young man had been to Wednesday night Bible Study. The pastor had shared about listening to God and obeying the Lord's voice. The young man couldn't help but wonder, "Does God still speak to people?"

After the service, he went out with some friends for coffee and pie to discuss the message. Several different ones talked about how God had led them in different ways. It was about ten o'clock when the young man started driving home. Sitting in his car, he began to pray, "God…if you still speak to people, speak to me. I will listen. I will do my best to obey."

As he drove down the main street of his town, he had the strangest thought: Stop and buy a gallon of milk. He shook his head and said aloud, "God, is that you?" He didn't get a reply and started on toward home. But again, the thought: Buy a gallon of milk. The young man thought about Samuel and how he didn't recognize the voice of God, and how little Samuel ran to Eli. "Okay, God, in case that is you, I will buy the milk." It didn't seem like too hard a test of obedience. He could always use the milk.

He stopped and purchased the gallon of milk and started toward home. As he passed Seventh Street, he again felt an urge: "Turn down that street." This is crazy, he thought, and drove past the intersection.

Again, he felt he should turn down Seventh Street. At the next intersection, he turned back and headed down Seventh. Half jokingly, he said out loud, "Okay, God, I will." He drove several blocks, when suddenly, he felt compelled to stop.

He pulled over to the curb and looked around. He was in a semi-commercial area of town—it wasn't the best but it wasn't the worst of neighborhoods either. The businesses were closed, and most of the houses looked dark, like the people were already in bed.

Again, he sensed something saying: "Go and give the milk to the people in the house across the street." The young man looked at the house. No lights were on, and it looked as if the people were either gone or already asleep.

He started to open the car door and then sat back in the seat. "Lord, this is insane. Those people are asleep and if I wake them up, they are going to be mad and I will look stupid."

Again, he felt he should go and give the milk. Finally, he opened the door, "Okay God, if this is you, I will go to the door, and I will give them the milk. If you want me to look like a crazy person, okay. I want to be obedient. I guess that will count for something, but if they don't answer right away, I am out of here."

He walked across the street and rang the bell. He could hear some noise inside. A man's voice yelled out, "Who is it? What do you want?" Then the door opened.

The man was standing there in jeans and t-shirt. Looking like he just got out of bed, he had a strange look on his face. He didn't seem too happy about some stranger standing on his doorstep. "What is it?" The young man thrust out the gallon of milk, "I brought this to you."

The man took the milk and rushed down a hallway speaking loudly in Spanish. Then from down the hall came a woman carrying the milk toward the kitchen, followed by the man holding a bawling baby. Sobbing, the man whispered brokenly, "We were just praying. We had some big bills this month and ran out of money. We didn't have any milk for our baby. I was just praying and asking God to show me how to get some milk."

His wife in the kitchen yelled out in broken English, "I asked him to send an angel with some. Are you an angel?" The young man reached into his wallet and pulled out all the money he had on him and put it in the man's hand. He turned and walked back toward his car, tears streaming down his face. He knew that God still speaks.

POST-IT MEDITATION FOR MARCH 22
I will set aside time each day and prepare my heart to hear God speak in the silence.

March 23

The love of God is greater far than tongue or pen can ever tell.
~F. M. Lehman, 20th century author, composer, and Nazarene minister

F. M. Lehman was at a camp meeting in a Midwestern state many decades ago when he heard an evangelist end his message with these words from an old Jewish poem:

> Could we with ink the ocean fill, and
> were the skies of parchment made,
> Were every stalk on earth a quill, and
> every man a scribe by trade,
> To write the love of God above would drain the ocean dry.

107

Struck by the weighty words that were so deep and insightful, Lehman was moved to preserve them for future generations, but it was years later when he was doing hard manual labor in 1917 that he picked up a scrap of paper during a break and with a pencil stub added the first two stanzas and chorus of the song, "The Love of God." All while sitting on an empty lemon crate.... More amazing than that environment was the place where the lines for the 3rd stanza (quoted above) were originally written—they had been penciled on the wall of a patient's room in an insane asylum and were found after he had been carried to his grave. From there, the words became a part of the Jewish poem "Haddamut," written in Aramaic in 1050 by Meir Ben Issac Nehorai, a cantor in Worms, Germany. Almost 900 years later they became the third verse of one of the greatest hymns ever written.

If an insane man could comprehend the love of God in such a profound way, how much easier it should be for us. Instead, we often make God's love perplexing by trying to understand in concrete, earthly terms. If we could only accept "how rich and pure...how measureless and strong" God's love is and that "it shall forever more endure," how much more peaceful our hearts might be.

Romans 8:38-39 (NIV) give us the assurance that "neither death nor life, neither angels nor demons, neither the present nor the future, nor any powers, neither height nor depth, nor anything else in all creation, will be able to separate us from the love of God that is in Christ Jesus our Lord." The love of God is indeed greater than tongue or pen can tell, but it is revealed to us in our earthly lives in remarkable ways and will stay with us through eternity.

POST-IT MEDITATION FOR MARCH 23
Thank you God for love that "goes beyond the highest star."

March 24

God is not unjust; he will not forget your work and the love you have shown him as you have helped his people and continue to help them.
~Hebrews 6:10 (NIV)

A couple, whom we shall call John and Mary, had a nice home and two lovely children, a boy and a girl. John had a good job and had just been asked to go on a business trip to another city and would be gone for several days. It was decided Mary needed an outing and would go along too. They hired a reliable woman to care for the children and made the trip, returning home a little earlier than they had planned.

As they drove into their home town, glad to be back, they noticed smoke, and they went off their usual route to see what it was. They found a home in flames. Mary said, "Oh well, it isn't our fire, let's go home."

But John drove closer and exclaimed, "That home belongs to Fred Jones who works at the plant. He wouldn't be off work yet; maybe there is something we could do."

"It has nothing to do with us," protested Mary. "You have your good clothes on—let's not get any closer."

But John drove up and stopped, and they were both horror stricken to see the whole house in flames. A woman on the lawn was in hysterics screaming, "The children! Get the children!" John grabbed her by the shoulder saying, "Get hold of yourself and tell us where the children are."

"In the basement," sobbed the woman, "down the hall and to the left."

In spite of Mary's protests, John grabbed the water hose and soaked his clothes, put his wet handkerchief on his head, and bolted for the basement, which was full of smoke and scorching hot. He found the door and grabbed two children, holding one under each arm like the football player he was. As he left he could hear some more whimpering. He delivered the two badly frightened and nearly suffocated children into waiting arms and filled his lungs with fresh air and started back, asking how many more children were down there. They told him two more, but Mary grabbed his arm and screamed, "John! Don't go back! It's suicide! That house will cave in any second!"

But he shook her off and went back by feeling his way down the smoke-filled hallway and into the room. It seemed an eternity before he found both children and started back. They were all three coughing, and he stooped low to get what available air he could. As he stumbled up the endless steps the thought went through his mind that there was something strangely familiar about the little bodies clinging to him, and at last when they came out into the sunlight and fresh air, he found he had just rescued his own children.

The baby-sitter had left them at this home while she did some shopping.

The wife had reacted normally. She hadn't wanted her husband to risk his life trying to save others, never imagining they might be her own children. It is in our human nature to be selfish and want to put our own safety above others. The Bible, however, gives well-defined guidance on our need to give glory to God by helping others in need. We are commanded to be generous in loving others and in doing so, Proverbs 22:9 tells us we will be blessed.

POST-IT MEDITATION FOR MARCH 24
***When I am tempted to pass by those needing
help, I will remember how John saved his
own children, thinking he was saving others.***

March 25

If you faint in the day of adversity, your strength is small.
~Proverbs 24:10 (ASV)

The story starts with a few carrots, a couple of eggs, and coffee. It was shared by a mother with her daughter, who complained about her hard life. Tired of trying and struggling, it seemed as soon as one problem was solved, another arose. The daughter appeared ready to give up.

Walking into the kitchen, the mother filled three pots with water and placed each on high on the gas burners of her stove. When the water boiled, the woman placed carrots in one pot, eggs in another, and in the last one, ground coffee beans. Silently, she stood and watched the pots continue boiling.

Twenty minutes later, the woman turned off the burners. She dipped the carrots up, fished the eggs out, and ladled the coffee—placing each in a separate bowl. Turning to her daughter, she asked, "Tell me, what do you see?"

The daughter replied with a quizzical look, "Just carrots, eggs, and coffee." But when her mother brought her closer and asked her to feel the carrots, she noted they were soft. The mother then asked her to take the eggs and crack the shell, releasing hard-boiled eggs. Finally, the mother asked the daughter to taste the coffee wafting its rich aroma in the air.

Mystified, the daughter asked, "What does it mean, mother?"

In simple terms, the mother explained that each of the objects had faced the same adversity—boiling water—but each reacted differently. The carrot went in strong, hard and unrelenting, but after being subjected to the boiling water, it softened and became weak.

The egg started out fragile, its thin outer shell protecting its liquid interior. After sitting in the boiling water, its inside became hardened.

The ground coffee beans were unique—after they were in the boiling water, they changed the water.

Which are you? A carrot that seems strong but with pain and adversity becomes soft and loses its strength? Or, are you like the egg that starts with a malleable heart but hardens with the heat? Did you have a fluid spirit, but after the trials of your life, become hardened and stiff? Does your shell look the same, but on the inside you are bitter and tough with a stiff spirit and a hardened heart?

Or, are you like the coffee bean, changing the hot water, the very circumstance that brings the pain, releasing its fragrance and flavor?"

POST-IT MEDITATION FOR MARCH 25
When adversity strikes, I want to be like coffee.

March 26

Give thanks in all circumstances, for this is God's will for you in Christ Jesus.
~1 Thessalonians 5:18 (NIV)

Giving thanks in all circumstances sounds absurd. It is tough enough to thank God for obstacles and troubles in our lives, but when a devastating tragedy strikes, the challenge becomes even greater. Why should we be grateful for an event that rips our lives apart? Where can we find faith when we are mired in daily problems, not to mention in times of deep despair?

One of the reasons we should give thanks every day, regardless of what it brings, is that we gain strength from practicing contentment despite daily anxieties and misfortunes.

Just as a weight-builder's muscles grow stronger with practice, so does our spirit. We become more resilient under pressure. And, like a diamond we can become beautiful because of the weight placed on us. A diamond is nothing more than a lump of coal that has gone through hard, hot pressure for up to a thousand years or more. But after it survives, it is a stone of great price and splendor. Put a lump of coal beside a diamond, and you will see the "before and after" that comes from intensive pressure over a long period of time.

In 1862, in the middle of the Civil War, General Stonewall Jackson wrote his wife, who was ill. Telling her he trusted God would hold her in his hands, he advised, "So live that your sufferings may be sanctified to you; remember that our light afflictions, which are but for a moment, work out for us a far more exceeding and eternal weight of glory."

The following year, on May 2, 1863, when the seemingly invincible Confederate Army won a significant victory at Chancellorsville, his troops were saddened when General Stonewall lost his left arm. Visited by a chaplain the next day, Jackson declared, "You see me severely wounded but not depressed.... I am sure my Heavenly Father designs this affliction for my good. I am perfectly satisfied, that either in this life, or in that which is to come, I shall discover that what is now regarded a calamity, is a blessing.... If it were in my power to replace my arm, I would not dare do it, unless I could know it was the will of my Heavenly Father."

Most of us would not have seen the loss of an arm as a blessing in disguise, but with practice we can learn to see through the apparent disaster and discern God's wisdom. Until that day comes, through faith, we can still give thanks in all things, seeing God's hand in all that happens to us.

When we are overwhelmed with what life has put upon us, if we can thank God, our attitude will change. And from a thankful heart, a soul grows in the spirit of God. When we are truly grateful, we walk in faith. We trust God in every circumstance. As someone once said, thanks and trust are Siamese twins.

St. Francis de Sales advised, "Take courage, and turn your troubles into material for spiritual progress." We can groan through our problems, or we can grow through them.

God is refining us with trials and tribulations in the same way he transforms a diamond. Like the lump of coal, we suffer heavy burdens, but if we endure and wait, we will become a shining jewel in God's kingdom.

POST-IT MEDITATION FOR MARCH 26
*I will thank God when blessings overflow
and when blessings are withheld.*

March 27

We who are strong have an obligation to bear with the failings of the weak, and not to please ourselves.
~Romans 15:1 (NIV)

A mother, in an effort to encourage her small son's piano lessons, purchased tickets to a performance by a great Polish pianist, Ignace Paderewski. The mother and child were both excited as they took their seats in the grand concert hall, where a splendid Steinway sat on the stage awaiting the hands of a master.

After a few moments, the mother began talking to the person beside her and didn't notice when her son got up from his seat and slipped away. When the lights were lowered, a stage spotlight revealed where the little boy had gone. There he sat on the bench of the majestic piano, where he began picking out "Twinkle, Twinkle Little Star." Mortified, his mother gasped and started toward the stage to retrieve her son. But before she could make her way through the aisles, Paderewski walked on stage and stood behind the little boy. The audience watched, agonizing, fearing what was coming. But they were wrong.

"Don't quit. Keep playing," the artist whispered. As the audience sat transfixed, the master leaned over and with his left hand began filling in bass notes. Then, with his right arm reaching around the child, he improvised a delightful treble accompaniment. The simple song had become a masterpiece. Everyone in the concert hall exploded in applause when the duet ended.

When he walked on stage and saw the little boy, Paderewski could have shooed the boy away. But he didn't. He took the opportunity to show grace and kindness.

What if we all had helping hands like the great master? How many opportunities do we pass by? It doesn't take a concert virtuoso and it doesn't require a well-lit stage to make a difference. We can all use our hands to make a person's life better. It matters not whether someone sees us—what matters is that we use whatever talent or resources we have to help a person who may be in over his head, a person who doesn't know how to get out of a bad situation, or anyone who needs something we have—a smile, a dollar, or just an encouraging word.

Few of us got where we are all by ourselves. Along the way, someone's helping hands gave us support. As part of our thanksgiving for the help we received, we can serve others.

POST-IT MEDITATION FOR MARCH 27
When I see an opportunity to
help someone, I will not pass it by.

March 28

Even so, it is well with my soul.
~Horatio P. Spafford, prominent 19th century lawyer

In 1870, Horatio Spafford, his wife Anna, and their five children had a wonderful life in Chicago, where he was a successful attorney. In early 1871, that began to change when their only son suddenly died. Not long afterward, another blow brought financial loss: a massive fire wiped out much of the city, and along with it, significant real estate holdings that had added to the Spaffords' financial security. Still, the family continued to serve God, opening their own home to some who had become homeless during the fire and helping many others find new housing.

When life had calmed down, Horatio booked passage to Great Britain—he and his family were going to help D.L. Moody with his overseas evangelism. At the last minute, Horatio had to delay the trip due to business responsibilities, and his family boarded the ship without him, knowing he would be catching up with them soon. Before that could happen, the ship the family was sailing on was struck by another vessel, sinking within twelve minutes. As soon as she could, Anna sent a two-word cable to her husband: "Saved alone." All four daughters had perished.

Horatio read the devastating news and immediately booked passage to England to rejoin his wife. Together, the heartbroken parents talked about how they could go on, how they could rebuild a life shattered by tragedy beyond understanding.

Several months later as they returned to America, Horatio heard the ship's engines stop. Then, a knock on his cabin door. A steward asked him to come to the bridge. When he arrived, the captain somberly told him the ship had stopped at the exact spot where his daughters had drowned to observe a moment of silence in their memory. The kind gesture sent Horatio reeling. Once again he was overwhelmed with pain and sorrow.

Returning to his cabin, Horatio looked to God for relief. As he sat with his head bowed, he penned the words to the great hymn, "It Is Well with My Soul."

Enveloped in his emotions, he wrote, "When peace like a river attendeth my way, when sorrows like sea billows roll, whatever my lot, Thou has taught me to say, 'It is well, it is well, with my soul.'"

His "lot" had been horrible beyond words, but Spafford's soul remained full of faith. God's presence in his life brought comfort and assurance that all was well in spite of his loss.

POST-IT MEDITATION FOR MARCH 28
God, grant me the wisdom and strength to know you are greater than any circumstance I shall ever face.

March 29

…The deeds of a man's hands will return to him.
~Proverbs 12:14 (NASB)

One night, at 11:30 p.m., an older African American woman was standing on the side of an Alabama highway trying to endure a lashing rain storm. Her car had broken down, and she desperately needed a ride. Soaking wet, she decided to flag down the next car.

A young white man stopped to help her, an action almost unheard of in the conflict-filled decade of the 60's. The man took her to safety, helped her get assistance, and put her into a taxi.

The lady seemed to be in a big hurry, but she wrote down his address and thanked him. Seven days went by and a knock came on the man's door. To his surprise, a giant console color TV was delivered to his home. A note was attached. It read:

"Thank you so much for assisting me on the highway the other night. The rain drenched not only my clothes, but also my spirits. Then you came along…. Because of you, I was able to make it to my dying husband's bedside just before he passed away…. God bless you for helping me and unselfishly serving others."

Sincerely,
Mrs. Nat King Cole

One of the laws of nature is that we reap what we sow. If we plant bulbs of tulips and irises in the fall, we will enjoy tulip and iris blooms the next spring. Surely, moles might eat the bulbs or a long drought might keep the flowers from blooming, but barring some natural intervention, we will reap what we sow. Likewise, good deeds we do may be overlooked or rejected, but many times we will be rewarded for our efforts. And, indeed, we may think our efforts have gone unrecognized, but just as the young man didn't receive a reward immediately, in time, we may be acknowledged. But if not, could it be we are looking for the wrong prize or compensation? Is the satisfaction of knowing we have done something for someone not enough? Perhaps our reward will come at a later time in another life.

My father, Kermit Howard, had little, but he never hesitated to help someone in need. I will forever remember how more than once he let a burned-out family or someone else who was down and out live rent-free in a small house whose rental income he counted on to pay his own bills. I don't recall that he ever received special blessings for his self-sacrifice, and I'm sure he never thought about Paul's words: "In due time we shall reap." He never expected anything in return, but I have no doubt he had rewards waiting on him in heaven for all of his selfless acts of kindness.

POST-IT MEDITATION FOR MARCH 29
God, help me to be patient as I wait to reap what I have sown.

March 30

"Why is it," Jonathan puzzled, "that the hardest thing in the world is to convince a bird that he is free, and that he can prove it for himself if he'd just spend a little time practicing? Why should that be so hard?"
~Richard Bach, author of Jonathan Livingston Seagull

A man found an eagle's egg and put it in the nest of a backyard hen. The eaglet hatched with the brood of chicks and grew up with them. All his life the eagle did what the backyard chickens did, thinking he was a backyard chicken. He scratched the earth for worms and insects. He clucked and cackled. And occasionally, he would thrash his wings and fly a few feet into the air.

Years passed and the eagle grew very old. One day he saw a magnificent bird far above him in the cloudless sky. It glided in graceful majesty among the powerful wind currents, with scarcely a beat of its strong golden wings. The old eagle looked up in awe, "What's that?" he asked.

"That's the eagle, the king of the birds," said his neighbor. "He belongs to the sky. We belong to the earth—we're chickens."

So the old eagle lived and died a chicken, for that's what he thought he was.

God had a grand plan for the eaglet, designed long before he was born. But the eaglet never fulfilled his potential as an eagle because he saw only what he thought he was destined to be. He had no vision for what he might become. In contrast, a seagull named Jonathan had big dreams.

Jonathan, a seagull, was bored with his flock's daily squabbles over food found by flying low over the ocean. Obsessed with a passion for flight far beyond what gulls are capable of, he practiced incessantly, unwilling to accept the limitations that came with his species. Other gulls called him foolish, eventually kicking him out of the flock for dishonoring them by refusing to be what he was—a seagull.

An outcast, Jonathan continued to learn everything he could about flying, soaring higher and faster than his fellow gulls thought possible. His goal was not reached without failures and heartaches, but he never gave up. One day at the height of a flight, he met two gulls who took him to bird heaven. While there, he learned from the Great Gull, who not only taught him about flight but also about life. After the Great Gull died, Jonathan left heaven, flying back to earth to teach other seagulls what he had learned and to spread the desire to soar.

We can learn from what the eaglet missed, and more importantly, what Jonathan taught the flocks—life is more than what we think. We can be free of the bonds of earthly existence and worldly obligations that confine our dreams and aspirations. God wants us to be everything we are capable of being. 1 Corinthians 12:31 (NIV) encourages us to "eagerly desire the greater gifts," and when we do, God will "show [us] the most excellent way."

Why should we settle for mediocrity in our Christian lives? When we anticipate greatness and excellence from God, he will exceed our expectations. God requires us to work with him and for him, dedicating our lives to him. Colossians 3 tells us that whatever we do, we should work at it with all our heart because we are working for the Lord, not men. As we strive for excellence as a Christian, we become a living testimony for God. Just as the naysayer seagulls watched Jonathan, ready to criticize and condemn, so do non-Christians observe our actions. We have an obligation to prove to them the heights a Christian can reach.

As we strive, we must remember that excellence doesn't mean the absence of mistakes. It simply means we will persevere with determination and faith to be all that God wants us to be.

POST-IT MEDITATION FOR MARCH 30
With God's help, I will live my gifts and talents at the highest level possible.

March 31

Comfort and prosperity have never enriched the world as much as adversity has.
~Billy Graham, evangelist

The story is told of an ancient king who had a boulder placed on a roadway and then hid to watch whether anyone would remove the huge rock from the path. He sat silently as some of his wealthiest merchants and courtiers strolled by, simply walking around it. Many vociferously blamed the King for not keeping the roads clear, but none attempted to move the stone.

Disappointed, the king was about to come from his hiding place when a peasant came along. Slipping back into the shadows, the king watched as the laborer laid down the bundle of vegetables he was carrying and tried to move the stone to the side of the road. After pushing and shoving for quite some time, he finally succeeded. As he leaned over to pick up his load of vegetables, he noticed a purse lying in the road where the boulder had been. Opening it, he found many gold coins, along with a note from the king indicating the gold was for the person who removed the massive rock from the roadway.

The peasant learned what many never understand: Every obstacle presents an opportunity to improve our condition. In the Bible, Joseph, after being sold into slavery by his brothers, spent years in prison but finally found favor in the eyes of the emperor. After his release, he eventually became the second highest ranking official in Egypt, just under the sovereign ruler. What his brothers intended as bad, God turned into good. The impediment they placed in Joseph's path brought good fortune, not only to Joseph, but to their entire family when their very existence was threatened by famine.

We never know to what extent God can use us. Only when we open our mind and spirit to him will he reveal what he has in store for our lives. He will show us that even the barriers in our lives can be transformed into tremendous opportunities. As Luke 1:37 (NIV) declares, "Nothing is impossible with God."

POST-IT MEDITATION FOR MARCH 31
With God's help, I will tackle every obstacle
and trust him to show me the possibilities they hide.

April 1

Live a life filled with love, following the example of Christ. He loved us and offered himself as a sacrifice for us….
~Ephesians 5:2 (NLT)

George Thomas, a pastor in a small New England town, came to church one Easter Sunday morning carrying an old, rusty, bent-up birdcage and set it by the pulpit. Several eyebrows were raised and, as if in response, Pastor Thomas began to speak:

I was walking through town yesterday when I saw a young boy coming toward me, swinging this birdcage. On the bottom of the cage were three little wild birds, shivering with cold and fright.

I stopped the lad and asked, "What you got there, son?"

"Just some old birds," came the reply.

"What are you gonna do with them?" I asked.

"Take 'em home and have fun with 'em. I'm gonna tease 'em and pull out their feathers to make 'em fight. I'm gonna have a real good time."

"But you'll get tired of those birds sooner or later. What will you do then?"

"Oh, I got some cats. They like birds. I'll take 'em to them."

I was silent for a moment, and then I asked, "How much do you want for those birds, son?"

"Huh! Why, you don't want them birds, mister. They're just plain old field birds. They don't sing; they ain't even pretty!"

"How much?" The boy sized me up as if I were crazy and said, "$10?"

Reaching in my pocket, I took out a ten dollar bill and placed it in the boy's hand. In a flash, the boy was gone. I picked up the cage and gently carried it to the end of the alley where there was a tree and a grassy spot. Setting the cage down, I opened the door, and by softly tapping the bars persuaded the birds out, setting them free.

Well, that explained the empty birdcage on the pulpit, and then the pastor began his sermon:

One day Satan and Jesus were having a conversation. Satan had just come from the Garden of Eden, and he was gloating and boasting. "Yes, sir, I just caught the world full of people down there. Set me a trap—used bait I knew they couldn't resist. Got 'em all!"

"What are you going to do with them?" Jesus asked.

"Oh, I'm gonna have fun! I'm gonna teach them how to marry and divorce each other. How to hate and abuse each other. How to be selfish and greedy. How to invent guns and bombs and kill each other. I'm really gonna have fun!"

"And what will you do when you get done with them?" Jesus asked.

"Oh, I'll kill 'em."

"How much do you want for them?"

"Oh, you don't want those people. They ain't no good. Why, you'll take them, and they'll just hate you. They'll spit on you, curse you, and kill you!! You don't want those people!"

"How much?"

Satan looked at Jesus and sneered, "All your tears and all your blood."

Jesus paid the price.

The pastor picked up the cage, opened the door, and walked from the pulpit.

POST-IT MEDITATION FOR APRIL 1
***Thank you, God, for caring enough to allow
your son to pay the price for my sins.***

April 2

If you do not wish to be prone to anger, do not feed the habit; give it nothing which may tend to its increase.
~Epictetus, Ancient Greek sage and philosopher

Anger is an emotion—and not a very pleasant one. When we feel furious, our heart rate increases, our palms sweat, and our stomachs knot. When we sense these reactions, we have two choices: Let our anger erupt or back away from it.

An old Cherokee grandfather said to his grandson, who came to him with anger at a friend who had done him an injustice:

"I, too, at times, have felt a great hate for those that have taken so much, with no sorrow for what they do. But hate wears you down and does not hurt your enemy. It is like taking poison and wishing your enemy would die. I have struggled with these feelings many times." He continued, "It is as if there are two wolves inside me. One is good and does no harm. He lives in harmony with all around him and does not take offense when no offense was intended. He will only fight when it is right to do so, and in the right way.

"But the other wolf, ah! He is full of anger. The littlest thing will set him into a fit of temper. He fights everyone, all the time, for no reason. He cannot think because his anger and hate are so great. It is worthless anger, for his anger will change nothing.

"Sometimes, it is hard to live with these two wolves inside me, for both of them try to dominate my spirit."

The boy looked intently into his Grandfather's eyes and asked, "Which one wins, Grandfather?"

The grandfather smiled and said quietly, "The one I feed."

And so it is with our anger. We can feed it or starve it.

When we feed our emotions, we let our feelings take control over logical thought. We surrender self-control to defensive mechanisms that protect our self-image. Defending our ego, we react negatively to those who threaten our position. In survival mode, our body pushes us in one of two ways: fight or flight. Instinctively, we think we have to stand our ground, and the natural way to do that is to respond with aggression. There is another way. Rationally, we can find a way to express our anger in a way that does not inflame the situation, but it takes willpower—and occasionally creativity.

Increasingly, atheists have reignited efforts to ban all prayer from educational institutions and even government entities. Many Christians feel righteous anger against what they perceive to be an intentional misinterpretation of the doctrine of separation of church and state. Although the courts often resolve disputes about the use of prayers at public events, sometimes Christians take the matter into their own hands.

They walked in tandem, each of the 93 students filing into the already crowded auditorium. With rich maroon gowns flowing and traditional caps perched on their heads, they looked almost as grown up as they felt. Dads swallowed hard behind broad smiles, and moms freely brushed away tears.

This class would not pray during the commencement—not by choice but because of a recent court ruling prohibiting it. The principal and several students were careful to stay within the guidelines allowed by the ruling.

They gave inspirational and challenging speeches, but no one mentioned divine guidance and no one asked for blessings on the graduates or their families. The speeches were nice, but they were routine...until the final speech received a standing ovation. A solitary student walked proudly to the microphone. He stood still and silent for just a moment, and then he delivered his speech...an astounding SNEEZE!

The rest of the students rose immediately to their feet, and in unison they said, "GOD BLESS YOU."

The audience exploded into applause. The graduating class had found a unique way to invoke God's blessing on their future...with or without the court's approval.

Virtuous anger is not bad if we handle it with the intent of correcting a wrong or improving a situation. In the Old Testament, we repeatedly see God's righteous rage when his children disobey him. In the New Testament, when challenged about healing on the Sabbath, Christ grieved at the hard hearts of his accusers. In annoyance, he challenged them: "Is it lawful on the Sabbath to do good or to do harm, to save life or to kill?" (Mark 3:4-5, KJ21).

Unrighteous anger, like Cain felt against God and his brother Abel, is destructive, bringing harm to self and others. It is this kind of resentment we should avoid. Proverbs 30:33 (ESV) says, "For pressing milk produces curds, pressing the nose produces blood, and pressing anger produces strife." Vicious and hurtful anger has no positive outcome.

POST-IT MEDITATION FOR APRIL 2
I will pray to discern when anger is righteous and when it is unrighteous.

April 3

As for God, his way is perfect....He is a shield for all who take refuge in him.
~2 Samuel 22:31 (ASV)

Me (in a tizzy): *God, can I ask you something?*
GOD: *Sure.*
Me: *Promise you won't get mad?*

GOD: *I promise.*

Me (frustrated): *Why did you let so much stuff happen to me today?*

GOD: *What do you mean?*

Me: *Well, I woke up late and my car took forever to start. Then, at lunch, the cook made my sandwich wrong and I had to wait. On the way home, my phone went dead, just as I picked up a call. And to top it all off, when I got home, I wanted to soak my feet in my foot massager and relax, but it wouldn't work. Nothing went right today! Why did you do that?*

GOD: *Well, let me see...the death angel was at your bed this morning, and I had to send one of the other angels to battle him for your life. I let you sleep through that. I didn't let your car start because there was a drunk driver on your route who might have hit you if you were on the road. The first person who made your sandwich today was sick, and I didn't want you to catch what he has; I knew you couldn't afford to miss work. Your phone went dead because the person calling was going to give a false witness about what you said on that call. I didn't let you talk to her so you would be covered.*

Me (softly): *I see, God.*

GOD: *Oh, and that foot massager, it had a short that was going to throw out all of the power in your house tonight. I didn't think you wanted to be in the dark.*

Me: *I'm sorry God.*

GOD: *Don't be sorry; just learn to trust me...in all things, the good and the bad.*

Me: *I WILL trust you God.*

GOD: *And don't doubt that my plan for your day is always better than your plan.*

Me: *I won't God. And let me just tell you God, thank you for everything today.*

GOD: *You're welcome child. It was just another day being your God—I love looking after my children.*

Does God really intervene in our lives on a daily basis? Only God knows...but if the very hairs on our head are numbered, then why is it so farfetched to think he knows all that is going to happen to us?

POST-IT MEDITATION FOR APRIL 3
When my day seems bad, I will remember
I can't always see God's way for my life.

April 4

Do to others whatever you would like them to do to you.
~Matthew 7:12 (NVT)

From birth until we reach young adulthood, most of us depend on our parents—for love, shelter, and support. If we and our parents live long enough, the tables may eventually turn, and one or both of our parents may become dependent on us. Payback time?

A frail old man went to live with his son, daughter-in-law, and four-year-old grandson. The old man's hands trembled, his eyesight blurred, and his step faltered. The family sat together at meals, but the elderly man's shaky hands and failing sight caused peas to roll off his spoon onto the floor. When he grasped a glass, milk spilled on the tablecloth. Soon, the son and his wife had enough of the mess and set a small table in the corner where the grandfather ate alone. Because he had dropped and broken several dishes, they served him in a wooden bowl.

When the grandson glanced in his grandfather's direction during meals, sometimes he saw a tear in his eye, especially if the parents sharply rebuked him when he dropped his spoon or spilled food. The four-year-old watched in silence as the old man sat, his shoulders slumped.

One evening before dinner, the father noticed his son playing with wood scraps on the floor. He asked the child what he was making. Innocently, the little boy responded, "Oh, I am making a little bowl for you and Mama to eat your food when I grow up." And with a sweet smile, the little boy went back to work.

The words struck the parents like a blinding light, and tears started to stream down their cheeks. Though no word was spoken, both knew what must be done. That evening the husband took Grandfather's hand and gently led him back to the family table. For the remainder of his days, he ate every meal with the family. And for some reason, neither husband nor wife seemed to care any longer when a fork fell, milk spilled, or the tablecloth became soiled.

The couple had an opportunity to change how they treated the man's father. Sometimes, that's not possible. Our parents die, and we must live with regrets for what we did or left undone.

If we follow the command in Leviticus 19:3 (ESV), "Every one of you shall revere his mother and father," our children will learn the Golden Rule and be there for us when we need them.

POST-IT MEDITATION FOR APRIL 4
Lord, help me treat my loved ones as I want to be treated.

April 5

A cloud does not know why it moves in just such a direction and at such a speed...it feels an impulsion...this is the place to go now. But the sky knows the reasons and the patterns behind all clouds, and you will know, too, when you lift yourself high enough to see beyond horizons.
~Richard Bach, American writer

Our lives can be like clouds from time to time. We don't know why we are moving in a certain direction, and sometimes the speed startles us.

We wonder, where does this sudden urge to form new patterns originate? Is it a message or signal from God? Perhaps. Just as he knows the reasons and patterns behind all clouds, we can discern the direction of our lives if we are willing to open our eyes and see beyond what lies on the immediate horizon.

The words written by Charles H. Scott in the old song, "Open My Eyes, That I May See," have a message for us: If we open our eyes, God will provide glimpses of truth for us. Scott also suggests how we need to prepare for this to happen: "Silently now I wait for Thee, ready, my God, Thy will to see."

The key, Scott reveals, is to open our heart so the Holy Spirit can illumine us. God's truth comes when we are ready to receive it—when our hearts are unlocked from the world, when everything false disappears. Without the distractions of the world, our soul's silence invites God's presence into our lives. With his presence come not only glimpses of truth but also his will for our lives.

But we don't have much practice with quietness. Linda Douty, a spiritual leader in Memphis, Tenn., suggests we try sitting silently for just 60 seconds. Why not try it right now?

What did you hear? Leaves blowing in the wind? Your air conditioner clicking on? A garbage truck clanging cans? A clock ticking? A bird trilling a melody? Most of us are so accustomed to sounds in our lives—many times a television or radio is turned on when we arise and is turned off when we go to bed—that we feel alone without noise pollution. Silence is uncomfortable, so we try to avoid it. When there is a pregnant pause in conversation, a pastor hesitates a few seconds too long, or an empty house has no background noise, it can be unnerving. And yet, if we never embrace moments of silence, how will we ever hear God's voice?

A Native American and his friend were in downtown New York City, walking near Times Square in Manhattan. It was during the noon lunch hour, and the streets were filled with people. Cars were honking their horns, taxicabs were squealing around corners, sirens were wailing, and the sounds of the city were almost deafening. Suddenly, the Native American said, "I hear a cricket."

His friend said, "What? You must be crazy. You couldn't possibly hear a cricket in all of this noise!"

"No, I'm sure of it," the Native American said, "I heard a cricket."

"That's crazy," said the friend.

The Native American listened carefully for a moment and then walked across the street to a big cement planter where some shrubs were growing. He looked into the bushes, beneath the branches, and sure enough, he located a small cricket. His friend was utterly amazed.

"That's incredible," said his friend. "You must have super-human ears!"

"No," said the Native American. "My ears are no different from yours. It all depends on what you're listening for."

"But that can't be!" said the friend. "I could never hear a cricket in this noise."

"Yes, it's true," came the reply. "It depends on what is really important to you. Here, let me show you."

He reached into his pocket, pulled out a few coins, and discreetly dropped them on the sidewalk. And then, with the noise of the crowded street still blaring in their ears, they noticed every head within twenty feet turn and look to see if the money that tinkled on the pavement was theirs.

"See what I mean?" asked the Native American. "It all depends on what's important to you."

POST-IT MEDITATION FOR APRIL 5
***Today, I will wait silently for God to
speak to me about his will for my life.***

April 6

Be still, and know that I am God….
~Psalm 46:10 (NIV)

Yesterday we talked about how noise permeates our lives, distracting us from the stillness necessary to hear God's voice. The spiritual director cited, Linda Douty, believes we subconsciously use noise to cover up feelings, thinking, and seeing. Some people sense that every second of silence must be filled. If no one else is talking, they talk. The words may be meaningless, but they fill the air, drowning silence needed for thoughtful contemplation.

Douty suggests that, as with Elijah, the whirlwinds of our lives and the tumultuous impact of society distract from our ability to hear God. Unless God shouts, he can't get our attention.

The good news remains: God is always there, waiting for us to listen. So, how then can we control our environment and our thoughts so they are open and ready for God's word?

The first step may be the hardest—committing to a time of silence every day to prepare our hearts to listen. This step is difficult because our tendency is to squelch silence even if it is only with thoughts in our heads. Have you ever been praying and suddenly realize your thoughts have taken a U-turn to something that transpired during the day? It happens to all of us, and God understands. After all, he made us—body and soul—and he knows our human limitations. What we must do is keep trying. If we fail—if we move from pure silence to thoughts unrelated to God—we simply need to start again.

The second step is to practice silence not just as an escape from noise but as a way to clear a space for God's voice to enter our hearts and minds. Thomas Merton, a Trappist monk, teaches that "Just remaining quietly in the presence of God, listening to him, being attentive to him, requires a lot of courage and know-how." The "know-how" is innate—in his creation God planted the seeds of desire for his voice. But it takes courage and commitment to abandon the sounds of television, iPods, and other invasive technologies, freeing up time for true communication with God. And it takes a willing ear—one ready to accept God's voice as real when he speaks.

Have you ever been just sitting there and all of a sudden you feel like doing something nice for someone you care for?

THAT'S GOD! He speaks to you through the Holy Spirit.

Have you ever been down and out and nobody seems to be around for you to talk to, but you feel a presence?

THAT'S GOD! He wants you to speak to him.

Have you ever received something wonderful that you didn't even ask for, like a debt that had mysteriously been cleared?

THAT'S GOD! He knows the needs of your life.

Have you ever been in a situation and you had no clue how you could survive, but now you look back on it, knowing you made it through the darkness?

THAT'S GOD! He passes us through tribulation to see a brighter day.

Author and psychiatrist M. Scott Peck reminds us we "cannot truly listen to anyone and do anything else at the same time." Yet, we rarely give God a moment when we aren't distracted by other messages—from others and from our own mind. To truly hear God, our hearts must be clear of all diversions. Only then can we listen completely. Only then will we hear his voice.

Will every need be met, every problem solved, and every situation improved? No, but listening to God brings support and strength for whatever we face in life. No doubt our spirit will expand and grow from his words. And the music in our heart will soar toward the clouds when we experience his presence.

POST-IT MEDITATION FOR APRIL 6
I will commit endless effort to escape the distractions that prevent me from listening for God's voice.

April 7

…Love each other deeply with all your heart.
~1 Peter 1:22 (NLT)

A teacher, frustrated with the crankiness of her students one day, decided to take a break from the lesson and do something different. She told the students to take two sheets of paper each and list the names of the other students in the room, leaving a space between each name. Then she told them to think of the nicest thing they could say about each of their classmates and write it down.

It took the remainder of the class period to finish the assignment, and as the students left the room, each one handed the teacher the papers. That Saturday the teacher wrote the name of each student on a separate sheet of paper and listed what everyone else had said about that individual. On Monday, she gave each student his or her list. Before long, the entire class was smiling. "Really?" she heard whispered. "I never knew that meant anything to anyone!" "I didn't know others liked me so much."

No one ever mentioned those papers in class again. The teacher never knew if they discussed them after class or with their parents, and it didn't matter. The exercise had accomplished its purpose. The students were happy with themselves and one another again.

Several years later the teacher was asked by one of the student's parents to attend their son's funeral—he had been killed in Vietnam. After the funeral, at a gathering of the soldier's friends and family, the parents pulled the teacher aside and told her they wanted to show her something. Taking a wallet out of his pocket, the father said, "They found this on Mark when he was killed. We thought you might recognize it."

Opening the billfold, the father carefully removed two worn pieces of notebook paper that had obviously been taped, folded, and refolded many times. Without looking at the papers, the teacher knew they were the ones on which she had listed all of the good things each of Mark's classmates had said about him. "Thank you so much for doing that," Mark's mother said. "As you can see, Mark treasured it."

Mark's classmates began to speak up. One smiled rather sheepishly and said, "I still have my list. It's in the top drawer of my desk at home." Another said, "I have mine, too…it's in my diary." Then another classmate reached into her pocketbook, took out her wallet, and showed her worn and frazzled list to the group. "I carry this with me at all times," she admitted without batting an eyelash. "I think we all saved our lists."

Later, in telling about the impact of the lists, the teacher (Sister Helen P. Mrosia) encouraged everyone "to compliment the people you love and care about. We often tend to forget the importance of showing our affections and love. Sometimes the smallest of things could mean the most to another."

POST-IT MEDITATION FOR APRIL 7
I will not forget that life can end at any time.
I will tell the people I love and care for that
they are special and important before it is too late.

April 8

And he said to him, "You shall love the Lord your God with all your heart and with all your soul and with all your mind."
~Matthew 22:37 (ESV)

Some people may not see the good in you, but there is good in everyone because God created us. Even knowing you have a good soul, do you show people the kind of good person you are? One little boy demonstrated the goodness of his soul even when being criticized:

Last week I took my children to a restaurant. My six-year-old son asked if he could say grace.

As we bowed our heads he said, "God is good. God is great. Thank you for the food, and I would even thank you more if mom gets us ice cream for dessert. Amen!"

Along with the laughter from the other customers nearby, I heard a woman remark, "That's what's wrong with this country. Kids today don't even know how to pray. Asking God for ice cream! Why, I never!"

Hearing this, my son burst into tears and asked me, "Did I do it wrong? Is God mad at me?"

As I held him and assured him he had done a terrific job, and God was certainly not mad at him, an elderly gentleman approached the table.

He winked at my son and said, "I happen to know God thought that was a great prayer."

"Really?" my son asked.

"Cross my heart." Then in a theatrical whisper he added (indicating the woman whose remark had started this whole thing), "Too bad she never asks God for ice cream. A little ice cream is good for the soul sometimes."

Naturally, I bought my kids ice cream at the end of the meal. My son stared at his for a moment and then did something I will remember the rest of my life. He picked up his sundae and without a word walked over and placed it in front of the woman. With a big smile he told her, "Here, this is for you. Ice cream is good for the soul sometimes, and my soul is good already."

So how do you show others the goodness in your heart and soul? By being kind...being open in defending yourself in ways that point them toward God...doing good deeds... sharing what you have...forgiving others when they are unkind...taking joy in being kind to others...doing all that you do with a smile? These and other acts of love come from the heart—others will see them and know all is well with your soul.

POST-IT MEDITATION FOR APRIL 8
*I will try to show what resides in my
soul through my words and actions.*

April 9

Lying lips are an abomination to the Lord, but they
that deal truly are his delight.
~*Proverbs 12:22 (KJV)*

Have you ever stood at the front of a courtroom, placed your hand on a Bible, and answered the question, "Do you swear to tell the truth, the whole truth, and nothing but the truth, so help you God?" If so, you've faced the weight of responsibility that comes when what you say may radically affect another person's life. And, in that situation, few of us would consider a lie. But in everyday life, when we haven't sworn on a Bible, we are not always as diligent about the truth. From little white lies or fibs to big whoppers, we mislead and exaggerate.

We lie to sidestep consequences and avoid accountability. Or, we lie because we don't want to do something but prefer another person not know that. Sometimes we just use falsehoods because it is easier than telling the truth, or we excuse ourselves by saying that a made-up story will keep from hurting someone's feelings. But a lie is a lie. As Thomas Aquinas said, "As a matter of honor, one man owes it to another to manifest the truth."

Remember "Honest Abe"? A timeworn story illustrates why Abraham Lincoln earned this nickname:

One day, while working at a country store in New Salem, Illinois, when he was about twenty-two years old, Abe sold some items totaling $2.06. When he closed out the accounts at the end of the day, he discovered the customer had paid him six cents too much. Abe knew he couldn't sleep if he cheated anyone, so as soon as he locked the doors, he walked to the customer's home, more than two miles away, and handed her the six cents.

Would Lincoln have called in sick when he was well? Would he have told his mother he didn't know how a vase was broken, hiding that he had knocked it off a table? Would he have cheated on his income tax? Doubtless, he would not have lied about these actions or any others. In both small and large matters, he was known to tell the truth. People knew when Abe Lincoln spoke, they could depend on what he said. Would our families, friends, and co-workers say that about us?

A modern-day man almost failed the test:

Several years ago a preacher moved to Houston, Texas. Some weeks after he arrived, he had occasion to ride the bus from his home to the downtown area. When he sat down, he discovered the driver had accidentally given him a quarter too much change.

As he considered what to do, he thought to himself, you better give the quarter back. It would be wrong to keep it. Then he thought, "Oh, forget it, it's only a quarter. Who would worry about this little amount? Anyway the bus company already gets too much fare; they will never miss it. Accept it as a gift from God and keep quiet."

When his stop came, he paused momentarily at the door, then he handed the quarter to the driver and said, "Here, you gave me too much change."

With a smile, the driver replied, "Aren't you the new preacher in town? I have been thinking lately about going to worship somewhere. I just wanted to see what you would do if I gave you too much change."

When the pastor stepped off the bus, he literally grabbed the nearest light pole, held on, and said, "O God, I almost sold your Son for a quarter."

Our lives are the only Bible some people will ever read.

POST-IT MEDITATION FOR APRIL 9
When I am tempted to lie, I will remember that lies, regardless of the size, are an abomination to God.

April 10

Why, you do not even know what will happen tomorrow. What is your life? You are a mist that appears for a little while and then vanishes.
~James 4:14 (NIV)

Our lives are like an early morning mist—visible but soon to fade away. Some people live a long life, while others live for what seem like only brief moments. But even if we live to be 100 years old, our time on earth is brief compared to eternity. Long or short, we have only one chance at physical life in this realm, and we all face heartache and despair. In the end, how we handle life's tribulations is what counts.

As I faced my Maker at the last judgment, I knelt before the Lord along with the other souls. In front of us lay our lives, like the squares of a quilt. Angels sat sewing our quilt squares together into a tapestry of each life.

As my angel took each piece of cloth off the pile, I noticed how ragged and empty each of my squares looked. They were filled with giant holes. Each square was labeled with a part of my life that had been difficult, the challenges and temptations I had faced in everyday life. The hardships I endured formed the largest holes of all.

I glanced around me. Nobody else had such squares. Other than a tiny hole here and there, the other tapestries were filled with rich color and all the bright hues of good fortune. I gazed upon my own life and was disheartened as my angel sewed the ragged pieces of cloth together, threadbare and empty like binding air.

*Finally the time came when each life was to be displayed, held up to the light...
the scrutiny of the truth. The others rose, each in turn, holding up their tapestries. So filled their lives had been.*

*When my angel looked upon me and nodded for me to rise, my gaze dropped to
the ground in shame. I hadn't had earthly fortunes. I had love and laughter in
my life, but I had also been through trials of illness, death, and false accusations
that took from me my world as I knew it.*

*I had to start over many times. I often struggled with the temptation to quit, only
to somehow muster the strength to pick up and begin again. I had spent many lonely
nights on my knees in prayer, asking for help and guidance in my life. I had often
been held up to ridicule, which I endured painfully: each time offering it up to the
Father in hopes that I would not melt within my skin beneath the judgmental gaze
of those who unfairly belittled or condemned me.*

*And now, I had to face the truth. My life was what it was, and I had to accept
it for what it had been.... I rose and slowly lifted the combined squares of my life
to the light. An awe-filled gasp filled the air. I gazed around at the others staring
at me with eyes opened wide.*

*Then I looked upon the tapestry before me. Light flooded the many holes, creating an image, the face of Christ. Then our Lord stood before me, with love and
warmth in his eyes. He said: "Every time you gave over your life to me, it became
my life, my hardships, and my struggles. Each point of light in your life is when
you stepped aside and let me shine thru, until there was more of me than there
was of you."*

POST-IT MEDITATION FOR APRIL 10
When facing life's trials, I will let God's love shine through.

April 11

Nothing endures but change.
~Heraclitus, Greek philosopher

Do you ever feel as if you are stuck in a rut and cannot get out? Do you
think the train of life is passing by and you are not on board? It happens
to all of us occasionally, and we need to be cautious not to get lulled into
complacency by the "same old, same old" of our lives.

Denis Waitley, in his book *Seeds of Greatness*, tells a story about
Switzerland's loss of world domination of watchmaking:

*In 1969, the Swiss had 65 percent of the world market share and Japan had
virtually none. But that changed when the quartz watch was introduced, even
though the Swiss invented it. Within 10 years, the Swiss market share dropped
to 10 percent, and 65,000 watchmakers had lost their jobs.*

Swiss lab researchers presented the quartz watch mechanism to Swiss watch manufacturers in 1967, but they rejected it, having no idea it would become the future of watches. It didn't have bearings, gears, or even a mainspring. Nobody would want a watch you didn't wind, they assumed. They were so confident in the style of watch they had manufactured for years they didn't even patent the quartz watch.

In 1969, the Swiss researchers presented the quartz watch as a new idea at an annual watch congress. The watch that had been handily dismissed by the Swiss industry was spotted by Texas Instruments and Seiko of Japan—and the rest is history.

Another story demonstrates the effect of an opposite reaction to change:

In 1879, Proctor and Gamble's best seller was candles. But the company was in trouble. Thomas Edison had invented the light bulb, and it looked as if candles would become obsolete. Their fears became reality when the market for candles plummeted since they were now sold only for special occasions.

The outlook appeared to be bleak for Procter and Gamble. However, at this time, it seemed that destiny played a dramatic part in pulling the struggling company from the clutches of bankruptcy. A forgetful employee at a small factory in Cincinnati forgot to turn off his machine when he went to lunch. The result? A frothing mass of lather filled with air bubbles. He almost threw the stuff away but instead decided to make it into soap. The soap floated. Ivory soap was born and became the mainstay of the Procter and Gamble Company.

Why was soap that floats such a hot item at that time? In Cincinnati, during that period, some people bathed in the Ohio River. Floating soap would never sink and consequently never got lost. So, Ivory soap became a best seller in Ohio and eventually across the country.

The stories about watches and soap are about much more than two industries—they are about any organization that has been so successful in the past it won't consider radically new ideas. Even more so, the stories illustrate that individuals must keep their eyes open to possibilities for the future. Whether we have been successful in the past or have experienced multiple failures, we must be willing to explore different ways to enrich our lives. Like Procter and Gamble, never give up when seemingly insurmountable problems arise. Creativity put to work can change a problem and turn it into a gold mine.

Change is the only constant in our lives, and it goes beyond new jobs, new homes, new friends, and other earthly issues. Change is necessary for spiritual maturity. As industries must adjust when their products stagnate or become obsolete, Christians should watch for opportunities to change direction when they languish or decline.

When the world changes, we must change. Even so, Romans 12:2 tells us we should not be conformed to this world but changed by the renewing of our mind; and by testing, we will discern the good and acceptable and perfect will of God. Change should be within his will.

POST-IT MEDITATION FOR APRIL 11
*I will be open and welcoming to change that
brings me closer to God's will for my life.*

April 12

Praise be to the Lord, who daily bears our burdens....
~Psalm 68:19 (NASB)

Monica slammed the bedroom door and leaned against it, groaning, "Why is my burden so heavy? Is there no rest from this life?" She stumbled to her bed and dropped onto it, pressing her pillow around her ears to shut out the noise of her existence. "Oh God," she cried, "let me sleep. Let me sleep forever and never wake up!" With a deep sob, she tried to will herself into oblivion, then welcomed the blackness that came over her.

Light surrounded Monica as she regained consciousness, and she focused on its source: The figure of a man standing before a cross. "My child," the person asked, "why did you want to come to me before I am ready to call you?"

"Lord, I'm sorry. It's just that...I can't go on. You see how hard it is for me. Look at this awful burden on my back. I simply can't carry it anymore."

"But haven't I told you to cast all of your burdens upon me, because I care for you? My yoke is easy, and my burden is light."

"I knew you would say that. But why does mine have to be so heavy?"

"My child, everyone in the world has a burden. Perhaps you would like to try a different one?"

"I can do that?"

He pointed to several burdens lying at his feet. "You may try any of these."

All of them seemed to be of equal size. But each was labeled with a name. "There's Joan's," Monica said. Joan, married to a wealthy businessman, lived in a sprawling estate and dressed her three daughters in the prettiest designer clothes. Sometimes she drove Monica to church in her Cadillac when her own car wouldn't start. "Let me try that one." How difficult could her burden be? The Lord removed Monica's load and placed Joan's on her shoulders, but she sank to her knees beneath its weight. "Take it off!" she pleaded. "What makes it so heavy?"

"Look inside." Untying the straps and opening the top, Monica found a figure of Joan's mother-in-law, and when she lifted it out, it began to speak. "Joan, you'll never be good enough for my son," it began. "He never should have married you. You're a terrible mother to my grandchildren...." Monica quickly placed the figure

back in the pack and withdrew another. It was Donna, Joan's youngest daughter. Her head was bandaged from the surgery that had failed to resolve her epilepsy. A third figure was Joan's brother. Addicted to drugs, he had been convicted of killing a police officer. "I see why her burden is so heavy, Lord. But she's always smiling and helping others. I didn't realize...."

"Would you like to try another?" he asked quietly.

Monica tested several. Paula's felt heavy: She was raising four small boys without a father. Debra's did too: A childhood of sexual abuse and a marriage of emotional abuse. When she came to Ruth's burden, she didn't even try. She knew that inside she would find arthritis, old age, a demanding full-time job, and a beloved husband in a nursing home.

"They're all too heavy, Lord," Monica said. "Give back my own." As she lifted the familiar load once again, it seemed much lighter than the others.

"Let's look inside," God said.

Monica turned away, holding it close. "That's not a good idea; there's a lot of junk in there," she said.

"Let me see." The gentle thunder of God's voice compelled her so Monica opened her burden. He pulled out a brick. "Tell me about this one."

"Lord, you know. It's money. I know we don't suffer like people in some countries or even the homeless here in America. But we have no insurance, and when the kids get sick, we can't always take them to the doctor. And I'm tired of dressing them in hand-me-downs."

"My child, I will supply all of your needs...and your children's. I've given them healthy bodies. I will teach them that expensive clothing doesn't make a person valuable in my sight."

Then he lifted out the figure of a small boy. "And this?" he asked.

"Andrew..." Monica hung her head, ashamed to call her son a burden. "But, Lord, he's hyperactive. He's not quiet like the other two. He makes me so tired. He's always getting hurt, and someone is bound to think I abuse him. I yell at him all the time. Someday I may really hurt him...."

"My child," he said, "If you trust me, I will renew your strength; if you allow me to fill you with my Spirit, I will give you patience."

Then he took some pebbles from Monica's burden.

"Yes, Lord," she said with a sigh. "Those are small. But they're important. I hate my hair. It's thin, and I can't make it look nice. I can't afford to go to the beauty shop. I'm overweight and can't stay on a diet. I hate all my clothes. I hate the way I look!"

"My child, people look at your outward appearance, but I look at your heart. By my spirit you can gain self-control to lose weight. But your beauty should not come from outward appearance. Instead, it should come from your inner self, the unfading beauty of a gentle and quiet spirit, which is of great worth in my sight."

Monica's burden now seemed lighter than before. "I guess I can handle it now," she said.

"There is more," he said. "Hand me that last brick."

"Oh, you don't have to take that. I can handle it."

"My child, give it to me." Again his voice compelled her. He reached out his hand, and for the first time she saw the ugly wound. "But, Lord, this brick is so awful, so nasty, so.....Lord! What happened to your hands? They're so scarred."

She placed the filthy brick into his wounded palm. It contained all the dirt and evil of her life: her pride, her selfishness, the depression that constantly tormented her. God turned to the cross and hurled her brick into the pool of blood at its base. It hardly made a ripple. "Now, my child, you need to go back. I will be with you always. When you are troubled, call to me and I will help you and show you what you cannot imagine now."

Monica reached to pick up her burden.

"You may leave that here if you wish. You see all these burdens? They are the ones that others have left at my feet. Joan's, Paula's, Debra's, Ruth's..... As Monica placed her burden, the light began to fade, and she heard him whisper, "I will never leave you, nor forsake you."

POST-IT MEDITATION FOR APRIL 12
Help me never forget, God, that others have heavy burdens, too. You are much better at carrying our loads than we are.

April 13

Look, the winter is past, the rain is over and gone; the flowers are springing up, the season of singing birds has come, and the cooing of turtledoves fills the air.
~Song of Solomon 2: 11-12 (NLT)

By mid-April, nature has painted a picturesque palette of colors across hills and valleys, on flat lands and mountains. Sometimes it is so breathtaking we can hardly take in the fields of wildflowers, trees bursting forth in green, and daylilies raising their heads toward the sky. As Longfellow penned, "Came the Spring with all its splendor, all its birds and all its blossoms. All its flowers, and leaves, and grasses." All sights to behold....

Although each season has its own beauty, spring is the only one that showers us with sparkling rebirth all around: a reawakening reminding us of God's mighty power to bring life from death; regeneration giving us comfort that we, too, will someday be reborn to a new, unmarred and unscarred body. I wonder if God planned spring for that purpose—to give evidence that death is not the end. If he can raise a daylily or iris after it has crumpled to the ground, lifeless, then surely he can and will raise us up after our earthly bodies have turned to dust. When we sorrow, what a comfort nature brings. The majesty nature creates fills our spirits with warmth in the seasons to come. One lady's story tells how just a simple buttercup did just that.

When I was a very little girl, my father's family would all gather at my great-grandmother's house for Sunday dinner after church every week. She lived down a mile-long dirt lane surrounded by acres of land, and after dessert, I loved nothing more than to go for a walk and explore with my daddy. In the spring, whenever the fields at Grandma Sally's would fill with golden sprigs, he would pick one and ask, "Do you like butter? Let's check to see," and as the flower cast a yellow glow onto my chin, he would pronounce once again that yes, I liked butter. I would eagerly snatch it from his hand and after doing the same, confidently announce that he liked butter, too. As I grew, we no longer played the butter game but instead made a game of who would find the first buttercup of the season to give to the other. Once I became a teenager and could no longer be bothered with such things, my daddy would still present me with a bouquet of buttercups each spring.

After my father died, as my family drove down the long country road to the cemetery in his funeral procession, I stared out the window in a teary fog, watching the green fields roll by. As the church came into view, I tried to focus my gaze onto anything but the blue tent and folding chairs that had been erected among the rows of headstones. And there, in the embankment across the church, grew a patch of buttercups.

There, and only there, until weeks later did I see my harbingers of spring. My heart leapt with joy and plummeted into my stomach just as quickly while I choked back a sob. As I stepped out of the car and made my way to the place where my mother and sisters awaited me, I reminded my husband of the buttercups and nodded after he asked if I wanted him to bring some to me. I sat through the graveside service with tissues and buttercups clutched in my hands. As we all made our way to the casket to stand in my father's presence one last time, I gently placed my unassuming, tiny yellow flowers near the large spray of vibrant red roses and said to my sister, "He gave me my very first buttercup, and I just gave him his last." With those words, we clung to each other and sobbed, because she knew just what that meant. Something seemingly so insignificant—a weed—was the most profound and precious thing in the world to me in that moment. That little flower, to both my father and me, represented pure love and being so made it the perfect way to say goodbye.

On a day in April, just a few days before my father's birthday, I was strolling through my backyard with my husband and daughters, staring out at an expanse of green grass peppered with the yellow blooms of dandelions. For no apparent reason, I paused and looked down at my feet and spotted a lone, golden flower. It was my first buttercup of the season and the only one in my entire yard. I knew this because I had been awaiting their arrival with a mixture of dread and delight, scanning my yard since the official beginning of spring. I kneeled down to the ground to reverently pluck the stem and whisper a prayer of thanks and love. I couldn't help but feel that my daddy had just given me the first buttercup of spring.

As the old hymn declares, "For the beauty of the earth, for the glory of the skies…we raise this hymn of grateful praise." To see the grandeur of a landscape touched by God's paintbrush is a gift greater than most. For those of us who have sight, it is difficult to imagine how deprived we would if we could not see a creamy crocus or a joyful jonquil push its way above the ground. And, as impressive a blessing sight is, if we were blind, perhaps we would, as Helen Keller did, learn that "The best and most beautiful things in the world cannot be seen or even touched. They must be felt within the heart." This very wise woman was blind in her eyes, but she felt God's blessings in her heart and thus in her life. Each spring, she couldn't see the glorious colors changing the terrain, but she felt the transformation: "To me, a lush carpet of pine needles or spongy grass is more welcome than the most luxurious Persian rug." Helen Keller was deprived of her sight, but she sensed beauty far deeper than we who are sighted may ever know.

SOURCE OF BUTTERCUP STORY: http://www.values.com/your-inspirational-stories/863-Song-of-Spring

POST-IT MEDITATION FOR APRIL 13
I will be grateful for eyes to see God's magnificent creation,
but I will also be sensitive to gifts that can't be seen.

April 14

The way to make learning a lesson of celebration instead of a cause for regret is to ask, "How can I put this to use today?"
~Jaroldeen Edwards, motivational speaker and author

A woman's daughter called her several times one week, urging her to "come and see the daffodils before they are over." The mother wanted to go, but it was a two-hour drive from her home in Laguna to Lake Arrowhead, and her schedule was packed. Finally, she reluctantly promised to come the next Tuesday.

The appointed day dawned cold and rainy. Still, she had promised, and so she unenthusiastically began her journey. By the time she started up the mountain, the trees were enshrouded in clouds; and soon she was driving through a blanket of wet, grey fog. Finally arriving at her daughter's home, relieved to be off the narrow, winding road, she declared she wasn't getting back in the car to see anything. "Forget the daffodils!" she exclaimed. But her daughter was insistent the daffodils would be worth the drive. Besides, she was accustomed to traveling the mountain roads in bad weather.

Although she felt like a hostage, the mother climbed in the car, muttering her misgivings. Soon, they parked in a small lot adjoining a little stone church. Following her daughter down a path winding through dense trees, the mother shivered, but as they turned a corner in the path, she looked up and gasped. "Before me lay the most glorious sight, unexpectedly and completely splendid. It looked as if someone had taken a great vat of gold and poured it down the mountain peak and slopes where it had run into every crevice and over every rise. Even in the mist-filled air, the mountainside was radiant, clothed in massive drifts and waterfalls of daffodils. The flowers were planted in majestic, swirling patterns, great ribbons and swaths of deep orange, white, lemon yellow, salmon pink, saffron, and butter yellow."

It no longer mattered that the sun was not shining.

"But who has done this?" the woman asked her daughter, overflowing with gratitude she had been forced to come. Her daughter pointed to a small sign:

"Answers to the Questions I Know You Are Asking"

50,000 bulbs

One at a time, by one woman.

Two hands, two feet, and very little brain.

Begun in 1958

One woman had forever transformed the mountain where she lived. She had created a massive display of beauty and inspiration for others to enjoy. The principle of the daffodil garden is simple: if we move toward our goals and desires a bit at a time, if we love what we are doing, the accumulation of our efforts can yield something spectacular.

Overwhelmed with the implication of what she had seen, the mother admitted to her daughter, "It makes me sad in a way. What might I have accomplished if I had thought of a wonderful goal thirty-five years ago and had worked away at it 'one bulb at a time' through all those years?"

Her daughter's response was simple but full of wisdom: "Start tomorrow."

Thinking of the lost hours of yesterday is pointless. How much more we can achieve if we think after reading the daffodil story, "How can I put this to use tomorrow?"

AUTHOR'S NOTE: The story of "The Daffodil Principle" originally appeared nearly ten years ago in Jaroldeen Edwards' book Celebration! The daffodil garden is reportedly located below Running Springs, California, in the San Bernadino Mountains.

POST-IT MEDITATION FOR APRIL 14
***Because it is pointless to think of the time I lost in all my yesterdays,
I will take the lesson I learned today and put it to use today and tomorrow.***

April 15

And if anyone gives even a cup of cold water to one of these little ones because he is my disciple, I tell you the truth, he will certainly not lose his reward.
~Matthew 10:42 (NIV)

A successful young executive was traveling too fast down a neighborhood street in his new Jaguar when he saw kids darting back and forth between parked cars. Slowing down to avoid hitting a kid, he suddenly heard something hit his Jag's side door. Slamming on the brakes, he backed up and jumped out of the car. He grabbed the nearest kid and shoved up him against a parked car, yelling, "What the heck do you think you are doing?"

The frightened child apologized, adding, "I couldn't get anyone to stop, and I didn't know what else to do, so I threw a brick at your car." Tears streaming down his face, he pointed to a kid on the ground a few feet away. "It's my brother. He rolled off the curb and fell out of his wheelchair, and I can't lift him up. Would you help me? He's hurt."

Suddenly, the man's rage melted. He lifted the boy back into his wheelchair, and with his expensive handkerchief, wiped the blood from his scrapes and cuts.

Turning to the stranger, the grateful child thanked him for helping, adding, "May God bless you," and started pushing his brother toward home.

The Jaguar driver, shaken beyond words, walked slowly back to his car. For a long time afterward, the man left the huge dent in his car door to remind him of this message: "Don't go through life so fast that someone has to throw a brick at you to get your attention!"

Like the driver of the fancy car, we sometimes get so caught up in our lives we don't pay attention to what is happening around us. We overlook those who may need our help even though they may be in our line of vision—we simply don't see them.

It is important to remember God speaks to us not only in shouts but also in whispers. When he speaks softly, we don't want to be so distracted he has to throw a brick at us to make us stop and pay attention.

SOURCE OF BRICK STORY: http://www.indianchild.com/inspiring_stories.htm

POST-IT MEDITATION FOR APRIL 15
God, help me see needs and feel compassion without your having to throw a brick at me.

April 16

Do you believe I am able to do this?
~*Matthew 9:28 (NKJV)*

Jesus asked the above question in Matthew 9:28 of two blind men who began following him one day. Excited, the men responded in unison, "Yes, sir!" With that assurance, Jesus said, "Let it happen, then, just as you believed." And the men's sight was restored. What we don't find in the scriptures is how many times the two men had prayed and the answer was "no" or "not now."

When the answer to our prayers is "no," or "maybe later," we may be disappointed or angry, Still, we should never doubt God's limitless power and his undeniable wisdom. If he says "no," as difficult as it may be, we can believe God has a wonderful plan for our lives.

When tempted to question God's wisdom or his goodness, we can turn to the scriptures for assurance he cares for us. Psalm 121:3, 8 (NKJV) reminds us, "God will not allow your foot to be moved. He who keeps you will not slumber…. The Lord shall preserve your going out and your coming in… forevermore." We can have confidence when we ask anything according to his will, he hears us (1 John 5:14). The key phrase in this verse is "according to his will." Sometimes we pray for actions or events that may not be in God's will for us. God can see the future, and if he gave us what we ask, it might not fit his plan for our lives.

I wonder what God thinks about some of our prayers. "Lord, please let Jeremy make the basket," a parent says silently as he watches his son toss the ball at the free throw line, a tie-game breaker. We pray for a vacant parking space, the money to buy a new car, or a different job. We pray about important issues and inconsequential ones. What if God answered all our prayers?

John Sittzer, author of *When God Doesn't Answer Your Prayer*, tells us, "Strange as it may sound, we need unanswered prayer." He adds it is a gift from God that protects us from ourselves. If we got everything we asked for, he suggests we might abuse the power to ask. So God decides when to say "yes" and when to say "no." The "no's" may break us, Sittzer concedes, but he also declares they deepen us and transform us. "Ironically, the unanswered prayers of the past, which so often leave us feeling hurt and disillusioned, serve as a refiner's fire that prepares us for the answered prayers of the future."

The story of Joni Eareckson Tada illustrates how unanswered prayer can lead to deeper faith. Not long after graduating from high school, while Joni was diving into the waters of Chesapeake Bay, her head struck the bottom of the estuary, leaving her paralyzed from the neck down. Joni, along with her parents and friends, prayed without ceasing for healing, but the answer they wanted never came. After months of being strapped into a bed, being turned upside down with only the floor to look at, and developing horrible bed sores, Joni begged a friend to help her commit suicide. Thankfully, that didn't happen, or the world would have missed the wonderful and powerful life of personal faith that Joni grew into. It wasn't easy, but today, as a quadriplegic, she is known worldwide for her books and paintings, which she does by holding a pen or brush in her mouth. Joni avows, in her book, WHEN GOD WEEPS, that "God uses suffering to purge sin from our lives, strengthen our commitment to him, force us to depend on grace, bind us together with other believers, produce discernment, foster sensitivity, discipline our minds, spend our time wisely, stretch our hope, cause us to know Christ better, make us long for truth, lead us to repentance of sin, teach us to give thanks in times of sorrow, increase faith, and strengthen character." Her unanswered prayer, tragic as it seemed at the time, led Joni into a life of blessings for millions of people.

POST-IT MEDITATION FOR APRIL 16
When God's says "no," I will remember he knows best.

April 17

Joy comes from simple and natural things, mists over meadows, sunlight on leaves, the path of the moon over water. Even rain and wind and stormy clouds bring joy….
~Sigurd F. Olson, American author

Beauty surrounds us—in the sky, on the ground, and in the waters. If we did nothing more than enjoy the simple gifts of nature, our lives would be rich indeed. Our souls ring with rapture as sunlight sparkles on dew-tipped leaves. Our faith is fulfilled as we watch a flower break into bloom. Our spirits lift with a field of goldenrod. And, to revive our land and our spirit, God "makes springs gush forth in the valleys; they flow between the hills" (Psalm 104: 10, ESV).

Have you ever stopped by the pure running water of a natural spring, fresh from melted snow, to taste its refreshing coolness? How long has it been since you paused to breathe in the fragrance of a freshly bloomed rose or to inhale a whiff of new-mown grass? All around us sit simple yet glorious pieces of nature to gladden our hearts. Whether your life is full of happiness or serious problems, nature has a gift to add a note of joy or strengthen your spirit. In God's handiwork are messages for your soul.

The little flower was so shy she hid in the shadow of a tall leaf, and there she spread her blossoms. From the hidden spot sprang an exquisite, delicate perfume.

One day an angel flew down to earth with a mission of love. As its white wings swept close to the earth, they brushed aside the tall leaf. There the angel discovered the purple and gold blossoms and inhaled the faint fragrance.

"You are too lovely to dwell alone in the shadows," the angel exclaimed. "You should be a flower in the garden of the angels." But then, the angel had another thought, one more beautiful. "You shall be the angel's blossom, but you shall bloom in the land of man." Then the angel stooped and kissed the flower, and the imprint of the kiss turned into the angel's face, and all of the little flowers from that time on had tiny faces. We call them pansies.

The next time you see a pansy, remember the kiss of the angel. And, never forget that every other flower, every leaf, every sunrise and sunset, every glimmer of the moon, every thundercloud, and every drop of dew were created by the hand of God to bring joy into our lives.

POST-IT MEDITATION FOR APRIL 17
I will look for God's messages not just in the Bible, but also in flowers, leaves, stars, rivers, oceans, clouds, rain showers, and storms—in all of God's creations.

April 18

In any of the towns in your land the Lord your God is giving you, if there is anyone poor among you, do not let your heart be hard and not be willing to help him. Be free to give to him. Let him use what is yours of anything he needs.
~Deuteronomy 15:7-8 (NLV)

Once, while riding through the country with some other lawyers, Abraham Lincoln disappeared from the party and was seen loitering near a thicket of wild plum trees where the men had stopped a short time before to water their horses.

"Where is Lincoln?" asked one of the lawyers.

"When I saw him last," answered another, "he had caught two young birds the wind had blown out of their nest and was hunting for the nest to put them back again."

As Lincoln joined them, the lawyers ribbed him about his tender-heartedness, and he said, "I could not have slept unless I had restored those little birds to their mother."

Such tenderness was typical of Lincoln, a man who stood six-foot, four-inches tall and whose physical prowess was widely known. One witness declared he had the strength of three men, once carrying a load of 600 pounds—three large logs. Another person said, "He could strike with a maul a heavier blow, could sink an axe deeper into wood than any man I ever saw."

But Lincoln was not all brawn and muscle. In describing him, the poet Carl Sandburg wrote, "Not often in the story of mankind does a man arrive on earth who is both steel and velvet, who is as hard as a rock and soft as drifting fog, who holds in his heart and mind the paradox of terrible storm and peace unspeakable and perfect."

The ultimate example of Lincoln's combination of steel and velvet was witnessed when General Robert E. Lee surrendered his army. The defeated general never expected the message he received from the commander of his enemy: "Tell your men they may keep their horses; they'll need them for plowing." The message continued with an offer to let the crushed soldiers keep their rifles: "They'll need them for hunting." Lee wept as he read Lincoln's noble words.

A tough general who fought with steel in his backbone showed a different side once the battles were won. Humanness undergirded the fighting man.

In one of the most chaotic and difficult times in our history, Lincoln applied a soft touch. Preserving the union and liberating four million slaves took a will of steel, but it was the blending of hardness and compassion that made Lincoln one of the most revered leaders in our history.

Author Steve Goodier points out that from Lincoln we learn, "There is a time for toughness and a time for tenderness. A time for resolve and a time for kindness." And he adds, "An iron will is not the same as an iron spirit."

As parents, we are expected to be tough on our children, but at the same time we should be compassionate. We should set high expectations for our employees, but we should care about them. We want our military to be daunting against enemies, but we expect them to show the benevolence of Lincoln when the battles end.

How we balance toughness and compassion takes wisdom. God can help us balance the scales for both friend and foe, family and stranger.

POST-IT MEDITATION FOR APRIL 18
I will pray for guidance about when I should be tough and when I should apply a soft touch.

April 19

Therefore, if anyone is in Christ, he is a new creation; the old has gone, the new has come!
2 Corinthians 5:17 (ESV)

There is a legend about a man who, through a lifetime of poor posture, became round-shouldered. One day this man asked a sculptor to cast a statue of him, instructing the artist to show him standing in a perfectly straight, upright position—shoulders back, head held high, and chin up—just as he looked when he was in the prime of life.

When the work was finished and delivered, the old man hid it in a remote corner of his garden. For a few minutes every day, he went to the secret place and looked at himself as he once stood. As time passed, the man's granddaughter noticed he was standing straighter, regaining his youthful posture. One day she decided to follow him as he walked to the back of his garden, where she often saw him go. At the secret hiding place, the little girl was startled to see what appeared to be two grandpas. One was shining like a golden god in the sun, straight and tall; the other standing nearby was a slightly stooped version.

As his granddaughter watched, the real grandfather stood straighter and straighter. "Grandpa," she said tenderly, "you're beginning to look like the other grandpa." He had transformed himself into the image he had created.

Like the grandpa, we can hold in our mind the image of the person we would like to be—the person God wants us to be. We can become that person.

What does that person we want to be look like? Would these descriptions be on your list?

- ✓ A person who benefits from a prayer-driven life
- ✓ A possibility thinker
- ✓ A person who values inner peace over possessions
- ✓ A person of faith who trusts God for all needs
- ✓ A discipline-driven disciple of Christ—in thought, word, and deed
- ✓ An energized force for God
- ✓ A courageous believer, not a fretter

Make your own list, put it in a secret place, and in quiet contemplation, stare at it, seeing yourself as the person you want to be.

POST-IT MEDITATION FOR APRIL 19
*I am a new creation; the old has gone, and the
new will be the person God wants me to be.*

April 20

For you see your calling, brethren, that not many wise according to the flesh, not many mighty, not many noble, are called. But God has chosen the foolish things of the world to put to shame the wise, and God has chosen the weak

things of the world to put to shame the things which are mighty; and the base
things of the world and the things which are despised God has chosen.
~1 Corinthians 1:27-28 (ASV)

A young woman named Brenda was invited to go rock climbing. Although she was scared to death, she went with her group to a tremendous granite cliff. In spite of her fear, she put on the gear, took hold of the rope, and started up the face of that rock. When she got to a ledge where she could take a breather and was hanging there for a moment, the safety rope snapped against Brenda's eye and knocked out her contact lens. There she was on a rock ledge, with hundreds of feet below her and hundreds of feet above her. Of course, she looked and looked and looked, hoping the lens had landed on the ledge, but it just wasn't there.

Far from home, her sight now blurry, Brenda was desperate and began to get upset, so she prayed to the Lord to help her to find it. Arriving at the top, a friend examined her eye and her clothing for the lens, but it was not to be found. She sat down, despondent, waiting for the rest of the climbers to make it up the face of the cliff. Looking out across range after range of mountains, a Bible verse came to her: "The eyes of the Lord run to and fro throughout the whole earth…" (AMP). She thought, "Lord, you can see all these mountains. You know every stone and leaf, and you know exactly where my contact lens is. Please help me."

Finally, the group walked down the trail to the bottom. At the bottom there was a new party of climbers just starting up the face of the cliff. One of them shouted out, "Hey, you guys! Anybody lose a contact lens?" Well, that would be startling enough, but you know why the climber saw it? An ant was moving slowly across the face of the rock, carrying it.

Brenda's father is a cartoonist. When she told him the incredible story of the ant, the prayer, and the contact lens, he drew a picture of an ant lugging that contact lens with the words, "Lord, I don't know why you want me to carry this thing. I can't eat it, and it's awfully heavy. But if this is what you want me to do, I'll carry it for you."

God can use the lowliest creature for his purpose. None of us should ever feel we aren't good enough or smart enough to serve God. The apostle Paul tells us God uses the foolish, the weak, the base, and the despicable. Undoubtedly, he can use us despite our shortcomings.

POST-IT MEDITATION FOR APRIL 20
I am thankful God can use me even with my inadequacies.

April 21

Give all your worries and cares to God, for he cares about you.
~1 Peter 5:7 (NLT)

We do not know what tomorrow will bring—sunshine or rain, happiness or pain, joy or grief—but what we do know is we can face whatever the future holds because God will be with us. An old song begins, "I don't know about tomorrow; I just live from day to day" and leaves us with the assurance that we do know *who* holds tomorrow and he holds our hand.

Why then, do we worry and fret? I sometimes wonder how many hours—and days—of my life have been wasted worrying about something that never happened, or something that I could not prevent occurring. And what did it accomplish? Nothing. Worry doesn't bring solutions to our problems or relief from our fears. It is wasted energy. Matthew 6:27 (NLT) asks, "Can all your worries add a single moment to your life?" No, not one. Neither can worries bring us peace or contentment.

There are two days in every week about which
we should not worry,
two days which should be kept free from
fear and apprehension.
One of these days is Yesterday with all its
mistakes and cares,
its faults and blunders, its aches and pains.
Yesterday has passed forever beyond our control.
All the money in the world cannot bring back Yesterday.
We cannot undo a single act we performed;
we cannot erase a single word we said.
Yesterday is gone forever.
The other day we should not worry about is Tomorrow
with all its possible adversities, its burdens,
its large promise and its poor performance;
Tomorrow is also beyond our immediate control.
Tomorrow's sun will rise,
either in splendor or behind a mask of clouds, but it will rise.
Until it does, we have no stake in Tomorrow,
for it is yet to be born.
This leaves only one day, Today.
Any person can fight the battle of just one day.
It is when you and I add the burdens of those two awful eternities,
Yesterday and Tomorrow, that we break down.
It is not the experience of Today that drives a person mad;
it is the remorse or bitterness of something that happened Yesterday and the
dread of what Tomorrow may bring.
Let us, therefore, live but one day at a time.

Fretting about the future is as futile as reliving the past, even to the point of making us physically ill. Proverbs 12:25 (NLV) tells us, "Worry in the heart of a person weighs it down…." It burdens our mind and our spirit, eclipsing our ability to smile because we are focusing on what may happen instead of trusting tomorrow to God. As Gaither wrote in "Because He Lives," we can face uncertain days because Christ lives—he died for our sins and wants us to believe his love is sufficient for all our needs.

One effective way to overcome worry is to replace it with prayer. As a message on Facebook asserted, "Feed your faith and your fear will starve to death." Prayer diminishes anxiety because it focuses us in the right direction, bringing us to the source of all life and comfort. When we take our needs and requests to God, we can be confident he will shape our future in a way that fulfills his will for our lives. After we have turned the days ahead over to the one who created our world and keeps it revolving, we should, as instructed in Philippians 4:6-7, thank him for all he has done and will do for us. Only then will we experience God's peace, which will guard our hearts and minds whatever the future holds.

POST-IT MEDITATION FOR APRIL 21
*I will replace worry with prayer, trusting God to hold
my hand, one day at a time.*

April 22

See to it that you do not refuse him who speaks. If they did not escape when they refused him who warned them on earth, how much less will we, if we turn away from him who warns us from heaven?
~Hebrews 12:25 (NIV)

Have you ever been headed for disaster but were too stubborn to turn and go in another direction? Some people continue in extramarital affairs despite knowing they are destroying their marriages. Others continue drinking excessively even though they are risking their jobs. Still others pile up credit card debt, knowing a financial crisis is looming. Why do we continue on a path when a crash is inevitable, when a collision is in clear view?

On the dark seas one night, a ship captain cautiously directed his ship through the fog. Along with his lookout, he kept his eyes strained on the hazy darkness, searching for dangers that might be lurking. Then, while standing on the bridge, he saw a bright light straight ahead. To avert disaster, he quickly told his signalman to send a message to the other vessel. "Signal that ship: 'We are on a collision course; advise you change course 20 degrees.'"

To the surprise of the captain, the light stayed still as a signal came back. "Advisable for you to change your course 20 degrees."

Appalled at the audacity of the message, the captain yelled, "Send, 'I'm a captain; change your course 20 degrees!'"

The light still didn't budge, and the captain was amazed at the next message: "I'm a seaman second class. Change your course 20 degrees."

Furious, the captain took over the signalman's job, sending the next message himself: "I am on a battleship. Change course 20 degrees now!"

Back came the flashing light, "I'm on a lighthouse. Advise you change course." The battleship changed course.

Are we like the captain, so confident in our position we refuse to consider another course? Are we so arrogant we think no one can do us damage or so obstinate we cannot consider other routes to get to our destinations in life? We take harmful paths, ignoring looming consequences, hoping we can avoid the inevitable end of the road. Deluding ourselves will not prevent disaster, and we should pray for strength from God to change course.

POST-IT MEDITATION FOR APRIL 22
God, help me heed the warning glow from your lighthouse, allowing you to guide me safely out of the line of life's perils.

April 23

Jesus Christ is the same yesterday, today, and forever.
~Hebrews 13:8 (NLT)

One day the employees of a large company in St. Louis, Missouri, returned from lunch break and were greeted with a sign on the front door: "Yesterday the person who has been hindering your growth in this company passed away. We invite you to join the funeral in the room that has been prepared in the gym."

At first everyone was sad to hear one of their colleagues had died, but after a while they started getting curious about who this person might be.

The anticipation grew as the employees arrived at the gym to pay their last respects. Everyone wondered: "Who is this person who was hindering my progress?" And then, the thought emerged, "Well, at least he's no longer here!"

One by one the employees got closer to the coffin, and when they looked inside, they suddenly became speechless. They stood over the coffin, shocked and silent, as if someone had touched the deepest part of their soul.

There was a mirror inside the coffin: everyone who looked inside could see himself. There was also a sign next to the mirror: "There is only one person who is capable of setting limits to your growth: it is YOU.

You are the only person who can revolutionize your life. You are the only person who can influence your happiness, your relationships, and your success. You are the only person who can help yourself.

Your life does not change when your boss changes, when your friends change, when your parents change, when your partner changes, when your company changes. Your life changes when YOU change, when you go beyond your limiting beliefs, when you realize you are the only one responsible for your life.

Even when we aren't facing a major obstacle in our lives, change is very much a part of our journey. The world changes daily—technology, climate, politics, and world economies all shift, and we must learn new skills and realities. The baby boomer generation has had its world turned upside down more than once, and those born later will find even more turmoil and revolution as the 21st century unfolds. Personal, national, or international circumstances will continue to force people to cope with unexpected change on a regular basis.

The only constant in our lives is the assurance we are given that God sent Christ to save us now and for eternity. When we are frustrated and frightened as the world shifts and threatens life as we know it, we can always rely on God. No matter how uncertain our environment or how calamitous our circumstances, faith in God and his power to control and direct our lives provides an anchor that cannot be moved. In Ruth Cave Jones' song, "In Times Like These," we are reminded to be sure our anchor grips the solid rock of Jesus. Another hymn of faith, "The Solid Rock," expresses similar sentiments, assuring us our hope is built on Jesus' blood and righteousness. As long as we stand on Christ, the solid rock, we need not worry about sinking sand. His love for us is endless—as strong and powerful tomorrow as it is today and was yesterday.

Resisting change is futile. With God's help, we can embrace change and make it a productive part of our lives. Faith calls on us to see opportunities—not problems—in change. If we are possibility believers, we can expect something good—perhaps even wonderful—to come with change. It may be the silver lining in the cloud, so we may have to go through a dark mist to find it, but positive anticipation has a way of transforming our future. The expectation of good brings its own reward—a bit of happiness that lifts our spirits even if the outcome isn't exactly what we envisioned. Cheerful faith is a gift all by itself.

POST-IT MEDITATION FOR APRIL 23
God, help me look for unanticipated dividends in every change, knowing I am responsible for how I respond.

April 24

For I have not come to call those who think they are righteous, but those who know they are sinners.
~Matthew 9:13 (NLT)

Have you ever felt unworthy of God's love? When our lives are filled with sin or we have wasted many years outside God's grace, we become hesitant to ask God back into the center of our lives. When we feel that way, we only have to look at the people Jesus associated with and assisted to remember that he came for people like us—imperfect human beings. He spent time with the poor, the lame, lepers, prostitutes, tax collectors, and people possessed by unclean spirits. He bypassed the rich and looked for those who were poor; those who were well had no need of him, so he came to heal the sick. He helped those who were persecuted. He was there for those who were burdened by sorrow. He had no patience with those who thought they were righteous but infinite mercy for those who knew they were sinners. He loved little children. And, he loves each of us.

In Matthew 18:2-4 Jesus tells us we must become like little children to enter the kingdom of heaven. Brennan Manning, author of *The Ragamuffin Gospel*, explains when Jesus tells us we need to be like little children, he is encouraging us to forget what lies behind. "What we have done in the past, be it good or evil, great or small, is irrelevant to our stance before God today."

Manning illustrates the value of living in the present through a Zen story about a monk being pursued by a vicious tiger:

As the monk approaches the edge of a cliff, he looks back and sees the tiger about to spring. Spotting a rope dangling over the edge of the cliff, the monk grabs it and begins to start down the cliff, hand over hand. About the time he thinks he is going to escape, he looks up and sees a mouse chewing on the rope. The ledge below is 500 feet away. Caught between the ferocious tiger above him and the dangerous fall he knows will kill him, the monk stops for a moment and looks sideways. There he sees a luscious strawberry, just within arm's reach. He plunks it and eats it, thinking, "That's the best strawberry I've ever tasted in my entire life."

Manning explains that the monk would have missed the strawberry God was giving him in the present moment if he had been preoccupied with the tiger above (his past) or the rock below (his future).

Yes, we are sinners, but God wants us to be like the monk—like children who live in the moment, not in the past or the future. He wants to put our past behind us, enjoy what he has given us, and leave the future to him.

POST-IT MEDITATION FOR APRIL 24
*I will accept God's forgiveness, his blessings of today,
and his promise for tomorrow.*

April 25

*Everyone has inside of him a piece of good news. The good news is that you
don't know how great you can be!
How much you can love! What you can accomplish! And what your potential is!*
~Anne Frank, Holocaust victim

God created all people equal, and when we closely examine life, we find
that in the 21st century all men and women are still equal. Granted, we
have gone through periods in history when inequality tarnished God's
creation both legally and socially. But in the ways that really matter, all
people were and still are equal—inside.

*In a small church in London many years ago, the pastor offered an unusual, and
remarkably short, sermon. Holding up an English walnut, the minister asked his
congregation to consider the nut. He then suggested that comparing the ugly, tough
shell to beautiful and exciting pieces of creation, the walnut seemed rather pitiful.
"It is common, rough, not particularly attractive, and certainly not valuable in any
monetary sense." He added, "Besides, it is small. Its growth is limited by the hard
shall that surrounds it—the shell from which it never escapes during its lifetime."*

*Holding out the walnut once again, the minister told his parishioners that judg-
ing the walnut by the shell was the wrong way to appraise it. Instead, he suggested,
to evaluate the walnut, it had to be cracked open so you could see inside. "See how
the walnut has grown to fill every nook and cranny available to it." Importantly, he
noted, the walnut didn't have any input in the size or shape of its shell, but given
its limitations, it had amazingly achieved its full potential. The short sermon ended
with these words. "How lucky we will be if, like the walnut, we blossom and bloom
in every crevice of the life that is given to us."*

What if the walnut had griped and complained about its misshapen
shell and size? What if it had spent its time wishing it had the smooth
skin of a pecan or the beauty of a hazelnut? If it had bemoaned its
God-given shape, it would never have filled its inside with tasty meats
the world could enjoy.

We are all created in God's image, and he loves each of us equally. We
all have an innate ability to love. We all have the capacity to respect others
and to treat them as we would like to be treated. We all have the opportunity to ask God for forgiveness for our sins and to expect pardon.

In a lifetime, most of us only scratch the surface of our potential because we don't make the most of what we have been given.

Self-help author Brian Tracy wrote, "The potential of the average person is like a huge ocean unsailed, a new continent unexplored, a world of possibilities waiting to be released and channeled toward some great good." What a vast wasteland exists between what we are and what we could be!

SOURCE OF THE WALNUT SERMON: Ed McManus, Leadership, published by The Economics Press, Inc.

POST-IT MEDITATION FOR APRIL 25
When I am tempted to think I am not capable, I will remember the walnut and take advantage of the life I have been blessed to receive from God.

April 26

We are either living a little more or dying
a little bit each moment of our lives.
~Norman Mailer, American novelist, journalist, poet, screenwriter, and film director.

A small boy walking down the street one day found a bright copper penny. He was so excited he found money that the experience led him to spend the rest of his days walking with his head down, eyes wide open, looking for treasure.

During his lifetime he found 296 pennies, 48 nickels, 19 dimes, 16 quarters, 2 half dollars and one crinkled dollar bill. For a total of $13.96.

He got money for nothing. Except that he missed the breathless beauty of 31,369 sunsets, the colorful splendor of 157 rainbows, the fiery beauty of hundreds of maples nipped by autumn's frost. He never saw white clouds drifting across blue skies, shifting into various wondrous formations. Birds flying, sun shining, and the smiles of a thousand passing people are not a part of his memory.

Do you know anyone living like this: Head bent down, burdened with trivial things, hoping to find that copper penny...missing the world for so little in return?

God created us to grow physically, mentally, and spiritually. Unless we are ill or have a genetic disorder, the physical part takes care of itself, although staying fit requires regular exercise. Our mental capacity entails more effort—like our bodies, it will grow stronger if we train and work out through reading, study, and mental gymnastics. Likewise, our spiritual growth requires activity. Bible reading and prayer grow muscles of spirit and soul. We stretch those muscles through service to God and others. In a spiritual sense, from the time we are "born again," we must develop as a Christian or our faith will begin to die, a bit at a time, each instant we fail to entrust our entire being to God.

With every breath we take, we have the opportunity to use each moment to live fully. We each travel different paths, but we can love those around us, help others in need, provide friendship and support to family and friends. Along the way, we will make mistakes, but we can use those times as learning moments, discovering the harmony that comes from asking forgiveness and giving forgiveness. We can turn moments of anger into moments of peace, times of sorrow into moments of rejoicing, phases of worry into points of trust. Every day we move closer to God or we move away from him. As we live, we should want to grow in the spirit.

In her column, "If I had my life to live over again," Erma Bomback wrote, "…given another shot at life, I would seize every minute, look at it and really see it, live it, and never give it back.

POST-IT MEDITATION FOR APRIL 26
I will not wait around to die—I will
attempt to grow with each moment of life.

April 27

Nature is a mutable cloud which is always and never the same.
~Ralph Waldo Emerson, American poet, essayist, and philosopher

A renowned Italian math professor at the University of Padua heard about an interesting discovery in another country and decided to investigate it. In 1608, someone in the Netherlands had invented a device described as "an instrument for looking into the distance." Today, we know that instrument as a telescope, from the Greek words tele (far) and scopeo (I see). Intrigued with the device, the Italian faculty member improved its original design, finally magnifying by twenty-one times anything seen through the glass. Then he tried something different: He turned his new telescope up, toward the sky. What he saw forever changed how mankind views the heavens. The man's name was Galileo, and he became the father of modern day observational astronomy because what he saw transformed how man viewed the heavens for hundreds of years to come. He brought part of God's creation closer not only for scientific purposes but also for non-scientists' viewing pleasure.

One of God's greatest gifts is the ever-changing nature—the sky included—we are privileged to witness every day of our lives. It not only varies from day to day but is also always the same. Perhaps that is what makes it so amazing.

The sun rises and sets every day, yet the breathtaking colors vary, new shades and tints creating colors we have never seen before. The ocean tides move with the moon, yet the size of the waves differs and their colors can go from deep to light. Clouds form often in the sky, but their shapes and sizes can surprise us. The Grand Canyon, formed by the ravages of nature, provides magnificent vistas of vegetation and rock formations, but at night it becomes a dark cavern.

Spring brings trees glowing in green; fall turns the leaves gold and crimson—but the sequence of seasons never changes. We know that after every fall, winter arrives, then spring and summer follow. The examples never end, all testifying that nature is God's art—painting, sculpture, even music that comes with a whistling wind or a babbling brook.

How blessed we are by nature. When we lean toward depression and sadness, a walk through God's studio can reawaken our slumping spirit. God speaks to us through nature. George Washington Carver once said he loved to "think of nature as an unlimited broadcasting station, through which God speaks to us every hour, if we will only tune in."

If we climb a hill at sunset or walk beside the ocean at sunrise, or even just stand outside our door and gaze at the sky, we will find perspective on our problems. If we trod through rain in a forest or stroll by a creek with an open heart, we can hear answers to our questions. With one of the most brilliant minds of all mankind, Albert Einstein had the wisdom to advise, "Look deep into nature, and then you will understand everything better." And with understanding comes healing, so nature is also our medicine. For that we should be eternally thankful.

A heartfelt prayer of thanksgiving for the beauty of the earth is found in the *Episcopal Book of Common Prayer*:

We give thanks, most gracious God, for the beauty of earth and sky and sea; for the richness of mountains, plains, and rivers; for the songs of birds and the loveliness of flowers. We praise you for these good gifts...grant that we may continue to grow in our grateful enjoyment of your abundant creation, to the honor and glory of your Name, now and forever. Amen.

POST-IT MEDITATION FOR APRIL 27
When budding flowers fill me with joy, a silky field of wheat moves me, or a rainbow reminds me of God's power to paint the sky, I will know my spirit is alive and all is well with my soul.

April 28

Give thanks to the Lord, for he is good....
~Psalm 107:1 (NIV)

Francie Baltazar-Schwartz wrote about an interesting guy named Jerry.

Amazingly, Jerry always had something positive to say and was constantly in a good mood. When someone asked him how he was doing, he always replied, "If I were any better, I would be twins!"

153

Jerry managed restaurants, and everywhere he went, several waiters went, too, because he was such a positive influence. A natural motivator, he encouraged employees to look on the bright side of any situation. Curious how he could constantly remain optimistic and upbeat, Baltazar-Schwartz asked him how he did it.

"Each morning I wake up and say to myself, 'Jerry, you have two choices today. You can choose to be in a good mood or you can choose to be in a bad mood.' I choose to be in a good mood. Each time something bad happens, I can choose to be a victim or I can choose to learn from it. I choose to learn from it. Every time someone comes to me complaining, I can choose to accept their complaining, or I can point out the positive side of life. I choose the positive side of life."

Jerry explained that life is all about choices, about how we react to situations. It is our choice, he said, and his life proved he lived what he preached. Several years later, the restaurant he was managing was held up at gunpoint by three armed robbers, and Jerry was shot. Seriously wounded, he says the expressions on the faces of the doctors and nurses scared him. He read the message in their eyes, "He's a dead man."

A big, burly nurse shouted questions at him before taking him in to surgery, including, "Are you allergic to anything?"

"Yes," Jerry responded, "Bullets!"

Over the laughter of the doctors and nurses, Jerry told them, "I am choosing to live. Operate on me as if I am alive, not dead." After 18 hours of surgery, Jerry began recovery, complete with his amazing attitude.

POST-IT MEDITATION FOR APRIL 28
Thank you, God, for the freedom to choose between a positive and a negative attitude.

April 29

Be strong and courageous and do the work. Do not be afraid or discouraged, for the Lord God is with you. He will not fail you or forsake you....
~*1 Chronicles 28:20 (NIV)*

One night a man sleeping in his cabin was awakened by a brilliant light, and in the center God appeared. God told the man he had work for him and instructed him to push against the huge rock in front of his cabin with all his might. So the man pushed, day after day, from sunup to sundown, his shoulders set squarely against the massive stone. Sore and worn out each night, he began to feel his whole days were being wasted.

Perceiving the man's discouragement, his adversary (Satan) began to put negative thoughts into his mind, telling him the task was impossible and he had failed. He even suggested to the disheartened man he was crazy to kill himself—he should just push the rock with minimum effort. Although he was tempted to slack off, the man decided to pray about his frustration.

"Lord, I labored long and hard according to your instructions, yet I have not even budged the rock at all. What is wrong?"

With compassion, the Lord responded, "My friend, when I asked you to serve me and you accepted, I told you that your task was to push against the rock with all your strength, which you have done. I never said I expected you to move it. Your task was simply to push. You haven't failed. Look at your arms—they are strong and muscled. Your legs have become massive and hard. Through your hard work, your abilities now surpass what they once were. True, you haven't moved the rock, but your calling was to be obedient. That you have done." And then God concluded, "Now I, my friend, will move the rock."

We humans tend to put our own spin on what God asks us to do, when all he may desire is simple obedience and faith. Yes, we should exercise our faith and push to move the obstacles we face, but we should never forget it is God who moves the huge boulders in our path of life.

POST-IT MEDITATION FOR APRIL 29
When the work I have to do gets me down,
*I will remember to P.U.S.H.: I will **P**ray **U**ntil **S**omething **H**appens.*
AUTHOR'S NOTE: *The original author of the P.U.S.H. acronym is unknown.*

April 30

When clouds appear like rocks and towers, the earth is refreshed by frequent showers.
~Unknown

We have all heard the old saying, April showers bring May flowers. Still, as much as we look forward to the buds about to burst into bloom, by the end of April, we sometimes feel so soggy and wet we just want the rain to cease.

Life is like that. When clouds constantly dump bucketsful of rain on our heads, we resent anyone telling us that after the deluge ends our lives will be better. While the volley of showers continues, we have trouble seeing brighter days that lie ahead, and words about tomorrow don't seem to help.

How much is enough and how much is too much—rain or trouble?

As a mother and daughter said goodbye at an airport departure gate, they hugged, and the mother said, "I love you and I wish you enough."

The daughter replied, "Mom, our life together has been more than enough. Your love is all I ever needed. I wish you enough, too, Mom."

As the daughter boarded the plane, the mother walked over to where another lady was sitting alone, clearly needing to talk. "Did you ever say goodbye to someone knowing it would be forever?" she asked. "I am old and my daughter lives so far away—the next time she comes back will be for my funeral. It's sad—I love her so much."

Touched, the stranger asked, "What did you mean by, 'I love you enough?'"

"That's a wish that has been used in my family for generations. When we said it, we were wanting the other person to have a life filled with just enough good things to sustain them." And then, she recited these lines from memory:

I wish you enough sun to keep your attitude bright.
I wish you enough rain to appreciate the sun more.
I wish you enough happiness to keep your spirit alive.
I wish you enough pain so that the smallest joys in life appear much bigger.
I wish you enough gain to satisfy your wanting.
I wish you enough loss to appreciate all that you possess.
I wish you enough hellos to get you through the final good-bye.

POST-IT MEDITATION FOR APRIL 30
I wlll pray for enough—not more or less—for my life.

May 1

Sometimes it is necessary to be cruel in order to be kind.
~William Shakespeare, English poet and playwright

Have you ever watched a butterfly's struggle to escape the cocoon in which it lives before emerging? If so, you know it is a painful process.

One man, observing a monarch butterfly trying to force its body through a tiny opening in its cocoon, became disturbed when it appeared the butterfly had stopped making progress. Fearing the butterfly was stuck, halfway inside and halfway outside its cocoon, he decided to help. Taking a pair of scissors, he snipped off the back part of the cocoon that was holding the butterfly prisoner. He then watched proudly as the butterfly easily emerged, but his pride soon turned to dismay when he saw the small, shriveled wings that held fast to a swollen body. Transfixed, the man waited hopefully for the wings to break free and expand, but it didn't happen. The butterfly was condemned to crawling around, never able to fly the rest of its short life. In trying to help, the man had deformed the beautiful creature.

What the man didn't understand was that God's perfect plan called for the butterfly to labor because the struggle strengthened its wings. The protracted, painful exit through the small opening of the cocoon was designed to force fluid from the body of the butterfly into its wings, shrinking its body and preparing it for flight.

Like the butterfly, we may need struggles and pain to prepare us for our flight through life. We may wiggle and thrash as we deal with problems that seem to restrict our growth as Christians, but battles with obstacles toughen us. When we think we may be paralyzed by our efforts, we should pause and remember the butterfly was crippled because his struggle was cut short.

We should also recall that Christ did not shy away from suffering. When he returned from the mount of transfiguration, he was painfully aware of his impending crucifixion. He knew he would not be spared suffering. Even so, he had confidence God's power would enable him to triumph over torment, that he would be resurrected three days after death. We, too, will someday triumph over agony. Even in the face of a disabling accident, terminal cancer, or mental incapacitation, we can be assured that, like Christ, we will rise again, free of agony and anguish. As Christians, our faith can hold firm, refusing to give in to discouragement, despair, and defeat.

POST-IT MEDITATION FOR MAY 1
***When I am struggling to escape from problems,
I will remember pain brings growth.***

May 2

Let your love flow through me.
~Rodger Strader, American composer

Sometimes we get so entangled in life's problems—or maybe just in its busyness—that we insulate ourselves from the hardships of others. As Strader's song reminds us, many people are lonely and crave for someone to care; broken hearts of others are filled with pain. Yet, we shield ourselves from their hurts and needs, excusing our lack of caring by saying we don't have time or money beyond our own commitments.

For more than 25 years, when I even happened to think about him, I found excuses why I did not write or visit a second cousin confined in a Georgia state prison. From the out-of-state city where I lived, I sent a few Christmas cards over the years and wrote several letters on his behalf to the parole board in Georgia, but there was so much more I could have done. Occasionally, I would feel guilty; but brushing the feeling aside, I convinced myself that others closer to him would surely help him. Belatedly, when I retired, I decided to make contact. The first time I visited him, I discovered that in his 30 years in prison, he had averaged less than one visit a year from family members. I was further saddened to learn my cousin had not had a single visitor in four years, even though he had requested and received a transfer to a facility less than three hours from most of his family members, thinking they would come see him if they didn't have to travel a long distance. Although one uncle stayed in touch by telephone and occasionally others would send a greeting card or small amounts of money, the few visits he had had over the years had ended long ago. That day, with a heart wrenched by regret, I made a commitment to myself that I would leave the ranks of those who made excuses for why they didn't visit and let God's love flow through me to this lonely, forgotten member of my family. Although my goal was to help him, I have found my own spirit uplifted by being in his presence—the strength of his faith is amazing. I have no doubt the blessing I have received is far greater than any joy he has found in my visits.

While everyone does not have a family member in prison, all of us are surrounded by people longing for love and kindness—family, friends, or strangers. When we look about and see a soul secluded from support and nurture, we should pray God will make us a blessing in that person's life. And then we need to put hands and feet behind that prayer.

AUTHOR'S NOTE: Several months after I started visiting my cousin, two other cousins began going with me to the prison on a regular basis. Now there are three of us who are committed to sharing our love. I pray daily that others will join this small number of visitors.

POST-IT MEDITATION FOR MAY 2
When I see someone in need, I will not be selfish because that person's only chance for compassion may be with me.

May 3

Oh, Great Spirit, grant me the wisdom to walk in another's moccasins before I criticize or pass judgment.
~Sioux Indian Prayer

You probably remember me from the other day. I was the one who reacted very slowly to the green traffic light. When you honked your horn, I realized I was holding up traffic, so please accept my apology. However, I do want you to know why I seemed in a daze. You see, I was just at the doctor's office getting the results of the biopsy I had two weeks ago, and I was wondering how I would tell my husband and children I have cancer. My eyes were still stinging from crying, so, quite simply I didn't even see the light change. Perhaps I should not have been driving, but I didn't want to miss my appointment, and there was no one else to take me. Please, accept my apology.

~~~

You over there—yes, you. I was the one in the express lane at the supermarket. I know you are only supposed to take 12 items or less and I had a basket full. I didn't even notice the express lane sign until my items were being taken from the basket. Please accept my apology. My mind was on my youngest daughter who ran away from home, and she's just sixteen. I was so distraught then. You see, she somehow got in with the wrong crowd and started using drugs and drinking. I was remembering what a pretty little girl she had been most of her life. I know you were perturbed along with others in line. Please, accept my apology.

~~~

I remember you from the department store last week. I was so mean to you, when you were doing your job to the best of your ability. I acted so childishly. Please accept my apology. You see, I arrived home from work just yesterday and discovered my wife had left me. But I should never have taken it out on you. Please, accept my apology.

~~~

Walking in another's moccasins—seeing through someone else's eyes—is not easy. We all view others through the lens of our own life experiences. If our children have never gone hungry, we can't imagine stealing a loaf of bread. If we don't carry an addiction gene, it is easy to condemn an addict struggling to escape the "gotta have it" craving he can't control. If we have never been without a job, we don't know what it feels like to be dependent on others.

How can we avoid the trap of passing judgment on those in whose moccasins we have never walked?

John 8:1-11 tells the story of an adulterous woman brought before Jesus by scribes and Pharisees for punishment. Reminding Jesus that Moses had commanded such women be stoned, they asked him what should be done. The answer: "Let him who is without sin among you be the first to throw a stone at her." Bewildered, the accusers walked away, one by one. And Jesus said that just as the scribes and Pharisees no longer condemned her, "Neither do I condemn you...."

Each of us sins daily, yet our transgressions never seem quite as horrible as our neighbor's offenses. Hypocritical, we ignore our own failings while condemning others, never realizing how insensitive and unfeeling we can become in our own smug, sanctimonious world. Matthew 7:3 (NIV) warns us about such hypocrisy, demanding we first get rid of the log in our own eye before we try to deal with the speck of sawdust in a friend's eye.

Someone once said we believe wrongs aren't wrong if they are actions *we* take. Conversely, if it isn't a wrong we have chosen to commit, then that's another story. Self-righteous, we criticize and condemn. We should be mindful of Shakespeare's words from *Henry VI*: "Forbear to judge, for we are sinners all." Matthew 7:1 (NIV) said it another way: "Do not judge, or you, too, will be judged."

SOURCE for three apologies: http://www.values.com/your-inspirational-stories/81-Please-Accept-My-Apology

POST-IT MEDITATION FOR MAY 3

Before I criticize and condemn others who act in ways I don't act or who are slow, absentminded, or angry, I will pause to admit to myself I can't possibly know the life experiences that have influenced their actions.

May 4

Therefore, I urge you, brothers, in view of God's mercy, to offer your bodies as living sacrifices, holy and pleasing to God—this is your spiritual act of worship.
~Romans 12:1 (NIV)

There was a school with a class of students no teacher had been able to handle. Two or three teachers had been run off from this school in one year by the unruly students. A young man, just out of college, heard about the class and applied to the school.

The principal asked the young man, "Do you not know what you are asking for? No one has been able to handle these students. You are asking for a terrible beating."

After a few moments of silent prayer, the young man looked at the principal and said, "Sir, with your consent I accept the challenge. Just give me a trial basis."

The next morning the young man stood before the class and said, "Young people, I came here today to conduct school. But I realize I can't do it by myself. I must have your help."

One big boy, called Big Tom, whispered to his buddies in the back of the room, "I'll not need any help. I can lick that little bird all by myself."

The young teacher told the class if they were to have school, some rules would be needed. But he also added he would allow the students to make up the rules, which he would list on the blackboard.

This was certainly different, the students thought!

One young man suggested "NO STEALING." Another shouted "BE ON TIME FOR CLASS." Soon they had 10 rules listed on the board.

The teacher then asked the class what the punishment should be for breaking these rules. "Rules are no good unless they are enforced," he said.

Someone in the class suggested if the rules were broken, they should receive 10 licks with a rod across their back with their coat off. The teacher thought that was pretty harsh, so he asked the class if they would stand by this punishment. The class agreed.

Everything went pretty well for two or three days. Then Big Tom came in one day very upset. He declared someone had stolen his lunch. After talking with the students, the teacher discovered someone had seen Little Timmy with Big Tom's lunch!

The teacher called Little Timmy up to the front of the room. Little Timmy admitted he had taken Big Tom's lunch. So the teacher asked him, "Do you know the punishment?" Little Timmy nodded that he did.

"You must remove your coat, then," the teacher instructed. The little fellow had come with a great big coat on.

Little Timmy said to the teacher, "I am guilty and I am willing to take my punishment, but please don't make me take off my coat." The teacher reminded Little Timmy of the rules and punishments and again told him he must remove his coat and take his punishment like a man.

The little fellow started to unbutton that old coat. As he did so, the teacher saw he did not have a shirt on under the coat. And even worse, he saw a frail and bony frame hidden beneath that coat. The teacher asked Little Timmy why he had come to school without a shirt on.

Little Timmy replied, "My daddy's dead and my mother is very poor. I don't have but one shirt, and my mother is washing it today. I wore big brother's coat so's to keep warm."

The young teacher stood and looked at the frail back with ribs sticking out, the spine protruding against the skin. He wondered how he could lay a rod on that little back without even a shirt on. Still, he knew he must enforce the punishment or the children would not obey the rules. So he drew back to strike Little Timmy.

Just then Big Tom stood up and came down the aisle. He asked, "Is there anything that says I can't take Little Timmy's whipping for him?"

The teacher thought about it and agreed. With that Big Tom ripped his coat off and stooped and stood over Little Timmy at the desk. Hesitatingly, the teacher began to lay the rod on the big back. But for some strange reason, after only five licks that old rod just broke in half. The young teacher buried his face in his hands and began to sob. He heard a commotion and looked up to find not even one dry eye in the room.

Little Timmy had turned and grabbed Big Tom around the neck, apologizing to him for stealing his lunch, begging his forgiveness. He told Big Tom he would love him till the day he died for taking his whipping for him.

Aren't you glad Jesus took our whipping for us, that he shed his precious blood at Calvary so you and I can have eternal life in glory with him? We are unworthy of the price he paid for us, but isn't it wonderful he loved us that much?

POST-IT MEDITATION FOR MAY 4
Help me not sit on the sidelines, God, when someone is in need or suffering.

May 5

Dogs are not our whole life, but they make our lives whole.
~Roger Caras, American wildlife photographer, preservationist, writer

Some dogs—perhaps all—are precious gifts from God. A story about a dog named Lucky illustrates how unique the relationship between a human and a dog can become.

Lucky's owners, Mary and Jim, always warned visitors to their home they should not leave their luggage open because Lucky would help himself to whatever struck his fancy. Inevitably, someone would forget and something would come up missing. Mary or Jim would go to Lucky's toy box in the basement and there the treasure would be, amid all of Lucky's other favorite toys he kept stashed in his box.

One day Mary discovered she had breast cancer and became convinced it was fatal. The night before a double mastectomy, she cuddled with Lucky, concerned what would happen to him if she died. The dog loved her husband, but he was her dog through and through. The thought that Lucky would feel abandoned made her even sadder than the possibility of her death.

When she returned home from the hospital, Mary felt worse than she had anticipated, so exhausted she couldn't even make it up the steps to her bedroom. Her husband made her comfortable on the couch and left her to nap. Lucky stood watching Mary but didn't come to her when she called. It made Mary sad, but sleep soon overcame her and she dozed. When Mary woke, she couldn't move her head and her body felt heavy and hot. For a second, she couldn't understand what was wrong, but panic soon gave way to laughter when she realized the problem. She was covered, literally blanketed, with every treasure Lucky owned! While she had slept, the sorrowing dog had made trip after trip to the basement bringing his beloved mistress all the favorite items he had hoarded. He had covered her with his love. Mary forgot about dying. Instead she and Lucky began living again. At her next checkup, Mary found she was cancer-free. Lucky? He still steals gems of all kinds and stashes them in his toy box, but Mary remains his greatest treasure.

Mary knew what many dog lovers know—a caring dog is a special, God-given blessing. They can be better than psychiatrists when we are depressed or suffering.

POST-IT MEDITATION FOR MAY 5
Thank you, God, for all your creatures
that brighten lives and lift spirits.

May 6

My grace is sufficient for you, for my power is made perfect in weakness.
~2 Corinthians 12:9 (ESV)

A well-known speaker started a seminar by holding out twenty dollars, asking of the 200 people in the room, "Who would like this $20 bill?"

Hands popped up all across the room.

The speaker then explained, "I am going to give this $20 to one of you, but first, I'm going to crumple it up." He then asked, "Who still wants it?"

The same number of hands went up.

"Well," the speaker continued, "What if I do this?" Then he dropped the $20 bill on the floor and ground it with his shoe. Picking up the crumpled and dirty bill, he asked, "Now who still wants it?" Not one person chose to drop his bid for the $20.

"You have just learned a valuable lesson. No matter what I did to the money, you still want it because it did not decrease in value. It is still worth $20."

Just as the value of the $20 was not diminished, we don't lose our worth when we are dropped, crumbled, or ground into dirt by decisions we make and the circumstances that come into our lives. We should never feel worthless, because no matter what has happened or will happen, we will never lose our value. We are accepted by God as imperfect human beings. Unlike Quasimodo, the hunchback of Notre Dame, we don't have to hide the unattractive and unpleasant parts of our lives.

We need to never forget, as Brennan Manning wrote, that "Jesus comes not for the super-spiritual but for the wobbly and the weak-kneed who know they don't have it all together...." We may be ashamed of our past, unhappy with our present, and fearful of our future, but God accepts us with understanding and grace. Our perception of ourselves does not matter—what counts is God's willingness to value us despite our sinful natures. We may be failures in our own sight; we may be guilt-ridden and discouraged, but God knows we want to be faithful even when we fall short. Our lives are never too sordid for the blood of Christ to cleanse our past and for God's grace to make us acceptable to him.

POST-IT MEDITATION FOR MAY 6
Even when I am battered and beaten down, I will not become discouraged because I know God still values and accepts me.

May 7

Wherever a man turns he can find someone who needs him.
~Albert Schweitzer, German/French theologian, philosopher, and medical missionary

Each day of our lives we pass people without really seeing them. Caught up in our own day, they remain faceless to us—often we don't even look close enough to see if they wear a smile or a frown. A waitress brings our meal, and we utter a quick "thanks" without raising our head. A department store clerk rings up our sale, but we are so busy texting someone we hardly notice her. The man in front of us at the grocery store is just someone slowing down our progress. Even at church, we may sit beside someone and not notice fluttering eyelids of a person unable to contain sorrow. Engrossed in our own lives, we aren't on the same wavelength as the people we encounter.

What would happen if we began to be more sensitive to those about us? What a difference it might make in another person's life if we paused to offer a warm smile, a genuine expression of gratitude, or a gentle touch. We never know what lies behind the masks people wear, but we may be able to lighten a load, even for a few seconds, if we make an effort to show we are concerned.

An Australian who delivers parcels for Australia Post gets to meet a lot of people because she delivers the parcels personally to each house. One day when she took a parcel to an elderly couple, the wife made the comment "age before beauty," saying the delivery lady was "beauty" and she was "age." Smiling, the delivery person responded that the lady was beautiful herself. The older lady didn't know what to say, but it had really touched her, and she commented that as you get older, the compliments you receive become less and less. She insisted on giving a tip, a $5 dollar note. The delivery agent thanked her and continued on her parcel run. She wasn't going to do anything special with the money but changed her mind. She decided to buy the elderly lady a flowering plant and go back and "deliver" it to her!

The same delivery agent was near the end of her parcel delivery run on another day and drove past an elderly gentleman who was obviously walking home from town. He was walking slowly and looked tired. "I felt sorry for him but kept on my way, driving to the next house on my run. After I had delivered this parcel, I turned into the next street, which runs up a long and quite steep hill. I noticed this same gentleman was still walking, by now looking quite weary and puffed. I pulled over, wound my window down and asked if he would like a lift." Noting she normally didn't do this sort of thing because she was a female, she felt good after the man looked most relieved and grateful. She drove him to his house, right up to the front door and told him to have a great day. He replied he definitely would, now that she had made his day!

Even within our own families, we are sometimes oblivious to the cares and concerns of those we love. We need to make time to notice if they require assistance or just need to talk. We need to take action or listen unconditionally, to voice our approval and support, and to make an effort to spend quality time. Likely, we do this with our immediate family, but what about distant relatives who may not have children or grandchildren in their lives? What about elderly friends or strangers who may be lonely?

Most people have an altruistic streak—we truly want to be unselfish, to help others, and to make a difference. Yet, we fail to see the opportunities surrounding us. Lofty openings to help others may not come our way, but small ones abound. Albert Schweitzer advised, "Always keep your eyes open to the little task, because it is the little task that is important to God.... The great flowing rivers represent only a small part of all the water that is necessary to nourish and sustain the earth. Beside the flowing river there is the water *in* the earth—the subterranean water—and there are the little streams which continually enter the river and feed it.... Without these other waters...the great river could no longer flow. Thus it is with the little tasks to be fulfilled by us all."

SOURCE for Australia Post story: http://payitforwardday.com/inspire-me/ best-pay-it-forward-stories/

POST-IT MEDITATION FOR MAY 7
*Help me, God, to see the importance of little actions
I can do in your service.*

May 8

Now ye may suppose that this is foolishness in me; but behold I say unto you, that by small and simple things are great things brought to pass; and small means in many instances doth confound the wise.
~Alma the Younger, Nephite prophet

For a long time, a young man had admired a beautiful sports car in a dealer's showroom. Knowing his father could well afford it, he told his dad that was all he wanted for his upcoming graduation from college.

As his commencement day approached, the young man began looking for signs his father had bought the car. Finally on the morning of his graduation, his father called him into his study. He told him how proud he was to have such a fine son and how much he loved him. Then he handed his son a beautifully wrapped gift box. Curious, but somewhat disappointed, the young man opened the box and found a lovely leather-bound Bible with his name embossed in gold. Angry, he raised his voice to his father and said, "With all your money, you give me a Bible?" He then stormed out of the house, leaving the Bible.

Many years passed and the young man was very successful in his own business. He had a beautiful home and wonderful family, but he realized his father was very old and thought perhaps he should go to him as he had not spoken to him since that long-ago graduation day. Regrettably, before he could make arrangements, he received a telegram that his father had passed away and had willed all his possessions to his son.

When he arrived at his father's home, sadness and regret filled the man's heart. As he began sorting through his dad's papers, he saw the still new Bible just as he had left it years ago. With tears in his eyes, he opened it and began to turn the pages, noticing his father had carefully underlined Matthew 7:11, "And if ye, being evil, know how to give good gifts to your children, how much more shall your heavenly Father which is in Heaven give to those who ask him?" As the man read these words, a car key dropped from the back of the Bible. It had a tag with a dealer's name, and on the tag was the date of his graduation and the words, "Paid in full."

How many times do we miss out on blessings because they are not packaged as we expected?

POST-IT MEDITATION FOR MAY 8
May I never underestimate the value of a small gift;
any gift of love is a blessing.

May 9

Through it all, I've learned to trust in God.
~Andrae Crouch, American gospel singer, songwriter, recording artist, and pastor

Crouch's song, "Through It All," tells the story of a Christian who has had many tears and sorrows, experienced questions about tomorrow, and been through times when he didn't know right from wrong. But, the words assure us, "In every situation, God gave blessed consolation that my trials only come to make me strong."

Carol Schuller lived this song after a motorcycle accident took her leg. The daughter of Robert Schuller, she was well versed in positive thinking. As her father and mother rushed to her side, they searched for ways to comfort her. Their struggle was unnecessary; Carol's first words were, "I know why it happened, Dad. God wants to use me to help others who have been hurt." Throughout the *ordeal of seven months in the hospital as she fought an infection that threatened her life, Carol's faith never faltered. After six surgeries following the amputation, Carol returned to playing softball and to skiing, even winning a gold medal in the qualifying races for the National Ski Championships.*

Carol learned the lesson her father had taught: "Tough times never last, but tough people always do." At the age of 17, although she was not a singer, she decided to participate in a talent show on a cruise. Describing her accident and amputation, she told the audience, "If I've one talent, it is this: I can tell you during that time my faith became very real to me."

A hush fell over the room as Carol continued, "I look at you girls who walk without a limp, and I wish I could walk that way. I can't, but this is what I've learned, and I want to leave it with you. It's not how you walk that counts, but who walks with you and who you walk with." Then, pausing, she sang,

> *And, He walks with me,*
> *And He talks with me,*
> *And He tells me I am His own.*
> *And the joy we share,*
> *[In our time of prayer],*
> *None other has ever known.*

Carol had learned to thank God for both mountains and valleys, for the storms he had brought her through. Through it all, she trusted God.

POST-IT MEDITATION FOR MAY 9
Without problems, I wouldn't know God could solve them— and I might never know what faith in God can do.

May 10

I wandered lonely as a cloud that floats on high o'er vales and hills.
~William Wordsworth, English poet

Mother Teresa described loneliness and the feeling of being unwanted as "the most terrible poverty." An unknown person once said loneliness is about the scariest thing there is. I would add that loneliness is one of the saddest of life's experiences. And poet John Milton avowed, "Loneliness is the first thing which God's eye named not good."

If you have never experienced the hell of loneliness, you are fortunate, and you likely do not understand its language. If American writer Thomas Wolfe is right, though, you may someday face this formidable enemy. Wolfe said, "The whole conviction of my life now rests upon the belief that loneliness, far from being a rare and curious phenomenon... is the central and inevitable fact of human existence."

So, you are not alone if you have endured loneliness—you know what it is like to feel alone, to be convinced you are not the most important person in anyone's life. Lonely people sometimes sense they are invisible to other people—they see you, but they don't recognize who you are or how you feel. Like a cloud floating high above the earth, do you move about unnoticed by those below?

A motley crowd of people took the same bus every day, most to work, a few others to various places. One of the passengers was a small somber man who took the bus to the center for senior citizens each morning. He walked with a stoop and a sad look on his face as he boarded the bus with difficulty and sat down alone behind the driver. No one ever paid very much attention to him.

Then one July morning he said good morning to the driver and smiled at others as he made his way to his seat. The driver nodded guardedly. The rest of the passengers remained silent.

The next day, the old man boarded the bus energetically, smiled, and said in a loud voice: "And a very good morning to you all!" Some looked up, amazed, and murmured "Good morning," in reply.

In the weeks to come the elderly man now dressed in a nice old suit and a wide, out-of-date tie, his thin hair carefully combed. Gradually, most of the passengers began to nod and smile in response to his cheerful greeting.

One morning the old man had a bunch of wild flowers in his hand. They were already dangling a little because of the heat. The driver turned around smilingly and asked: "Have you got yourself a girlfriend, Charlie?" (No one knows if his name was Charlie, but everyone began to call him that.) In response to the driver's question, he nodded shyly and admitted he did. The other passengers whistled and clapped at him. Charlie bowed and waved the flowers before sitting down.

Every morning after that Charlie always brought a flower. Some of the regular passengers began bringing him flowers for his bouquet, gently nudged him, and said shyly: "Here." Everyone smiled. The men started to jest about it, talk to each other, and share the newspaper.

The summer went by, and autumn was closing in, when one morning Charlie wasn't waiting at his usual stop. When he wasn't there the next day and the day after that, the group of people who had become more than fellow passengers started wondering if he was sick or—hopefully—on holiday somewhere. When the bus came near the center for senior citizens, one of the passengers asked the driver to wait. All held their breaths when she went to the door.

Yes, the staff said, they knew whom we were talking about. The elderly gentleman was fine, but he hadn't been coming to the center that week. One of his very close friends had died over the weekend. They expected him back on Monday. How silent everyone was the rest of the way to work.

The next Monday Charlie was waiting at the stop, stooping a bit more, a little bit more ashen, and without a tie. He seemed to have shrunk again. Inside the bus, the air screamed with silence. Even though no one had talked about it, all the riders sat with their eyes filled with tears and a bunch of wild flowers in their hands. And Charlie knew, they cared.

No one will ever know how many of the passengers on that bus were lonely themselves or how many of them found their spirits lifted by caring for the old man. Nor will anyone know if the old man's affection and flowers had lifted his fellow senior citizens from aloneness.

Author Dag Hammarskjold admonished us to "pray that our own loneliness may spur us into finding something to live for, great enough to die for." In helping someone, we may unearth a purpose for our lives, and in doing so, we will discover we are no longer bound by loneliness when we are alone. Our loneliness becomes solitude, described by Paul Tillich, a German-born theologian and philosopher, as "the glory of being alone," so different from loneliness, which he defines as "the pain of being alone."

As long as we stay inside ourselves, it is difficult to climb out of the chasm. But, if we turn toward others, we find love can save us. Even if we feel unloved, we can love someone else. Lifting someone else's loneliness will heal our own. We will never be lonely if we befriend others.

Adapted from a story by Jean Hendrichson. Accessed at: http://www.inspirationalarchive. com/1096/flowers-on-the-bus/#ixzz24yfcDyCc

POST-IT MEDITATION FOR MAY 10
*When clouds of loneliness hang over my head,
I will choose to offer love to others.*

May 11

The world is not divided into the strong who care and the weak who are cared for. We must each in turn care and be cared for....
~Sheila Cassidy, British doctor

In an old-fashioned twist of words, "What goes around, comes around." Each of us goes through life helping and being helped, playing different roles at different times in our lives.

A poor Scottish farmer named Fleming spent his days trying to eke out a living for his family. One day, while working on his farm, he heard a cry for help coming from a nearby bog. Dropping his tools, he ran to the quagmire and saw a terrified young boy mired to his waist. The more the boy struggled, the deeper he sank. Farmer Fleming came to his rescue, pulling the lad from an almost certain death.

The next day, a fancy carriage pulled up to the old farmhouse, and an elegantly attired nobleman stepped down, introducing himself as the father of the boy Fleming had saved.

"I want to pay you," the dapper nobleman explained, "for saving my son's life."

But the farmer insisted no payment was necessary. About that time, the farmer's own son stepped to the door of the dilapidated farm house.

"Is this your son?" the nobleman inquired. Proudly, the farmer responded that it was.

"Then let me take your son and give him a good education," the nobleman offered. "If he is anything like his father, he'll grow up to be a man you will be proud of."

So, reluctantly, the farmer let his son go with the rich man. In time, the boy graduated from St. Mary's Hospital Medical School in London, eventually becoming known throughout the world as Sir Alexander Fleming, the man who discovered penicillin.

Many years later, the nobleman's son was stricken with pneumonia—and he was saved by the penicillin the farmer's son had created.

The name of the nobleman was Lord Randolph Churchill, and his son, saved first by Farmer Fleming and again by his son, was Winston Churchill. If the nobleman hadn't helped the farmer's son after the first rescue, his own son would still have died.

We should all be helpers—one person at a time. We should go through life easing the burdens of others. We never know when the person we aid will in turn assist us.

POST-IT MEDITATION FOR MAY 11
I will do my share of helping, and in turn, I will be helped.

May 12

Let your father and mother be glad; let she who bore you rejoice.
~*Proverbs 23:25 (ESV)*

A businessman left work late the day before Mother's Day and had to rush to get to the flower shop to order flowers for his mother, who lived just over 200 miles away. As he dashed from the car to the shop, he noticed a young girl sitting on the steps, sobbing. Despite his hurry, he couldn't pass her by and stopped to ask why she was crying.

"I wanted to buy a rose for my mother, but they cost two dollars and I only have 75 cents," the young girl said through her tears.

Smiling, glad he could help, the man asked the young girl to come into the flower shop with him, telling her he would gladly buy the rose she wanted for her mother. Inside, he ordered the flowers to be delivered to his mother and bought a rose for the girl. As they started to leave, it began to rain, and the man asked if the young girl would like a ride home.

"That would be wonderful. You can take me to my mother," said the grateful girl.

As they drove down a tree-lined street, the girl told him to turn right. The man was shocked to see they were entering a cemetery. The girl, tears brimming, directed him to her mother's grave, where she tenderly laid the rose.

After dropping the girl by her home, the man turned his car around, went back to the flower shop, and cancelled the wire order. He put the bouquet of flowers he had ordered in his car and drove the 200 miles to his mother's home to deliver them himself.

None of us know how long we will have our loved ones on this earth. Their presence should never be taken for granted. All hang onto life with a tenuous thread that can be easily broken. If we treasure those we love, our efforts to stay connected should not be the most expedient way; it should be with a personal touch. The Bible commands in both Exodus 20:12 and Ephesians 6:2 that we should honor our father and our mother. It is a command that should be heeded 365 times a year, not just on special days.

POST-IT MEDITATION FOR MAY 12
If my mother is alive, I will honor her with my presence as often as possible; if she now resides in heaven, I will thank God for the time we shared on earth.

May 13

What is impossible with men is possible with God.
~Luke 18:27 (ESV)

A number of stories exist about the invention of the ice cream cone, and one of the most often told is from the Louisiana Purchase Exposition held in St. Louis in 1904. That year, more than 1200 acres in the city sported new buildings— Japanese pavilions, Civil War diorama, neoclassical palaces, and many more. Of course, to feed the thousands of people expected at the fair, a number of vendors offered their specialties. Among the vendors were one with an ice cream concession and one selling waffles. Crowds exceeded estimates, and as throngs flowed through the grounds, the waffle vendor ran out of the cardboard plates on which he had been selling his waffles with toppings. He quickly went to other vendors, asking them to sell him plates, but no one wanted to take a chance on running out himself, so they all refused. Next door, the ice cream vendor had a smile on his face. "That's the way it goes," he told the waffle vendor. "Why don't you just work for me selling ice cream?"

Without any other choice, the waffle vendor agreed to buy ice cream from the vendor next to him and resell it at his booth. But that didn't take care of all the waffle batter ingredients he had bought, so he was still dismayed at the money he was losing. Then, in what appeared to be a revelation from heaven, an idea came to him.

At home that night, with his wife helping, the waffle vendor cooked up a batch of 1000 waffles. While they were still hot, he pressed them very thin with a flat iron and then rolled them into a circular pattern with a point at the bottom. The next morning he stuffed the waffles with ice cream, and the waffle cone became history. A stumbling block had become a stepping stone.

When facing an obstacle, Christians must have faith and then act. That's what the Israelites did when God commanded them to take the Ark of the Covenant and stand in the water at the edge of the River Jordan. The river was at flood stage, but the Israelites believed God would do wonders among them. And he did—As soon as the priests who carried the ark reached the Jordan and their feet touched the water's edge, the water from upstream stopped flowing. It piled up in a heap a great distance away. The ark was carried across on dry ground (Joshua 3).

With God, there is always a way.

POST-IT MEDITATION FOR MAY 13
God, I trust you to make a way for me on the journey you want me to travel.

May 14

When we are sure we are on the right road, there is no need to plan our journey too far ahead. No need to burden ourselves with doubts and fears as to the obstacles that may bar our progress. We cannot take more than one step at a time.
~Orison Swett Marden, writer and physician

Pierre Vincent Eckhart tells about a game he and his fellow Boy Scouts played when new Scouts joined the troop. The boys lined up chairs in a pattern, creating an obstacle course. After the Scoutmaster gave the boys a few moments to study the pattern, the new Scouts were blindfolded and told to maneuver through the chairs without hitting any. But as soon as the eyes of the participants were secured behind the cloths tied around their heads, the older Scouts quietly removed all of the chairs. The boys stumbled through the imaginary chairs, hitting one another but never a chair.

Eckhart says life is like the game the Scouts played. We spend our lives avoiding obstacles we have created for ourselves or impediments we think are in our path to success. Most of the obstructions we dread exist only in our minds. We fear applying for a job, taking guitar lessons, traveling to a foreign country, challenging a bully, calling someone we once hurt, or something else we imagine to be much worse than it is. Eckhart advises we need to learn not to fear any chairs until we have run smack-dab into one.

When we believe a hurdle lies in our path, we should not overestimate it. After all, as an unknown person once said, the problems we face in life wouldn't be called "hurdles" if there wasn't a way to get over them. With God's help, we can put the obstacle in proper perspective—what is the worst thing that could happen? And then we need to submit the obstacle to God so he can guide our path around it, over it, under it, or even through it.

No one is exempt from hurdles or difficulties—in fact, success itself can create problems. But no problem is impossible to overcome if God is on our side. Philippians 4:13 says, "I can do all things through Christ who strengthens me" (ESV). Our job is to identify the stumbling blocks that can be transformed into stepping stones. Then we choose to move on with faith that God will get us through problems and lead us to the other side on the newly created stepping stones. When we expect positive results, the chairs others place in our paths will be moved by unseen hands.

POST-IT MEDIATION FOR MAY 14
I believe everything is possible when I put my trust in God.

May 15

And he shall be as the light of the morning, when the sun rises, even a morning without clouds.
~2 Samuel 23:4 (KJ21)

Morning mists may mute the start of a day, but when the sun rises, the mist burns off, leaving the glory of light to shine down on earth. Our lives are like that, sometimes shrouded in the fog that envelopes us for a time. But eventually the fog dissipates, and sunshine prevails.

British preacher C.S. Spurgeon reminded us, "The path of the Christian is not always bright with sunshine; he has his seasons of darkness and of storm. True, it is written in God's word."

Spurgeon is right. At times, we have walked in the bright light of our faith, but we also wake some mornings to murky days when our happiness is dimmed, convinced if we were truly a child of God, our lives would not be so bleak. Christians are not protected from gloom or despair. In the words of a song by Annie Johnson Flint, we were never promised our skies would always be blue or we would walk on "flower-strewn pathways all our lives through." We were not promised "sun without rain, joy without sorrow, peace without pain." What we *were* promised by God is "strength for the day, rest for the labor, light for the way, grace for the trials, help from above." And most of all, our creator promised "unfailing sympathy and undying love."

So we should not bemoan the fog or beg for a day without clouds. Even under an overcast sky, the morning is a reminder that God has given us another day. If we start the day with a quiet time with him, seeking his wisdom, God will change the bleak day into a thankful one. Then, we should ask him to send his sunshine into every corner of our heart, letting the sunrays bounce off us onto others. When we face the day with a joyful heart, we find our faith is contagious.

Tom White, president of The Voice of Martyrs, was captured by Cuban authorities on May 27, 1979, after his plane crashed on a Cuban highway. The Cuban authorities, irate he had been dropping Christian literature from his plane, tried to break his spirit by isolating him in a dark, ice-cold cell. The frigid draft coming into the room through the vents made White miserable, and at first he was discouraged. He tried everything to keep himself warm—walking around, curling himself into a fetal position, and stuffing his pant legs into his socks so the icy air couldn't blow up his pants. He even put his head inside his shirt and tried to warm himself with his breath. Nothing helped more than a few minutes. Shivering all over, he started to panic. But then he remembered why he was in prison. Realizing he was approaching his problems the wrong way, he invited God's Spirit to come dwell in him and started to praise God out loud by singing every Christian song he knew. This confused the Cuban guards, and they asked how he could sing when he was so miserable. He responded, "Because I love Jesus!" As he continued to praise God through song, he noticed he wasn't freezing any more. God had come to his rescue, warming him despite the bitterly cold cell.

Someone once advised, "Happy moments, praise God. Difficult moments, seek God. Busy moments, bless God. Quiet moments, worship God. Waiting moments, trust God. Painful moments, touch God. Lovely moments, thank God." We can follow this advice if we keep God at the center of our lives. With him in control, there is nothing in our life we won't be able to handle. And, when others see our faith, they, too, may find the way.

SOURCE OF TOM WHITE STORY: *http://www.answers2prayer.org/praise_principle.html*
(*Original source cited on website: Jesus Freaks, Albury Publishing, 1999*)

POST-IT MEDITATION FOR MAY 15
When my path is cloudy and rough, I will exercise my faith.

May 16

A man's heart plans his way, but the Lord directs his steps.
~Proverbs 16:9 (NKJV)

Three trees once stood on a hill in the woods, discussing their hopes and dreams. The first tree said, "Someday I hope to be a treasure chest. I could be carved with intricate designs and filled with gold, silver, and precious jewels. Everyone would admire my beauty."

The second tree wanted to be a mighty ship. "I will take kings and queens across the waters and sail to the corners of the earth. They will feel safe because of the strength of my hull."

The third tree's desire was to be the tallest and straightest tree in the forest. "People will see me on top of the hill and look up at my branches, thinking of the heavens and God and how close to them I am reaching."

After a few years of praying for their dreams to come true, the trees saw a group of woodsmen coming toward them. When one came to the first tree, he said, "This looks like a strong tree—I can sell the wood to a carpenter" and began cutting it down.

Another woodsman liked the second tree because it was so strong. He said, "I will sell it to a shipyard," and the tree smiled.

The third tree was frightened—if he was cut down his dream would be ruined. And it happened, even though the man who cut it down had no special plans for the tree.

The first tree also lost its excitement when the carpenter carved it into a feed box for animals instead of a treasure chest, and the second tree's dreams were crushed when he was cut and made into a small fishing boat.

The years went by, and the trees forgot their dreams of greatness. Then one day, a man and woman came to the barn. She gave birth, and they placed the baby in the hay in the feed box made from the first tree. The hay box had become a manger. Years later, a group of men got in the fishing boat made from the second tree. One of them was tired and went to sleep, but a great storm arose and the tree was afraid he couldn't keep the men safe. Then the stranger awoke and said, "Peace," and the storm stopped. Finally, someone came and got the third tree. It was carried through the streets as the people mocked the man who was carrying it. Then, he was nailed to the tree and raised in the air to die at the top of a hill. Finally, the tree was as close to God as possible.

When our dreams are crushed, and we believe our lives will never be worth anything important, we can know God has a plan for us, just as he had a grand design for the three trees.

POST-IT MEDITATION FOR MAY 16
I may not know God's plan, but I know he has a purpose for my life.

May 17

Expect people to be better than they are; it helps them to become better.
~Merry Browne, author

In the early days of this country there was said to be a very wise man who lived on the edge of the Western frontier. He ran a general store, where in addition to selling supplies for travelers he freely gave advice and information.

One of the questions many people anxiously asked as they began their journey out West was, "What kind of people will we find up ahead?"

The shopkeeper would ponder the query for a minute and then respond, "What kind of people did you have in the place you just left?"

If the traveler said they were ornery folks, the merchant would shake his head forlornly and say, "I'm sorry to tell you, but where you are heading you'll find plenty of those types, too."

But if the wayfarer told the store owner he was sad to leave old friends—generous, warm, and kind—the man would tell him. "Don't worry, you're going to find hundreds of people just like you left behind."

It is said the man was never wrong.

Another story about a place known as the House of 1000 Mirrors illustrates the same truth:

Long ago in a small, far away village, a small, happy little dog learned of the House of 1000 Mirrors and decided to visit. When he arrived, he bounced happily up the stairs to the doorway of the house. He looked through the doorway with his ears lifted high and his tail wagging as fast as it could. To his great surprise, he found himself staring at 1000 other happy little dogs with their tails wagging just as fast as his. He smiled a great smile and was answered with 1000 great smiles just as warm and friendly. As he left the House, he thought to himself, "This is a wonderful place. I will come back and visit it often."

In this same village, another little dog, who was not quite as happy as the first one, decided to visit the house. He slowly climbed the stairs and hung his head low as he looked into the door. When he saw the 1000 unfriendly looking dogs staring back at him, he growled at them and was horrified to see 1000 little dogs growling back at him. As he left, he thought to himself, "That is a horrible place, and I will never go back there again."

All the faces in the world are mirrors. What kind of reflections do you see in the faces of the people you meet?

Each day as you encounter people on the job, in the grocery store, at the hospital, or a multitude of other places, what are your expectations? Do you expect them to be kind and helpful, or do you expect them to treat you rudely? Do you expect them to respect you or look down on you? Or do you simply have no expectations? At least, if you expect nothing, you will not be disappointed.

Is that really where we want to be—expecting nothing or the worst from people and getting what we expect? How much better our lives will be if we anticipate the best of other people. When we exhibit a positive expectation, it is much more likely people will react in ways that boost our spirits while lifting them up at the same time. If we walk around with a chip on our shoulder, someone will always be ready to knock it off; but, if we have a smile on our face and a song in our heart, we may find our attitude is catching. As Proverbs 17:22 (NLT) tells us, "A merry heart is good medicine." Do you see a merry face when you look in the mirror?

POST-IT MEDITATION FOR MAY 17
I will expect the best in other people—and my life will reflect that expectation.

May 18

At sunrise I offer my prayer and await your answer.
~Psalm 5:3 (GNT)

The first part of the psalmist's words are easy—we pray to God each morning (and perhaps during the day and again at evening), placing our problems, our hurts, and our desires before him. The second part—waiting for God's response—requires discipline.

The age in which we live demands instant feedback or reaction. We key in a word or phrase on a search engine like Google or Bing and WHAMMO—we have hundreds of selections from which to choose—and instantly get myriad answers. We are in immediate contact with others through texting. We order an e-book and seconds later we're reading it. ATMs give us instantaneous access to cash. We order food at a drive-up window, and it's in our hands in mere moments. The examples are endless—we have been trained to expect immediate gratification. And so, we have become an impatient people who don't tolerate waiting very well.

We say we trust God, but that doesn't change our disappointment with postponements. 1 Peter 3:9 tells us the Lord is not slow to fulfill his promises as some count slowness. But on an earthly timetable, the wait sometimes seems intolerable. Abraham and Sarah waited many years for a child. Later, Abraham laid that same son on the altar, lingering for God (for what likely seemed an eternity) to provide another sacrifice. Jacob worked 14 years for Rachel. Joseph suffered in slavery for 13 years. Fifteen years passed after David was anointed as a future king before he ascended the throne. Each had moments of doubt, but in the end, all trusted God

Delays can be painful, but they exercise our faith in the same way that lifting weights makes our bodies more fit. As Hebrews 12:11-12 (NIV) declares, "No discipline seems pleasant at the time…later on, however, it produces a harvest of righteousness and peace for those who have been trained by it." Waiting helps us grow spiritual muscle.

One day a woman's minister told his congregation, "If you want results from prayer, pray for thirty days without ceasing." The lady didn't know why it was thirty days, but she was willing to give it a try. The following became her daily prayer: "…Guide me, precious Lord, and lead me in what I say and do. May my words and actions be a witness that you are living in me. To the one that is lonely, may I be a friend. To those with heavy burdens, help me to meet their needs…I know I don't have much to offer, but I will give you my all…Amen."

On the twenty-first day of this prayer, the woman was working an extremely busy 12-hour night shift in Labor and Delivery when a phone call came from a friend working in the Emergency Room. An 18-year-old boy had been brought to the ER for alcohol and drug overdose and was very close to death. Nothing could be done to help him. The father of this boy was requesting a priest or minister, and they were having difficulty locating one, so her friend said, "We know you're a Christian, and we need you to come and try to comfort this father. Please help."

As the Christian lady walked into the ER and approached the father, she took his hand and silently led him to the chapel. Before she could even say, "I am not a minister," the six-foot, 220-pound man sank into a chair and became a broken-hearted child.

Through his non-stop sobbing he spoke, "Christian, pray for Raymond. I remember the first time I held my boy. I felt so proud and I just kept saying, 'I have a son.' As the years passed those tiny feet became bigger and walked away from his family's love and entered a strange, hardened, and destructive world. Tonight, too much alcohol and an overdose of drugs are taking his life. It's as though he wants to rebel against everything his family stood for. He knew what he was doing was wrong. Sometimes he seemed so afraid, but he wouldn't stop. Now it is too late. Christian, you have to pray for Raymond." The large hands trembled in the lady's, and as she looked into his eyes, she mourned with him. Silence fell between them as she searched for the words that would comfort the crumbling tower of a man. Feeling inadequate, she wanted to scream, "Lord it has only been twenty-one days since I began that prayer! I am not ready for this!"

Time was running out, and she knew she couldn't stall any longer. Clutching his hands, now wet with tears, she began to pray. The words came easy, much to her surprise.

"Lord I am asking for a miracle, and I know you can do it."

*She stayed with them both until Raymond was taken to Intensive Care. Then, visiting Raymond on a daily basis, she continued to pray for him. Eight days passed with little improvement. On the ninth day she entered the ICU, and a miracle had taken place. Raymond was awake and talking with his father. CPR had taken on a new meaning for her: "**C**hristian **P**ray for **R**aymond." As she left the ICU with tears falling down her face, she realized it was the 30th day of her prayer.*

POST-IT MEDITATION FOR MAY 18
*I will trust God to answer my
prayers however long it takes.*

May 19

…for the joy of the Lord is your strength.
~Nehemiah 8:10 (NIV)

A sad-looking man arrived at a psychologist's office and said to him, "Doctor, I always feel depressed. No matter what I do, I still feel depressed. I just don't know what to do."

The psychologist looked at him and said, "Come with me to the window."

The man followed and then the psychologist pointed outside and said, "Do you see that tent over there in the distance? Well, there is a circus in town, and it is really good. There are lots of acts to watch, especially the clown acts. And there is one clown in particular who is extremely funny. He will make you rock with laughter over and over again. Go and see that clown, and I guarantee you will have no reason to be depressed again!"

The man turned to the psychologist with pitiful eyes and said, "Doctor, I am that clown!"

The simplest way to be happy may not work—especially if you are the clown. That's because cheeriness doesn't come from a big smiley face painted on your skin—it comes from within.

We can experience the gladness God gives in good times and bad, under cloudy or sun-kissed skies. He extends the gift, and we simply have to accept. Joyfulness is free because it comes from within, where God places it in our hearts, always present regardless of the circumstances in our lives.

Author James Russell Miller penned these words about such Christian contentment more than 100 years ago, and they are as true today as they were then: "To the happiest heart that really makes room for Christ within, there is always the assurance of a world of spiritual blessings, hopes, and joys, lying concealed in the luster of human gladness, like stars in the noonday sky, but ready to pour their brightness upon us the moment the night falls with its shadows. Whether, therefore, the earthly light be bright or dark, Christ in the heart gives great blessedness and peace."

Sometimes we forget the stars shine in the sky even on sunny days—their brightness is just outmatched by the sun. But the stars are always there, ready to shine when darkness descends. So it is with God's love. It is ever present, even when we can't see it, ready to bring us joy and contentment when we ask in the midst of blackness.

Our lives ebb and flow, dim to bright to dim again. Like waves coming to shore, the return of joy is always certain. We may not be able to change the direction of the tide on dark days, but, because we have God's love, lending hope and spiritual peace, we can be assured the tide will go out again—just as the stars return with their light after clouds roll away.

POST-IT MEDITATION FOR MAY 19
I will draw strength from assurance of joy in my life.

May 20

People are lonely because they build walls instead of bridges.
~Joseph Newton, author

Many years ago two brothers who lived on adjoining farms had a disagreement. Although it started as a small misunderstanding, it grew into a major dispute. The first conflict experienced in 40 years of farming side-by-side caused wounds that ran deep. After heated words, the two brothers went weeks in stark silence.

One morning a young man knocked on the older brother's door, asking for work as a carpenter. After a few moments of thought as he stared toward his brother's house, the man told the carpenter he would like for him to build a fence between his property and his brother's farm. He explained a meadow once stood where now a creek ran—his younger brother had taken a bulldozer and pulled down a river levee so the running creak now separated the property. In exchange, the older brother wanted an 8-foot high fence so he wouldn't be able to see his brother's property at all.

After helping the carpenter get the materials together for the fence, the older brother went into town to take care of some errands. All day, the carpenter measured, sawed, and nailed, finishing just before the farmer returned at dusk. The farmer's mouth fell open at what he saw: instead of a fence, the carpenter had built a bridge between the two properties. As he stood in amazement, the older farmer saw his brother walking across the bridge, his arms outstretched. "You could have been mad because I created the creek, but instead you had a bridge built so we could still work together," the younger brother exclaimed.

Turning to the carpenter, the older brother paid him and asked him to stay for a few days to complete more projects. But the carpenter said he couldn't, explaining, "You see, I have more bridges to build."

When people make us mad or hurt our feelings, we often erect walls to protect ourselves in the future. But those walls become prisons, keeping us inside even as they keep others outside. We can only escape the pain and isolation if we tear down barriers and build bridges in their place.

POST-IT MEDITATION FOR MAY 20
**I will not shut out those who hurt me;
instead, I will seek connections that will heal the wounds.**

May 21

For God, who said, "Let light shine out of darkness," has made his light shine in our hearts so we could know the glory of God that is seen in the face of Jesus Christ.
~2 Corinthians 4:6 (NLT)

When God commanded light to appear in a universe engulfed in total darkness, he was pleased with what he saw. Like the creator of our world, we find light in dark places to be good. But cheerless conditions still exist in our earthly lives, and it is human nature to seek out light to brighten the blackness.

Years ago, during World War II, a small child was walking in the remote village where he lived. A poor lad, he didn't have much to play with so he picked up the broken pieces of a mirror from a Nazi motorcycle that had wrecked nearby.

The young child tried to find all the pieces and put them together, but it was not possible so he kept only the largest piece. By scratching it on a stone, he made it round and smooth.

The child began to play with the fragment of mirror as a toy and became fascinated by reflecting light into dark places where the sun would never shine—in deep holes and crevices and dark closets. It became a game for the child to get light into the most inaccessible places he could find.

The child kept the little mirror, and as he grew up, he would take it out in idle moments and continue the challenge of the game. As he became a man, he grew to understand this was not just a child's game, but a metaphor for what he might do with his life.

He came to understand he was not the light nor the source of the light. But light—truth, understanding, knowledge—is there, and it will only shine in many dark places if it is reflected.

God created the light of his word, but it is up to us to shine it in dark places. So many people have darkness in their lives, unable to see how their lives could be better. If we have been given a sliver of a mirror—if blessed with light in our own lives—we can reflect it so others find the truth of God's promises. Like the lesson the boy learned from the mirror, when we devote ourselves to help others find the way, we are shining light into blackness, extending hope.

POST-IT MEDITATION FOR MAY 21
*Today and tomorrow I will reflect the light of my own
life into the lives of others.*

May 22

The Lord will guide you always; he will satisfy your needs in a sun-scorched land...you will be like a well-watered garden, like a spring whose waters never fail.
~Isaiah 58:11 (NIV)

One day a man was crossing a bridge with God. Scared, he asked God, "Can I hold your hand so I won't fall into the river?"

God said, "No my child, I should hold your hand..."

The man asked, "What's the difference?"

God replied, "If you hold my hand and something happens, you might let go. If I hold your hand, no matter what happens, I'll never let go...."

The question is not "Are you holding on to God's hand?" but "Are you letting God hold your hand?"

It is not God who lets go and distances himself from us; it is we who don't hold on.

Sometimes we get so caught up in our lives we forget he is there, his hand out-stretched, waiting for us to grasp it. But God loves us. He is steadfast and faithful while he waits for us.

Despite the admonition in Psalm 37:1 that we shouldn't worry, most of us fume and fret more than we should. We whine and even allow anger to simmer when life isn't going the way we think it should. From problems with our families or jobs to world crises that affect us personally, we wrestle. Or, we express envy we don't have as much as others. Finding peace and contentment in a world that sends us burdens and tempts our minds, we become like the woman at the well who was seeking answers and possessions that won't satisfy. The song, "Fill My Cup, Lord," tells us, though, if we listen closely, we can hear our Savior speaking, "Draw from this well; it never shall run dry." Earthly pleasures we crave leave us thirsty and hungry, but the spring that fills God's well never runs dry, and the bread of heaven supplies us until we need nothing else.

Norman Vincent Peale, known for his book *The Power of Positive Thinking*, suggested several techniques we can use when we agonize, including:

➢ Imagine your mind as the tumultuous surface of a lake in a storm. Then, picture the subsiding of the tossing waves, leaving the lake unruffled and smooth.

➢ Create an image in your mind of one of the most beautiful and peaceful scenes you have experienced—perhaps a surreal sunrise or sunset, a field dressed with wildflowers, a quiet walk in the woods, or a rapturous rainbow over the ocean—and relive the moments of peace you felt at that time.

➢ Repeat Isaiah 26:3 (GNT), "You, Lord, give perfect peace to those who keep their purpose firm and put their trust in you" several times each day.

God's peace can permeate us when we turn our thoughts from worldly treasures and desires to concentrate on his creation that surrounds us and on his word that assures he will never leave us alone to face life's problems. Fear diminishes when we focus on faith.

POST-IT MEDITATION FOR MAY 22
With God's help, I will draw from his well
that never runs dry to fill my spirit
and strengthen my faith.

May 23

I am only one, but I am one. I cannot do everything, but I can do something. And I will not let what I cannot do interfere with what I can do.
~Edward Everett Hale, American author, historian, and Unitarian clergyman

Two men, both seriously ill, shared the same hospital room. One man, who lay by the room's only window, was allowed to sit up in his bed for an hour each afternoon to help drain fluid from his lungs. The other man couldn't raise his head.

Every afternoon, while sitting up, the first man passed the time by describing to his roommate everything he could see outside the window. Swans and ducks played on a lake in a lovely park within view, while children glided tiny sail boats. He also depicted young lovers walking arm in arm among flower-strewn pathways. One day, he told about a colorful band marching by, though he couldn't hear its music. Every day brought a view of nature and mankind, enlivening the men's dreary existence.

After many weeks passed, the man in the bed beside the window died peacefully in his sleep. As soon as it seemed okay, the totally bedridden man asked if he could be moved next to the window. Then he asked that his bed be raised enough so he could glimpse the park outside. Straining, he turned to look—but he was shocked to see only a blank wall. Unbelieving, the man asked the nurse what could have compelled his roommate to describe delightful scenes outside.

The nurse responded, "Your roommate was blind and could not even see the wall."

Setting aside his own sightless condition, unable to see even his nurse or his roommate, the man had wanted to encourage the person in the bed beside him. No doubt, it brought him a good feeling to know he was brightening another person's day. In bringing joy to his roommate, he likely lifted his own spirit despite his personal situation.

When we are feeling sorry for ourselves, perhaps we will find our own hearts made lighter if we seek ways to encourage others who are dealing with their own circumstances and disappointments.

POST-IT MEDITATION FOR MAY 23
God, help me look beyond my own life and bring joy into the lives of others.

May 24

Whatever is true, whatever is noble, whatever is right, whatever is pure, whatever is lovely, whatever is admirable—if anything is excellent or praiseworthy—think about such things.
~Philippians 4:8 (NIV)

In a world filled with temptations, frustrations, and disappointments, our thoughts sometimes stray from God. We get angry at others who hurt us and resent people whose lives seem better than our own. Instead of good thoughts, our heads become filled with bad feelings. Because negativity consumes our time and energy, dragging us down, we need to find ways to combat it.

The first step is to admit our thoughts are not good and recognize they damage us more than anyone else. Forgiving others frees us from the burden of hate and anger.

Pope John Paul II walked into a prison and said to Mehmet Ali Agca, the hired assassin who had tried to kill him, "I forgive you." Shot as he rode in an open car across St. Peter's Square on a late spring day in 1981, the Pope took two hits to his stomach, one to his right arm, and one to his left hand. Emergency surgery saved his life, but his spirit was saved when he held the hand that shot him and forgave his would-be killer. The violence of St. Peter's Square was transformed into peace and pardon in that instant.

Hatred hurts the hater more than it hurts the hated, and it needs to be removed from our lives. Otherwise, it will control our thoughts and our very existence.

The second effort we should make is to pray about our feelings. Sadly, at the time we most need to kneel and pray, we find it difficult because we aren't quite ready to relinquish our views about others, our desires, and our fears. *The Kneeling Christian* suggests the only way to have real growth in our spiritual lives: "All victory over temptations, all confidence and peace in the presence of difficulties and dangers, all repose of spirit in times of great disappointment or loss, all habitual communion with God—depends upon the practice of secret prayer."

Some pray openly and loudly, but prayers that come from our souls are whispered in secret, in continuous conversations with God. Those are the prayers enabling us to be the person God wants us to be. They also empower us to think on those things that are right, lovely, and true. Within such thoughts, anger and hurt find no room to survive.

POST-IT MEDITATION FOR MAY 24
I will pray in private, sharing my innermost thoughts, even bad ones, with God, asking for his healing power to bring peace despite the actions of others.

May 25

God's solid foundation still stands….
~2 Timothy 2:19 (PNT)

G. K. Chesterson, an English writer, once noted, "There are no rules of architecture for a castle in the clouds." Just as there are no design rules for a castle formed by ephemeral curls of white clouds—it can be as expansive and elaborate as we like—there is no assurance the castle will survive the first wisp of wind that blows its way.

Clouds are not the only insecure place to build a castle. Matthew 7:24-27 tells us a wise man builds his house upon a rock, while the foolish man builds his house upon the sand. When the rain falls, the floods come, and the winds blow, the house built on a rock will stand firm, but the house built on sand will fall.

Our lives, like houses and castles, will not survive if they are not built on a solid foundation. Clouds and sand blow away, but the rock of our faith is firm, grounded in everlasting truths. We have no guarantee we will be totally protected against calamity, but we do have the assurance our faith will not waiver if our trust is placed in God. Our physical bodies may suffer damage and our physical homes may be wiped out, but our spirit stands strong. Faith fortifies us against the forces that would destroy our spiritual being.

Most of the flight from Atlanta to Ft. Lauderdale was delightful. We sailed high, in clear skies, without a bump to bother us. As the pilot announced the initial descent, though, that changed. The cloud cover was thick, and we would have to go through it to land. As I peered out the window into murky emptiness, I felt frightened. There was nothing I could do except put my trust in the pilot and those in the control tower. We bounced and jarred until it seemed the plane was a roller coaster, but finally we broke through the clouds. How relieved I was, being able to see once again and having the smooth ride resume. Breaking through the clouds was exhilarating and relieving.

Life hands us cloudbanks of dark and dismal times. We may have some warning, as the pilot likely warned the passengers, or we may just hit the turbulent clouds of life with a bang. Either way, the ride through them is usually bumpy and uncomfortable, to say the least. But the old saying that there is light at the end of the tunnel is so true. Light returns after we ride through the dark, unsettling clouds of life. The question is how we weather the storm. In whom do we put our trust as we face difficult times? We need to turn our eyes toward heaven and ask God, who created this universe, for guidance and help during the cloudy times we endure. Then, when we make the transition out of darkness into his wonderful light, we can be reminded he was with us all the while.

The underpinning for both planes and castles must be substantive if they are to withstand the ravages of nature. Similarly, we must undergird our souls with the strength of God's word if we are to survive life's tempests. Then we can be assured of the promise in Matthew 9:29 (PNT): "You have believed, and you will not be disappointed." We must make sure our foundation is firm in the uncertainty of this ever-changing world. When times are tough, when our lives and homes are ripped by tornados or hurricanes, illness, bankruptcy, abuse, divorce, or loss, we must not just dream of a castle in the clouds, of a brighter tomorrow. We must put feet to our faith; and, with God's help, build a new life on a firm foundation that earthly winds cannot destroy.

SOURCE OF FLIGHT STORY: http://www.inspirationalstories.com/11/1145.html

POST-IT MEDITATION FOR MAY 25
When the storms of fear and disaster threaten my life, they will not prevail if I stay close to the mighty fortress of my God. With his help and my labor, I can rebuild.

May 26

Like an eagle that stirs up its nest and hovers over its young, that spreads
its wings to catch them and carries them aloft, the Lord alone led him....
~Deuteronomy 32: 11-12 (NIV)

The writer of Deuteronomy shares a number of addresses given to the Israelites while they were in Moab, just before they entered the promised land of Canaan. The verses at the beginning of today's devotion are some of the last spoken by Moses before his death, and they are part of a song of celebration Moses chants to remind God's people he is always faithful. He tells the people of Israel what God does is right and fair, even though they have sometimes proved themselves to be unworthy. By taking away their comforts and privileges at times, God made them a stronger and better people.

Hard times build stamina and reliance. When God exposes us to the storms of life, he never leaves us alone. Like an eagle protecting its young, God spreads his wings to catch and carry us through tumultuous times. Granted, when he lets us get so near the edge of the cliff our heart beats in fear, we cannot see how we can possibly be saved. But when we are thrust from the precipice, if we cannot fly on our own, he sweeps under us and bears us up.

Thirty-one years after my husband killed a man in self-defense, he was indicted and faced a trial for first-degree murder. At the time, it was the longest time in U.S. history between an alleged crime and an indictment. Facing not only the possibility of a conviction and prison but also massive media coverage from coast to coast, we both felt we had been thrown from a precipice and did not know if we would survive the fall. But God put his wings under us, and in the difficult days ahead he sent incredible encouragement and hope that kept us from hitting the bottom of the abyss. Like the writer of the words in the hymn, "Never Alone," we felt the lightning flash and the thunder roll in our lives, but we claimed God's promise that he would never leave us—and he didn't. I can't say we were free of worry about the outcome of the trial, but there was never a time when we didn't feel God was with us. He gave us strength to get through each day, and though the jury's verdict was not unequivocal, we learned that God's grace is. (The story of my husband's life and historic trial is told in A MATTER OF CONSCIENCE: Redemption of a hometown hero.)

POST-IT MEDITATION FOR MAY 26
When I am in free fall, unable to help myself, I know
God will catch me and lift me up.

May 27

Love bears all things, believes all things, hopes all things, endures all things.
~1 Corinthians 13:7 (ESV)

Most of us have heard the haunting song, "Taps," a melody that kindles a lump in our throats, goose pimples on our arms, and tears in our eyes. Do you know the story behind the song? It's a captivating tale with humble beginnings.

Reportedly, it all began in 1862 during the Civil War, when Union Army Captain Robert Ellicombe was with his men near Harris Landing in Virginia. The Confederate Army was on the other side of the narrow strip of land. During the night, Captain Ellicombe heard the moaning of a soldier as he lay severely wounded on the field. Not knowing if it was a Union or Confederate soldier, the Captain risked his life and brought the suffering man back for medical attention. Crawling on his stomach through the gunfire, he reached the stricken soldier and began pulling him toward his encampment. When the Captain finally reached his own lines, he discovered it was actually a Confederate soldier, but the soldier was dead. Lighting a lantern, the Captain caught his breath and went numb with shock. In the dim light, he saw the face of the soldier. It was his own son. The boy had been studying music in the South when the war broke out. Without telling his father, he enlisted in the Confederate Army. The following morning, heartbroken, the father requested permission from his superiors to give his son a full military burial, despite his enemy status. His request was only partially granted. The Captain had asked if he could have a group of Army band members play a funeral dirge for his son. The request was turned down since the soldier was a Confederate, but, out of respect for the father, they did give him one musician. The Captain chose a bugler and asked him to play a series of musical notes he had found on a piece of paper in the pocket of the dead youth's uniform. This wish was granted. The haunting melody we now know as "Taps"...used at military funerals...was born:

Day is done...gone the sun...from the lakes...from the hills...from the sky.... All is well...safely rest...God is nigh.... Fading light...dims the sight...and a star...gems the sky.... Gleaming bright...from afar...drawing nigh...falls the night.... Thanks and praise...for our days...'neath the sun...'neath the stars... 'neath the sky.... As we go...this we know...God is nigh....

Both the father and his son bore great tragedy through giving of themselves to others, but both knew, because God is on his throne, they could endure all that happened to them. We can have the same assurance in our own battle-beleaguered and conflict-scarred lives.

May 28

So encourage one another and build one another up....
~1 Thessalonians 5:11 (NLT)

A group of frogs was traveling through a woods when two of them fell into a deep pit. Seeing the depth of the hole, the other frogs told the two they might as well accept that their fate was to die in the pit. The two frogs were young, and they didn't want to die, so they started jumping as high as they could, hoping they could hop out. The other frogs kept telling them they might as well save their energy—they were doomed. Exhausted, one of the frogs finally accepted the advice and stopped trying, eventually dying at the bottom of the pit. But the other frog continued to jump. The group on the edge of the pit yelled louder and louder, trying to convince the frog there was no hope and thus he should not struggle, making his last hours miserable. But the determined frog just kept jumping, and eventually, after many unsuccessful attempts, he made one last strong effort, heaving himself out. When he rested a bit, his fellow frogs asked him why he didn't pay attention to what they had been yelling. Reading their mouths, the frog explained, "I couldn't hear you because I am deaf. I thought you were encouraging me."

We can find at least two lessons from this story. As we look at the frog who gave up, we see that discouraging words can cause a person to abandon hope. We never know when a negative comment will be the final straw, causing someone to stop trying. Second, as seen with the second frog, when someone receives encouraging words, he can achieve a seemingly impossible task.

The deaf frog didn't even hear words; he just interpreted sounds as encouragement—which shows that sometimes we don't have to do much to hearten someone who is struggling. Still, in life, what we say and how we say it can make a tremendous difference—perhaps even the difference between life and death—to another person. We can lift an individual up, or we can push him down. The choice is whether we inflate or deflate the spirit of someone who may be at a critical point in his life. Even when it is not a life or death matter, simple words of encouragement can help a person be stronger or happier while words of discouragement dampen and dishearten.

May 29

The earth has music for those who listen.
~George Santayana, Spanish/American philosopher, poet, essayist, and novelist

The movie <u>Mr. Holland's Opus</u> tells the story of a musician who wants to be a composer. Rather grudgingly, he takes a job teaching music at the local high school, because it gives him time to write music while providing an income for his family.

Not all of his students are talented, of course, and one of the worst is a very serious, red-headed girl who plays the clarinet terribly despite constant practice. Finally, she decides she is a failure and comes into the music classroom to tell Mr. Holland she's going to give it up.

As she walks away, Holland asks her, "Is it any fun?"

With a shrug, she answers, "I wanted it to be."

"You know what we've been doing wrong, Miss Lang? We've been playing the notes on the page."

The bewildered girl asks, "Well, what else is there is to play?"

"There's a lot more to music than notes on a page. Playing music is supposed to be fun. It's about heart. It's about feelings and moving people and something beautiful and being alive, and it's not about notes on a page. I could teach you notes on a page. I can't teach you that other stuff." With those thoughts, Holland takes away her music and asks, "What do you like best about yourself?" With a shy smile she says, "My hair—my dad says it reminds him of a sunset."

"Then play the sunset."

The frustrated musician closes her eyes, and begins to play with nothing in front of her—she plays not just the notes she had memorized, but the emotion and mood of the music. Amazingly, she even plays the hard part perfectly. And we know that this time, it is fun.

Just as the young girl began enjoying music when she played more than just notes, we can be virtuoso Christians if we realize it takes more than following rules. We must play the game of life with soul.

All people are not equally blessed with intelligence and wealth; all have opportunities, but all don't have the capacity or luck to capitalize on them. Some of us will always have more than others. Some will be great performers; some will never be more than mediocre musicians. Some will have marriages; others will not; some marriages will fail while others succeed. Some will have children who make their parents proud; others will have children who push them to the limits. Some will have exciting, lucrative careers while others will struggle to make ends meet. Some lose all their earthly possessions when Mother Nature turns nasty, but others are sheltered.

Place and status in life are not equally distributed, and we don't all deal with the same circumstances, but what we all have in common, if we are blessed with eyes to see and ears to hear, is the beauty of the earth and sky and sea.

This morning as I walked outside to get the morning paper, not a cloud shaded the sapphire sky. The expanse of pure blue drew my spirit upward, and I experienced the clear canopy God created over the earth. Only days ago the sky had been filled with dark clouds that brought thunderstorms and tornados, destroying houses and lives, but today God had cleared the skies, inviting me to gaze toward heaven. Just moments after seeing the sky, I read of local families who had lost everything, and my heart went out to those who had been left homeless. I prayed that even in their darkness, they had found a moment of peace and renewal of faith in the splendor of the blue sky after such massive devastation.

When we have nothing else, we have nature. It costs nothing to emotionally sense the sights and sounds of a sunset like the one Miss Lang played on her clarinet, a scarlet-winged cardinal in splendid song, a mountain stream making its way through a tree-clad forest, an ocean wave crashing against the silent shore, or just dazzling sunshine breaking through a cloudy day. I love the old song, "Heavenly Sunlight," because it celebrates how the sun God created to light the day can "flood our soul with glory divine." Shadows around us and shadows above us can't conceal the light of God, because in him there is no darkness.

We owe God thanks and praise for his resplendent creations—for the blessing of boundless beauty that enriches our lives and lifts our souls to the Lord.

POST-IT MEDITATION FOR MAY 29
God is blessing me always, and I will be thankful at all times for the wondrous world all around me.

May 30

Whatever you do, work at it with all your heart, as working for the Lord, not for human masters.
~*Colossians 3:23 (NIV)*

An elderly carpenter told the owner of the construction company for which he worked that he was ready to retire—he wanted to spend more time with his wife and family. He admitted he would miss the weekly paycheck, but he had decided he preferred to get along with less money and lead a more leisurely life.

The contractor appreciated the good work the carpenter had done for him over many years and was sorry to hear he wanted to retire. As a special favor, he asked the man to build just one more house for him. The carpenter reluctantly agreed, but his heart wasn't in the work, and for the first time in his life, his workmanship became shoddy. He didn't even ensure that the materials he used were of the best quality.

When the house was finished, the contractor came by to inspect the work. Then, he handed a key to the man. "This is your house...I'm giving it to you to express my thanks for the excellent work you have done for me over the years."

The carpenter was shocked—and dismayed. If he had known he was building his own house, he would have made it the best it could be instead of sloughing off on quality materials and workmanship.

In many ways we are like the carpenter. As we frame and build our lives, we don't always give our best effort. How will we feel in our final days? Will we be proud of the life we constructed? Now is the time to think about the house we are building. At the end, it will be too late. Every day we hammer a nail, erect a wall, or install a floor in the structure of our lives. We cannot go back later and rebuild, so we would be wise to use quality products (prayer, Bible study, works, and faith) to build a life that will be soundly formed for our final days on earth and for eternity. If we expect to have a mansion in the sky, we need to build it now.

POST-IT MEDITATION FOR MAY 30
Each day I will remember I am building "a mansion over the hilltop in that bright land where [I'll] never grow old."

May 31

But if anyone does not provide for his relatives, and especially for members of his household, he has denied the faith and is worse than an unbeliever.
~1 Timothy 5:8 (NIV)

Timothy's words sound harsh, but the message is undeniable. Each of us has an obligation to take care of family members if they are in need. No if's, and's, or but's. Timothy expects us to provide for them regardless of the circumstances.

One of the most difficult situations families face arises from the disease of addiction. Addicts lie, manipulate, and steal to feed their abuse, and family members often feel like victims. And, experience indicates they can fall into the role of enablers. So what is a family member to do, turn his back on the addict? Timothy does not give us that option. Yet, surely we should not hand out money freely if we know a person is using it to buy drugs or alcohol. Should we apply tough love? No easy answers exist, but whatever actions we take should be with care and support. Even if we choose to stop the flow of funds, we can ensure the addict has a place to live and food to eat—and especially unequivocal love.

Addiction is not the only condition causing family members to turn away. A teenager is disrespectful and rebellious to the point a parent becomes tempted to throw him out of the house. A brother squanders his money on gambling and then asks for help with rent. A nephew is in prison for a terrible crime. A sister spends excessive amounts on luxuries but is unable to make her car payments. A parent is too controlling. Another is quarrelsome. Still another turns into a person we don't know because she is afflicted with Alzheimer's disease.

How much are we expected to bear when a family member becomes a burden—financially or emotionally? Should we provide for a relative when the person appears to be a "lost cause"?

Under God's grace, lost causes don't exist. All are worthy of love and redemption. Isaiah 43:4 tells us all are precious in God's sight. When we can't handle a family member any more, we can turn the person over to God in prayer. With faith that God can change the person's life, we will find peace as we continue to provide for needs that once brought resentment and anger.

Willie was adopted when he was five. By that time he was already strong-willed and independent. Being abandoned as a baby and shuffling through four foster homes had taken its toll, and by the time he started school he was rebellious and belligerent. Teachers, hearing about him long before he arrived in their classrooms, expected the worst—and got it. Likely, he passed every grade because no teacher wanted to put up with him twice. After graduation from high school, Willie started running around with a bad crowd, stole a car, and was charged with drunken driving and theft. His parents, stalwart Christians, were at their wits' end. No matter how much they prayed, he never changed. But they never turned their backs on Willie. Once they put him out of the house when he became violent, but they let him know he would be welcomed back into the home when he could act civilly. Time after time they bailed him out of jail but rarely got even a begrudging word of appreciation. One night after taking drugs, he walked into the path of an oncoming car, leaving him paralyzed. His parents now care for him around the clock. Amazingly, their son's attitude has been one of contrition and thanksgiving for his parents' love. Although God didn't answer their prayers the way they hoped, he had healed Willie's spirit.

POST-IT MEDITATION FOR MAY 31
I will pray for God's guidance and grace
when family members are in need.

June 1

Love the Lord your God with all your heart and with all your soul and with all your mind and with all your strength.
~**Mark 12:30 (NIV)**

Paul Schenk tells of a lesson learned from his father:

During a visit from his dad, the older man had offered to help his son with major basement renovations. About halfway through the day, the son had lamented he would be glad when the project was complete; he was tired. His father responded with an anecdote Schenk never forgot:

"This reminds me of the time Harry Johnson and I had to bench-test hundreds of electronic parts for a NASA contract," the elder Schenk began. The job was laborious and had taken most of the day when Schenk commented to his colleague that he would surely be glad when the testing of the parts was finished. Johnson looked over at him and remarked, "Oh, have you been testing transistors, Bill? I've helping send a man to the moon." Turning to his son, Bill Schenk asked, "Is that what you've been doing, Paul, putting up corner molding? I've been spending the morning working with my son."

Years later, Paul was planting bulbs with his 10-year-old-son Peter, who had a green thumb and treasured time in the garden. The goal for the day was to set out 80 bulbs along a sidewalk border; but the Georgia red clay was stubborn, and at one point Paul was about to comment he would be glad when they had all of the bulbs planted. But then he recalled the anecdote his father had told, and time stopped seeming so important. What mattered was spending time with his son.

Each task we do can be boring or exciting, inspiring or depressing. It is all a matter of perspective—what we focus on as the meaning of our mission. If it is simply a chore, then it has little or no significance. But if we refocus on a broader view—how the activity affects a larger endeavor or enriches relationships—the value increases, and our motivation emanates from a spirit of love and companionship.

Treasuring time spent together begins with cherishing God's blessings.

POST-IT MEDITATION FOR JUNE 1
I will hold love tightly in my heart, reflecting it in my actions.

June 2

Oh, that a hand would come down from heaven and deliver me from my besetting sin!
~*Seneca, Roman philosopher, statesman, dramatist*

I am your constant companion. I am your greatest helper or heaviest burden. I will push you onward or drag you down to failure. I am completely at your command.

Half of the things you do might just as well be turned over to me, and I will be able to do them quickly and correctly. I am easily managed—you must merely be firm with me. Show me exactly how you want something done, and after a few lessons, I will do it automatically.

I am the servant of all great men; and alas, of all failures as well. Those who are great, I have made great. Those who are failures, I have made failures.

I am not a machine, though I work with all the precision of a machine plus the intelligence of a man. You may run me for profit or run me for ruin—it makes no difference to me.

Take me, train me, be firm with me, and I will place the world at your feet. Be easy with me, and I will destroy you. Who am I? I am habit!

Habits are easy to form and difficult to break; temptation surrounds us constantly; and, sin besets all humans. An old proverb tells us bad habits are like a comfortable bed, easy to get into, but hard to get out of. Should we just give up, using the sinful nature we inherited from Adam as an excuse?

Some habits seem relatively insignificant—we routinely speed, but not much, maybe just setting the cruise control two or three miles over a 70-mile-per-hour limit. Does the degree we are breaking the law matter, or can we slide by, convincing ourselves the habit isn't that bad?

The number and kinds of habitual behaviors and emotions are limitless—smoking, gambling, cursing, lusting, overeating, laziness, anger, pride, fear, bitterness, sexual perversions, and on and on. Each of us has a personal list that nudges our consciences but may not control our actions. The cycle is inevitable: We indulge ourselves, experience shame or guilt, make a pledge never to do it again. With pride, we pat ourselves on the back. But it doesn't last. Soon, we give in to the lure of the good feeling generated by the habit, or we succumb to emotional tugs that send us off into rage or self-pity or some other overreaction.

Despite our best efforts, old habits return again and again. Our weakness takes control, and we fall back into a rut that is uncomfortable but familiar as a place bringing us pleasure or release. How then can we emphatically say "no" when we are tempted to do something we don't want to do or that is harmful to us? Romans 5:20 (NIV) has the key: "… but where sin increased, grace increased all the more."

We have the assurance we will be given grace greater than our sin. As the words of the old hymn go, we can expect marvelous grace from a loving Lord, "grace that exceeds our guilt and our sin." But we can't sit back and wait for grace to fall upon us like morning dew and save us from our bad habits. Saying no is possible, but it requires turning the offensive behavior over to God, asking him for help, and believing he will give us the power to overcome temptation. God's goodness is so great he will help us over and over if we continue to ask, even when we repeatedly fail. He will take away our weaknesses and desires if we give him control.

POST-IT MEDITATION FOR JUNE 2
With God's help, I will say no to bad habits, even when I want to say yes.

June 3

We are what we pretend to be, so we must be careful what we pretend to be.
~ Kurt Vonnegut, 20th century American writer

Do you ever feel as if you are the "great pretender"? Do you sometimes wonder if you are fake, a cubic zirconia and not a diamond? We want to be real, but the world demands we act in many different ways to be accepted. A job may require behavior that puts our conscience in turmoil. A church friend offends us, but we hide our hurt feelings. We resent a family member but pretend it doesn't bother us. We criticize a person behind his back but act as if we admire him in his presence. Sometimes, as American cartoonist Bill Watterson wrote, we wonder if the face we see in the puddle is real and we are just a reflection of him.

A father and his son were walking high on a mountain one day when the son fell. In great pain from his injury, he screamed, "AAAhhhhhhhhh!!!" To his surprise, he heard his cry of pain repeated from a distance: "AAAhhhhhhhhh!!!"

Curious, the boy yelled back, "Who are you?"

The answer came back from afar, "Who are you?"

Enjoying himself, the boy shouted, "I like you!"

Again, the voice came back, "I like you!"

Angered at not getting his questions answered, frustrated the voice from another part of the mountain just repeated his words, the boy screamed, "Coward!" Back came the answer, "Coward!"

Finally, the boy turned to his father and asked what was going on. The father explained his son was hearing an echo, adding that an echo is really life. "Life gives you back everything you say or do."

Our lives reflect all that we do. If we give love, we get more love. If we care for others, they will care for us. Who and what we become is not a coincidence. Whether we are real or fake is a reflection of our actions. As Christians, we should not *pretend* we live a Christian life. We should be known by our actions as sons and daughters of God.

Funny how someone can say "I believe in God" but still follow Satan who, by the way, also "believes" in God.

Funny how you can send a thousand jokes through e-mail and they spread like wildfire, but when you start sending messages regarding the Lord, people think twice about sharing.

Funny how the lewd, crude, vulgar, and obscene pass freely through cyberspace, but the public discussion of Jesus is suppressed in the school and workplace.

Funny how someone can be so fired up for Christ on Sunday but be an invisible Christian the rest of the week.

Funny how a person can be more worried about what other people think of him than what God thinks of him.

FUNNY, ISN'T IT?

Are you laughing?

POST-IT MEDITATION FOR JUNE 3
With God's help I will be true to myself—and to him.

June 4

But the one who is right and good will live by his faith.
~*Habakkuk 2:4 (NLV)*

Howard Hendricks, in the Foreword to Edwin Lutzer's *FAILURE: The Back Door to Success*, admits that "Failure is one of the ugly's of life. We deny it, run away from it, or upon being overtaken, fall into permanent paralyzing fear." But failure is not the end, because, as actress Mary Pickford wrote, "You may have a fresh start any moment you choose, for this thing we call failure is not the falling down, but the staying down."

Einstein was considered unteachable in his youth. Beethoven was told by his music teacher he was hopeless as a composer. Michael Jordan was cut from his high school basketball team. An MGM testing director wrote about Fred Astaire after his first screen test, "Can't act. Slightly bald. Can dance a little." Vince Lombardi was told by an expert that he possessed minimal football knowledge and lacked motivation. Kentucky Fried Chicken's Colonel Sanders was told "no" by over a thousand restaurants while he lived in his car trying to sell his chicken recipe. He was 65 years old when he opened his first restaurant. Walt Disney was fired from his newspaper job because he lacked ideas and was turned down by over a hundred banks when he tried to get funding to start Disneyland. The stories are endless. And, of course, not all of them end in success. But when you have honestly given a project your all with confidence, you are never a failure.

Did you know Bill Gates' first business, Traf-o-Data, failed before he started Microsoft? Most people know Oprah Winfrey endured an abusive childhood and had numerous career setbacks, including being fired from a job as a reporter because she was "unfit for television," but few know former Vice President Dick Cheney flunked out of Yale not once, but twice. Every cartoon submitted by Charles Schutz to his high school newspaper was rejected, and Walt Disney turned him down for a job before he became famous for his <u>Peanuts</u> comic strip. The first book submitted by Stephen King (<u>Carrie</u>) was rejected by thirty publishers, and King was so discouraged he threw it in the trash. His wife fished it out and persuaded him to submit it one more time—today King is one of the best-selling authors of all times.

Like Einstein, Jordan, Astaire, Lombardi, Sanders, Disney, Gates, Winfrey, Cheney, Schutz, and King, we can find new opportunities if we don't let failure determine our future. We cannot always control what happens to us, but we can control whether we respond negatively or positively.

Lutzer suggests the best way to respond is to "live from the inside out." In other words, if we let our lives be filled with God's word and his Holy Spirit, we can have Christ-like responses to life's negative experiences. "To be controlled by the Spirit means we are not controlled by what happens on the outside but by what is happening on the inside." We may not be famous like the individuals named above, and we may not know what enabled them to overcome failure, but we can be assured walking in faith gives *us* the power to live confidently, and that's enough to overcome any setback life sends us.

POST-IT MEDITATION FOR JUNE 4
I will commit my failures to God and trust him to handle tomorrow.

June 5

Can you by searching find out God?
~Job 11:7 (AKJV)

An old story tells about a man stumbling through the woods, totally drunk, when he comes upon a preacher baptizing people in the river. The drunk proceeds to walk into the water and subsequently bumps into the preacher. The preacher turns around; and, almost overcome by the odor of whiskey, he asks the drunk, "Are you ready to find Jesus?"

The drunk responds with a slur, "Yes, I am."

So the preacher grabs him and dunks him in the water. Pulling him up, he asks, "Brother, did you find Jesus?"

The sputtering drunk replies, "No, I didn't find Jesus."

Shocked at the answer, the preacher dunks him into the water again, leaving him under a little longer this time. When he pulls him up, he asks again, "Have you found Jesus, my brother?"

The water-logged drunk again answers, "No, I haven't found Jesus."

By this time, the preacher is so frustrated he dunks the drunk in the water again and holds him down until the man begins kicking his arms and legs in desperation.

Once again, the preacher asks, "For the love of God, did you find Jesus?"

Wiping his eyes, the drunk heaves out water before responding angrily, "*%$#%$! Mercy, man! Are you sure this is where he fell in?"

God gave us a sense of humor and the grace to see a joke. He also gave us the ability to see him, but like the drunk, sometimes we can't find him because we don't know what we are searching for. Even if we know what we are looking for, we may hunt in the wrong places.

How many times are we disillusioned because "godly" people don't act godly? We won't find God in other people's lives, even if they are righteous. We will find him in our own hearts and souls. When we are floundering around underwater, desperate for someone to save us, we can find God's help simply by acknowledging his presence and power.

POST-IT MEDITATION FOR JUNE 5
Give me the wisdom, God, to search for you in the right places.

June 6

We saw clearly how the Lord was with you.
Genesis 26:28 (NIV)

A young man planted a rose garden in early spring and watered it faithfully. After many weeks, he became discouraged because he saw only thorns. Not noticing the tiny buds about to erupt, he pondered, "I don't know why I bothered to plant these ugly creatures—it is impossible for lovely flowers to come from stems filled with so many hurtful thorns." Saddened by this thought, he stopped watering the roses, and just before the tiny buds would have emerged as beautiful blooms, the rose bushes died.

Many people resemble rose bushes, filled with disfiguring thorns—faults and weaknesses that mar them and prickle others. They look at themselves and see only their thorny side, the defects they feel make them ugly and undesirable. In despair, they think nothing good can possibly come from them, so they don't water the sprouts within them, and their spirit eventually dies without reaching its potential.

Everyone has a rose within the soul, planted by God to grow and blossom in all its beauty. But some people cannot see the inner rose by themselves. Someone else must show it to them. Unfortunately, we are sometimes put off by the thorns we see in others. It takes a great gift to see past the thorns of another and find the rose waiting within. But that's what love is—looking at people, knowing their true blemishes, accepting and nurturing them until their hidden goodness bursts forth.

We can help others (and ourselves) if we recognize faults don't outweigh virtues implanted before birth. Weaknesses can be overcome. If we look for the rose within, in time the flower will be able to blossom amid its thorns. Only then can Christians achieve the level of love we should feel for each other; only when we help others can we produce the most beautiful blooms in our own garden.

In Luke 5, when Jesus heals the leper, he reminds us we must reach out to others with love, just as he does with us. Then, as the words from Genesis illustrate, others see clearly that we live in God's love. Both we and they will bloom in a garden of care.

Adapted from an essay called "The Rose Within," author unknown

POST-IT MEDITATION FOR JUNE 6
As God loves me despite my weaknesses,
I will accept others as they are and help them find
the beauty within their souls.

June 7

Human life is purely a matter of deciding what's important to you.
~Anonymous

Kids can teach us more than we can learn in books, hear from media pundits, or acquire at the feet of master teachers in K-12 or postsecondary schools. When we get confused about what's important in our lives, the little piece of writing that follows can put our existence on this earth in perspective.

Big Mud Puddles and Sunny Dandelions

When I look at a patch of dandelions, I see a bunch of weeds that are going to take over my yard. My kids see flowers for Mom and blowing white fluff you can wish on.

When I look at an old drunk and he smiles at me, I see a smelly, dirty person who probably wants money and I look away. My kids see someone smiling at them and they smile back.

When I feel wind on my face, I brace myself against it. I feel it messing up my hair and pulling me back when I walk. My kids close their eyes, spread their arms and fly with it, until they fall to the ground laughing.

When I pray, I say "thee" and "thou" and "grant me this, give me that." My kids say, "Hi, God! Thanks for my toys and my friends. Please keep the bad dreams away tonight. Sorry, I don't want to go to Heaven yet. I would miss my Mommy and Daddy."

When I see a mud puddle, I step around it. I see muddy shoes and dirty carpets. My kids sit in it, run through it, or stand in the middle of it, splashing their feet.

I wonder if we are given kids to teach or to learn from? No wonder God loves the little children of the world—they are precious in his sight!

Children welcome each new day. With fresh eyes, they see sunshine and rain as equal opportunities to smile and laugh. We should learn from them and do the same.

POST-IT MEDITATION FOR JUNE 7
From this day forward, I will enjoy the little things in life, knowing one day I may look back and realize they were the big things.

June 8 ✦

Do not neglect to do good....
~Hebrews 13:16a (ESV)

Taxi drivers see a window on life that most of us never envision. For those who see their jobs as a ministry, the cab can become a moving confessional. Passengers climb in, sit behind the driver in total anonymity, and tell him about their lives. One such passenger touched the life of a cabbie on a hot June night in an unusual way.

Picking up his fare after midnight, the cab driver waited at the door of a small brick quadplex in a quiet part of town for several minutes. When no one appeared, he walked to the door and knocked, knowing that occasionally a person needed help to get to the cab. On this particular night, an elderly woman answered the door and asked for assistance with her small bag. After she settled herself in the back seat, the frail woman asked the cabbie to drive through downtown. The honest driver told her that wasn't the shortest way.

"Oh, I don't mind," she said. "I'm in no hurry. I'm on my way to a hospice." Her eyes glistening, she added, "I don't have any family left, and the doctor says I don't have very long."

Touched, the cab driver quietly reached over and shut off the meter. "What route would you like me to take?" For the next couple of hours, the two strangers drove through the city. The lady showed him the building where she had once worked as an elevator operator. They drove through the neighborhood where she and her husband had lived when they were newlyweds. And they pulled up in front of a furniture warehouse that had once been a ballroom where she had gone dancing as a girl. Sometimes she just sat and stared after asking the driver to pull over. Finally, as the first hint of sun crested the horizon, she suddenly said, "I'm tired. Let's go now."

At the small convalescent home, as the driver pulled under a portico, two orderlies came out and helped the woman out of the cab. Turning to the cabbie, she asked how much she owed him. When he said, "Nothing," she protested, telling him he had to make a living.

"There will be other passengers," he responded and then spontaneously hugged her.

"You gave an old woman a little moment of joy," she said gratefully. "Thank you."

Then the door of the hospice center closed, and the cabbie thought, "That's the sound of the closing of a life." For the rest of the day, he drove aimlessly, lost in thought.

What if the cabbie who went to pick up the lady had honked once and then driven away? What if that woman had gotten an angry driver, or one who was impatient to end his shift?

We are conditioned to think our lives revolve around great moments. But meaningful moments often catch us unaware—beautifully wrapped in gifts of caring for strangers.

POST-IT MEDITATION FOR JUNE 8
I will not let great moments pass me by because of indifference or haste.

June 9

Every good gift and every perfect gift is from above.
~James 1:17 (ESV)

A group of students were asked to list what they thought were the present "Seven Wonders of the World." Though there were some disagreements, the following received the most votes:

1. Egypt's Great Pyramids
2. Taj Mahal
3. Grand Canyon
4. Panama Canal
5. Empire State Building
6. St. Peter's Basilica
7. China's Great Wall

While gathering the votes, the teacher noted one quiet student hadn't turned in her paper yet. So she asked the girl if she was having trouble with her list. The girl replied, "Yes, a little. I couldn't quite make up my mind because there were so many." The teacher said, "Well, tell us what you have, and maybe we can help. The girl hesitated, then softly said she thought the "Seven Wonders of the World" are:

1. *to see*
2. *to hear*
3. *to touch*
4. *to taste*
5. *to feel*
6. *to laugh*
7. *to love.*

The room became so quiet you could have heard a butterfly flutter its wings.

The aspects of life we overlook as simple and ordinary—the ones we take for granted—are truly wondrous! The most precious parts of our lives cannot be built by hand or bought by man. As Ruth Ann Schabacker noted, "Each day comes bearing its own gifts. Untie the ribbons."

POST-IT MEDITATION FOR JUNE 9
Today I will be thankful for eyes to see, ears to hear, hands to touch,
a tongue to taste, and a heart to feel, laugh, and love.

June 10

Do not remember the things that have happened before. Do not think about the things of the past. See, I will do a new thing. It will begin happening now. I will even make a road in the wilderness, and rivers in the desert.
~Isaiah 43:18-19 (NLV)

Do you sometimes wish you could step back in time? Just as we tend to think the grass is greener on the other side of the pasture, we think yesterday was better than today. If we are honest, the "good old days" weren't all that good. In many ways, today's problems mirror those of yesteryear. The *Boston Globe* headline for November 13, 1857, read, "Energy Crisis Looms." Sound familiar? An article from the June 16, 1833, edition of the *Atlantic Journal* reads as if it were written in the 21st century: "The world is too big for us. Too much going on, too many crimes, too much violence and excitement. Try as you will, you get behind in the race, in spite of yourself...the political world moves so rapidly you're out of breath trying to keep pace with who's in and who's out. Everything is high pressure. Human nature can't endure much more."

Good old days? Sure, bread, clothes, cars, and gas were cheaper decades ago, but salaries were lower. And, how many would want to go back to outdoor privies and clothes lines? A wood-burning fireplace still brings charm and coziness to a room, but would we want to depend solely on it for our heat? Most of us can't even imagine what it would be like to live without air conditioning in our homes and cars. Again, the question, good old days?

Instead of looking backward with regret, we need to look to the past to see what we can learn to help us solve our current dilemmas. Football teams regroup after most plays, huddling to discuss why a play didn't work or to decide on a new strategy. Companies also regularly evaluate their business plans, regroup, and come up with better schemes for the future.

Reassess, regroup, and move forward. As Robert Schuller says, "The walk of faith is a moving sidewalk!" Walking in the right direction on a moving sidewalk or escalator is critical. Trying to walk backward when the steps are going forward is a slow—and sometime dangerous—process. God expects us to go with the flow of our lives, to keep moving after we surrender our problems to him.

One day, while searching for food, a fat frog and a skinny frog inadvertently jumped into a vat of milk. At first, they thought how fortunate they were—a big supply of nutritious liquid was all around them. But when they had drunk their fill, they couldn't get out, as the sides were too slippery, so they were just swimming around. In retrospect, what had seemed so good wasn't.

Finally, the fat frog said to the skinny frog, "Brother frog, there's no use paddling any longer. We're just going to drown, so we might as well give up." The skinny frog replied, "Hold on brother, keep paddling. Somebody will get us out." And they continued paddling for hours.

After a while, the fat frog said, "Brother frog, I told you before, there's no use. I'm becoming very tired now. I'm just going to stop paddling and drown. It's Sunday and nobody's working. We're doomed. There's no possible way out of here." But the skinny frog said, "Keep trying. Keep paddling. Something will happen; keep paddling." Another couple of hours passed.

The fat frog said, "I can't go on any longer. There's no sense in doing it because we're going to drown anyway. What's the use?" And the fat frog stopped. He gave up and drowned in the milk. But the skinny frog kept paddling.

Ten minutes later, the skinny frog felt something solid beneath his feet. He had churned the milk into butter. Now, he easily hopped out of the vat.

When we think we can't paddle any more, we need to remember the two frogs. God can use our forward movements to solidify the swirling waters threatening to drown us. Then, we can hop out of the dangerous waters and move on to safety.

POST-IT MEDITATION FOR JUNE 10
With God's help, I will move forward even when the way seems impossible.

June 11

It is one of the most beautiful compensations of this life that no man can sincerely try to help another without helping himself."
~Ralph Waldo Emerson, American poet, essayist, and philosopher

On a stormy night many years ago, an elderly man and his wife entered the lobby of a small hotel in Philadelphia only to find the hotel had no vacancies. Feeling sorry for the couple, the clerk on duty offered them his own room, insisting he couldn't send them back out in the rain. The couple hesitated but finally gave in after the clerk told them he had to work all night.

The next morning, as he paid his bill, the elderly man said to the clerk, "You are the kind of manager who should be the boss of the best hotel in the United States. Maybe someday I'll build one for you."

The clerk looked at the man and his wife and smiled. The three had a good laugh over the old man's little joke, and then the clerk helped them with their bags to the street.

Two years later, the clerk received a note from the man he had helped, inviting him to come to New York—a round-trip train ticket was enclosed.

When he reached New York, the young man was led to the corner of Fifth Avenue and Thirty-Fourth Street. Gazing up, he was dumbfounded at the great new building there, a palace of reddish stone, with turrets and watchtowers, like a fairyland castle thrusting up into the air.

"This," said the older man, "is the hotel I built for you to manage."

"You must be joking," the young man said, not quite knowing whether to believe his friend or not.

"I most assuredly am not," said the older man, a sly smile playing around his mouth.

"Who—who are you?" stammered the other.

"My name is William Waldorf Astor."

The hotel was the original Waldorf-Astoria and the young clerk, who became its first manager, was George C. Boldt.

This story, which has been printed many times and has circulated on the Internet, has a few exaggerations. But the basic facts in the story are true, and the hyperbole doesn't affect the impact of the story's moral: You never know what reward a good deed may bring you.

POST-IT MEDITATION FOR JUNE 11
*How much richer our lives might be if our hearts are
so touched by the needs of others
that we willingly give up something to help them.*

June 12

Surely there is a future, and your hope will not be cut off.
~*Proverbs 23:18 (ESV)*

Two kinds of birds fly over the California desert—the hummingbird and the vulture.

All the vulture can see is rotting meat because that's all he looks for. He thrives on that diet. But the hummingbird ignores the carcasses and the smelly flesh of dead animals. Instead, it looks for the tiny blossoms of cactus flowers, buzzing around until it finds the colorful blooms, almost hidden from view by the rocks.

Each bird finds what it is looking for!

What are you looking for in life? Or, a more piercing question might be: What are you finding in life? For what you are finding reveals what you are looking for.

Are there hidden diamonds you will never find because you fail to look? Is there unseen goodness in people because you look for the worst in them? Is there a purpose for your life that remains veiled from your eyes?

Each morning we awaken to face a new day. We can choose to look for flowers in nooks and crannies or complain about the weeds in the cracks of the sidewalk. We can marvel at the fiery grandeur of a thunderstorm threatening the horizon, or we can dread the pelts of rain about to pummel our heads. We can see the heart-wrenching need of a homeless man with his out-stretched hands or silently berate him for making us face his human wretchedness.

Each new day demands to be filled. Sights and sounds color our thoughts as we make our choices. To lend a helping hand or pass a stranger by. To offer a heartfelt smile or remain absorbed in the demands of our own lives. To be hopeful or hopeless.

If blessed with two eyes to see, we should look for the best in other people. Like the hummingbird, we should search for wildflowers secreted among the rocks. We should seek splendor in the shadows of our lives.

POST-IT MEDITATION FOR JUNE 12
With my future safely in God's hands, I will look
for the best in all circumstances,
knowing my hope will not be cut off.

June 13

Now no one can look at the sun, bright as it is in the skies, after the wind has swept them clean.
~Job 37:21 (NIV)

Clouds mute the sun's rays, protecting our eyes from its blinding beams of light. And, they create their own beauty, building castles in the sky, forming shapes of wild animals, and casting fluffy white mounds of ephemeral glory in the blue skies. But some clouds paint the sky dark and dreary. They cover the light with haze, obscuring the radiance. As beautiful as Seattle is, I'm not sure I could endure the endless clouds and rain. Likewise for London—somehow its splendor is overshadowed by overcast skies rarely broken by sunlight. Yet, God created both the dark rain clouds and the frothy, cumulous puffs, each with its own purpose.

Like the changing clouds overhead, our lives have both happy swirls and dark veils. Behind each, the sun still exists. It may be blocked from our view, but its light is never dimmed. In the same way, when our lives seem draped in darkness, the power and love of God has not diminished, although we may not be able to see the beauty within his plan.

If we could only fly above the clouds and look down on our earthly lives, we might see a different picture. With the radiance of heaven shining down, we might see light reflected in dark places. And we could see that the clouds never stand still—they are always moving. God knows how long we can bear our troubles and sorrows, and he commands the wind to blow the desolate clouds away before we succumb to their darkness. Then he sends brightness back into our lives.

In 1980, the Pacific Northwest forests were annihilated; rivers were choked by ash, fish and wildlife were destroyed, and the air was poisoned—all by the devastating force erupting from Mt. St. Helen. Yet, less than a year later, despite the overwhelming damage, life emerged from the ashes. Thanks to moles, gophers, and ants that survived because they were buried when the explosion occurred, the soil was turned over, allowing new plants, shrubs, and trees to quickly take root. Large animals like elk returned faster than scientists predicted. And, clogged rivers were bypassed by the salmon, who returned to their native environment by alternate routes. Those who feared the area would never come back were wrong. God's nature righted itself.

Henry van Dyke, author and educator, reminds us we worry too much: "Do we know that more than half our trouble is borrowed? Just suppose we could be sure of final victory in every conflict, and final emergence out of every shadow into brighter days; how our hearts would be lightened...

This is the courage to which we are entitled." All that is necessary to find the light is to claim God's promise for victory over destruction and despair.

POST-IT MEDITATION FOR JUNE 13
I can be sure of final victory in every misfortune or suffering because I will someday join God above the clouds.

June 14

Have I not commanded you? Be strong and courageous. Do not be frightened, and do not be dismayed, for the Lord your God is with you wherever you go."
~Joshua 1:9 (ESV)

A pastor had been on a long flight from one city to another. The first warning of approaching problems came when the sign on the airplane flashed on: Fasten your seat belts. Then, after a while, a calm voice said, "We will not be serving beverages at this time as we are expecting a little turbulence. Please be sure your seat belt is fastened."

As he looked around the aircraft, it became obvious many passengers were becoming apprehensive. Later, the voice of the announcer said, "We are so sorry we are unable to serve the meal at this time. The turbulence is still ahead of us."

And then the storm broke. The ominous cracks of thunder could be heard above the roar of the engines. Lightning lit the dimming skies, and within moments the great plane was like a cork tossed about on a celestial ocean. One moment the airplane lifted on terrific currents of air like a retracting bungee cord; the next, it plummeted.

The pastor confessed he shared the discomfort and fear of those around him. "As I looked around the plane, I could see that nearly all the passengers were upset and alarmed. Some were praying. The flight gyrations seemed ominous, and many were wondering if we would make it through the storm. Then, I suddenly saw a little girl. Apparently the storm meant nothing to her. She had tucked her feet beneath her as she sat on her seat; she was reading a book, and all within her small world was calm. Sometimes she closed her eyes, then she would read again; then she would straighten her legs, but worry and fear were not in her world. When the plane was being buffeted by the terrible storm, when it lurched this way and that, as it rose and fell with frightening severity, when all the adults were scared half to death, that marvelous child was completely composed and unafraid." The minister could hardly believe his eyes.

Not surprisingly, when the plane finally reached its destination and all the passengers were hurrying to disembark, the pastor lingered to speak to the girl whom he had watched for such a long time. Having commented about the storm and behavior of the plane, he asked why she had not been afraid.

The sweet child replied, "Sir, my Dad is the pilot, and he is taking me home."

There are many kinds of storms that buffet us. Physical, mental, financial, domestic, and other tempests can easily and quickly darken our skies and throw our plane into apparently uncontrollable movements. We have all known such times, and let us be honest and confess, it is much easier to be at rest when our feet are on the ground than when we are being tossed about a darkened sky. But even in turbulent times, knowing God is our pilot can bring peace.

POST-IT MEDITATION FOR JUNE 14
I will remember my father is the pilot. He is in control, and he is taking me home.

June 15

As a man thinketh in his heart, so is he.
~Proverbs 23:7 (KJV)

The awful clanging box that wakes us is called an ALARM clock. When it jars us from slumber, we have two choices: We can exclaim, "Oh my god, I've got to face another day or we can proclaim, "God has given me another day—I will enjoy it!" If we choose the latter of the two options, it is more likely that we will think positive thoughts all day. We become what we think.

The full text of Proverbs 23:7, from which the above excerpt comes, suggests we consider the true motivations of a person who is being uncharacteristically generous before accepting his generosity, but the part often quoted is used to apply not to another person but to the reader himself.

British philosophical writer James Allen, in a 1902 essay titled "As a Man Thinketh," opened with this statement: "Mind is the master power that molds and makes." He goes on to say the tool of thought can bring forth a thousand joys or a thousand ills. We think in secret, he explains, and it comes to pass: "Environment is but [man's] looking glass." Consequently, a man is what he thinks, his character formed from the sum total of his thoughts. Those thoughts are to be cherished because they can produce visions, ideals, and music that stir our hearts.

Allen avowed, "Every action and feeling is preceded by a thought. Right thinking begins with the words we say to ourselves." He continued that circumstances don't *make* us who we are—they simply *reveal* to us who we are. In other words, we are responsible for who and what we become; and, we can shape that being by how we think. Marcus Aurelis, Roman emperor and philosopher, said it this way: "The world in which we live is determined by our thoughts."

One day I hopped in a taxi, and we took off for the airport. We were driving in the right lane when suddenly a black car jumped out of a parking space right in front of us. My taxi driver slammed on his brakes, skidded, and missed the other car by just inches! The driver of the other car whipped his head around and started yelling at us. My taxi driver just smiled and waved at the guy. And I mean, he was really friendly. So I asked, "Why did you just do that? This guy almost ruined your car and sent us to the hospital!"

This is when my taxi driver taught me what I now call, "The Law of the Garbage Truck." He explained that many people are like garbage trucks. They run around full of garbage, full of frustration, full of anger, and full of disappointment. As their garbage piles up, they need a place to dump it and sometimes they'll dump it on you. Don't take it personally. Just smile, wave, wish them well, and move on. Don't take their garbage and spread it to other people at work, at home, or on the streets.

The bottom line is successful Christians do not let garbage trucks take over their day. Life's too short to wake up in the morning with regrets, so... Love the people who treat you right. Pray for the ones who don't. Life is ten percent what you make it and ninety percent how you take it!

It has been said the first four minutes in the morning set the tone for the entire day. How you respond to the alarm clock is the beginning. If you thank God for another day, you begin with a grateful heart. A good way to follow that thought is to focus on the one who has given you the day—even a moment or two thinking specifically about what God has done for you and what he will do in the future can prepare you for a day that may be filled with circumstances you would prefer not to face. Equipped with that preparation, no one else's garbage can destroy your positive thoughts.

POST-IT MEDITATION FOR JUNE 15
Each day I will thank God for the gift of life and his blessings—
and then refuse to take on anyone else's garbage.

June 16

Neither height nor depth, nor anything else in all creation, will be able to separate us from the love of God that is in Christ Jesus our Lord.
~Romans 8:39 (NKJV)

One Father's Day a six-year-old boy decided to fix his father breakfast. Both of his parents were still asleep, so he made his way downstairs, found a big bowl and spoon, and pulled a chair to the counter. Perched precariously on the edge of the chair, he stretched up to open the cabinet and pulled out the heavy bag of flour. To his dismay, the bag slipped from his hands, and flour spilled everywhere. Not to be deterred, he scooped some of the flour into the bowl with his hands, mixed in a cup of milk, and added some sugar, just as he had seen his mother do. But he also did something he had never witnessed from his mother—he left a floury trail on the floor. Covered with the white powder himself, the little boy watched in dismay as he saw his kitten licking from the bowl of mix. As he tried to push her away, he knocked the egg carton to the floor. Frantically trying to clean up the monumental mess, he grabbed some paper towels and started wiping; but the floor was slick, and down he went. By now, he was sticky from head to toes. About then, his father appeared at the kitchen door. Knowing he was about to get the scolding of his life, maybe even a spanking, the child began to cry crocodile tears. He had wanted to surprise his parents, but not this way. As he sobbed, he looked through tears at his father, who was watching him. Then, gingerly walking through the disaster zone, the man picked up his crying son, hugged him, and held him close, getting the gummy batter on his own pajamas in the process.

The father had two choices: punish his child for wrecking the kitchen, or recognize the little boy was trying to do something good and love him for his efforts. That's the same two choices God has when we turn our lives upside down, creating disorder and disarray. Like the little boy's father, he sees in our heart and treats us with compassion, knowing we tried. He picks us up and shows us he loves us despite our failures. We may make a mess of our marriage or our job; we may hurt others in spite of our best intentions; we may break the law or blunder in other ways. Whatever we do, we will not be separated from God's love.

POST-IT MEDITATION FOR JUNE 16
I am thankful God's love is unconditional.

June 17

He will turn the hearts of the fathers to their children, and the hearts of the children to their fathers.
~Malachi 4:6 (NIV)

Some parents attempt to give their children everything they want, almost as if they are trying to earn love with "things." But material possessions are fleeting parts of a child's life, and they are not the cloth from which memories are made. In a *Guideposts'* story, a man named Ray Payleitner shares a time when his father's actions created a sense of security and caring that lasted far longer than any gift might have. Now a father himself, one day a bridge stirred a distant memory:

As a Boy Scout, Payleitner's troop made a two-day, 40-mile canoe journey down the Fox River. His dad dropped his brother and him at the launch spot and, after making sure their life jackets were secure, wished them a safe journey when the flotilla of canoes set off. As the two boys plunged their paddles into the water and began moving down the river, Payleitner recalls thinking, "I wish Dad could see us."

At the next bridge along the river, Payleitner looked up and was surprised to see his dad standing, looking out over the side of the bridge. After the boys passed underneath the span, he waved at them. He then walked back to his car. When Payleitner looked back, he was gone.

Another mile or so downstream, at the second bridge, the young boy glanced up and saw his father again, waving them by. And he was there at the next bridge and the next one. After the second time, the whole troop started watching for him. Payleitner recalls every time they rounded a bend and a bridge was up ahead, someone would yell, "There's Mr. Payleitner!" All the boys began to wave at him at each span.

In a simple way, Payleitner's father had gone the extra mile to show his boys his love. It was a demonstration of caring Payleitner never forgot. Years later, as he crossed the Fox River, it reminded him of the nightly prayer he had said when his kids were younger—asking God's guidance to help him be the kind of dad his kids needed. Thinking of the day his dad followed him and his brother down the river, he closed his story with, "At last I understood the most important thing I could do for my children—just be there, even if it meant going the extra mile."

POST-IT MEDITATION FOR JUNE 17
With God's help, I will cheer my children (and grandchildren) or neighborhood kids on, encouraging and supporting them with care and love.

June 18

...share what you have because God is pleased with these kinds of sacrifices.
~Hebrews 13:16b (CEB)

In a small Idaho community, a man sold fresh produce from a roadside stand. It was during the Great Depression, and food and money were extremely scarce and bartering was extensively used. One day the man, Mr. Miller, stopped to ask a young boy who was gazing at a display of fresh green peas if he wanted to buy some.

"Got nuthin to pay for 'em with," the child responded.

The kind man asked, "Well, what have you to trade me for some of those peas?"

"All I got's my prize marble here," came the response. "But she's a dandy."

With a twinkle in his eye, the owner of the produce said, "I can see that. Hmmmmm, only thing is this one is blue and I sort of go for red. Do you have a red one like this at home?"

"Not zackley...but almost."

"Tell you what. Take this sack of peas home with you and next trip this way let me look at that red marble."

With a grateful smile, the boy thanked Mr. Miller.

Mrs. Miller, who had been watching, came over and explained to another customer: "There are two other boys like him in our community; all three are in very poor circumstances. Jim just loves to bargain with them for peas, apples, tomatoes, or whatever. When they come back with their red marbles, and they always do, he decides he doesn't like red after all and sends them home with a bag of produce for a green marble or an orange one."

Years later, when Mr. Miller died, three young men stood in line to pay their respects. One wore an army uniform, and the other two sported good haircuts, dark suits, and white shirts. They approached Mrs. Miller and hugged her and moved on to the casket. Each young man stopped briefly and placed his own warm hand over the cold pale hand in the casket. Each left the mortuary awkwardly, wiping his eyes.

Now, at last, when Mr. Miller could not change his mind about the color or size, they came to pay their debt. In the lifeless fingers of the deceased man lay three exquisitely shined red marbles.

When our own time on earth ends, we will not be remembered by our words, but by our kind deeds.

POST-IT MEDITATION FOR JUNE 18
When I am prone to hoard what I have, I will remember the story of Mr. Miller and the marbles.

June 19

There comes a special moment in everyone's life, a moment for which that person was born. That special opportunity, when he seizes it, will fulfill his mission—a mission for which he is uniquely qualified.
~Sir Winston Churchill, British prime minister

Once upon a time a pencil maker took a pencil aside before putting him into the box, telling him that there were five points he needed to remember to be the best pencil he could be.

"First, you must allow yourself to be held in someone's hand if you are to do great things.

"Second, be prepared to endure a painful sharpening occasionally and know that it will make you a better pencil.

"Third, you can correct any mistakes you might make.

- 213

"Fourth, the most important part of you will always be inside.

"And last, you must leave your mark on every surface you are used on. Regardless of the condition, you must continue to write."

Humans are like pencils.

First, we can do great deeds but only if we allow ourselves to be held in God's hand.

Second, we will go through times of painful sharpening as we experience life's problems and breaking points. But we will come from the sharpening stronger and ready to write again on the pages of our lives.

Third, we can correct mistakes we make in our lives, erasing them and starting again.

Fourth, the most important part of who we are is inside us.

And, fifth, we should always leave our mark on the people we pass by in life. Regardless of the situation, we should give of ourselves to help others.

Each person has lead inside, lead that can be used to create marks on our lives and the lives of others. No human being is created without this lead, so everyone has the potential to contribute, fulfilling the purpose we were born to accomplish. And, as American writer John Maxwell reminds us, "A difficult time can be more readily endured if we retain the conviction that our existence holds a purpose—a cause to pursue, a person to love, a goal to achieve."

SOURCE OF PENCIL STORY: http://www.indianchild.com

POST-IT MEDITATION FOR JUNE 19
I will use the lesson from the pencil story to sustain and guide me.

June 20

For as the heavens are higher than the earth, so are my ways higher than your ways and my thoughts than your thoughts.
~Isaiah 55:9 (NIV)

Sir Christopher Wren, British architect and designer, was walking among artisans and stonecutters who were building St. Paul's Cathedral, which he had designed. Unrecognized by the laborers, he asked the first one he saw, "What are you doing?"

"I am cutting a piece of stone," the workman replied.

Continuing his walk through the work site, Wren stopped beside another stonecutter and asked the same question.

"I am earning five shillings two pence a day," the second workman replied.

When Wren asked a third workman the same question, he received a much different response:

"I am helping Sir Christopher Wren build a magnificent cathedral to the glory of God."

In the age St. Paul's Cathedral was built, such structures often took more than 50 years to construct. Consequently, those who designed and built them knew they might not be alive when they were finished. But they also realized they were creating something glorious and grand that would survive for not just decades but centuries.

In the 21st century, too few of us think at this level. If we project far at all, it is usually only to our retirement years. And that's often because we want to escape the drudgery of jobs we consider meaningless.

So why do we set our sights so low? What would it take to get out of the rut of just getting through the daily grind? It's simple. Look at the big picture—the whole and not just its parts. In addition, we should not merely know how and what we are doing, but we should also know why. In other words, we should seek to understand the significance of the work. And, we should look for how the work of our hands and minds will live on, whether in the stones of a cathedral or in the impact made on others' lives.

The choice is ours. We can be like the first stonecutter, who knew what he had to accomplish that day, a narrow task that brought little satisfaction. Or, we can be like the second one, caring nothing about the work, focused only on the money it will bring. A better option is to look beyond earning a living or achieving personal goals to see the bigger picture—how we can use our work to make a difference in others' lives or in the world in which we live.

The first step is to abandon apathy, which is the biggest enemy of success—personally and spiritually. Staying in a mindless routine is easier than thinking big. We need to let go of our little ideas and find ways to change our lives for God's purpose.

POST-IT MEDITATION FOR JUNE 20
I will look at the big picture for my life, seeking meaning even in small tasks that can have significance and make a difference.

June 21

And without faith it is impossible to please God, because anyone who comes to him must believe that he exists and that he rewards those who earnestly seek him.
~Hebrews 11:6 (NIV)

The following is supposedly a true story of something that happened in 1998:

A well-known University of Southern California professor of philosophy was a deeply committed atheist. His primary goal for one required class was to spend the entire semester attempting to prove God couldn't exist. His students were always afraid to argue with him because of his impeccable logic. For twenty years, he had taught this class and no one had ever displayed the courage to go against him. Sure, some had argued in class at times, but no one had ever really challenged him because of his reputation. At the end of every semester on the last day, he would say to his class of 300 students, "If there is anyone here who still believes in God, stand up!"

In twenty years, no one had ever stood up. They knew what he was going to do next. He would say, "Because anyone who believes in God is a fool. If God existed, he could stop this piece of chalk from hitting the ground and breaking. Such a simple task to prove that he is God, and yet he can't do it." And every year, when he dropped the chalk onto the tile floor of the classroom, it shattered into a hundred pieces. The students could do nothing but stare. For 20 years, Christians in the class had been too afraid to stand up.

But finally, a young freshman Christian, who had heard the stories about the professor, was required to take the class for his major. He was afraid, but for three months that semester, he prayed every morning that he would have the courage to stand up no matter what the professor said, or what the class thought. Nothing they said could ever shatter his faith...he hoped.

Finally, the day came. The professor said, "If there is anyone here who still believes in God, stand up!" The professor and the class of 300 students looked at the young Christian, shocked, as he stood up at the back of the classroom. The professor shouted, "You FOOL!!! If God existed, he would keep this piece of chalk from breaking when it hit the ground!"

He proceeded to drop the chalk, but as he did, it slipped out of his fingers, off his shirt cuff, onto the pleat of his pants, down his leg, and off his shoe. As it hit the ground, it simply rolled away unbroken. The professor's jaw dropped as he stared at the chalk. He looked up at the young man—and then ran out of the lecture hall.

Over 20 years, thousands of students had lacked the faith necessary to stand up for God. When one finally did, God rewarded him with a miracle.

SOURCE OF PROFESSOR STORY: http://www.websites-host.com/insp/istories.html

POST-IT MEDITATION FOR JUNE 21
I will never doubt God's power or his promises.

June 22

The hardest arithmetic to master is that which enables us to count our blessings.
~Eric Hoffer, American writer

> I've never made a fortune, and it's probably too late now.
> But I don't worry about that much; I'm happy anyhow.
> And as I go along life's way, I'm reaping better than I sowed.

I'm drinking from my saucer, 'cause my cup has overflowed.
Haven't got a lot of riches, and sometimes the going's tough.
But I've got loving ones all around me, and that makes me rich enough.
I thank God for his blessings, and the mercies he's bestowed.
I'm drinking from my saucer, 'cause my cup has overflowed.
I remember times when things went wrong; my faith wore somewhat thin.
But all at once the dark clouds broke, and the sun
peeped through again.
So Lord, help me not to gripe about the tough rows
I have hoed.
I'm drinking from my saucer, ' cause my cup has overflowed.
If God gives me strength and courage, when the way grows steep and rough.
I'll not ask for other blessings; I'm already blessed enough.

When we think how many people in this world have it worse than we do, we realize just how blessed most of us really are. When we are consistently grateful, we build force in our faith. The more we are thankful, the stronger our spiritual lives become. Like the muscle in our bodies, if we don't use the gift of thankfulness, then our muscle of appreciation will lose its capacity to keep us resilient.

An attitude of gratefulness helps us find blessings all around us—in everything we see, in whatever happens to us, and in everything we are given. Sadly, in our quest for more and more, we fail to appreciate the good fortune of sight and sound. Helen Keller recognized this when she said, "I have always thought it would be a blessing if each person could be blind and deaf for a few days during his early life. Darkness would make him appreciate sight; silence would teach him the joys of sound."

Many of life's blessings come from being able to see the rapturous beauty of nature. A striking sunset, a blossoming rose, a vibrant field of wildflowers, the soft shades of a stunning rainbow, a snow-capped mountain range, lightning flashing fire across the ocean—it is difficult to imagine what it would be like not to be able to see God's handiwork in the world he created for us. We can't envision not being able to view such sights or hear the majestic music of a pipe organ, the symphonic sound of crashing waves, or a choir of birds in our backyard.

How can we learn to appreciate gifts from God without ever having been deprived of most of them? One way is to train ourselves when we awaken, or to simply stop sometime during the day and look around us at God's handiwork. It is so easy to take sights and sounds for granted, never noticing the grandeur of dew drops on a leaf or the rich beauty of a cloudless sky. We should look for blessings in all that we see—and in all that happens to us, we can ask ourselves, "What is the blessing here?"

June 23

For the love of money is a source of all kinds of evil. Some have been so eager to have it that they have wandered away from the faith and have broken their hearts with many sorrows.
~1 Timothy 6:10 (GNT)

Once upon a time there was a White Knight looking for adventure. He came to a village where legends told of a terrible ogre in a pit. Bravely, the White Knight took up the challenge. He would do battle with the underground monster. The people remembered several courageous men who had climbed down into the pit, but no one could ever remember one of those champions returning.

The White Knight stood looking at the deep, dark hole. The opening was so narrow that he stripped himself of armor and all unnecessary clothing. He took only a long dagger, which he tied around his neck with a leather strap. After securing a rope at the opening and testing its strength, he gripped it firmly and began lowering himself, hand under hand, letting the rope slip between his feet. Soon he felt the smooth cool floor of the chamber. It took several minutes for his eyes to adjust to the darkness, but soon he focused on a large mound. Then he realized it was the bones of his predecessors, along with their assorted weapons. A little way off, he spotted another mound, but he wasn't sure what it was.

Suddenly he was surprised by the inhabitant of the pit...surprised because he didn't anticipate the ogre would be only as tall as a rabbit. The ogre raised its arms and screeched with its squeaky voice, trying to appear as fierce as possible. The White Knight picked up a sword from the floor and prepared to do battle, but quick as a rat, the ogre ran into a hole near the second mound.

The White Knight followed, and the second mound became clearer—again he was surprised. Before his eyes glittered balls of gold as big as grapefruit and diamonds as big as plums. With only a small part of that treasure even a commoner would be a prince for life. The ogre lost its importance in view of this great treasure.

But the Knight had a problem. How would he carry it out of the hole? He had no pockets. Who would believe him if he didn't bring back at least a piece?

He suddenly had an idea. He would take one of the diamonds in his mouth and carry it that way until he climbed out of the hole. He could always come back later for the rest. Hurriedly he chose one of the larger diamonds. It fit comfortably into his mouth, and he began the arduous climb out of the pit, hand over hand, gripping the rope with his feet. Higher and higher he climbed until the heavy exertion began to render him breathless. He would have to breathe through his mouth in order to get enough air. As he took a large gulp of air, the diamond slipped and stuck in his throat. The White Knight choked on his treasure, lost consciousness, and fell to his death on the mound of bones below.

You see, the terrible ogre in the pit was not the little troll. The ogre in the pit was greed...greed in the hearts of men who desire easy treasure and the hope of unearned gain. The glitter of this world choked the Knight to death.

Greed is a destructive force. 1 Timothy 6:9 (GNT) warns us of the depraved condition it can bring upon us: "...those who want to get rich fall into temptation and are caught in the trap of many foolish and harmful desires, which pull them down to ruin and destruction." It is not, of course, wealth that causes harm—it is greed and temptation. If people seek wealth for the right reasons and use their money wisely, they can use their prosperity in good ways. The key is not to love money more than we love God and others.

POST-IT MEDITATION FOR JUNE 23
I will be wary of greed.

June 24

Guilt, regret, resentment, grievances, sadness, bitterness, and all forms of non-forgiveness are caused by too much past, and not enough presence.
~Eckhart Tolle, German-born, Canadian author

I ran into a stranger as he passed by, "Oh, excuse me, please" was my reply.
He said, "Please excuse me, too; I wasn't watching for you."
We were very polite, this stranger and I. We went on our way saying good-bye.
But at home a difference is told, how we treat our loved ones, young and old.
Later that day, cooking the evening meal, my son stood beside me very still.
As I turned, I nearly knocked him down. "Move out of the way," I said with a frown.
He walked away, his little heart broken. I didn't realize how harshly I'd spoken.
As I lay awake in bed, God's still small voice came to me and said, "While dealing with a stranger, common courtesy you use, but the children you love, you seem to abuse. Go and look on the kitchen floor, you'll find some flowers there by the door. Those are the flowers he brought for you. He picked them himself: pink, yellow and blue. He stood very quietly not to spoil the surprise, and you never saw the tears that filled his little eyes."
By this time, I felt very small, and now my tears began to fall.
I quietly went and knelt by his bed; "Wake up, little one, wake up," I said. "Are these the flowers you picked for me?"

He smiled, "I found 'em, out by the tree. I picked 'em because they're pretty like you. I knew you'd like 'em, especially the blue."

I said, "Son, I'm very sorry for the way I acted today; I shouldn't have yelled at you that way."

He said, "Oh, Mom, that's okay. I love you anyway."

The rhyming story above has a happy ending, but sometimes we don't get or take the opportunity to re-do a particular incident we wish never happened. Sometimes we carry guilt, resentment, or embarrassment longer than the situation warranted.

Do you have a memory that will not heal? Did you ever humiliate someone so terribly the person wanted to die on the spot? Has someone helped you over and over and yet you resent everything they say or do? Did you destroy your family through adultery? Or, did a friend betray you at a critical point in your life? Are you ashamed you intentionally hurt someone? Are you a recovering addict who cannot stand to look at the shambles you made of your life? Did you kill another person in self-defense and are plagued with guilt that you took a human life? Maybe it was something far less dramatic—if no less traumatic at the time—but we all have memories we would like to erase because they cripple a part of our emotions and haunt a hidden place in our minds.

How can we live with our hurtful memories? Psychiatrist Rollo May declares any moment that can be taken as a crippling curse can also be taken as a blessing for growth. The first step toward growth is to admit our feelings. Christ himself did not hide from his state of mind: "My soul is deeply grieved, to the point of death..." (Matthew 26:38, NASB). Admitting our own resentment, bitterness, anger, or hatred is essential to coping with our hurts. This may entail making a list of all of the wrongs we have suffered, but once the list is made and we have acknowledged the injuries someone has inflicted on us, we should tell God how we feel and ask him to release us from the pain. Then we should tear the list in shreds. Keeping a catalogued list of wrongs we have suffered does no good. Reading it again and again deepens depression and harms us more than it hurts the person we hate. Moreover, it creates a barrier between us and God's love and plan for our happiness. Blessings follow forgiveness. As St. Francis of Assisi knew, "It is in pardoning that we are pardoned." Or, as an unknown person wrote, "To forgive is to set a prisoner free and discover the prisoner was you." We all need forgiveness, and we should follow God's example, forgiving others as we have been forgiven.

POST-IT MEDITATION FOR JUNE 24
I will forgive those who have hurt me, whether they have asked for forgiveness or not.

June 25

Shall we live in mystery and yet conduct ourselves as though everything were known?
~Christopher Fry, English playwright

Do events in our daily existence happen randomly, or does God intervene directly, opening and closing doors in accordance with his plan for our lives?

The only survivor of a shipwreck was washed up on a small, uninhabited island. He prayed fervently for God to rescue him, and every day he scanned the horizon for help, but each day passed with no help. Accepting his fate—and God's presumed lack of caring—he built a little hut out of driftwood to protect him from the elements and in which to store his few possessions.

But then one day, after a foray for food, he arrived home to find flames consuming his little hut, the smoke billowing toward the sky. The worst had happened; what little he had was lost. He was overcome with rage and despair.

"God, how could you do this to me!" he cried.

Early the next day as he lay on the beach, the distraught man was awakened by the sound of a ship approaching the island. It had come to rescue him.

The weary man asked his rescuers: "How did you know I was here?"

They replied: "We saw your smoke signal."

Was the fire a random act, or is it possible God was looking out for the man? It is easy to get discouraged when tragedies befall us. But we shouldn't lose heart, because God is at work in our lives, even in the midst of discouragement and trouble.

People in grief often feel God sends them signs their loved ones are okay. A flower blooms out of season. A special song is heard on the radio at a critical time. A lost ring is found among indescribable rubble. A single live rose falls from an icy spray of dead flowers. A blue heron returns. A monk in a faraway cathedral talks about a lost son. A windmill turns when no breeze stirs nearby leaves. A bright star follows a sorrowful wife wherever she walks or drives. All of these are real stories, told by people recovering from losses, in *Faces of Grief: Stories of Surviving Loss and Finding Hope* (Hoppe, 2011). All were considered gifts from God.

Heaven's Postcards *also tells of astonishing signs and miracles a family received to assure them their 25-year-old son was in heaven following a car accident in December 2007:*

"God showed us many signs that Zach was in Heaven. He used the clouds, the stars, birds, butterflies, the radio, and words from friends. I was amazed at how clearly God spoke to us. He used the clouds to show us a perfect heart, a

cross, an "I love you" sign, the word Hi, and a hand writing the letters Z a c in the clouds. God used birds to hug us, wave at us, and do flips in the air at us. He used stars and butterflies to show he controls everything in our universe…. God's presence was everywhere."

The next time we are discouraged and down because we think God doesn't care, the story of the shipwrecked man and those from grieving hearts can be a reminder that mysterious events may be gifts from God. *Excerpt from HEAVEN'S POSTCARDS, by Kim Todd, ZMH Press, 2009.*

POST-IT MEDITATION FOR JUNE 25
I will not question whether mysterious events I encounter are signs or inter-pretations; I will accept them as gifts from God bringing light to dark days.

June 26

Success is never final; failure is never fatal. It is courage that counts.
~Winston Churchill, British prime minister

Humans have a tendency to judge themselves by benchmarks against others. We question whether we are as pretty or handsome as another; we gage our possessions by those of others; we compare our abilities, jobs, and recreational opportunities to our friends, neighbors, or co-workers. We worry about what other people say about us; and worse, we berate ourselves because we don't measure up to our own standards or goals.

When we use an earthly yardstick to calculate our worth, we will never be good enough. There will always be "things" we don't have and places we haven't been. We will never be able to please everyone, and likely we won't be able to satisfy ourselves. None of that matters. If God says we are good enough for him, then we are okay. God will never reject us based on our own merit or what others think of us. He calculates our worth based on his grace, not our ability or actions. When we accept this truth, we can begin what Brennan Manning calls the second journey of our lives.

The second journey may be triggered by loss of wealth or fame—or the realization that job titles and possessions no longer matter to us. It can also be sparked by infidelity, a car accident, or any other event making us rethink our priorities. The question prompting a new direction may be like the one uttered by the heroine in Anne Tyler's *Breathing Lessons*, when this middle-aged lady turns to her husband and utters, "Oh Ira, what are we going to do with the rest of our lives?"

The courage to face life anew comes, Manning declares, from giving some things up, letting some things die, and accepting human limita-tions. "It is a wisdom that [comes when a person] has faced the pain caused by parents, spouses, family, friends, colleagues, business associates, and has truly forgiven them and acknowledged with unexpected compassion that these people are not angels nor devils, but only human."

Another realization necessary for the second journey is an awareness that we have only a limited amount of time left to give attention to what really matters, what really counts in our lives. With this consciousness comes a desire for a deeper, more fulfilling faith; an undeniable belief that God loves us as we are.

The last perception we must acquire is whether we truly want a different life—one of service to God and others. The opportunity to help those less fortunate is never far away.

Just up the road from my home is a field where two horses graze. From a distance, each horse looks like any other horse. But if you look closer, you will notice something quite interesting: One of the horses is blind. His owner has chosen not to have him put down and provides a safe and comfortable existence for the sightless horse. This alone is pretty amazing. But if you stand nearby and listen, you will hear the sound of a bell. It is coming from a smaller horse in the field. Attached to the horse's halter is a small, copper-colored bell. It lets the blind friend know where the other horse is so he can follow. As you stand and watch these two friends, you'll see that the horse with the bell is always checking on the blind horse and that the blind horse will listen for the bell and then slowly walk to where the other horse is, trusting he will not be led astray. When the horse with the bell returns to the shelter of the barn each evening, he will stop occasionally to look back, making sure his blind friend isn't too far behind to hear the bell.

Like the owner of the two horses, God does not throw us away just because we are not perfect. Or because we have problems or challenges. He watches over us and even brings others into our lives to help us when we are in need. Sometimes we are the blind horse, being guided by the little ringing bell of those God places in our lives. And at other times we are the guide horse, helping others find their way.

POST-IT MEDITATION FOR JUNE 26
I will leave behind the desires of the past and focus on the future where faith overlooks failures and gives me desire and fortitude for tomorrow.

June 27

Listen to the whispers of your heart.
~Unknown

Once upon a time, when God was creating mankind in his likeness and image, there was an Executive Council meeting for all of heaven's divisions. All the top angels were asked to attend, even though everyone had much work to be done with impending deadlines. God wanted opinions on an extremely grave and pressing matter. He was considering giving mankind the "Secret of Life." He wanted to know where to hide this precious gift, so it would be very difficult to find and then only by the most dedicated individuals. One angel thought it should be sunk in the depths of the sea. Another suggested it should be buried in the bowels of the earth. A third felt it should be hidden very near the sky, at the pinnacle of the highest mountain, in the most desolate region possible. Yet, a fourth angel had a different point of view. "No, mankind will be a tricky breed. Somebody will swim the deepest sea. Someone will dig down into the bowels of the earth. Some determined, industrious individual will even scale the highest mountain. We should place this secret someplace where mankind would never dream of looking…right inside himself." God nodded in agreement, and it was done.

And so it is that the secret to our lives resides right inside each of us—to find it, we must be silent and still, listening for God's whisper in the din of noise that surrounds us.

Psalm 46 declares God is with us though the earth be removed, though the waters roar and storms rage, though the mountains shake with swelling, and though the winds blow. He is there when we lose our jobs. He is there when the bills are due, and we don't have enough money to pay them. He is there when someone betrays us. He is there when a family member won't act right. He is there though our children disappoint us. He is there when our bodies are racked with illness. He is there when a loved one dies.

When we encounter problems and troubles, the secret to getting our lives back on track is within us. God is there waiting to help and heal us. We can cast our cares on him when our hearts are breaking and our souls are in despair. His whispered words will comfort our hearts, calm our fears, and give us hope for a better tomorrow.

POST-IT MEDITATION FOR JUNE 27
When I am overwhelmed with life, I will look inside my soul, waiting to hear God's whispers of encouragement.

June 28

Nothing is predestined: The obstacles of your past can become the gateways that lead to new beginnings.
~Ralph Blum, writer and cultural anthropologist

The story is told of an old mule that fell into his owner's well. The water wasn't very deep, so the mule could stand on the bottom. Scared, he began braying (or if mules can pray, he may have been praying), and the farmer came to check on him. Sadly, he decided the old mule nor the well was worth the trouble of saving, so he began hauling dirt to bury the creature in the well to put him out of his misery.

When the first shovelfuls of dirt hit his back, the mule was hysterical, braying louder and louder. As the soil kept tumbling in, the old mule was shaking so hard the dirt fell off. And then it dawned on him that every time a shovel load of dirt landed on his back, he could shake it off and step up. This he did, blow after blow. No matter how hard the blows or how distressing the situation seemed, he kept shaking the dirt off and stepping on top of it. It wasn't long before the old mule, all tuckered out and dirty, stepped triumphantly over the wall of the well, taking the farmer by surprise.

What appeared to be burying the mule actually helped him. Our lives are no different. If we refuse to give in to adversities but find opportunities within the wreckage of our lives, we may find the potential to rise above them. When we appear to be sinking, the solution is prayer, asking God's help in examining all of the possibilities. Next, we wait on God to renew our strength and then work toward the best possibility. God may open doors for us himself, or he may strengthen us or help us through another person whom he sends to encourage or assist us. Still another possibility is that he will give us an epiphany—a clear vision of what we should do. Through his guidance (in whatever form it may take), we may find a new route to our goals, a new approach to our problems, a new path to progress and prosperity. Our job is to have faith to climb up even if the dirt keeps descending—not deplore the situation.

POST-IT MEDITATION FOR JUNE 28
When I am about to be buried by life's perils, I will shake it off and step it up, having faith God will help me find a way out.

June 29

The effects of our actions may be postponed but they are never lost. There is an inevitable reward for good deeds and an inescapable punishment for bad. Meditate upon this truth, and seek always to earn good wages from destiny.
~Wu Ming Fu

A wealthy man and his son loved to collect rare works of art. They had everything in their collection from Picasso to Raphael. They would often sit together and admire the great works of art. When the Vietnam conflict broke out, the son went to war. He was very courageous and died in battle while rescuing another soldier. The father was notified and grieved deeply for his only son.

About a month later, just before Christmas, there was a knock at the door. A young man stood on the porch with a large package in his hands. He said, "Sir, you don't know me, but I am the soldier for whom your son gave his life. He saved many lives that day, and he was carrying me to safety when a bullet struck him in the heart, and he died instantly. He often talked about you, and your love for art." The young man held out his package. "I know this isn't much. I'm not really a great artist, but I think your son would have wanted you to have this."

The father opened the package. It was a portrait of his son, painted by the young man. He stared in awe at the way the soldier had captured the personality of his son in the painting. The father was so drawn to the eyes that his own eyes welled up with tears. He thanked the young man and offered to pay him for the picture. "Oh, no sir, I could never repay what your son did for me. It's a gift."

The father hung the portrait over his mantle. Every time visitors came to his home, he took them to see the portrait of his son before he showed them any of the other great works he had collected.

The man died a few months later. A great auction of his paintings took place. Many influential people gathered, excited over seeing the great paintings and having an opportunity to purchase one for their collection. On the platform sat the painting of the son. The auctioneer pounded his gavel. "We will start the bidding with this picture of the son. Who will bid for this picture?"

There was silence. Then a voice in the back of the room shouted, "We want to see the famous paintings. Skip this one."

But the auctioneer persisted. "Will someone bid for this painting? Who will start the bidding? $100, $200?" Another voice shouted angrily, "We didn't come to see this painting. We came to see the Van Goghs, the Rembrandts. Get on with the real bids!" But still the auctioneer continued, "The son! The son! Who'll take the son?"

Finally, a voice came from the very back of the room. It was the longtime gardener of the man and his son. "I'll give $10 for the painting." Being a poor man, it was all he could afford.

"We have $10, who will bid $20?"

"Give it to him for $10. Let's see the masters."

"$10 is the bid, won't someone bid $20?" The crowd was becoming angry. They didn't want the picture of the son. They wanted the more worthy investments for their collections. The auctioneer pounded the gavel. "Going once, twice, SOLD for $10!"

A man sitting on the second row shouted, "Now, let's get on with the collection!"

The auctioneer laid down his gavel. "I'm sorry, the auction is over."

"What about the paintings?" the man raged, his sentiments shared by the crowd.

"I am sorry. When I was called to conduct this auction, I was told of a secret stipulation in the will. I was not allowed to reveal that stipulation until this time. Only the painting of the son would be auctioned. Whoever bought that painting would inherit the entire estate, including the paintings. The man who took the son gets everything!"

God gave his son more than 2000 years ago to die on a cruel cross. Much like the auctioneer, his message today is, "The son, the son, who'll take the son?" Because you see, whoever takes the son gets everything.

June 30

Be merciful, just as your Father is merciful.
~Luke 6:36 (NIV)

Some people court those who wear the latest fashions or have much money, wanting to associate with people who represent what they aspire (or wish) to be. Those who have been blessed with great beauty, wealth, or fame often look down on those with less, not wanting to waste their time on anyone who can't do something for them. What these people fail to realize is that those with less may be the friends they will someday need.

In an Aesop fable, a lion lay asleep in the forest, his great head resting on his paws. A timid little mouse came upon him unexpectedly, and in her fright and haste to get away, ran across the lion's nose. Awakened from his nap, the lion laid his huge paw angrily on the tiny creature to kill her.

"Spare me!" begged the poor mouse. "Please let me go, and some day I will surely repay you."

The lion was so amused at the idea of the little mouse being able to help the King of Beasts, he lifted up his paw and let her go.

Some weeks later, the lion was caught in a net. The hunters, who desired to carry the lion alive to their King, tied him to a tree while they went in search of a wagon to carry him.

Just then the little mouse happened to pass by, and seeing the lion's sad plight, went up to him and soon gnawed away the ropes of the net, freeing the lion.

"You have helped me, and now I have returned the favor. Was I not right— even a mouse can help a lion!" exclaimed the little mouse.

Whether you are the mouse or the lion, the moral is: Never forget the smallest friend is worthwhile. One version of Luke 6:36 instructs us to be compassionate, just as our Father is compassionate to us, while Job 34:19 avows God shows no partiality to princes, nor regards the rich more than the poor. Likewise, we should help anyone in need, regardless of his or her circumstances in life—or the ability to return the favor or give us something in return.

POST-IT MEDITATION FOR JUNE 30
I will remember all people are worth helping.

July 1

Let all who run to you for protection always sing joyful songs. Provide shelter for those who truly love you and let them rejoice.
~Psalm 5:11 (CEV)

Some years ago on a hot summer day in south Florida a little boy decided to go for a swim in the old swimming hole behind his house. In a hurry to dive into the cool water, he ran out the back door, leaving behind shoes, socks, and shirt as he went. He flew into the water, not realizing that as he swam toward the middle of the lake, an alligator was approaching the shore. His mother was watching out the window and gasped in terror as she spotted the huge alligator close to her son. In utter panic, she ran toward the water, yelling to her son as loudly as she could. The little boy became alarmed when he heard his mother's voice and made a U-turn to swim to her. It was too late. Just as he reached the edge of the dock, the alligator attacked.

From the dock, the mother grabbed her little boy by the arms as the alligator snatched his legs. That began a staggering tug-of-war between the two. The angry alligator was much stronger, but the mother doggedly determined not to let go. A farmer happened to drive by, heard her screams, raced from his truck with a rifle, took aim, and shot the alligator. Amazingly, after weeks in the hospital, the little boy recovered. His legs were savagely scarred by the vicious attack of the animal, and deep scratches marked his arms where his mother's fingernails dug into his flesh in her effort to hang on to her son. The newspaper reporter, who interviewed the boy after the trauma, asked if he would show him his scars. The boy lifted his pant legs. And then, with obvious pride, he said to the reporter, "But look at my arms. I have great scars on my arms, too. I have them because my mom wouldn't let go."

Most of us can identify with the little boy. We have scars, too. Not from an alligator but from our painful past. Many of the scars cut deeply and are ugly. Be that as it may, some serve as evidence God refused to let go. In the midst of our battles, he has been there holding on to us. God is always there to protect us, but sometimes we swim away from him. If we, like the little boy, will swim *toward* him, God will grab hold of us and pull us from the perils of life. Yes, we will have scars, but we can show them with pride as evidence that God held on to us in the struggles of our lives.

POST-IT MEDITATION FOR JULY 1
I am thankful, God, for the scars on my arms.

July 2

See how the farmer waits for the precious fruit of the earth, waiting patiently for it until it receives the early and the latter rain. You also be patient.
-James 5:7-8 (NKJV)

Digging in the earth, planting vegetables or fruits, and waiting for the harvest take work and patience. It would be easy to forget to water the ground when not even a green sprout can be seen, but gardeners know both early and late watering are required. If nature's rains fail to be sufficient, a wise person intervenes and keeps the soil moist until a tomato stalk or other plant raises its head toward the sky. Even then, waiting for the plant to grow high enough and strong enough to bear the weight of its fruit can be tiresome. But the anticipation, knowing in time a vine-ripe tomato or a sumptuous grape will be ready for picking, holds impatience at bay.

Many of life's activities reap instant products or gratification, and sometimes the quality is in direct relation to the time spent. In contrast, farming and gardening teach us homegrown vegetables and fruits are worth the wait. I can't think of anything more delicious than a freshly picked strawberry—a fruit that initially requires two years before blooming. But the taste of a sun-warmed, hand-picked strawberry cannot be matched by one purchased in a store.

Waiting on nature to do its work can teach us patience in other parts of our lives. In the 21st century, kids grow up wanting what they want when they want it. But some things are worth waiting for, and the expectancy of delight in the future brings hope. One man tells how prison changed the way he looked at life:

Over the last six years I have learned what patience is. Growing up I did not have this value, and it is a very important value to have. Now I can see if you are patient, you will almost always get what you want if you are supposed to have it. I gained patience when I lost my freedom. I knew I would eventually get it back in time.

I was locked up in prison for a period of six years. The first couple of years were the hardest. I was always stressed out about any and everything. Time was dragging by because I was always paying attention to it. Then, a fellow prisoner helped instill the value of patience in me. He told me it was possible he would never make it home, but being forbearing and believing he would made him a better man. After a while I realized he was right. Once I stopped paying attention to the days and just kept in mind I would be released when it was my time to go, it seemed my time got a little easier.

Now I am home and use the value of patience in a lot of my daily activities. I know for a fact sometimes life gets hard; if you don't get discouraged and stay serene, it will pay off it the end. So if you are having a hard time in life, be patient and it will eventually work out one way or the other.

Another man who has been in prison for 30 years also says the first few years were the most difficult. Faced with two life sentences, unable to envision the possibility of parole even in the distant future, he rebelled against rules and lashed out against guards. But then a prison minister told him his attitude only made his life more miserable. Even though his freedom might be decades away, he needed to accept where he was and quit counting the days until a possible parole. He didn't give up hope, but he learned patience—praying someday he will be released but living one day at a time without constantly fretting about his confinement.

Even though we may not be in prison, life can be tough for us in other ways. If we stay patient and refuse to be discouraged, our waiting will pay off in the end, just as it does for farmers and gardeners.

POST-IT MEDITATION FOR JULY 2
I will pray for patience as I wait for what I hope for in life.

July 3

Death and life are in the power of the tongue.
~*Proverbs 18:21 (ASV)*

Rev. A. Purnell Bailey told about a woman who bought eggs and butter from a farmer with a fine reputation not only for the quality of his products, but also for his promptness of delivery. Then one day, when the lady was expecting guests, he failed to come. On the next delivery, she spoke harshly to him. At the end of her tirade he said quietly, "I'm sorry if I caused you any inconvenience, but I had the misfortune of burying my mother yesterday."

Ashamed, the woman determined never to speak critically to anyone again until she fully understood the cause of the delay or other issue that irked her.

Have you ever wished you could recall something you said? Or, have your words ever gotten you in trouble? Have you created problems in relationships because of harsh or careless words? If we are truthful, most of us must answer "yes" to these questions. Despite our best intentions, we fall victim to our tongues.

Many of our errors in speech come because of haste. We speak before we think, often because we are defensive or argumentative. Proverbs 25:8 cautions us not to hastily argue our case. This is good advice since we can quickly make fools of ourselves when we react before gathering the facts.

When we speak impulsively, we are prone to interrupt others because we are so anxious to give our opinion we can't wait until we hear the other person's ideas. The bottom line—this reflects a tendency to think we know more than the individual who is talking.

Another negative habit of the tongue is being facetious, often saying one thing when we mean the opposite, attempting to soften the message with humor. We may pretend we are joking, but words can cut deeply. And, it's phony. Likewise, overly flattering someone is deceptive and in some instances, manipulative. We brag on someone with an ulterior motive in our heart—we "butter the person up" to get something we want. Proverbs 26:28 (NIV) advises, "A flattering mouth works ruin," so we need to be cautious not to hurt others in this way.

A third type of speech to avoid is gossip. Few of us will call ourselves "gossips," but most people participate in this negative form of communication at one level or another. At the worst extreme, gossip entails rumors and innuendos, often nasty and malicious. If we pass along stories others share with us, even without being intentionally hurtful, we fit the larger definition of a gossip. And, unfortunately, when we reveal secrets, whether accidentally or on purpose, we break the trust of another person. Such breaches can damage or destroy relationships, for as Proverbs 17:9 (NIV) states, "He who repeats a matter separates intimate friends."

The key to avoiding undesired ramifications of an idle or wicked tongue? Don't talk without thinking and don't talk too much. Proverbs 10:19 (NASB) reminds us, "When there are many words, transgression is unavoidable."

Adapted from Proverbs for Easier Living by Jo Berry

POST-IT MEDITATION FOR JULY 3
I will pray for restraint in what, how, and when I use my tongue.

July 4

For I the Lord thy God will hold thy right hand, saying unto thee: "Fear not, I will help thee."
~Isaiah 41:13 (NKJV)

Fear is an emotion we all experience; and when it takes hold, it can be difficult to shake.

One Fourth of July, after returning from a tour of duty in Iraq, a soldier found himself yelling, "Incoming!" at the sound of fireworks. As he screamed the warning, he dove to the ground, hands covering his head, his heart pounding as he waited for the all-clear signal.

Neighbors at the backyard barbeque quickly surrounded him, asking him if he was alright. As his wife crouched beside him, he got his bearings and realized the explosive sounds weren't from IEDs (improvised explosive devices).

The next year, the ex-soldier refused to go to the annual Fourth of July celebration held in his town, afraid he would embarrass himself again. While his wife and son went to the city park, he shut himself in his bedroom, cranking up the television volume to mute the terrifying booms.

The fear of fireworks wasn't the only challenge the Army veteran faced. He lost his job two years after returning from Iraq. After months of job-searching, the position he found paid only one-third of his former salary. But one day, when he visited a church that had helped his family financially, the pastor's words hit him in the gut: "We often feel alone with the challenges we face," he said, "but God is always with you." His eyes filled with tears, the man walked forward and accepted God in his life. Now, he wondered, could God help him overcome his deep fear of fireworks? His young son was begging him to go to the annual celebration, and he didn't want to disappoint him.

At a church meeting that week, the man told everyone how fireworks affected him. "About how sometimes, wars are never over." His church family gathered close to him. His wife put him on the prayer chain and posted a story about his struggle on the church's Facebook page. Encouraging messages came from everywhere, letting him know prayers were going up for him. "It was like having a whole new band of brothers I could count on."

Finally, the holiday arrived. The day went well, but at dusk, the new Christian got antsy. And then, someone said, "We've got your back, Patrick." Others came up to tell him they were praying for him, and then a whole crowd of his church friends gathered around. "So many people asking God to watch over me," the man thought. "Of all those I could surround myself with, was there anyone more powerful than God?" As the team lit the fuses, he prayed, "Lord, I know you're here and you'll be with me." As the first firework whistled into the air, he took a breath and kept watching.

For the first time in years, as he held his son on his shoulders and clasped his wife's hand, surrounded by people who loved him, Independence Day was beautiful.

When we know someone is afraid—whether realistically or unrealistically—we should do everything in our power to help alleviate the fear. The first step is to let the person know they are not alone in their anxiety—that we will be beside them in their distress. Second, we can pray for God to lift the burden of panic or terror from the person's heart and mind. Our presence and the power of God can turn apprehension into peace.

Adapted from a story in Guideposts

POST-IT MEDITATION FOR JULY 4
***I will say special prayers for those who protect our freedom
and for God's healing of their wounds—
physical and psychological.***

July 5

There is no fear in love, but perfect love drives out fear, because fear has to do with punishment. The one who fears is not made perfect in love.
~1 John 4:18 (NIV)

Holidays come and go. Yesterday across America, families celebrated Independence Day with cookouts and homemade ice cream, fireworks and cannon blasts. How many of those enjoying independence have ever wondered what happened to the 56 men who signed the Declaration of Independence?

Five signers, captured by the British as traitors (after all, we were British subjects at the time and were fighting the homeland for our freedom), were tortured to death. Twelve had their homes ransacked and burned. Two others lost their precious sons serving in the Revolutionary Army, while another had both of his sons captured. Nine of the signers fought themselves and died from wounds or hardships during the war.

These men came from all walks of life: Twenty-four were lawyers; eleven were merchants; nine were farmers and owned large plantations. They all believed in America and its ideals for freedom so fervently they were willing to risk death or capture. Some lost everything they had. Thomas McKeon, hounded by the British, was forced to move his family time and time again. While his family stayed in hiding, he served in Congress without pay. Before the war ended, he had lost all his possessions and lived in poverty. Similarly, Carter Braxton, a wealthy planter and trader from Virginia, had his ships stolen by the British Navy. Selling his home to pay his debts, he died in rags.

Eight men had their properties looted by vandals or soldiers. One man's wife was jailed by the British and died within a few months. John Hart was taken from his wife's bedside as she lay dying, while his 13 children fled for their lives. His fields and gristmill lay untended while he lived in forests and caves for more than a year. When he returned home, he found his wife dead and his children vanished. Not long afterward, he died of exhaustion and a broken heart.

These and similar stories tell of the sacrifices of men who believed in a cause: Men who risked their wealth and possessions—and even their families and their own lives—because they valued liberty. More importantly, in signing the Declaration of Independence, they relied "on the protection of the divine providence" as they "mutually pledge[d] to each other [their] lives, [their] fortunes, and [their] sacred honor." Today, that reliance is more critical than ever for all Americans.

POST-IT MEDITATION FOR JULY 5
The celebrations are past. I will pause to remember those who sacrificed for liberties too often taken for granted and will pray for God's providence.

July 6

For the Lord will be your confidence and will keep your foot from being caught.
~Proverbs 3:26 (ASV)

As a man was passing elephants standing outside a circus tent, he suddenly stopped, confused by the fact that these huge creatures were being held by only a small chain tied to their front legs. No fences, no cages. It was obvious the elephants could, at any time, break away from their bonds but for some reason, they did not.

The man saw a trainer nearby and asked why these animals just stood there and made no attempt to get away. "Well," the trainer said, "when they are very young and much smaller we used the same size chain to tie them and, at that age, it was enough to hold them. As they grow up, they are conditioned to believe they cannot break away. They believe the chain can still hold them, so they never try to break free."

The man was amazed. These animals could at any time break free from their bonds, but because they believed they couldn't, they were stuck right where they were.

A similar story about fleas illustrates the same moral:

Fleas can be trained by putting them in a jar with a top on it. Jumping is a natural movement for fleas, so they jump up and hit the top over and over again. As you watch them jump and hit the top, you will notice something interesting. The fleas continue to jump, but they are no longer jumping high enough to hit the top.

Then, you can take the top off and though the fleas continue to jump, they won't jump out of the jar. Once they conditioned themselves to jump just so high, that's all they can do.

Many times, people do the same thing. They restrict themselves and never reach their potential. Just like the fleas, they fail to jump higher, thinking they are doing all they can do. Or, like the elephants, who don't jerk on the chain because they don't believe they are strong enough to pull up the stake, they stay imprisoned by their past failures.

How many of us go through life hanging onto a belief that we cannot do something, simply because we failed at it once before?

Failure is part of learning; we should never give up against the struggles in life.

Like the elephants and fleas, if we believe we are locked into our existence, however bad it may be, we will never try to improve our lives. Perhaps, like the young elephants and the fleas, we learned early that when we tried, we failed, so we stopped trying. But if our faith kicks in, we can escape our defeatism and expect positive results by trusting God to give us the courage and strength to challenge the prison in which we are trapped. With God, we can break the chains holding us captive. After all, he "has begun a good work in [us] and will complete it..." (Philippians 1:6, ESV).

POST-IT MEDITATION FOR JULY 6
God wants me to have the life he has planned for me, and through belief in his direction and power, I can chart a course for my life.

July 7

For whoever wants to save their life will lose it, but whoever loses their life for me will find it.
~Matthew 16:25 (NIV)

"They Kept the Faith," a poem by Joseph Auslander, was published in the *Saturday Evening Post* on July 7, 1945. It begins with these lines:

> *Four men of God put out to sea;*
> *(Washington, Poling, Fox, and Goode)*
> *Their God was one, though their faiths were three,*
> *And the men who worshipped their God were free*
> *Where the Cross and Star together stood.*

The poem explains the men were of three different faiths: *Two were Protestant, one was Catholic, and the fourth was Jewish. They were off the coast of Greenland one cold, grey morning, when their ship, the Dorchester, was blasted. As the four men watched, the troops on board "stood frozen stark with fright" and "the fearsome waters boiled and burned." Jumping into action, the four men of God comforted the frantic, urging them to the floats. As they quieted terror, they also took time to bless the dead and pray as they strapped boys into life belts, leading the wounded into the boats. When the last life raft was filled and the last life jacket strapped on, a few still had no belts.*
Standing together, the four men of God knew the Dorchester was sinking fast; a cold, tumultuous sea beckoned the remaining few on the boat to a watery grave. Without a word among them, the four men stripped off their own life belts and handed them to the troops doomed to death without them. "Take these belts...God go with you as well," they spoke without a qualm. The poem closes, "They asked of no man whence he came, or at what altar did he pray."
In the eyes of the four men of God, religion made no difference—Jew and Gentiles were all the same—as they gave their own life belts to save others. In the same way, God sees every one of his children as worthy of saving—he doesn't care about our nationality, our gender, our ethnicity, our ideologies,

our financial status, our failures, or even our sins. All he sees is a child he created, and he sent his son to give up his own life to save each one.

POST-IT MEDITATION FOR JULY 7
I am thankful for true men of God. And I am thankful for a God who cares about everyone he created.

July 8

Like a welcome summer rain, humor may suddenly cleanse and cool the earth, the air, and you.
~Langston Hughes, American writer

A summer rain interrupted today's intense rays of sunlight, first with dark clouds and then with rolling claps of thunder before a deluge of water poured from the sky. I love such summer rains because they disappear as quickly as they open heaven's faucets—and because they cleanse and cool everything they touch. Green leaves become brighter and flowers become perkier. Hughes compares this refreshing of the earth and man to the effects of laughter. We can see the similarity, for at some time in our lives, most of us have remarked, "I'm laughing to keep from crying."

Laughter brings an immediate physical and emotional release from stress and worry. It distracts us from negative emotions like anger and guilt. And, laugher is contagious and can release tension in relationships. Quicker than a summer shower can refresh the earth and air, humor alters our feelings. Laughter is thus to be treasured—and should never be abandoned. Even during our darkest hours, we can remember past laughter and know we will one day laugh another time. As Bildad reminded Job in Job 8:21, God will always let us laugh again. If laugher was possible after all Job lost, then surely we can hope to find laughter, even in sorrow. Indeed, when grief over the death of my husband threatened to drown me in a torrent of tears, a funny story about my beloved brought me momentary relief. And, a picture of my spouse lying on the sofa with all three of his massive Old English Sheepdogs sprawled on top of him brought a smile to my sad face and a chuckle to my tight throat.

Laughter is so good for us we should seek it out. One way is to spend time with kids. As Art Linkletter knew, kids say the darndest things. A couple of examples for today:

One little boy was overhead praying, "Lord, if you can't make me a better boy, don't worry about it. I'm having a real good time like I am."

A three-year-old girl had her own interpretation of the Lord's Prayer, including this line, "Lead us not into temptations," she prayed, "but deliver us from email."

Evil and email—they not only sound alike but have some of the same attributes!

POST-IT MEDITATION FOR JULY 8
God, thank you for rain, laughter, and children.

July 9

Love each other deeply. Honor others more than yourselves.
~Romans 12:10 (NIRV)

Once upon a time all feelings and emotions went to a coastal island for a vacation. According to their nature, each was having a good time. Suddenly, a warning of an impending storm was announced, and everyone was advised to evacuate the island.

The announcement caused sudden panic. All rushed to their boats. Even damaged boats were quickly repaired and commissioned for duty.

Yet, Love did not wish to flee quickly. There was so much to do. But as the clouds darkened, Love realized it was time to leave. Alas, there were no boats to spare. Love looked around with hope.

Just then Prosperity passed by in a luxurious boat. Love shouted, "Prosperity, could you please take me in your boat?"

"No," replied Prosperity, "my boat is full of precious possessions, gold and silver. There is no place for you."

A little later Vanity came by in a beautiful boat. Again Love shouted, "Could you help me, Vanity? I am stranded and need a lift. Please take me with you."

Vanity responded haughtily, "No, I cannot take you with me. My boat will get soiled with your muddy feet."

Sorrow passed by after some time. Again, Love asked for help. But it was to no avail. "No, I cannot take you with me. I am so sad. I want to be by myself."

When Happiness passed by a few minutes later, Love again called for assistance. But Happiness was so happy it did not look around, hardly concerned about anyone.

Love was growing restless and dejected. Just then somebody called out, "Come Love, I will take you with me." Love did not know who was being so magnanimous but jumped on the boat, greatly relieved she would reach a safe place.

On getting off the boat, Love met Knowledge. Puzzled, Love inquired, "Knowledge, do you know who so generously gave me a lift just when no one else wished to help?"

Knowledge smiled, "Oh, that was Time."

"And why would Time stop to pick me and take me to safety?" Love wondered.

Knowledge smiled with deep wisdom and replied, "Because only Time knows your true greatness and what you are capable of. Only Love can bring peace and joy in this world."

The important message is that when we are prosperous, we overlook love. When we feel important, we forget love. Even in happiness and sorrow we neglect love. Only with time do we realize the importance of love. Why wait that long? Why not make love a part of your life today?

POST-IT MEDITATION FOR JULY 9
God, may I never let other emotions come before love.

July 10

For God so loved the world that he gave his only son....
~John 3:16 (ESV)

Sometimes we doubt extraordinary experiences, but this story removes all doubt:

In a church service long ago, a pastor introduced one of his dearest friends, who was to be the guest minister that evening. With that, an elderly man stepped up to the pulpit and began to speak. "A father and son and a friend of his son were sailing off the Pacific coast," he began, "when a fast approaching storm blocked any attempt to get back to shore. Even though the father was an experienced sailor, the waves were so high he could not keep the boat upright, and the three were swept into the ocean as the boat capsized."

The old man hesitated for a moment, making eye contact with two teenagers who were, for the first time since the service began, looking somewhat interested in his story. The aged minister continued: "Grabbing a rescue line, the father had to make the most excruciating decision of his life—to which boy he would throw the other end of the life line. He only had seconds to make the decision. The father knew his son was a Christian but knew his son's friend was not. The agony of his decision could not be matched by the torrent of waves. As the father yelled out, "I love you, son!" he threw the life line to his son's friend. By the time the father had pulled the friend back to the capsized boat, his son had disappeared beneath the raging swells into the black of night. His body was never recovered.

By this time, the teenagers were sitting up straight in the pew, anxiously waiting the next words to come out of the old minister's mouth. "The father," he continued, "knew his son would step into eternity with Jesus, and he could not bear the thought of his son's friend stepping into an eternity without Jesus. Therefore, he sacrificed his son to save the son's friend. How great is the love of God that he should do the same for us. Our heavenly father sacrificed his only son that we could be saved. I urge you to accept his offer to rescue you and take hold of the life line he is throwing out to you." As silence filled the room, the old man turned and sat back down in his chair.

Within minutes after the service ended, the two teenagers were at the old man's side. "That was a nice story," politely stated one of the boys, "but I don't think it was a very realistic for a father to give up his only son's life with only a hope that the other boy would become a Christian."

"Well, you've got a point there," the old man replied, glancing down at his worn Bible. A big smile broadened his narrow face. He once again looked up at the boys and said, "It sure isn't very realistic, is it? But I'm standing here today to tell you that story gives me a glimpse of what it must have been like for God to give up his Son for me. You see, I was that father—and your pastor is my son's friend."

POST-IT MEDITATION FOR JULY 10
Dear Father, help me truly appreciate the great sacrifice you made.

July 11

The pride of your heart has deceived you, you who live in the clefts of the rocks and make your home on the heights, you who say to yourself, "Who can bring me down to the ground?"
~*Obadiah 1:3 (NIV)*

I once loved yucca plants, and years ago, despite his reservations, my husband agreed to a small bed of the prickly bushes. I carefully tended the three plants I had placed in the ground, and the first year they were strikingly beautiful. The next year the three plants had become five, and by the third year, we had twelve yuccas spilling outside their bed into our yard. Now I understood my husband's reluctance. After about five years, when the prolific plants threatened to take over our back yard, I agreed they had to go. So we started digging. What we found was an intricate, knotty root system that fought us every step of the way. Finally, after days of chopping with a pickax, we removed every smidgen of yucca roots. I would miss them, but I knew I couldn't keep even one.

About two years later, one spring day as I walked through the yard, I saw the heads of several yuccas poking their way through the ground. They had not been so easily defeated. For the rest of our years at that location, we fought them mightily, but we never totally won.

In her book *Proverbs for Easier Living*, Jo Berry compares pride to such plants: "a sin that is deeply imbedded in our soul, intrinsic to our nature, one that gives birth to many other sins; that rears its ugly head when we are certain we have extracted it." Berry notes that just as plants need roots to grow, evil also needs roots—"an unholy source that will keep it alive: and that root in the lives of God's righteous is the sin of pride."

Pride puts down intricate roots that expand our ego, making it difficult for us to consider how other people feel; when we glorify ourselves, we look down on them, thinking we are better than they. And just as the yuccas sent new sprouts out of the ground, our pride generates new sins—often jealousy, greed, and even disgust. Pride can also cause us to be stubborn; just as the yucca roots refused to be eradicated, our pride lets our willful ways find the way to the surface even when we think we have them conquered. Only when we yield the fertile ground of our lives to God can humility imbed so deeply in our lives that pride can't regrow.

POST-IT MEDITATION FOR JULY 11
God, help me dig out pride in my life, and with your grace, replace it with humility.

July 12

Whoever belongs to God accepts what he says.
~John 8:47 (ERV)

A man was hiking in the Rocky Mountains when he spied a cougar staring at him from the trail below. As the cougar took his first running leap, the man started scurrying up the mountain, fearing for his life. He ran as hard as he could until he was at the edge of a cliff with the cougar in hot pursuit. Looked over the edge, the man knew he faced certain death if he jumped.

Shaking, the man looked back at the cougar and felt hopeless as the ferocious animal closed in. The man again glanced down to the drop of a thousand feet and then looked up to the heavens and yelled out, "Dear God, if you are there, please help. I will do anything you ask but please help."

Suddenly a voice came booming down from heaven, "You will do anything I ask?" it questioned.

The man, shocked to hear a reply to his plea, yelled back, "I will gladly do anything you ask, but please save me."

The voice from heaven then replied, "There is one way to save you, but it will take courage and faith."

The cougar was still growling a few feet above the man. "Please, Lord, tell me what I must do and I will do it. Your will is my will."

The voice from heaven then said, "All right then, jump."

The man looked down again, seeing nothing but death below. He looked up at the hungry cougar a few feet away. Then he glared up at the heavens and yelled, "Is there anyone else up there?"

Many times we are like the man tottering on the edge of the cliff—praying for God's help but failing to recognize it when it is offered. We should know God's voice because we know *him*, just as Christ said his sheep hear his voice and know him (John 10:14-15). If we listen carefully with a heart full of faith, we can hear not only the father, but also his son and his holy spirit. Faith is the key—the man trapped on the cliff heard God's voice, but he didn't trust him enough to accept his instruction as his salvation. We must not only hear God's voice; we must follow his command.

POST-IT MEDITATION FOR JULY 12
I will seek to know God more fully so I can recognize his voice when he speaks to me.

July 13

Therefore I do not run like someone running aimlessly; I do not fight like a boxer beating the air.
~I Corinthians 9:26 (NIV)

Have you ever been forced to reconsider your priorities—after it is too late? The man in the following story couldn't make up for time lost with one person, but he could change his focus for the future.

It had been some time since Jack had seen the old man. College, girls, career, and life itself got in the way. In fact, Jack moved clear across the country in pursuit of his dreams. There, in the rush of his busy life, Jack had little time to think about the past, and often no time to spend with his wife and son. He was working on his future, and nothing could stop him.

Over the phone, his mother told him, "Mr. Belser died last night. The funeral is Wednesday." Memories flashed through his mind like an old newsreel as he sat quietly remembering his childhood days.

"Jack, did you hear me?"

"Oh, sorry, Mom. Yes, I heard you. It's been so long since I thought of him. I'm sorry, but I honestly thought he died years ago," Jack said.

"Well, he didn't forget you. Every time I saw him he'd ask how you were doing. He'd reminisce about the many days you spent over 'his side of the fence' as he put it," Mom told him.

"I loved that old house he lived in," Jack said.

"You know, Jack, after your father died, Mr. Belser stepped in to make sure you had a man's influence in your life," she said.

"He's the one who taught me carpentry," he said. "I wouldn't be in this business if it weren't for him. He spent a lot of time teaching me things he thought were important...Mom, I'll be there for the funeral," Jack said.

As busy as he was, he kept his word. Jack caught the next flight to his hometown. Mr. Belser's funeral was small and uneventful. He had no children of his own, and most of his relatives had passed away.

The night before he had to return home, Jack and his Mom stopped by to see the old house next door one more time. Standing in the doorway, Jack paused for a moment. It was like crossing over into another dimension, a leap through space and time. The house was exactly as he remembered. Every step held memories. Every picture, every piece of furniture...Jack stopped suddenly.

"What's wrong, Jack?" his Mom asked.

"The box is gone," he said.

"What box?" Mom asked.

"There was a small gold box that he kept locked on top of his desk. I must have asked him a thousand times what was inside. All he'd ever tell me was 'the thing I value most,'" Jack said.

It was gone. Everything about the house was exactly how Jack remembered it, except for the box. He figured someone from the Belser family had taken it.

"Now I'll never know what was so valuable to him," Jack said. "I better get some sleep. I have an early flight home, Mom."

It had been about two weeks since Mr. Belser died. Returning home from work one day Jack discovered a note in his mailbox. "Signature required on a package. No one at home. Please stop by the main post office within the next three days," the note read.

Early the next day Jack retrieved the package. The small box was old and looked like it had been mailed a hundred years ago. The handwriting was difficult to read, but the return address caught his attention.

"Mr. Harold Belser" it read. Jack took the box out to his car and ripped open the package. There inside was the gold box and an envelope. Jack's hands shook as he read the note inside.

"Upon my death, please forward this box and its contents to Jack Bennett. It's the thing I valued most in my life." A small key was taped to the letter. His heart racing, tears filling his eyes, Jack carefully unlocked the box. There inside he found a beautiful gold pocket watch. Running his fingers slowly over the finely etched casing, he unlatched the cover. Inside he found these words engraved: "Jack, Thanks for your time! Harold Belser."

"The thing he valued most...was...my time." Jack held the watch for a few minutes, then called his office and cleared his appointments for the next two days. "Why?" Janet, his assistant asked.

"I need some time to spend with my son," he said.

"Oh, by the way, Janet...thanks for your time!"

POST-IT MEDITATION FOR JULY 13
Every day, every minute, every breath truly is a gift from God.
I will try not to waste even one, giving some to those I love.

July 14

Always be humble and gentle. Be patient and accept each other with love.
~Ephesians 4:2 (ERV)

If someone exasperates us, we quickly accuse them of wrongdoing—of being hateful to us, trying to control us, disrespecting us, treating us harshly, or any other number of actions that annoy or aggravate us.

It is unlikely we can change another person's behaviors, so we may just need to be tolerant, realizing the person may be going through problems or be worried about situations about which we know nothing. We may not like what the other person says or does, but in the absence of control, compassion and charity may be less stressful than resentment.

The following story exemplifies such charity at the highest level:

A doctor entered the hospital in a hurry after being called in for an urgent surgery. He changed his clothes and went directly to the surgery block where he found the boy's father pacing back and forth in the hall. Seeing him, the dad yelled: "Why did you take all this time to come? Don't you know that my son's life is in danger? Don't you have a sense of responsibility?"

The doctor gently said: "I am sorry, I wasn't in the hospital and I came as fast as I could after receiving the call…. And now, I wish you'd calm down so that I can do my work."

"Calm down? What if your son was in this room right now, would you calm down?" the father asked angrily.

The doctor smiled somberly and replied: "I will say what Job said in the Holy Book: 'From dust we came and to dust we return, blessed be the name of God.' Doctors cannot prolong lives. Go and intercede for your son; we will do our best by God's grace."

"Giving advice when you're not concerned is so easy," grumbled the father.

The surgery took some hours, after which the doctor came out, telling the man, "Thank goodness, your son is saved!" And without waiting for the father's reply, he rushed out the door, saying, "If you have any questions, ask the nurse!"

"Why is he so arrogant? He couldn't wait long enough for me to ask about my son's state?" the father asked with obvious irritation when he saw the nurse minutes after the doctor left.

The nurse answered, tears falling down her face: "His son died two days ago in a road accident—he was at the cemetery when we called him for your son's surgery. And now that he saved your son's life, he left running to finish his son's burial."

Never judge when you don't know what is happening in another person's life. Instead, as the Swiss psychiatrist Carl Jung advised, use an exasperating situation to examine your own life.

SourcE OF DOCTOR STORY: http://www.turnbacktogod.com/category/stories

POST-IT MEDITATION FOR JULY 14
With love, I will pray for patience to allow for what appear to be others'
faulty and uncaring attitudes, realizing they may have
deeper concerns than my own.

July 15

Seek first the kingdom of God and his righteousness, and all these things
will be given to you as well.
~Matthew 6:33 (NIV)

God created humans with a free will—we were not programmed to love him or others, to do good, or to serve him. We have the capacity to choose between right and wrong. But our choices have consequences, some we might never expect. The following questions by an unknown writer should shake us up—what would we do if our actions boomeranged on us?

What if God couldn't take the time to bless us today because we couldn't take the time to thank him yesterday?

What if God decided to stop leading us tomorrow because we didn't follow him today?

What if we never saw another flower bloom because we grumbled when God sent the rain?

What if God didn't walk with us today because we failed to recognize he made the day?

What if God took away his message because we failed to listen to the messenger?

What if God didn't send his only begotten Son because he wanted us to pay the price for sin?

What if the door to the church was closed because we did not open the door of our heart?

What if God stopped loving and caring for us because we failed to love and care for others?

What if God would not hear us today because we would not listen to him yesterday?

What if God answered our prayers the way we answer his call to service?

What if God met our needs the way we give him our lives?

God encourages us to make the right choices, but he doesn't force his will upon us. Just as he told the Israelites, "Today I have given you the choice between life and death, between blessings and curses," he also challenges us to choose. At the same time, we should heed the consequences of our choices, for once again, the words spoken to the Israelites apply to us: "Now I call on heaven and earth to witness the choice you make. Oh, that you would choose life…you can make this choice by loving the Lord your God, obeying him, and committing yourself firmly to him. This is the key to your life… (Deuteronomy 30:19-20, NLT).

POST-IT MEDITATION FOR JULY 15
With God's help, I will choose wisely, seeking his path to righteousness.

July 16

He has told you, O man, what is good; and what does the LORD require of you but to do justice, and to love kindness, and to walk humbly with your God?"
~Micah 6:8 (ESV)

Moses and Hitler were both charismatic leaders. Each had the ability to convince others to follow him, regardless of the cost. Yet, one used his power and influence to lead his people out of bondage—to save a nation, while the other led his people to destroy and be destroyed.

Although God formed us with a free will, allowing us to choose between right and wrong, after we become Christians, he does have expectations, prescribing a way of life that mirrors the example his son set while on earth. The framework for these expectations comes from Romans 8:29: God created us for the purpose of glorifying him by becoming more like Christ. The actions and attributes of Christ dictate that we live with compassion, humility, justice, kindness, loyalty, love, self-sacrifice, submission, and wisdom—such a Christ-like life benefits us now and in the future.

Claiming to be a Christian carries an obligation to live up to the name, because the word "Christian" can become tainted if what we profess doesn't line up with our conduct. 1 John 2:3-6 tells us that whoever alleges to live in him must walk as Jesus walked. Our very nature is sinful, so how is this possible? The key is getting to know Christ—to read about him, his life, and his works.

As we learn more about the man who walked on earth, faced temptation, experienced physical needs, and had friends who denied and betrayed him, we see how he handled life's trials. Because he confronted the everyday challenges we tackle, like the imprisoned Paul we should say, "I want to know Christ and the power of his resurrection and the fellowship of sharing in his sufferings…" (Philippians 3:10, NIV).

The most touching story I have ever heard about one human being sharing in the sufferings of another tells of Dick Hoyt, a 66-year-old man, whose 46-year-old son was born a spastic quadriplegic with cerebral palsy, a non-speaking person who achieved independence and inclusion in community activities, sports, school, and the workplace, and graduated from Boston University. Dick, determined to raise his son as "normally" as possible, gave him extraordinary experiences, pushing and pulling him across the country and over hundreds of finish lines—when Dick runs, Rick is in a wheelchair that Dick is pushing. When Dick cycles, Rick is in the seat-pod from his wheelchair, attached to the front of the bike. When Dick swims, Rick is in a small but heavy, firmly stabilized boat being pulled by Dick.

Dick Hoyt raised his son as Christ would have raised him. He is an inspiration to all parents.

AUTHOR'S NOTE: You can read about the Hoyts' adventurous life at http://www.teamhoyt. com/about/index.html. To get the full impact of the inspiring story, watch the YouTube video that depicts this father's extraordinary love for his son:

http://www.youtube.com/watch?v=flRvsO8m_KI&feature=player_embedded.

POST-IT MEDITATION FOR JULY 16
God, help me to be inspired to live a Christ-like life.

July 17

And let us not grow weary of doing good, for in due season we will reap, if we do not give up.
~Galatians 6:9 (NKJV)

It's harvest time—after tilling, planting, fertilizing, and weeding, gardeners can pick fresh okra, tomatoes, and whatever else went in the ground many weeks ago. Key words—whatever we put in the ground. If we didn't plant watermelons, we can't harvest watermelons. If we didn't plant squash, we can't harvest squash. We can only harvest what we planted. So it is with our lives.

Denis Waitley tells about a speech by Madame Chiang Kai-shek that his grandmother had copied by hand while hearing it on the radio during World War II.

It was a tough time for the Chinese as they struggled against the Japanese armies, but Madame Chiang had wisdom beyond the daily newscasts that predicted the Japanese would take over not only China but also the United States. And so she told her people and all the people of the world:

If the past has taught us anything, it is that every cause brings its effect, every action has a consequence. We Chinese have a saying: "If a man plants melons, he will reap melons; if he sows beans, he will reap beans." And this is true of everyone's life; good begets good, and evil leads to evil.

True enough, the sun shines on the saint and the sinner alike, and too often it seems that the wicked prosper. But we can say with certainty that, with the individual as with the nation, the flourishing of the wicked is an illusion, for unceasingly, life keeps books on us all.

In the end, we are all the sum total of our actions. Character cannot be counterfeited, nor can it be put on and cast off as if it were a garment to meet the whim of the moment. Like the markings on wood which are ingrained in the very heart of the tree, character requires time and nurturing for growth and development.

Thus, also, day by day, we write our own destiny; for inexorably…we become what we do.

As Christians, we will reap what we sow in our lives. Our salvation is assured—we do not earn it by works; it is a free gift if we accept it. But if we sow seeds of kindness, love, generosity, and other worthy plants, our harvest will be bountiful.

POST-IT MEDITATION FOR JULY 17
God, help me to sow plants pleasing
to you and nourishing to me.

July 18

Give to others, and you will receive. You will be given much. It will be poured into your hands—more than you can hold.
~Luke 6:38 (ESV)

Just as we reap what we sow, we are given back what we give and more.

A woman named Pam gave her unborn son to God. Serving as a missionary in the Philippines, along with her husband Bob, she had prayed for a fifth child. Before discovering she was pregnant, she contracted amoebic dysentery, an infection of the intestine caused by a parasite found in contaminated food or drink. In a coma, not knowing she was pregnant, Pam was treated with strong antibiotics.

Not much later, when the doctor discovered Pam was pregnant, he advised her to abort the baby for her own safety and because the medicines had caused irreversible damage to the fetus. Her fervent faith would not allow an abortion, and Pam hoped and believed God would give her an unblemished child, one without the devastating disabilities physicians had predicted.

Over the next few months, Pam almost lost the baby four times, but she still refused to abort the fetus. Together, she and her husband prayed, committing the child to God. If he would give them a son, they would name him Timothy and make him a preacher.

Despite all of her problems during pregnancy, Pam gave birth to a healthy boy on August 14, 1987. Today, Pam's youngest son is fulfilling the promise his parents made to God. He is a preacher—preaching in prisons, serving with his father's ministry in the Philippines when he can, and making hospital visits. He also plays football. Pam and Bob's son is Tim Tebow, the University of Florida star quarterback who became the first sophomore in history to win college football's highest award, the Heisman Trophy. From there he moved to a star quarterback role with the Denver Broncos, where he used his position as an incredible platform for Christian witness. Some call him the Mile-High Messiah. In 2012, Tim was traded to the New York Jets, where undoubtedly he will still take the knee in homage to his Christ.

Pam and Bob Tebow gave their son to their Lord, and he has given back good measure, running over, not just to his parents, but to the world.

POST-IT MEDITATION FOR JULY 18
With God's help, I will give him my life and my family for his glory.

July 19

When the storms of life are raging, stand by me.
~Charles A. Tindley, American minister and gospel song writer

In his master design for creation, God gave the eagle exceptional ability to know a storm is approaching long before it comes close. When the eagle senses the coming threat, it flies to a high spot and waits for the winds to arrive. As the storm hits, it sets its wings at a precise tilt, allowing the currents to pick it up and lift it above the storm. While the storm rages below, the eagle soars above it, using the very danger that threatened it to escape peril.

Like the eagle, when the storms of life loom in the distance, we can rise above them by using the gale to lift our minds toward God. Instead of being overcome, we can use our faith to protect us. If sickness strikes, tragedy hits, disappointment descends, or failure beats us down, we may not be able to escape the turmoil, but we can allow God's power to raise us up, enabling us to soar above the storm.

Tindley's old song, "Stand by Me," captures the essence of surviving storms:

If the world tosses us like a ship upon the sea, the God who rules wind and water will stand by us.

In the midst of tribulation when the hosts of hell attack and our strength begins to fail, the God who never lost a battle will stand by us.

Even with our faults and failures, God will stand by us just as he did David and Moses.

When our friends misunderstand us, the God who knows our heart will stand by us.

When we are being persecuted, the same God who saved Paul and Silas will stand by us.

And most importantly of all, when we grow old and feeble and our lives become a burden, our God will stand by us.

The burdens in life can't weigh us down if we claim God's promise that he will "ride across the heavens to help us, across the skies in majestic splendor" (Deuteronomy 33:26, NLT).

POST-IT MEDITATION FOR JULY 19
I will count on God to help me rise above the storms of life.

July 20

That day is lost if one has not laughed.
~French proverb

How many days of our lives do we go without smiling—even one time? What wonderful benefits we miss if we walk around with a frown or stoic expression on our faces! When we are sad or depressed, and find it difficult to smile, sometimes a child can lighten our mood and bring a peal of laughter to our day.

One day a four-year-old was at her pediatrician's office for a checkup. Trying to relax the child, as the doctor looked into her ears with an otoscope he asked, "Do you think I'll find Big Bird in here?" The scared little girl didn't say a word. Next, as the doctor pressed her tongue down and looked at her throat, he wondered aloud if he would find a Cookie Monster down there. Still, the child stayed silent. Then, the doctor put a stethoscope to her chest. As he listed to her heart beat, he asked, ""Do you think I'll hear Barney in there?" Without a blink, the little girl replied, "Oh, no. God is in my heart. Barney's on my underpants."

If you read this story without a smile or a laugh, you need to recalibrate your humor meter.

Proverbs 15:13 tells us a glad heart makes a cheerful face. And we can have a glad heart because, as the little girl knew, God lives within it. Though we may have problems and even tragedies in our lives, we can be grateful we have a God who cares, a God who will give us the strength to bear our burdens, and a God who will walk with us wherever we go.

Isaiah 41-43 gives us the assurance we are never alone: When we go through deep waters, he will be with us. When we walk through fire, he will not let it consume us. For, he says, "Fear thou not, for I am with thee; be not dismayed, for I am thy God" (41:10, ESV). These words don't mean we will never be hurt. Certainly, we know people drown and people die in fires; others die in earthquakes and tornados—or car wrecks or plane crashes. The assurance is not that such events will never happen; it is simply that God will be with us through fire or flood, through good times and bad. With this assurance, we should pause when life seems overwhelming and look for a child or another source of a good laugh. It will help relieve our stress and show God we can leave our problems in his capable hands.

POST-IT MEDITATION FOR JULY 20
When life is tough, I will remember the old adage, "Laughter is the best medicine," knowing laughter is one of God's gifts.

July 21

Set your mind on things above, not on things on the earth.
~*Colossians 3:2 (NKJV)*

In many ways, humans sometimes act like buzzards, bats, and bumblebees.

*If a **buzzard** is put in a pen six or eight feet square, open at the top, it will be a total prisoner, despite its ability to fly. Just as an airplane goes down a runway before soaring toward the sky, in its natural habitat the buzzard begins flight from the ground after running 10 to 12 feet, But, without space to run, the buzzard will not attempt to fly, remaining jailed in a cage with no top. Nothing in science says the buzzard couldn't begin its flight without its customary 10-12 feet of running—6 or 8 feet would be sufficient. But the buzzard doesn't know that, and he doesn't even try to fly upward toward freedom.*

We sometimes act like a buzzard when an escape route from our problems lies straight above. The passageway to peace is open, if we just look up. We don't need a running start—all we have to do is look skyward, allowing our spirit to lift us toward God.

Bats *fly at night, and they are quite nimble, but they never take off from a level place. If a bat is placed on flat ground, all it does is shuffle about helplessly until it finally reaches some slight elevation from which it can throw itself into the air. Then, it takes off like a flash.*

When our lives seem hopeless, we shuffle around. Like bats, we fear trying to fly without certain conditions, so we amble about until we find the right place and the right time and place to take a leap toward our heavenly father.

*And, then there is the **bumblebee**. If it is dropped into an open glass, it becomes like the buzzard, failing to fly out the opening at the top. Although quick and agile* *in the air, in its glass-walled prison, it flounders round and round, hitting the glass on all sides but never seeing the exodus just above its head.*

Human beings, like the bumblebee, struggle mightily against problems and frustrations, hitting our head against a wall, never realizing the answer is right there above us. All we have to do is look up and let God do the rest.
SOURCE OF BUZZARD, BAT, AND BUMBLE STORY: http://www.indianchild.com

POST-IT MEDITATION FOR JULY 21
When the problems, worries, and anxieties of life come,
I will look up for help.

July 22

I assure you that when you have done it for one of the least of these brothers and sisters of mine, you have done it for me.
~Matthew 25:40 (CEB)

Christians occasionally get caught up in activities they believe serve God and miss the ones that would bring him the most joy.

Ruth opened the letter from her mailbox and noticed it had no stamp or post-mark—only her name and address—then read its short message: "Dear Ruth: I'm going to be in your neighborhood Saturday afternoon, and I would like to visit. Love always, Jesus."

Ruth's hands were shaking as she placed the letter on the table. "Why would the Lord want to visit me? I'm nobody special. I don't have anything to offer; my kitchen cabinets are bare. I'll have to run down to the store and buy something for dinner." Reaching for her purse, she counted out its contents. Five dollars and forty cents. "Well, I can get some bread and cold cuts, at least." She threw on her coat and hurried out the door. She bought a loaf of French bread, a half-pound of sliced turkey, and a carton of milk, leaving a grand total of twelve cents to last her until Monday. Nonetheless, she felt good as she headed home, her meager offerings tucked under her arm.

Ruth had been so absorbed in her dinner plans she hadn't noticed two figures huddled in the alleyway until she heard the words: "Hey, lady, can you help us?" A man and a woman, both of them dressed in little more than rags, stood looking at her. "Look lady, I ain't got a job, and my wife and I have been living out here on the street, and, well, now it's getting cold and we're getting kinda hungry and, well, if you could help us lady, we'd really appreciate it." Ruth looked at them both. They were dirty and smelled badly. "Sir, I'd like to help you, but I'm a poor woman myself. All I have is a few cold cuts and some bread, and I'm having an important guest for dinner tonight, and I was planning on serving that to him." "Yeah, well, okay lady. I understand. Thanks anyway."

The man put his arm around the woman's shoulders, turned, and headed back into the alley. As she watched them leave, Ruth felt a familiar twinge in her heart. "Sir, wait!" The couple stopped and turned as she ran down the alley after them. "Look, why don't you take this food. I'll figure out something else to serve my guest." She handed the man her grocery bag. "Thank you, lady. Thank you very much!"

"Yes, thank you!" It was the man's wife, and Ruth could see now that she was shivering. "You know, I've got another coat at home. Why don't you take this one?" Ruth unbuttoned her jacket and slipped it over the woman's shoulders. Then smiling, she turned and walked back to the street...without her coat and with nothing to serve her guest. Ruth was chilled by the time she reached her front door, and worried, too. The Lord was coming to visit, and she didn't have anything to offer him. As she started in her door, she noticed another envelope in her mailbox. "That's odd. The mailman doesn't usually come twice in one day." She took the envelope out of the box and opened it. "Dear Ruth: It was so good to see you again. Thank you for the lovely meal. And thank you, too, for the beautiful coat. Love always, Jesus."

The air was still cold, but even without her coat, Ruth no longer noticed.

SOURCE: http://www.websites-host.com/insp/istories.html

POST-IT MEDITATION FOR JULY 22
When I see a stranger in need, I will remember Matthew 25:40.

July 23

Treat others the same way you want them to treat you.
~Luke 6:31 (NASB)

Healthy relationships—between parents and children, brothers and sisters, husbands and wives, or friend and friend—don't carry unresolved baggage. That's because resentment and anger that aren't dealt with create tension, even when it is unspoken. And tension makes it difficult to let the positives in a relationship outweigh the negatives. Every relationship has both good and bad, and communication about both is essential if love is to prevail.

Every harsh word, every angry gesture, and every indignant look chip away at love, damaging the relationship. Why is it that so often we treat strangers with respect and consideration and then treat someone we love with contempt and criticism? Even worse, if a person extends an olive branch and we reject it, more injury occurs.

When the relationship becomes so broken we cannot discuss our hurts, then it may be impossible to heal the wounds. Unfortunately, some people see communication about past or present injuries as an opportunity to win. And while one person may win in a given situation, human nature ensures the defeated person will go to extraordinary lengths to make sure the next victory doesn't go to the winner of the last confrontation.

Communication shouldn't be a win-lose proposition. The purpose of communication is to understand the other person's perspective, not just to present our side of the issue. The goal is to have two winners. A win/win, although it may be difficult to see at the time, builds a better, more trusting relationship than a win/lose situation. That doesn't mean two people must agree on every point or in every discussion. The key is to disagree about the matter in question, not to attack one another. As Proverbs 10:12 (NIV) says, "Hatred stirs up strife, but love covers all wrongs."

If we love someone, we should be tolerant of him or her. No one is perfect, and few of us have room to criticize the faults of others. If we act with love instead of bitterness and contempt, healthy relationships that honor not only the other person but also God will be produced.

High on a hilltop overlooking the beautiful city of Venice, Italy, there lived an old man who was a genius. Legend had it he could answer any question anyone might ask of him. Two of the local boys figured they could fool the old man, so they caught a small bird and headed for his residence.

One of the boys held the little bird in his hands and asked the old man if the bird was dead or alive. Without hesitation the old man said, "Son, if I say to you that the bird is alive, you will close your hands and crush him to death. If I say the bird is dead, you will open your hands and he will fly away. You see, son, in your hands you hold the power of life and death."

In your hands you hold the power to destroy relationships or set them free for new life by releasing resentment and anger. Your hands are capable, but they must be used—and for the right actions—to reap the rewards that result from healthy relationships.

POST-IT MEDITATION FOR JULY 23
I will try to prevent turning little annoyances into major disagreements by letting love rule.

July 24

For who knows what is good for a person in life, during the few and meaningless days they pass through like a shadow? Who can tell them what will happen under the sun after they are gone?
~Ecclesiastes 6:12 (NIV)

Two traveling angels stopped to spend the night in the home of a wealthy family. The family was rude and refused to let the angels stay in the mansion's guest room. Instead, the angels were given a space in the cold basement. As they made their bed on the hard floor, the older angel saw a hole in the wall and repaired it. When the younger angel asked why, the older angel replied, "Things aren't always what they seem."

The next night the pair came to rest at the house of a very poor, but very hospitable, farmer and his wife. After sharing what little food they had, the couple let the angels sleep in their bed where they could have a good night's rest. When the sun came up the next morning, the angels found the farmer and his wife in tears. Their only cow, whose milk had been their sole income, lay dead in the field.

The younger angel was infuriated and asked the older angel, "How could you have let this happen? The first man had everything, yet you helped him," she accused. "The second family had so little but was willing to share everything, and you let their cow die."

"Things aren't always what they seem," the older angel replied. "When we stayed in the basement of the mansion, I noticed there was gold stored in that hole in the wall. Since the owner was so obsessed with greed and unwilling to share his good fortune, I sealed the wall so he wouldn't find it. Then last night as we slept in the farmer's bed, the angel of death came for his wife. I gave her the cow instead."

When situations don't turn out the way we think they should, there may be more to them than we can see. The Bible promises, "And we know that for those who love God all things work together for good, for those who are called according to his purpose" (Romans 8:28, ESV). Surely we can trust the Lord to work things out for our good even though we can't see beyond the hole in the wall or the dead cow. Just remember, things are not always as they seem.

POST-IT MEDITATION FOR JULY 24
When I don't understand why something happens,
I will remember the angel story and know
God may have an unseen purpose.

July 25

Life is not what happens to you, but how you react to it...for what caused you to react will surely pass, but how you continue to react can only be dispatched by you.
~Anonymous

There once was a woman who woke up one morning, looked in the mirror, and noticed she had only three hairs on her head. "Well," she said, "I think I'll braid my hair today." So she did, and she had a wonderful day.

The next day she woke up, looked in the mirror, and saw that she had only two hairs on her head. "Hmmm..." she said, "I think I'll part my hair down the middle today." So she did, and she had a grand day.

The next day she woke up, looked in the mirror, and noticed that she had only one hair on her head. "Well," she said, "Today I'm going to wear my hair in a ponytail." So she did, and she had a fun, fun day.

The next day she woke up, looked in the mirror, and noticed that there wasn't a single hair on her head. "YAY!" she exclaimed. "I don't have to fix my hair today!"

Attitude is everything. A negative attitude propels you into a gloomy state of mind. A positive attitude leads to an upbeat, happy life. If you look at the bright side of life, refusing to allow dark clouds to color your sky, your whole life will become filled with light. In the glory of that light, you will see the world differently—people and happenings take on a cheerful, optimistic aura.

With a positive attitude, we can overcome difficult times in our lives. We can look at failures and problems as blessings in disguise. Psalm 11:71-72 (CEB) reminds us afflictions can be good because we learn about God through them. And that instruction is worth more than thousands of pieces of silver and gold.

An intimate relationship with God is accompanied by an attitude that is not only positive but also righteous. Prayer brings us close to the one who can give us grace and strength. In his presence, we can embrace an uplifted attitude, a measure of enthusiasm and confidence, and determination.

POST-IT MEDITATION FOR JULY 25
Today I will praise God for whatever happens in my life.

July 26

He will be like rain falling on the fields; he will
be like showers watering the earth.
~Psalm 72:6 (NIRV)

The tender hearts of children lead them to make decisions in crises that adults might fail to recognize as important.

It was one of the hottest days of the dry season. We had not seen rain in almost a month. The crops were dying. Cows had stopped giving milk. The creeks and streams were long gone back into the earth. It was a dry season that would bankrupt several farmers before it was through.

Every day, my husband and his brothers would go about the arduous process of trying to get water to the fields. Lately this process had involved taking a truck to the local water rendering plant and filling it up with water. But severe rationing had cut everyone off. If we didn't see some rain soon, we would lose everything. It was on this day that I learned the true lesson of sharing and witnessed the only miracle I have seen with my own eyes.

I was in the kitchen making lunch for my husband and his brothers when I saw my six-year-old son, Billy, walking toward the woods. He wasn't walking with the usual carefree abandon of a youth but with a serious purpose. I could only see his back. He was obviously walking with a great effort, trying to be as still as possible. Minutes after he disappeared into the woods, he came running out again, toward the house. I went back to making sandwiches, thinking that whatever task he had been doing was completed. Moments later, however, he was once again walking in that slow, purposeful stride toward the woods. This activity went on for an hour: walking carefully to the woods, running back to the house. Finally I couldn't take it any longer, and I crept out of the house and followed him on his journey, being cautious not to be seen. He was cupping both hands in front of him as he walked, being very careful not to spill the water he held in them. Maybe two or three tablespoons were held in his tiny hands. I sneaked close as he went into the woods. Branches and thorns slapped his little face, but he did not try to avoid them. He had a much higher purpose. As I leaned in to spy on him, I saw the most amazing sight.

Several large deer loomed in front of him. Billy walked right up to them. I almost screamed for him to get away. A huge buck with elaborate antlers was dangerously close. But the buck did not threaten him—he didn't even move as Billy knelt down. Then I saw a tiny fawn, lying on the ground, obviously suffering from dehydration and heat exhaustion, lift its head with great effort to lap up the water cupped in my beautiful boy's hand. When the water was gone, Billy jumped up to run back to the house as I hid behind a tree.

I followed him back to the house to a spigot to which we had shut off the water. Billy opened it all the way up and a small trickle began to creep out. He knelt there, letting the drip, drip slowly fill up his makeshift "cup," as the sun beat down on his little back. And it came clear to me: The trouble he had gotten into for playing with the hose the week before. The lecture he had received about the importance of not wasting water. The reason he didn't ask me to help him. This time it took almost twenty minutes for the drops to fill his hands. When he stood up and began the trek back, I was there in front of him.

His little eyes filled with tears. "I'm not wasting," was all he said. As he began his walk, I joined him—with a small pot of water from the kitchen. I let him tend to the fawn. I stayed away. It was his job. I stood on the edge of the woods watching the most beautiful heart I have ever known working so hard to save another life. As the tears that rolled down my face began to hit the ground, other drops...and more drops...and more...suddenly joined them. I looked up at the sky. It was as if God, himself, was weeping with pride.

Some will probably say that this was all just a huge coincidence. Those miracles don't really exist. That it was bound to rain sometime. And I can't argue with that...I'm not going to try. All I can say is the rain that came that day saved our farm...just like the actions of one little boy saved the life of another of God's precious creations.

Thank you, God, for the reminder that caring for your creatures is blessed.

July 27

Fools show their annoyance at once, but the prudent overlooks an insult.
~Proverbs 12:16 (NIV)

A World War II veteran told about an experience when he and other American soldiers had captured a group of German fighters. Forced to stand in formation, each German soldier was required to give up all personal belongings, including watches, rings, and wallets. Some protested the loss of their wedding rings, but Army regulations gave the captors no choice.

One man refused to be forced to give up his most prized possession. Looking at the line of American soldiers, he turned to one and handed him his gold watch.

Years later, recounting the story, the American says he was stunned. He had no idea why he had been chosen to receive the watch, but looking back, he realized it was the only way the German could control a difficult situation. Pausing, looking down at the floor and reliving that moment in his mind, he said, "He took control. Knowing that someone was about to take everything from him, that German soldier chose not to have it stolen but to present it as a gift to someone he selected."

In the midst of the humiliating act of surrender, one soldier eschewed being dominated by the enemy. In a similar way, we can rebuff bad situations in our lives by refusing to surrender power to those who try to dishonor or demean us. We can win the battle—not through guns or harsh words, but through taking command of the battle within us. We may want to fight back, but sometimes we are in a circumstance that is not winnable. It is then we take the contest within, controlling what we can and responding in a way that does not escalate the incident.

Instead of bemoaning our fate, when negative circumstances seek to dominate our thinking, all we need to do is decline to allow another person's attitudes or actions to influence our own. Through the power of prayer, we can reclaim control in spite of our inability to change the other person. By spending time with the one omnipotent person who can help, we will change how we think, which ultimately changes how we act. Our attitude and thus our thoughts need to reflect our belief that we can leave control of our lives in God's capable hands.

POST-IT MEDITATION FOR JULY 27
*God, give me the strength to think right thoughts
and to have the right attitude to live as you would have me live.*

July 28

No man is an island.

~John Donne, English poet, satirist, lawyer, and Protestant priest

Being independent is good. We should all want to stand on our own two feet. But, if we become so insular we don't let others close, we may not have the support system we need when storm clouds and strong winds threaten our lives.

In California forests, a redwood tree can grow over 300 feet tall—and if a tunnel were cut in its 30-foot base, a car could be driven through it. Standing in the middle of a cathedral of massive trees, one imagines their roots must go deep into the ground; otherwise, the huge trunks towering toward the sky could never stay upright. But the opposite is true. The roots of redwood trees go only a few feet into the ground. Their ability to stay upright comes not from depth but from how the roots grow tightly together just beneath the surface. The interlinking of the roots creates a strength that holds the trees steady against powerful winds and other ravages of time.

The redwood forests have a lesson for us: If our lives are closely bound to others, we strengthen each other, even when the gales of life threaten to uproot us. Whether family or friends, other people can help us survive tough times.

Donne shared an internal truth: every man is a piece of the continent, a part of the main. If we are involved with mankind, we build lives that have power and stamina. If we try to go it alone, we may find the slightest wind can uproot us. Christians share a foundation of faith, and being part of a Christian body reinforces our convictions and our trust in God that the storms of life won't prevail.

An effective way to stay positive is to unite with others of common mind and heart. Living on an island alone generates discouragement and despondency. Though it may be tempting to withdraw and isolate ourselves when life brings troubling times, we should seek help from others whose roots of faith are joined with ours.

POST-IT MEDITATION FOR JULY 28
I will not live my life in a bubble. I will form positive relationships with other Christians, and in doing so, I will build a foundation of faith.

July 29

How wonderful it is that nobody need wait a single moment before starting to improve the world.

~Anne Frank, *Holocaust victim*

When we watch movies about heroes, view documentaries about individuals who build orphanages, or read newspaper articles about people who start soup kitchens for the homeless, we feel an urge to make a difference in the lives of others. But we hold back, fearful that what little we can do will not make a nickel's worth of difference. Perhaps Loren Eiseley's well-known "Starfish Thrower" story can serve as a reminder that it doesn't take education, money, or a grand scheme to change the world or to save a life. The vision and effort can be small yet make a difference to one or a few—or even many.

An old man was walking on the beach early one morning when he saw a younger man in the distance. From where he was, the older man thought the other one was dancing from the sandy beach to the shoreline. But as he walked closer, he saw that the young man was picking up starfish, one at a time, loping to the water's edge, and tossing them into the water.

When the old man asked the young one what he was doing, he received a simple answer: "I'm saving starfish. If I don't throw them back in before the tide goes out, they will die."

"But young man, there are miles and miles of shore and hundreds of starfish, you can't possibly make a difference," the old man responded with what he thought was the wisdom of the ages.

Without breaking his stride, the young man picked up another starfish, danced to the water and threw it in. As he jogged back to the sandy beach, he said quietly, "Made a difference to that one."

In the same way the young man helped one starfish at a time, we can make a difference in the lives of others. We may not have the resources to build an orphanage or start a community kitchen, but we can be a friend to one child or offer a meal to a neighbor who is confined to his home by age or illness. We may not be able to start a charter school, but we can tutor one child. We may not have seminary training, but we can share our belief in God with a neighbor or a person with whom we work. All it takes is a willingness to make a difference, one at a time.

After leaving the beach, the words of the young man spun like a broken record in the old man's head. The next morning, as he walked on the beach, he stopped where the young man continued his self-appointed task—and joined him in picking up starfish, one at a time, and throwing them back into the water.

I may not have the talent or resources to change the world, but I can make a difference to someone each day—and with God's help, I will.

July 30

Ask the Lord your God for a sign, whether in the deepest depths or in the highest heights.
~Isaiah 7:11 (NIV)

When clouds hang low for days and even months on end, when rain soaks our spirits and hail hits our heads, when prayers go unanswered and our faith fails, we can ask God for a sign while we wait.

When Elijah was called up into heaven, he left behind Elisha, whom he had trained well over several years. Almost immediately, Elisha realized he needed help, and he called out, "Where is the Lord, the God of Elijah?" (2 Kings 2:14, NLT). He wanted a sign that God was with him, and so he struck the water in the Jordan River. When the sons of the prophets on the other side of the river saw the water part and Elisha walked over on dry ground, they said, "The spirit of Elijah rests on Elisha" (2 Kings 2:15, NLT). God had demonstrated his power in response to Elisha's plea.

Elisha prayed for a sign, and it came. He didn't call on Elijah, his mentor; he called on God. We, too, need our own relationship with God; he must reside in our hearts. We can't count solely on the prayers of others to see us through the cloudy days of our lives. Our own faith has to be strong enough to ask God directly; and, if his answer demands patience, we can then ask for a sign.

We need clear insight about where God dwells. Psalms 145:18 (NLT) reminds us, "The Lord is near to all who call on him...." When God is in our hearts, then we can pray for both large and small gifts—or for a sign that he is in control and that we are in his care.

A man had a little daughter—an only and much beloved child. He lived only for her; she was his life. So when she became ill and her illness resisted the efforts of the best obtainable physicians, he became like a man possessed, moving heaven and earth to bring about her restoration to health.

His best efforts proved fruitless, however, and the child died. The father was totally irreconcilable. He became a bitter recluse, shutting himself away from his many friends, refusing every activity that might restore his peace and bring him back to his normal self.

Then one night he had a dream. He was in heaven and witnessed a grand pageant of all the little child angels. They were marching in an apparently endless line past the Great White Throne. Every white-robed, angelic tot carried a candle. He noticed, however, that one child's candle was not lit. Then he saw that the child with the dark candle was his own little girl. Rushing towards her, while the pageant faltered, he seized her in his arms, caressed her tenderly, and asked, "How is it that your candle is the only one not lit?"

"Father, they often re-light it, but your tears always put it out again," she said.

Just then he awoke from his dream. The lesson was crystal clear, and its effects were immediate. From that hour on he was no longer a recluse but mingled freely and cheerfully with his former friends and associates. No longer would his little darling's candle be extinguished by his useless tears.

I received my own sign, following my husband's death, that he had made it across the great divide to live in God's presence. As I related in *SIPS OF SUSTENANCE: Grieving the Loss of Your Spouse*, trains had a special significance for us most of our married life. On the night my husband died, as I lay awake in the wee hours of the morning with my heart shattered, I heard the faint sound of a train whistle in the distance. Stunned, I sat up in bed and listened carefully, but I didn't hear it again. Since we had never heard a train while at home before, and because I never heard it again, I like to think my husband was the conductor that night—that he was passing by on his way to heaven to tell me all was well.

SOURCE OF THE Candle story by Odain: http://godslittleacre.net/inspirationalstories/the_dark_candle.html

POST-IT MEDITATION FOR JULY 30
Thank you, God, for being ever close, for showing me you rule in the deepest depths and in the highest heavens.

July 31

What has been will be again, what has been done will be done again; there is nothing new under the sun.
~Ecclesiastes 1:9 (NIV)

Every human being has strengths and weaknesses. As a university president, I tried to balance them when I had an employee who contributed significantly to the institution's goals but who also had irritating flaws and faults. I weighed the good against the bad, and if the good prevailed, I kept the employee and helped him or her work on the weaknesses. Other employees sometimes complained that a certain person's actions were inappropriate or bad and didn't understand why the person wasn't fired. I tried to explain what the person brought to the university and that the drawbacks didn't outweigh the advantages. Sometimes, the strengths and weaknesses of two employees complemented each other, enabling both to benefit.

An old Eastern parable tells of two beggars who formed one such symbiotic relationship. One, who was blind from birth, had strong muscles—strong enough to pick up the other beggar, who had no legs, and carry him on his back. As he carried the legless man around, he in turn became the eyes for the blind man. One man provided the eyes for direction; the other provided the legs for mobility.

When we work with other people—on the job, at church, or in volunteer organizations, we sometimes think we bring more to the table than others do. Or, we complain others don't do enough. If we open our minds to other ways of accomplishing goals, we may find working with those whose strengths and weaknesses differ from ours can make both us and them successful.

As Christians, we can become stale in how we think and act. We get in ruts so deep it becomes difficult to navigate them. In Romans 7:6, we are told to serve in the newness of the spirit and commanded to let go of the oldness. When we are open to new ideas, we can discover different ways to find happiness, innovative paths to prosperity, previously unexplored secrets to success, or even newfound truths in the Bible. Many times these alternative approaches are encountered as we team up with other people, just as the two beggars did. There may be nothing new under the sun, but we can always dig up new solutions to old problems.

POST-IT MEDITATION FOR JULY 31
I will be open to new situations and creative solutions.

August 1

May mercy, peace, and love be multiplied to you.
~Jude 1:2 (ESV)

Growing physically is part of the natural order—it occurs in fairly set stages for all of us. But growing emotionally, psychologically, and spiritually depends on the people with whom we interact, the experiences we have, and the time we spend working on our development as spirituals beings with human bodies.

Just as the beggars from yesterday's devotion teamed up for physical accomplishments, we can team up for faith and spiritual growth. Ecclesiastes 4:9 (ERV) asserts, "…When two people work together, they get more work done." Two oxen pulling together can carry a heavier load. Two Christians working side-by-side can move a project farther and faster than one can do alone.

In the same way that we will die if our physical heart stands still, our spirit will expire if we don't keep it moving and growing. Just as we make to-do lists for chores and other tasks, we should have a task list for growing spiritually. In addition to prayer and Bible studies, we should list activities that will develop habits of helping others. As we go through life, we can be on the alert for opportunities to lend a supportive hand or ear, for ways we can show mercy and grace, and for occasions when we can demonstrate forgiveness. All of these will help us nurture our spiritual side, and in doing so, mercy, peace, and love will be multiplied to us.

One man named Robert Peterson told how he missed such an opportunity to help someone:

The little girl was six years old when he first met her on the beach where he drove whenever the world began to close in on him. Wendy was a friendly kid, and he talked with her occasionally. One day he learned from her that "sandpipers come to bring us joy." A few months later, when Peterson was feeling particularly bad, he drove to the beach to try to find peace. Wendy saw him walking and came running, ready to carry on their conversations, but Peterson said crossly, "Look, if you don't mind, I'd rather be alone today." When Wendy questioned him, he shouted, "Because my mother died!" After sympathizing, Wendy asked softly, "Did it hurt?"

"Of course it hurt!" Peterson exclaimed, wrapped up in himself.

A month or so later, back at the beach, Peterson looked for Wendy to apologize for his bad temper, but she was nowhere to be found. Finally, he walked to the door of her cottage and knocked, asking her mother where she was.

"Mr. Peterson, please came in. Wendy spoke of you so much. I'm so sorry to tell you Wendy died last week. She had leukemia. I guess you didn't know."

In shock, Peterson fell silent, his mind returning to the day Wendy asked if dying hurt. The mother filled in the lapse, telling him Wendy had left something for him. She handed him a smeared envelope with MR.P printed in bold childish letters. Inside was a drawing in bright crayon colors—a yellow beach, a blue sea, and a brown bird. Underneath was carefully printed: A SANDPIPER TO BRING YOU JOY. Today the picture hangs in Peterson's study—a gift from a child with sea blue eyes and hair the color of sand who taught him the gift of love.

When we focus on others more than ourselves, we can rise above our moods, frustrations, disappointments, and problems. We become more tolerant and intuitively understand who we are, what we are, and why we were sent to earth. In doing so, we distance ourselves from worldly desires and problems, focusing more on our heavenly home than on our earthly life. None of this means we have to detach from life; it simply means our focus and priorities change, leading to inner peace.

POST-IT MEDITATION FOR AUGUST 1
I will give the central core of my being care and attention,
becoming more aware of who I am.

August 2

…When I am weak, then I am strong.
~2 Corinthians 12:10 (NIV)

> *There once was an oyster whose story I tell,*
> *who found that some sand had got into his shell.*
> *It was only a grain, but it gave him great pain,*
> *for oysters have feelings, although they're so plain.*
> *Now, did he berate the harsh workings of fate*
> *that brought him to such a deplorable state?*
> *Did he curse at the government, cry for election,*
> *and claim that the sea should have given him protection?*
> *"No," he said to himself as he lay on a shell,*
> *"since I cannot remove it, I shall try to improve it."*
> *Now the years have rolled around, as the years always do,*
> *and he came to his ultimate destiny—a stew.*
> *And the small grain of sand that had bothered him so,*
> *was a beautiful pearl all richly aglow.*
> *Now the tale has a moral, for isn't it grand*
> *what an oyster can do with a morsel of sand?*
> *What couldn't we do if we'd only begin,*
> *with some of the things that get under our skin?*

For most of us, gain is preceded by pain. Anything worth having is worth working for, even when dark clouds and dark places leave us hurting, just as the oyster ached from the grain of sand while creating an exquisite stone. If we but endure the agony of the people or circumstances that irritate us, we will not only become stronger from our suffering but also be made more beautiful in God's sight.

POST-IT MEDITATION FOR AUGUST 2
I will bear my burdens, knowing God can turn pain into gain.

August 3

Behold, I send an angel before you to guard you on the way and to bring you to the place that I have prepared.
~Exodus 23:20 (AMP)

It is impossible to doubt God's existence when he operates where we can see his loving hands.

A woman was driving to the grocery store, her mind filled with everything on her to-do list. Taking the kids to soccer practice, cleaning the house, getting groceries, having the oil changed in the car...the list went on and on. Feeling overwhelmed, she was tired before she started.

Just before she arrived at the store, as she was about to cross a railroad track, the lady saw something horrible. A train had hit a car as it crossed the track. She was the closest car to the tracks, so she put her gear in park and got out. Running to the car, she looked inside and was horrified. The driver, a young woman who was obviously dead, was alone in the front seat. In the backseat a baby in its car seat was bleeding everywhere and next to the baby was a little girl about four-years-old, who was also bleeding. Just then the little girl spoke.

Turning to the stranger, the little girl asked, "Are my mommy and baby sister okay?" The woman just looked at her and said, "Honey I don't know. A doctor is on his way right now." Just then the little girl started crying, saying, "Don't take my mommy and my baby sister—take me with you too!! Please!!" She was pleading at someone the stranger couldn't see to take her—but take her where? The woman asked the little girl who she was talking to and she said, "Don't you see? That angel is taking my mommy and my baby sister! I want to go with them too! My mommy is waving goodbye to me, smiling, and she is holding my baby sister!" The little girl started to cry because she did not want to stay; she wanted to go with her mommy and her baby sister. The passerby, who didn't believe in God herself, was shocked. Where did an angel come from? What kind of God would take a mommy and a baby but not the little sister?

At that moment she saw the little girl's sad face transformed into a beautiful smile as she held her arms out to something, someone to pick her up. The woman thought to herself that the little girl must be delirious, and maybe she was hurt worse than she thought. Just then the little girl closed her eyes and slumped over in her seat. She was dead! Still in shock, the lady couldn't be sad even though the beautiful little girl had just died. The smile on her face was radiant. Her thoughts in turmoil, the woman guessed the mommy and baby sister came back to get her. That was also the day God came to get the passerby—that was the day she became a believer and turned her life over to the living God.

POST-IT MEDITATION FOR AUGUST 3
***May I be as anxious and happy to follow God as the little
girl was to follow her mother.***

August 4

We are hard pressed on every side, yet not crushed; we are perplexed, but not in despair.
~2 Corinthians 4:8 (NIV)

When tragedy invades our lives, many of us understandably hit the "woe is me" button. When serious illness threatens, when a job or home is lost, when death strikes a sudden blow, when an accident disables, or when countless other misfortunes disrupt our lives, we can't be blamed if we momentarily feel sorry for ourselves. Negative feelings and reactions pull us down; and when we are in the throes of heartbreak, we need something to build us up, not unhelpful, pessimistic thoughts that send us further into the tunnel of despair.

In his Inspirational Writings' *book Robert Schuller tells how he prayed for emotional strength as he and his wife flew from Korea to be at the side of their 13-year-old daughter whose left leg had just been amputated in an Iowa hospital. Schuller candidly concedes their "hearts were bleeding, and [their] spirits were crushed...." But, in an instant, God answered his prayer with a short sentence: "Play it down and pray it up." A strange response, but after thinking, Schuller realized the calamity could have been much worse—his daughter might have lost both legs or even died. He and his wife began to count other blessings for which they could be thankful—their daughter's spinal cord had not been severed; her beautiful face was not marred; she didn't lose her sight or hearing, and on and on.*

Albert Ellis, a well-known psychotherapist, used this same line of reasoning in his rational emotive therapies when he taught patients to compare what was happening to them to the worst possible thing that might happen. In all cases, he avowed, it could always be worse. Compared to the mother of all possibilities, what is happening isn't the cruelest circumstance we might face. Sometimes that is hard to see, but if we think it through, it is true.

The omnipotent God knew what Ellis deduced long before rational emotive theory was developed. In simple terms, he showed Schuller and his wife—and us—that with faith we can play down the negative events in our lives and play up the positives. Granted, as Schuller notes, we may not be able to alleviate a problem or disaster, but we can keep it in perspective.

Today upon a bus, I saw a lovely girl and envied her:
She seemed so happy. And I wish I were as fair.
And then, suddenly, she rose to leave, and I saw her hobble down the aisle.
She had one leg and carried a crutch,
But as she passed, a smile.

Oh God, forgive me when I whine, I have two legs;
I am blessed indeed. The world is mine!
Later, walking down the street,
I saw a man with eyes of blue.
But he just stood and watched the others play.
So, I stopped a moment and then I said,
"Why don't you join the others, sir?"
But he looked ahead without a word,
And then I knew he could not hear.
Oh God, forgive me when I whine, I have two ears;
I am blessed indeed. The world is mine!
And later, I stopped to buy some sweets;
The lad who sold them had such charm,
I talked with him. If I were late, it would do no harm.
But as I turned to go, he said to me,
"I thank you sir. You've been so kind.
It's nice to talk with folks like you."
"You see," he said, "I am blind."
Oh God forgive me when I whine, I have two eyes,
I am blessed indeed. The world is mine!
With legs to take me where I want to go,
With ears to hear the things I need to know,
With eyes to watch that radiant sunset glow.
Oh God, forgive me when I whine;
I am blessed indeed!
The world is mine!

POST-IT MEDITATION FOR AUGUST 4
*With prayer and faith, I will attempt to be
thankful even when bad things happen.*

August 5

Misfortunes often sharpen the genius.
~Ovid, Roman poet

An old man lived alone in Minnesota. He wanted to spade his potato garden, but it was very hard work. His only son, who would have helped him, was in prison. The old man wrote a letter to his son and mentioned his situation:

Dear Son,

I am feeling pretty bad because it looks like I won't be able to plant my potato garden this year. I hate to miss doing the garden because your mother always loved planting *time. I'm just getting too old to be digging up a garden plot. If you were here, all my troubles would be over. I know you would dig the plot for me, if you weren't in prison.*

Love,
Dad

Shortly, the old man received this telegram: "For Heaven's sake, Dad, don't dig up the garden!! That's where I buried the GUNS!"

At 4 a.m. the next morning, a dozen FBI agents and local police officers appeared and dug up the entire garden without finding any guns.

Confused, the old man wrote another note to his son telling him what had happened and asked him what to do next.

His son's reply was: "Go ahead and plant your potatoes, Dad. It's the best I could do for you from here."

No matter where you are in the world, if you have decided to do something deep from your heart, you can do it. It is the thought that matters, not where you are or where the person is. What counts is drawing a mental picture of the outcome you want and then finding a creative way to achieve it. Explore all possible alternatives and choose the one that best solves the problem. The straightest route to our desire to help is often not possible, so we have to explore other options. The way may be hidden to us at first, but God will bring the path to light.

POST-IT MEDITATION FOR AUGUST 5
God, give me faith to find new ways to help those I love,
even when it seems impossible.

August 6

...And the eyes of man are never satisfied.
~Proverbs 27:20 (ASV)

We have all, at some time in our lives, probably been in the presence of someone who appears to see life through rose-colored glasses. Even in the midst of hard times, the person glows with peace and joy, displaying confidence and radiating enthusiasm. What a delight to be with someone who sees the silver lining in every cloud, a person who laughs instead of complaining and crying.

On the other hand, it is likely we have also spent time with someone whose face looks like a dried prune—a person who habitually wears a scowl or carries a chip on his shoulder. What a downer to be with someone who envisions being drowned in a downpour every time clouds hang low overhead. Similarly, isn't it miserable to be around someone who is never satisfied?

One old man finally got tired of people who were never content, regardless of the circumstances. He decided to teach his son a lesson on this very subject.

The next day the man caught his mule and jumped on his back, then rode into town while he had his son walk behind him. Everyone in the town talked about how awful the old man was, making his son walk to town while he himself rode the mule.

After a few days, the old man went out again and got on the mule's back, but this time he had his son climb on, too, and they both rode the mule to town. Once again, when he returned, the town folk were talking about how awful, even disgraceful, it was for the old man and the son to ride the mule at the same time—it was too much for the mule, they murmured.

After a few more days, the old man brought the mule in from the pasture. This time, the man and his son walked into town and led the mule. The tongues started wagging again—how stupid the old man and the son were for leading the mule instead of riding it.

The old man had made his point: people are never satisfied. We see this every day, even in our houses of religion. We criticize the choir, we berate the preacher. At work, we complain we are never paid what we are worth. At home, our children aren't as well behaved as they should be, or our spouse doesn't express love often enough. We even get mad when our favorite television series is discontinued. We want life our way, and no matter how good our life is, we can be like the townspeople who were never satisfied with how the farmer used his mule.

Our failure to be satisfied with our lives is likely displeasing to God, who gives and gives and gives. Granted, we don't get everything we want, and sometimes not even everything we need, but we have much to be grateful for, blessings for which we should give continuous thanks. As we are told in the first book of Timothy (6:6 ESV), "Now there is great gain in godliness with contentment."

POST-IT MEDITATION FOR AUGUST 6
Help me, God, to see good in all things.

August 7

Hope is such a marvelous thing. It bends, it twists, it sometimes hides, but rarely does it break. It sustains us when nothing else can. It gives us reason to continue and courage to move ahead, when we tell ourselves we'd rather give in. Hope puts a smile on our face when the heart cannot manage. Hope puts our feet on the path when our eyes cannot see it. Hope moves us to act when our souls are confused of the direction.
~Unknown writer

A little tugboat was moving down the Mississippi River toward a drawbridge. Although the drawbridge operator was watching as the tug approached and threw the gears to raise the bridge, a malfunction occurred and the bridge failed to open.

The little tugboat saw what was happening and tried to shift gears and back up to avoid hitting the bridge; but the river was running too fast, and the tugboat was pulled under the bridge sideways.

Moments passed, and from the other side of the bridge the bridge operator saw the little tugboat's flag begin to rise from the water. "She's low, but the flag is still flying." As he watched, the tugboat slowly appeared and righted itself.

Reminds me of a few Christians I know. They sometimes get sucked under, but the desire for life and their hope in God is so strong that they survive being underwater and reappear as strong as ever after a while.

In *FACES OF GRIEF: Stories of Surviving Loss and Finding Hope*, I wrote about amazing Christians whose strength and faith are an inspiration to many who have lost loved ones. One woman, whose husband was killed at sea during World War II, leaving her with three young boys, later had to endure the loss of one of her sons being electrocuted in high voltage lines during a routine parachute jump. In these and other tragedies she faced, she says she never felt strong going through a death, but somehow she was able to "right herself" multiple times. Like Thomas Merton, she found the goodness of God—and thus hope—even in tragedy.

Other faith-reliant Christians whose stories were told in *FACES OF GRIEF* include parents who lost a precocious eleven and one-half year old daughter, a husband who watched his wife suffer excruciating pain as she succumbed to cancer, a young wife whose beloved husband died tragically in a small plane crash, parents who watched a vibrant young man sink into a disabling illness that led to his death, a woman whose husband committed suicide, and siblings whose younger brother was taken from them by a freak accident with a charcoal grill. In all of these incredibly sad stories and others, the survivors righted themselves because of faith—an unshakable conviction they will be reunited with their loved ones. While they await that day, they are once again sailing upright, finding hope and joy on the other side of the bridge.

If you can look at the sunset and smile, and find beauty in the colorful petals of a small flower, then you still have hope.

If you can find pleasure in the movement of a butterfly, and if the rain breaking on a roof top can lull you to sleep, then you still have hope.

If you can see the good in other people, and if the smile of a child can warm your heart, then you still have hope.

If the sight of a rainbow makes you stop and stare in wonder, and if the soft fur of a favored pet feels pleasant under your fingertips, then you still have hope.

If you meet new people with a trace of excitement and optimism, and if you give people the benefit of the doubt, then you still have hope.

If you offer your hand in friendship to others who have touched your life, and if receiving an unexpected card or letter brings a pleasant surprise, then you still have hope.

If the suffering of others fills you with pain and frustration, and if you refuse to let a friendship die, or accept that it must end, then you still have hope.

If you look forward to a time or place of quiet and reflection, and if you watch love stories or want the endings to be happy, then you still have hope.

If you can look to the past and smile, and when faced with the bad, when told everything is futile, you can still look up and end the conversation with this, "… yes, but God…," then you still have hope.

AUTHOR'S NOTE: *The tugboat incident was captured in a series of photographs taken by an amateur photographer in 1979 at the Rooster Bridge on the Tombigbee River in western Alabama.*

POST-IT MEDITATION FOR AUGUST 7
With God on my side, I will never lose hope. I will have faith to right myself when I am sucked underwater by life's misfortunes.

August 8

In the town they tell the story of the great pearl—how it was found and how it was lost again.
~John Steinbeck, author

In Steinbeck's book, <u>The Pearl</u>, Kino, a young pearl diver in La Paz, enjoys the simple life of his village until his young son Coyotito is stung by a scorpion. Because Kino is poor and has very little money, the village doctor refuses to treat his child. But then, the next day Kino finds a huge pearl while diving, the largest he has ever seen. Word spreads quickly through the village, and the doctor changes his mind about treating Coyotito. Others in the village start plotting about how to steal the pearl. Throughout the rest of the story, Kino meets calamity after calamity while trying to protect and sell the pearl of great price—the pearl that offers a new life for his family, and especially for his son, who will now have the opportunity to go to school.

Despite killing a man trying to steal the pearl, his hut burning down after raiders dig up the floor looking for the pearl, and hiding in the mountains from trackers determined to take the precious stone, Kino refuses to give up. The pearl is his son's future, and ignoring pleas from his wife and his brother to throw the pearl back into the sea, Kino continues to run with his family and the pearl. One night while cowering in a cave, in the wee hours of the morning Kino sneaks down to kill the trackers; but before he can attack them, his son cries out. Thinking he is a coyote, the trackers shoot toward the dark cave where Kino's wife and son are hiding.

Tragically, Coyotito is killed by the gunshot. The pearl that held the promise of a rich and satisfying future had brought misfortune that could not be measured by any price.

Realizing the pearl is cursed and has destroyed his family (as his wife had feared), Kino and Juana travel back to La Paz and throw the cursed pearl into the sea.

The Prologue to *The Pearl* reads, "And, as with all retold tales that are in people's hearts, there are only good and bad things and black and white things and good and evil things and no in-between. If this story is a parable, perhaps everyone takes his own meaning from it and reads his own life into it."

Each of us looks for "pearls"—and sometimes finds them—in our own lives, but they don't always bring the happiness and contentment we dream of. Only God can do that.

Jesus' warning was wise: "Watch out! Be on your guard against all kinds of greed; a man's life does not consist in the abundance of his possessions" (Luke 12:15, NIV).

POST-IT MEDITATION FOR AUGUST 8
I will pray for strength not to depend on pearls for peace and prosperity.

August 9

Give your way over to the Lord. Trust in Him also. And He will do it.
~Psalm 37:5 (NLV)

In Steinbeck's book, Kino found the great pearl by accident, but most of us find the pearls in our lives by design and determination. Those pearls aren't fully formed like the valuable one people tried to steal from Kino, but if we are patient, the pearls growing in our lives will develop into priceless pieces of our being—here and in the life to come.

Just as it takes time for a grain of sand to be transformed into a pearl, for a mighty oak to grow from a sapling, or for an iris bulb to break through the barrier of the soil and rise to be a vision of beauty, it takes time for God to work his will in our lives. And, just as an oyster broken open too soon or a cocoon torn apart before the butterfly is complete leads to a disfigured life, our spiritual lives will be less than fulfilled if we become too impatient for God to stop our pain or release us from our prison of problems. We must be cautious about interfering in God's timing.

Instead of impatience, we need to develop faith—trust that enables us to turn a situation or person over to God and let go.

Dr. Edward Payson, an American Congregational preacher in the early 1800's, once wrote to a mother who was burdened with anxiety about her son: "You give yourself too much trouble about him. After you have prayed for him, as you have done, and committed him to God, should you not cease to feel anxious respecting him? The command, 'Be careful for nothing,' is unlimited...."

God's timing is impeccable—it is perfect. Sometimes when our lives are interrupted unexpectedly, we wonder why we should have to pause on our journey. Occasionally, God lets us see how interference and interruptions work for our good:

An army runner made his way across the dead and dismembered bodies strewn across the ravaged battlefield back to his company with orders from the battalion commander. The sound of bullets and bombs had been silenced. With a relative sense of safety, he walked on, thankful that, at least for a while, there was a calm in the senseless storm.

Approximately two-thirds of the way across the devastated field, he was suddenly stopped by an unusual sight. It hovered right before him, at perfect eye level. At first, he thought he was suffering from fatigue and was seeing a mirage.

"It can't be," he said to himself, "not out here in the midst of a raging war!"

But it not only was real, it came right up to him and stopped no more than three inches from his face. He started to step forward when it lunged forward, pushing him a couple of steps backward.

And then it happened!

A gigantic shell hurled through the air and landed right in the very spot from which he had been literally pushed.

"I would have been killed!" he gasped. "I would have been killed!"

But that little object, probably less than an ounce in weight, kept him from losing his life. It was a definite miracle because he had not seen one since he had gone off to war... and surely not right out in the middle of an all-out war, in the midst of an awful battle.

But it was there, and it did save his life.

The strange little object? It was a butterfly! It interrupted the man's path across the field, but like a pearl, it used its own timing to turn an irritation into something priceless.

POST-IT MEDITATION FOR AUGUST 9
God, give me the faith to know your timing is always right.

August 10

And now I give you a new commandment: Love one another. As I have loved you, so you must love one another.
~John 13:34 (GNT)

In our walk through life, we cross paths with people of all appearances and abilities. When we see someone who is quite different, we may turn our head to avoid facing something unlovely or inadequate. Or, we can open a caring heart to make the person feel loved and accepted.

A little girl named Annie, born with a cleft palate, grew up knowing she was different, and she hated it. When she started school, her classmates—who were constantly teasing—made it clear how she looked to others: a disfigured child with a misshapen lip, crooked nose, lopsided teeth, and hollow and somewhat garbled speech. She couldn't even blow up a balloon without holding her nose; and as she bent to drink from a fountain, the water spilled out of her nose. When her schoolmates asked, "What happened to your lip?" she'd tell them she had fallen as a baby and cut it on a piece of glass. Somehow it seemed more acceptable to have suffered an accident than to have been born different.

By the age of seven, Annie was convinced no one outside her own family could ever love her. Or even like her. And then she entered the second grade and was placed in Mrs. Leonard's class. Her new teacher was round and pretty and fragrant, with chubby arms and shining brown hair and warm dark eyes that smiled even on rare occasions when her mouth did not. Everyone adored her. But no one came to love her more than Annie. And for a special reason. The time came for the annual "hearing tests" at the school. Annie was barely able to hear anything out of one ear and was not about to reveal yet another problem that would single her out as different. And so she cheated. She had learned to watch other children and raised her hand when they did during group testing. The "whisper test" however, required a different kind of deception: Each child would go to the door of the classroom, turn sideways, close one ear with a finger, and the teacher would whisper something from her desk, which the child would repeat. Then the same thing was done for the other ear. Annie had discovered in kindergarten that nobody checked to see how tightly the untested ear was being covered, so she merely pretended to block hers. As usual, she was last, but all through the testing she wondered what Mrs. Leonard might say to her. She knew from previous years that teachers whispered words like "The sky is blue" or "Do you have new shoes?" When her turn came, Annie turned her bad ear to the teacher, plugging up the other solidly with her finger, then gently backed her finger out enough to be able to hear. Annie waited and then came the words that God had surely put in her teacher's mouth, seven words that changed her life forever. Mrs. Leonard, the pretty, fragrant teacher she adored, said softly, "I wish you were my little girl."

And with those words, Mrs. Leonard utterly changed the little girl's self-image—and thus her life.

POST-IT MEDITATION FOR AUGUST 10
With God's grace, I will treat every person with compassion.

August 11

...when the desire comes, it is a tree of life.
~Proverbs 13:12 (NKJV)

Faith without desire and drive is like a car without an engine and gas. To grow as Christians, we must yearn for God's presence in our lives. We must crave conversation with him; we must covet his word. When we remain close to God's presence, our faith will be strengthened—it will become our tree of life. If we wander too far away from him, if we find ourselves watching movies that don't reflect Christian values, if we let ourselves be enticed into bars or other places where our values might be cast aside, or if we choose to expose ourselves to countless other places and people that pull us in the wrong direction, we lose sight of God's purpose for our lives. Instead, we begin to focus on earthly pleasures more than heavenly goals.

Our lives are no different than computers. Remember the old saying, "Garbage in, garbage out?" We need to pray to God, as Solomon did in 1 Kings 3:9 (ASV), to be able to "discern between good and evil." With that discernment, we also need the strength and willpower to stand firm against those activities and people who would drag us away from a Christian focus.

A young pastor, whose story is told in <u>*HOOKED BUT NOT HOPELESS:*</u> <u>*Escaping the Lure of Addiction*</u> *(Hoppe and Yates, 2011), found that the wrong environment moved him back into addiction, even after he had turned his life over to God. Three months after he had been through rehab and had started preaching all over—from Louisiana to New York—, thinking his recovery was unshakable, the charismatic man of God went back to the drug world to try to save two friends. Instead, he was sucked back into the drug culture and before he escaped, he had blown $28,000 on heroin and cocaine. His wake-up call came from a waitress in a bar who was serving him drinks. Despite his inebriated condition, the cocky young pastor tried to win her to Christ and was stunned when she challenged him: "For someone who knows so much about Jesus, you sure don't act like it." In trying to lead the lady in the bar to a new life, the pastor found his way back to the tree of life, from which he has never again strayed.*

Lives can be transformed by faith and hope—and God's grace. The tree of life is available to all of us; we just have to let go of the activities and people that obscure it.

POST-IT MEDITATION FOR AUGUST 11
I will stay close to God, knowing he is the source of life unending.

August 12

Keep yourself in training for a godly life.
~1 Timothy 4:7 (GNB)

Many of us routinely attempt to keep our bodies in good shape, and even more people occasionally make a commitment to exercise regularly and eat healthy foods before soon falling away. As 1 Timothy 4:7 tells us, training has value. And, indeed, that applies to both our bodily and spiritual welfare. With exercise, we feel better both physically and psychologically—and typically live longer. Nevertheless, the next verse in 1 Timothy goes further: "For physical training is of some value, but godliness has value for all things, holding promise for both the present life and the life to come." Recognizing that value, we wonder how to grow spiritually—how to understand the truths in God's words. A teacher once used a physical exercise to teach her students one of these spiritual truths:

The teacher instructed each of her students to bring a clear plastic bag and a sack of potatoes to school. For every person a student had refused to forgive in his life's experience, he chose a potato, sliced it in two pieces, wrote on one piece the offense and on the other the name of the offender and the date, and put the pieces in the plastic bag. Some of the students' bags were quite heavy.

They were then told to carry this bag with them everywhere for one week, putting it beside their bed at night, on the car seat when driving, next to their desk at school, and when they went shopping or to a movie.

The hassle of lugging the bags around with them made it clear what a weight they were carrying spiritually, and how they had to pay attention to it all the time to keep from leaving it in embarrassing places. Naturally, the condition of the potatoes deteriorated to a nasty, smelly slime—a great metaphor for the price we pay for keeping our pain and heavy negativity. Too often we think of forgiveness as a gift to the other person, and it clearly is for ourselves.

No doubt our commitment to train our spiritual being is far more important than training our bodies to carry potatoes. The habit of exercise brings results. It might just be a truth learned, as with the potatoes—or it may be a more fit body. Both commitments—to our body and to our spirit—require consistency and endurance, and both build strength. One lasts for a lifetime; one lasts for eternity. Still, we can learn from the benefits of physical training—changes in our lives are evident. If we devote the same level of energy and time to our spirit as many do to their bodies, we will see a tremendous difference in our attitude, our desire to help others, and especially in our faith.

Training our spiritual being seems simple—we must dedicate ourselves to daily Bible reading and prayer. But growing spiritually also requires a high level of introspection and action. We need to increase our thoughts about God and his purpose for our lives and spend less time focusing on worldly ambition and earthly possessions. Thinking about self-control, brotherly kindness, forgiveness, and unconditional love based on Biblical teachings will enhance our "faith goodness"—the personal qualities of our lives that undergird our obligation to serve God through helping others and spreading his word. Moreover, spiritual growth gives a personal sense of well-being that will sustain us in times of anxiety, stress, difficulty, trouble, and tragedy. When we increase the measure of our faith, we benefit now as we enjoy a sense of contentment that goes beyond anything we can understand. Spiritual peace is the antidote for whatever comes our way in earthly life and prepares the path to eternity.

POST-IT MEDITATION FOR AUGUST 12
I will spend time exercising my spiritual being, growing in God's grace and claiming his promises, increasing my spiritual muscle for the present and claiming life in the next dimension.

August 13

So all of you should live together in peace. Try to understand each other. Love each other like brothers and sisters. Be kind and humble.
~1 Peter 3:8 (ERV)

Danny hit the red button in front of him, but no words came from his mouth before the buzzer rang out. The scholastic bowl was over, and he had missed the answer to the last question: "Who wrote Grapes of Wrath?"

The scholastic bowl coach had watched in amazement as Danny let waves of laughter roll over him and allowed the buzzer to sound without a response.

As Danny left the room, his coach pulled him aside, remarking, "You caused your team to lose the championship. And I know why. Ernest Hemingway made you think of Ernest, didn't it?"

Shamefaced, Danny admitted that when he tried to say "Ernest," he lost it. A fellow classmate, Ernest weighed about 300 pounds, had a terrible odor, and dressed like a homeless person. Imagining Ernest writing Grapes of Wrath was so hysterical Danny couldn't contain his raucous laughter.

Despite his crestfallen look, the coach couldn't let Danny leave without pushing the point: "What gives you the right to treat Ernest that way? No one is so unlovable that he doesn't deserve respect."

Danny sheepishly looked down and then apologized before leaving.

How many times do we look down on another human being because of how he looks or acts? How often do we treat people with disdain and disrespect, telling them with our actions that they are unlovable. A neighbor who insulted us…we never speak to him again, but do we have the right to judge? The woman serving us lunch at a restaurant, who gets our order wrong and doesn't even apologize—do we know what she faced before she came to work that day? The derelict who sits on the street corner with a sign, "Hungry: will work for food"—do we pass him by because we fear he would spend the money on drugs, not food? The examples are all around us: dirty people, rednecks, mean people, grumpy people, disrespectful people, annoying people. As a Christian, we should love them all.

POST-IT MEDITATION FOR AUGUST 13
When people seem unlovable to me, I will remember
God loves them and wants me to love them, too.

August 14

Thus says the LORD, "Restrain your voice from weeping and your eyes from tears; for your work will be rewarded," declares the LORD…. "There is hope for your future and your children will return to their own territory."
~*Jeremiah 31:16-17 (NASB)*

Several years ago in a small fishing village in the Netherlands, a young man taught the world what a person can get by putting aside one's own needs.

All of the people in the young man's village earned a living in the fishing industry; therefore, volunteers for rescues were often needed in emergency situations.

One night as the wind blew strongly, the clouds moved quickly, spawning a great storm that almost sank a fisherman's boat. In panic and fear, the ship's crew sent an S.O.S.

The captain of the rescue team sounded the alarm, and villagers quickly gathered, looking anxiously toward the harbor to see what was happening. When the rescue team ran their boat and tried to pass through the wild waves, the villagers worried, waiting at the shore with lanterns held high in their hands to give light to the way back. An hour later, the rescue boat returned, and the villagers cheered happily to welcome them.

As they exhaustedly fell on the sand, the volunteers reported that the rescue boat was not capable of taking more passengers with them, and one person had been left back. If they had taken the person, the rescue boat might have sunk so slow it would have been swept over by the waves. Even though it was only one person, he would have endangered the lives of all of the passengers. The captain asked one more group of volunteers to save the person who was left behind.

Hans, a young man of 16 years of age, stepped forward.

However, his mother held his arm and begged, "Don't go. Your father died in a shipwreck 10 years ago, and your older brother Paul has been missing at sea for three weeks. Hans, you're the only one I've got."

Hans replied, "Mother, I have to go. What would happen if all people say, 'I can't go, let others do it?' Mother, this time I've got to do my duty. When there's a calling for serving, we all have to join and play our role."

Hans kissed his mother, joined the rescue team, and soon disappeared in the darkness of the night.

A few hours passed, but for Han's mother it felt like forever. Finally, the rescue team's boat returned with Hans standing at the edge of it.

Clasping his two palms, the captain shouted, "Did you find the last person?"

Unable to restrain himself, Hans shouted excitedly, "Yes, we've found him. Tell my mother: He's my brother Paul!"

Hans had no reason to believe the missing fisherman was his brother, but his willingness to risk his own life to save another person brought a much greater reward than he could have imagined. And his mother, despite her fears and misgivings, had both sons returned to her safely.

August 15

Listen to advice and accept discipline, and at the end you will be counted among the wise.
~Proverbs 19:20 (NIV)

Sometimes a person's biggest weakness can become his or her biggest strength.

This truth is illustrated by the story of one 10-year-old boy who decided to study judo even though he had lost his left arm in a heartrending car accident. An old Japanese judo master taught him, and the boy did well, but after three months of training, he couldn't understand why the master had taught him only one move. He finally asked, "Shouldn't I be learning more moves?"

"This is the only move you'll ever need to know," the old man replied. Not understanding, but believing in his teacher, the boy kept training. Several months later, at his first tournament, the boy easily won his first two matches. The third match proved to be more difficult, but after some time, his opponent became impatient and charged; the boy deftly used his one move to win the match. Still amazed by his success, the boy was now in the finals. This time, his opponent was bigger, stronger, and more experienced. For a while, the boy appeared to be overmatched. Concerned the boy might get hurt, the referee called a time-out. He

was about to stop the match when the boy's teacher intervened. "No," the master insisted, "let him continue."

The match resumed, and soon the boy's opponent made a critical mistake: he dropped his guard. Instantly, the boy used his move to pin him. The boy had won the match and the tournament. He was the champion. On the way home, the boy and his teacher reviewed every move in each match. Then the boy summoned the courage to ask what was really on his mind. "Master, how did I win the tournament with only one move?"

"You won for two reasons," the old man answered. "First, you've almost mastered one of the most difficult throws in all of judo. And second, the only known defense for that move is for your opponent to grab your left arm."

The boy's greatest flaw had become his most powerful potency. In the same way, we may find our weaknesses hold the key to our success because victory often comes from strategies and maneuvers that move us from being on the defensive to being on the offensive. God can help us with those moves, just as the old master taught the boy.

JUDO STORY adapted from: http://www.websites-host.com/insp/istories.html

POST-IT MEDITATION FOR AUGUST 15
I will depend on God's teachings to help me win life's contests.

August 16

The soul's order can never be destroyed.
~Parker Palmer, author and educator

In his book, A Hidden Wholeness, Parker Palmer describes how, years ago, farmers on the Great Plains ran a rope from the back door out to their barn at the first sign of a blizzard. Too many times farmers had wandered off and frozen to death, a whiteout obscuring their homes a few feet away. The rope represented safe passage back to the house—such a simple task to complete, but many a farmer didn't take the time or effort to protect themselves, and they fell victim to the whiteout.

"Today," Parker notes, "we live in a blizzard of another sort." Getting lost in the gales of life—financial, physical, or spiritual—happens far too often. And, Parker declares, in the squall we find it easy to believe our soul "has lost all power to guide our lives." Still, his position is in stark contrast to the lyrics of Leonard Cohen's song that "The blizzard of the world…has overturned the order of the soul." Parker avows the soul can never be shattered and decimated. While it may be hidden for a period of time by a blinding blizzard, it is right there, offering us shelter and safety if we keep our lifeline attached to it.

How do we know our lifeline is secure? Watchman Nee, a Chinese Christian author, wrote about the evidence of staying soul-centered in the Holy Spirit in his book, *The Spiritual Man*:

"One quality which characterizes a spiritual person is the great calm he maintains under every circumstance. Whatever may happen around him or however much he may be provoked, he accepts it all calmly and exhibits an unmovable nature. He is one who is able to regulate his every feeling because his emotion has been yielded to the cross, and his will and spirit are permeated with the power of the Holy Spirit. No extreme provocation has the strength to unsettle him. But if one has not accepted the dealing of the cross upon his emotion, then he will be easily influenced, stimulated, disturbed, and even governed by the external world. He will undergo constant change, for emotion shifts often. The slightest threat from outside…shall upset him and render him helpless. Whoever genuinely desires to be [safe] must let the cross cut deeper into his emotion."

If we allow the Holy Spirit to hold sway over our emotions, we will remain safe.

POST-IT MEDITATION FOR AUGUST 16
Grace is that lifeline to the security of the soul where all is calm.

August 17

He paid for our sins with his own blood….
~1 John 2:2 (NLV)

A poor boy, who was selling goods from door to door to pay his way through school, found he had only one thin dime left. Hungry, he decided he would ask for a meal at the next house. However, he lost his nerve when a lovely young woman opened the door. Instead of a meal he asked for a drink of water. She thought he looked hungry, so she brought him a large glass of milk. He drank it slowly, and then asked, "How much do I owe you?"

"You don't owe me anything," she replied. "Mother has taught us never to accept pay for a kindness."

The grateful boy said, "Then I thank you from my heart."

As Howard Kelly left that house, he not only felt stronger physically, but his faith in God and man was deeper also. He had been ready to give up and quit.

Years later that young woman became critically ill. The local doctors were baffled. They finally sent her to the big city, where they called in specialists to study her rare disease. Dr. Howard Kelly was called in for the consultation. When he heard the name of the town she came from, a strange light filled his eyes.

Immediately he rose and went down the hall of the hospital to her room, recognizing her at once. He went back to the consultation room determined to do his best to save her life. From that day he gave special attention to the case.

After a long struggle, the battle was won. Dr. Kelly requested the business office to pass the final bill to him for approval. He looked at it, then wrote something on the edge and the bill was sent to her room. She feared to open it, for she was sure it would take the rest of her life to pay for it all. Finally she looked, and something caught her attention on the side of the bill. She read the following words:

"Paid in full with one glass of milk"

Signed, Dr. Howard Kelly

Christians can rest easy—no need to worry about a huge bill at the end of life. Christ's death paid our debt in full with his blood.

Source OF HOWARD KELLY STORY: http://academictips.org/blogs/a-glass-of-milk-paid-in-full/

POST-IT MEDITATION FOR AUGUST 17
Thank you God, for freely sending your son to save my life.

August 18

…What matters is faith expressing itself through love.
~Galatians 5:6 (GNT)

As John Lennon realized before he was gunned down in a driveway, every day is precious: "Life is what happens while you are busy making other plans." Like Lennon, we never know when our lives will be snuffed out like a candle, so we need to do more than just exist in the days we are given.

Have you ever known anyone on a deathbed to say, "I wish I had spent more time at the office"? Or: "I wish I had told that person what I really think." "I wish I had spent more time keeping my house clean." "I wish I had been depressed more often." "I wish I had worked in the yard more." "I wish I had had a nicer home or a more expensive car or more beautiful clothes." No, these aren't the desires people think about when their lives are drawing to an end. More likely, we will wish we had shown love more fully and more often, laughed more than we cried, read in the backyard under the shade trees, enjoyed the splendor of nature more.

As Pultizer Prize winning American author and journalist Anna Quindlen's father once wrote on a postcard to her, "If you win the rat race, you're still a rat." Confusing work and other activities with real life is a mistake. In a commencement address at Villanova in 2000, Quindlen stated, "People don't talk about the soul very much anymore," noting, "It is easier to craft a resume than to craft a spirit." She added that accomplishments you list on a resume are "a cold comfort on a winter night, or when you're sad, or broke, or lonely, or when you've gotten back the medical tests results and they're not so good." Her advice to the graduates: get a life. That doesn't imply we shouldn't do a good job at work or keep our houses or yards neat. It simply means we should keep our priorities in focus.

A real life, Quindlen said, is not a rat race for the next promotion, a bigger house, or other worldly possessions. Urging the graduates to think, she asked: "Do you think you'd care so very much about those things if you blew an aneurysm one afternoon or found a lump in your breast?"

A real life is comprised of being a good friend, a loving parent or grandparent—or sucking in the smell of salt water at the beach. Pausing to watch a squirrel sit atop a fence or a line of turtles sunning on a log. Stopping in a park to watch a child learning to ride a bike. Visiting a neighbor who is ill. Letting a puppy sit in your lap and lick your face. Picking up the phone and calling your parent.

Real life is treasuring your connection to others. And when you do that, your spirit will be filled and overflowing.

Adapted from a commencement speech at Villanova by Anna Quindlen

POST-IT MEDITATION FOR AUGUST 18
God, help me live a life focused on the treasures you give me.

August 19

Then people everywhere will know about the glory of the LORD.
~Habakkuk 2:14 (ERV)

A homeless man sitting on the boardwalk at Coney Island taught Anna Quindlen one of life's most important lessons. It was December, and she was doing a story about how the homeless survive in the winter months. Sitting with one of the men living adrift, she dangled her feet over the side of the pier, and the man told her about how he panhandled the streets when the summer crowds were gone, sleeping in a church if the temperature dropped below freezing. In the warmer months, when a police officer came by during the day, he hid behind the Tilt-a-Whirl. But when they weren't around, he stayed on the boardwalk, even in the winter, when he wore newspapers to keep warm. Quindlen asked him why he didn't go to one of the shelters, why he didn't check himself into a hospital for detox.

The homeless man continued staring at the ocean and said, "Look at the view, young lady. Look at the view."

That's what we need to do every day—look at the view. Quindlen described it as words of wisdom from a man with not a dime in his pocket, no place to go, nowhere to be.

What do you see from where you sit as you read this? A blank wall? If so, tomorrow put a picture of a shimmering seashore or a towering mountain on that wall. Your back yard? Does it have at least one flower blooming? If not, plant one. If you don't have a view, you can walk outside, down a tree-lined street, or through a grassy park. You can watch a yellow-tipped butterfly sipping nectar from a budding flower, holding your breath as it flies toward you, landing on your shoulder.

When you have nothing else, you can always find a view. You can arise early to see a spectacular sunrise or stay outside to watch the sun go down in fiery splendor. You can stare at a star-sprinkled sky or contemplate a crescent moon on a dark, velvety night. All free gifts. As the psalmist sang, "Shout joyfully to God...How awesome are [his] works" (Psalm 66:1, 3, NASB).

Adapted from a commencement speech at Villanova by Anna Quindlen

POST-IT MEDITATION FOR AUGUST 19
*Thank you, God, for the glorious views
you created for my pleasure and uplifting.*

August 20

But if we confess our sins to him, he is faithful and just to forgive us our sins and to cleanse us from all wickedness.
~1 John 1:9 (NLT)

While visiting his grandparents on their farm, a little boy was given a slingshot to play with in the woods. Although he practiced among the trees, he never hit the target, so he headed back to the farm for dinner, discouraged. As he walked, he saw his Grandma's pet duck. An impulse propelled the slingshot to fly, and he hit the duck square in the head, killing it. Shocked and grieved, he hid the dead duck in the wood pile. As he finished, he looked up to see his sister watching. Sally had seen it all, but she said nothing.

After lunch the next day, his Grandma asked Sally to help her with the dishes, but Sally said, "Grandma, Johnny told me he wanted to help in the kitchen." Then, she whispered to him, "Remember the duck?" So Johnny did the dishes.

Later that day, Grandpa asked if the children wanted to go fishing and Grandma said, "I'm sorry, but I need Sally to help make supper." Sally just smiled and said,

"Well, that's all right because Johnny told me he wanted to help." She whispered again, "Remember the duck?" So Sally went fishing and Johnny stayed to help.

After several days of Johnny doing both his chores and Sally's, he finally couldn't stand it any longer. He went to Grandma, confessing he had killed the duck. Grandma knelt down, gave him a hug, and said, "Sweetheart, I know. You see, I was standing at the window and saw the whole thing, but because I love you, I forgave you. I was just wondering how long you would let Sally make a slave of you."

Each of us has something in our past, something we have done, that the devil keeps throwing up in our face (lying, stealing, cheating, drinking, drugs, debt, divorce, fear, bad habits, hatred, anger, abortion, bitterness, etc.). Whatever it is, we need to know God was standing at the window, and he saw the whole episode. He hasn't missed one event in our whole life, yet like the little boy's grandma, God loves us and forgives us. He's just wondering how long we will let the devil keep us in slavery. Like Johnny, all we need to do is confess to feel better.

POST-IT MEDITATION FOR AUGUST 20
God was standing at the window; I might as well confess!

August 21

...do not be so hard on your children that they will give up trying to do what is right.
~Colossians 3:21 (NLV)

Arguing with children can be risky.

In a grade school lesson, a teacher was teaching about whales.

A little girl in class piped up and said: "I just learned in the Bible that Jonah was swallowed by a whale."

The teacher said it was physically impossible for a whale to swallow a human because even though it was a very large mammal, its throat was relatively small.

The girl said: "I am sure Jonah was swallowed by a whale."

The teacher reiterated that a whale could not swallow a human; it was physically impossible.

The little girl replied: "My Sunday school teacher told me Jonah was swallowed, and she would not lie to me."

A bit perturbed by this, the teacher proclaimed: "That is a 'story' from the Bible; it is not factual, and I will not argue with you."

After a little thought, the girl responded: "Well, when I get to heaven, I will ask Jonah."

Now challenged, the teacher spouted: "What if Jonah didn't go to heaven?"

Not at all daunted, the girl quipped, "Okay, then you ask him."

~~~

A kindergarten teacher was observing her classroom of children while they drew. Stopping by a desk where one little girl was working diligently, she asked what she was drawing.

"I'm drawing God," the child replied.

Pausing, the teacher thought for a moment and then remarked, "But no one knows what God looks like."

Without slowing down her pencil or looking up from her drawing, the child said, "They will in a minute."

Children fill us with laughter and keep us humble. Anyone who has children knows how exasperating they can occasionally be, but the blessings they bring cannot be measured.

POST-IT MEDITATION FOR AUGUST 21
Thank you, God, for children who delight and teach us.

August 22

For anger rests in the bosom of fools.
~Ecclesiastes 7:9 (ASV)

The Living Bible translation of the above verse advises us to keep our temper under control, declaring it is foolish to harbor a grudge. Other versions of this scripture put the same thought in different words, but all are based on the premise that having patience in dealing with our fellowman is wiser than being so filled with pride that we respond in haste and anger.

Woodrow Wilson advised, "Let us sit down and take counsel together, and if we differ from each other, understand why it is we differ, just what the points at issue are. We will presently find we are not so far apart after all, that the points on which we agree are many, and if we only have the patience and the candor and the desire to get together, we will get together."

Frequently, though, we fail to pause and consider how another person feels about a situation or an issue. Puffed up with self-importance, we see our views as superior or right. And, if our pride has been insulted, we think we have the right to strike back. As the writer of Ecclesiastes tells us in the eighth verse of the seventh chapter, "The end of a thing is better than the beginning," but the outcome of anger expressed in haste has little chance of making a situation better.

How can we control our temper? Perhaps we can learn from the little boy whose father tried to alter his son's bad temper.

The father gave his son a bag of nails and told him every time he lost his temper, he must hammer a nail into the back of the fence.

The first day the boy drove 37 nails into the fence. Over the next few weeks, as he learned to control his anger, the number of nails hammered daily gradually dwindled down. He discovered it was easier to hold his temper than to drive those nails into the fence.

Finally the day came when the boy didn't lose his temper at all. He told his father about it, and the father suggested that the boy now pull out one nail for each day he was able to hold his temper. The days passed and the young boy was finally able to tell his father all the nails were gone.

The father took his son by the hand and led him to the fence. He said, "You have done well, my son, but look at the holes in the fence. The fence will never be the same. When you say words in anger, they leave a scar just like these."

You can put a knife in a man and draw it out. It won't matter how many times you say, "I'm sorry," the wound is still there.

POST-IT MEDITATION FOR AUGUST 22
When my heart fills with anger, I will pause,
ask God for control, and hold my heated words.

August 23

Have mercy on those who doubt.
~Jude 1:22 (CEB)

Have you ever felt like the man in Mark 9, who came to Jesus one day, asking him to heal his son of an affliction that no one else had been able to cure? Convinced if anyone could help his son, Jesus was the one, he also confessed his faith wasn't strong: "I do believe! Help me to believe more!" (vs. 24, NCV).

If we are honest, even when God has been very good to us, when we have seen his grace and power in our lives, we sometimes have doubts. Even ministers feel uncertainties and misgivings occasionally. Those who have lived through doubts with their faith intact can help others, adhering to the admonition of Proverbs 9:9 (NLT): "Instruct the wise, and they will be even wiser; teach a righteous man, and he will learn even more."

A young, new preacher was walking with an older, more seasoned preacher in a garden one day. Feeling a bit insecure, doubting what God had for him to do, he asked the older preacher for guidance. The older preacher walked up to a rosebush and handed the young preacher a rosebud and told him to open it without tearing off any petals. The young preacher looked in disbelief at the older preacher and was trying to figure out what a rosebud could possibly have to do with his wanting to know the will of God for his life and for his ministry. But, because of his high respect for the older preacher, he proceeded to try to unfold the rose, while keeping every petal intact. It wasn't long before he realized it was impossible to do so.

Noticing the younger preacher's inability to unfold the rosebud while keeping it whole, the older preacher began to recite the following poem:

> *It is only a tiny rosebud, a flower of God's design;*
> *But I cannot unfold the petals with these clumsy hands of mine.*
> *The secret of unfolding flowers is not known to such as I.*
> *God opens this flower so sweetly, when in my hands they fade and die.*
> *If I cannot unfold a rosebud, this flower of God's design,*
> *Then how can I think I have wisdom to unfold this*
> *life of mine?*
> *So I'll trust in him for his leading each moment of every day.*
> *I will look to him for his guidance each step of the*
> *pilgrim way.*
> *The pathway that lies before me, only my heavenly*
> *Father knows.*
> *I'll trust him to unfold the moments, just as he unfolds*
> *the rose.*

Billy Graham once wrote that our doubts come when we take our eyes from God and put them on our circumstances. He illustrates this point with two examples: Elijah's doubts arose when he became fearful and exhausted, worried his life was a failure (I Kings 19:1-10). In the New Testament, John 20:24-25 shows that Thomas' doubts overcame his beliefs when he refused to listen to first-hand witnesses who had seen Christ after his resurrection.

Graham avows our doubts will either drive us away from God or push us closer to him. His advice: "Don't allow doubts to take root in your soul, but immediately turn them over to God and draw closer to him."

If we spend time in Bible reading and prayer every day of our lives, the lower our threshold for doubting will be. But we are human, and even our closeness to God is no guarantee the devil won't put doubts in our hearts. We are not helpless, though, for just as Jesus reached out and took Peter's hand when his faith wavered as he walked on water, he will take ours, exclaiming, "What little faith you have! Why did you doubt?" (Matthew 14:31, GNT). Though the waves of our lives are rough, Christ's hand is always there waiting to lead us to safety. Why do we doubt?

POST-IT MEDITATION FOR AUGUST 23
I am safe as long as I keep my eyes and my heart focused on God.

August 24

And to all these things, you must add love. Love holds everything and every-body together and makes all these good things perfect.
~Colossians 3:14 (NLV)

Back in the fifteenth century, in a tiny village near Nuremberg, a family with 18 children lived. Merely to keep food on the table for this throng, the father and head of the household, a goldsmith by profession, worked more than 15 hours a day at his trade and any other paying chore he could find. Despite their seemingly hopeless condition, two of Albrecht Durer the Elder's children had a dream. They both wanted to pursue their talent for art, but they knew full well their father would never be financially able to send either of them to Nuremberg to study at the Academy.

After many long discussions at night in their crowded bed, the two boys finally worked out a pact. They would toss a coin. The loser would go down into the nearby mines and, with his earnings, support his brother while he attended the academy. Then, in four years, when the brother who won the toss completed his studies, he would support the other brother at the academy, either with sales of his artwork or, if necessary, also by laboring in the mines.

They tossed a coin on a Sunday morning after church. Albrecht Durer won the toss and went off to Nuremberg. Albert went down into the dangerous mines and, for the next four years, financed his brother, whose work at the academy was almost an immediate sensation. Albrecht's etchings, his woodcuts, and his oils were far better than those of most of his professors, and by the time he graduated, he was beginning to earn considerable fees for his commissioned works.

When the young artist returned to his village, the Durer family held a festive dinner on their lawn to celebrate Albrecht's triumphant homecoming. After a long and memorable meal, punctuated with music and laughter, Albrecht rose from his honored position at the head of the table to drink a toast to his beloved brother for the years of sacrifice that had enabled Albrecht to fulfill his ambition. His closing words were, "And now, Albert, blessed brother of mine, now it is your turn. Now you can go to Nuremberg to pursue your dream, and I will take care of you."

All heads turned in eager expectation to the far end of the table where Albert sat, tears streaming down his pale face, shaking his lowered head from side to side while he sobbed and repeated, over and over, "No ...no ...no ...no."

Finally, Albert rose and wiped the tears from his cheeks. He glanced down the long table at the faces he loved, and then, holding his hands close to his right cheek, he said softly, "No, brother. I cannot go to Nuremberg. It is too late for me. Look…look what four years in the mines have done to my hands! The bones in every finger have been smashed at least once, and lately I have been suffering from arthritis so badly in my right hand that I cannot even hold a glass to return your toast, much less make delicate lines on parchment or canvas with a pen or a brush. No, brother, for me it is too late."

More than 450 years have passed. By now, Albrecht Durer's hundreds of masterful portraits, pen and silver-point sketches, watercolors, charcoals, woodcuts, and copper engravings hang in every great museum in the world, but the odds are good that you, like most people, are familiar with only one of Albrecht Durer's works. More than merely being familiar with it, you very well may have a reproduction hanging in your home or office.

One day, to pay homage to Albert for all that he had sacrificed, Albrecht Durer painstakingly drew his brother's abused hands with palms together and thin fingers stretched skyward. He called his powerful drawing simply "Hands," but the entire world almost immediately opened their hearts to his great masterpiece and renamed his tribute of love, "The Praying Hands."

POST-IT MEDITATION FOR AUGUST 24
The next time I see a copy of the praying hands, I will take a second look.
They will be a reminder that no one—no one—ever makes it alone!

August 25

We are called to be fruit and drink for one another.
~Wendy M. Wright, professor of theology

In an earlier devotion, I talked about a second cousin I regularly visit in prison. Today, I received a letter from him thanking me for my most recent visit: "For days after you come, my time in here goes so much easier. You don't know just how much it means to me to know you take time out of your life to come down to visit me. I appreciate it more than you will ever know." By the time I read this much, my eyes were misting from guilt for all the years I had not stayed in touch. But the next words broke my heart: "I am grateful to have someone who cares enough. Other family members know where I am, and sometimes I wonder why I can't even get a postcard or a letter from them telling me how they are or what they are up to." Despite the kind words about my current visits, I felt like I had been stabbed in the heart. For more than 28 years I had been one of the neglectful ones. How many times had I not heeded the urging to slow down long enough to write a letter? On how many occasions did my husband and I talk about stopping by the prison in Georgia on a trip to Florida? I doubt I will live long enough to make up for those years where self-interest pushed down love for one who felt no one cared. When I read 1 John 3:17-18 (ESV), I feel the weight of my sin: "But if anyone has the world's goods and sees his brother in need, yet closes his heart against him, how does God's love abide in him? Let us not love in word or talk but in deed and in truth."

For most of us, love of family members falls just short of our love for God. And yet, occasionally, we desert a sister or brother, a parent or grandparent, a niece or nephew—perhaps someone who brought shame to the family, someone who deeply hurt our feelings, or someone who angered us or stole from us. We all know of parents who have become so estranged from their children that their son or daughter doesn't come to the funeral of a mother or father.

Family members are a gift from God. If we become distanced from them through neglect or resentment, it might help to reread 1 Corinthians 13 (NIV), which says, in part, "If we speak in the tongues of men or angels but have no love, we are only a resounding gong or clanging cymbal...if we have faith that can move mountains but have no love, we are nothing." If we need to examine our hearts, we should do it without delay. Today, we can change how we love others; tomorrow it may be too late.

AUTHOR'S NOTE: As I noted previously, two cousins now join me in my visits to the prison. The above referenced letter was written before their visits began.

POST-IT MEDITATION FOR AUGUST 25
***I will examine relationships with family members
and with love restore any that are neglected or broken.***

August 26

**Yet God raised Jesus to life! God's Spirit now
lives in you, and he will raise you to life by his Spirit.**
~Romans 8:11 (CEV)

Years ago a monastery had fallen on hard times. It was decimated to the extent there were only five monks left in the mother house: the Abbott and four others, all of whom were over seventy. With heavy hearts, they shuffled through the cloisters, serving God but worried. Clearly, it was a dying order.

On the edge of the woods stood an old hut where a rabbi from a nearby town sometimes came to fast and pray. The monks never talked with him, but they felt his presence, finding peace when he was nearby.

One day the Abbott decided to visit the Rabbi and ask for advice. After talking, both men were in tears, with the Rabbi concluding, "I know how it is. The spirit has gone out of people. Almost no one comes to the synagogue anymore."

The Abbott pressed the rabbi, pleading with him for advice that might save the monastery. Finally, the rabbi told him, "The only thing I can tell you is that the Messiah is among you."

When the other monks heard the Rabbi's words, they were startled. "The Messiah is one of us? One of us, here at the monastery?" Each ran the list of monks through his head: "Do you suppose he meant the Abbott? Of course, it must be the Abbott, who has been our leader for so long. Or, could it be Brother Thomas, who is certainly a holy man? Or is it possible he meant Brother Elrod, even though he is so crotchety? But then Elrod is very wise. Surely he could not have meant Brother Phillips—he's too passive. But then, magically, he's always there when you need him. Of course, he didn't mean me—yet supposing he did?"

As they contemplated, the old monks began to treat each other with extraordinary respect, believing that one of them might be the Messiah.

Because the forest surrounding the monastery was quiet and beautiful, people occasionally came to visit, to picnic or wander along the old paths. Over time, they sensed the aura of extraordinary respect now permeating the monastery. They began to come more frequently, bringing their friends, and their friends brought friends. Some of the younger men who came to visit began to engage in conversation with the monks. After a while, one asked if he might join. Then another, and then another. Within a few years, the monastery once again became a thriving order—and thanks to the Rabbi's gift—a vibrant community of light and love for the whole realm.

Like the monks, we have the choice to serve God with heavy hearts or to let Christ dwell among us, bringing peace and harmony.

MONK STORY adapted from "The Rabbi's Gift" by William R. White

POST-IT MEDITATION FOR AUGUST 26
I will try to live in a way that reflects the presence of Christ within me.

August 27

But after you have suffered for a little while, the God of all grace, who calls you to share his eternal glory in union with Christ, will himself perfect you and give you firmness, strength, and a sure foundation.
~1 Peter 5:10 (GNT)

Susannah Spurgeon, wife of the renowned Dr. Charles Spurgeon, suffered many years from a disability and later endured the sorrowful loss of her husband. In 1892 she wrote, "Oh! My husband, my husband, every moment of my now desolate life I wonder how I can live without thee! The heart that for many years has been filled and satisfied with thy love must needs be very empty and stricken now that thou are gone!"

Whether suffering health tribulations or deep grief, Mrs. Spurgeon not only had great faith, but she also had humanness. She was not afraid to admit agony. Once she wrote, *"At the close of a dark and gloomy day, I lay resting on my couch as the deeper night drew on; and though all was bright within my cozy room, some of the external darkness seemed to have entered into my soul and obscured its spiritual vision. Vainly, I tried to see the hand that I knew held mine and guided my fog-enveloped feet along a steep and slippery path of suffering."*

From her troubled soul, Mrs. Spurgeon asked God why he had dealt with her in this way? Like many of us, she wanted to know why her Lord so often sent sharp and bitter pain. She related that, for a while, "Silence reigned in the little room, broken only by the crackling of the oak log burning in the fireplace." And then, she says, she heard a clear musical note, small and gentle, like a robin beneath her window. At first she thought she was mistaken—no bird would be singing at that time of year in the pitch blackness of the night. But the tender trill came again, and she turned her head toward the sound, realizing that it came from the log on the fire.

"The fire is letting loose the imprisoned music from the old oak's inmost heart!" exclaimed a friend sitting with her.

Musing, the friend thought aloud that the oak log had stored this song in the days "when all was well with him, when birds twittered merrily on his branches, and the soft sunlight flecked his tender leaves with gold. But he had grown old since then, and hardened; ring after ring of knotty growth had sealed up the long-forgotten melody, until the fierce tongues of the flames came to consume his callousness, and the vehement heart of the fire wrung from him at once a song and a sacrifice."

So it is with us—we can become so roughened and scarred from pain that the melodious songs we once heard can only be set free by more pain. Strangely, Mrs. Spurgeon felt sweet comfort in her suffering as the log sang in the fire. "Singing in the fire. Yes, God helping us, if that is the only way to get harmony" out of our hardened hearts, we will survive.

For those who struggle with sorrow, it is helpful to know that even a person of great faith like Mrs. Spurgeon can feel the deep intensity of loss. Like others who lose a dearly loved one, she felt desolation and wondered how she could go on without her husband. The story of her sorrow and how she survived it shows on many days she had a pathetic longing to join her beloved. But there was more: "Ah! My husband," she wrote in one passage, "the blessed earthly ties which we welcomed so rapturously are dissolved now, and death has hidden thee from my mortal eyes; but not even death can divide thee from me or sever the love which united our hearts so closely. I feel it living and growing still, and I believe it will find its full and spiritual development only when we shall meet in the glory land and worship before the throne." Written approximately seven years after the words of despair quoted at the beginning of this devotion, these words reveal a Christian who grew in faith, reaffirming her belief that love can keep us linked to our beloved ones beyond the grave, until the time when we can be with them once again. Perhaps Henry Scott Holland (1847-1918), Canon of St. Paul's Cathedral in London, said it best:

Death is nothing at all—
I have only slipped away into the next room.
I am I and you are you
Whatever we were to each other
That we are still.
Call me by my old familiar name;
Speak to me in the easy way you always used;
Put no difference into your tone.
Wear no forced air of solemnity or sorrow;
Laugh as we always laughed
At the little jokes we always enjoyed together
Play, smile, think of me, pray for me.
Let my name be ever the household word that it always was;
Let it be spoken without effort,
Without the ghost of a shadow in it...
Why should I be out of mind
Because I am out of sight?
I am waiting for you for an interval
Somewhere very near,
Just around the corner.
All is well.
Nothing is past; nothing is lost;
One brief moment and all will be as it was before.
How we shall laugh at the trouble of parting when we meet again!

POST-IT MEDITATION FOR AUGUST 27
I will endure the fire, knowing God will someday release singing from my soul once again because I can take comfort in knowing I will see my loved ones again.

August 28

And Jesus said to them, "Go everywhere in the world, and tell everyone the good news."
~Mark 16:15 (GW)

On August 15, 1976, a regular daily flight originated in Quinto, Ecuador, and departed for the southern Ecuadorian city of Cuenca. The four engine Vickers Viscount plane carried 55 passengers and 4 crew members. When the plane disappeared from radar screens, the normal flight of 40 minutes became a painful mystery that wasn't resolved for more than two decades.

Flight #232 never reached its destination. It completely vanished—for 26 years. Ongoing investigations turned up nothing, until finally they were terminated, recording the fact that 59 human beings and a 727 Boeing jet had evaporated into nothingness. Despite countless rumors about the fate of the plane, families and friends were denied peace of mind and closure as to the plight of their loved ones. That changed in October 2002 when Chimborazo Mountain climbers discovered the Boeing jet imbedded in the snow and ice of one of the highest volcanic mountains in the world. Further investigation in February 2003 confirmed the flight was Saeta 232. Amazingly, the plane was almost intact—and the bodies had been kept well-preserved by the icy conditions. After 26 years, bodies were removed, identified, and returned to families.

Sadly, the story does not end there. Upon examining the wrecked plane and preserved bodies, investigators knew they were not the first ones to discover the wreckage. The passengers had been stripped of their jewelry, wallets, and other possessions. No one knows when, and no one will likely ever know who made the initial discovery. What is known is that they never bothered to inform authorities so loved ones of those who perished on that fateful flight could know what happened. They apparently valued jewelry and money over bringing closure to loved ones. The sin of theft was minor compared to knowing the truth, possessing yet concealing the knowledge that could free grieving hearts. It is hard to imagine such selfish greed reigning over mercy and loving kindness.

Christians have a knowledge that can bring peace and comfort to people who are lost without God and without hope. Do we understand the critical and moral need to share what we know? Why do we not bother to share with unbelievers the saving message of Jesus Christ? As Mark Creech said, "Perhaps the greatest of all sins is to know the truth, to possess the knowledge that can free others, and then to conceal it for reasons that are essentially selfish."

SOURCE OF FLIGHT #32 STORY: http://www.actsweb.org/articles/article. php?i=517&d=2&c=2Agape Press (Richard Inness) and http://headlines.agapepress.org/archive/7/152003mc.asp

POST-IT MEDITATION FOR AUGUST 28
I may not have great gifts of
eloquent speech, but I know the truth
and can share it in my own way.

August 29

I know there is nothing better for people than to be happy and to do good while they live....
~Ecclesiastes 3:12 (NIV)

The best way to keep troubles from pulling us down is to confront them with a smile. An impossible possibility? Not so. We decide whether we will be happy or unhappy, regardless of what happens to us. It is a daily choice we can all make. When we arise, we can face the day with an energetic enthusiasm or a pessimistic attitude. Which one do you think has the greatest potential to chase away dark clouds that may fill our skies that day? American writer William Arthur Ward knew the answer: "A cloudy day is no match for a sunny disposition."

About now, the pessimist is thinking, "That's crazy. It doesn't matter whether I am happy or gloomy, my problems will be the same." But the optimist is thinking, "While this may be an oversimplification of life's ups and downs, maybe I should try it."

Abraham Lincoln once said people are just about as happy as they make up their minds to be. So why not try it—make up our minds to be happy regardless of the clouds hanging low in the sky. And if we get off track, if we let a problem bring a frown to our face, we should remove it as quickly as possible. Children seem to innately get over their fits of anger or crying spells swiftly. They let their emotions out, and then a smile magically returns to their faces.

But the question remains, "How can we be happy in bad times as well as good times?" Norman Vincent Peale tells about one of his friends, H. C. Mattern, who was consistently and genuinely happy. He spread his happiness to others by handing out a unique business card that had the following on the reverse side:

The way to happiness: keep your heart free from hate, your mind from worry. Live simply, expect little, give much. Fill your life with love. Scatter sunshine. Forget self, think of others. Do as you would be done by. Try this for a week and you will be surprised.

Will it work? We'll never know until we do it for a week—and a week is such a short time to invest in something that has the potential to reap lifetime benefits of happiness.

Smiles can work magic, but the following piece of writing adds a godly twist and thus a deeper perspective to the different ways we can react to what happens in life:

A man fell into a pit and couldn't get himself out.
A subjective person came along and said, "I feel for you down there."

An objective person walked by and said, "It's logical
that someone would fall down there."
A Pharisee said, "Only bad people fall into pits."
A mathematician calculated how deep the pit was.
A news reporter wanted the exclusive story on the pit.
A self-pitying person said, "You haven't seen
anything until you've seen my pit."
A fire-and-brimstone preacher said, "You deserve your pit."
A psychologist observed, "The pit is just in your mind."
A psychiatrist noted, "Your mother and father are
to blame for your being in that pit."
A self-esteem therapist said, "Believe in yourself and
you can get out of that pit."
An optimist said, "Things could be worse."
A pessimist claimed, "Things will get worse."
Jesus, seeing the man, took him by the hand and lifted him out of the pit.

Yes, smiles can brighten our days, but the best way to have a smile is to know Jesus because he is the answer to all of our problems.

POST-IT MEDITATION FOR AUGUST 29
I can spread sunshine among dark clouds because
I know God can help wipe them away.

August 30

Set me as a seal upon your heart, as a seal upon your arm, for love is strong as death…. Many waters cannot quench love, neither can floods drown it.
~Song of Solomon 8:6-7 (ASV)

I once read a list called "Some Things You Keep." The unknown author of the list included good teeth, warm coats, and bald husbands because *"They're good for you, reliable and practical and so sublime that to throw them away would make the garbage man a thief."* So, she said, we hang on to something old sometimes because it is better than something new. More importantly, what we know is often better than something unknown.

I grew up in an age when, like the above writer, we made do with old things. Like the author, I had practical parents—my mother mended clothes, I wore hand-me-downs, my dad had his shoes resoled, and we used aluminum foil again after wiping it off. And, again like the author, I sometimes became cantankerous—rebelling at reusing and reusing anything and everything.

The desire to be wasteful once in a while occasionally arises in all of us. After all, waste means you are so affluent you can throw things away because there will be more.

But, the writer found, when her father died, "On that clear autumn night, in the chill of the hospital room, I was struck with the pain of learning that sometimes there isn't any more. Sometimes what you care about most gets all used up and goes away, never to return."

So, the writer reminds us, "While you have it...it's best to love it, and care for it, and fix it when it's broken, and heal it when it's sick. That's true for marriage and old cars and children with bad report cards and dogs with bad hips and aging parents. You keep them because they're worth it...." And you keep other beings..."like a best friend who moved away...or a classmate you grew up with. There are just some individuals who make life important...people you know are special, and you keep them close."

Colossians 3:14 tells us love binds things together in perfect unity. Love is a virtue we should keep. It seals the relationships we treasure.

POST-IT MEDITATION FOR AUGUST 30
I will not be wasteful—with possessions or with people.

August 31

Why, O Lord, do you stand far away? Why do you hide yourself in times of trouble?
~Psalm 10:1 (ESV)

Sometimes it seems as if God is oblivious to our pain. Or, if he is aware of it, he doesn't care. We pray for relief from troubles, but none comes. We pray for healing, but a loved one dies. We pray for a child, but we remain barren. We pray for a job, but we cannot find one. We are left to feel like C.S. Lewis, who said, when we ask for God's help, we not only hear a door slamming in our face—we hear it being bolted and locked. "After that, silence. You may as well turn away. The longer you wait, the more emphatic the silence will become."

Although Lewis' frustration was connected to the death of his wife, the feeling of being shut out by God can come to us in any circumstance. We have all experienced unanswered prayer, prayer that may have been uttered in desperation or despair.

When God says, "Knock and it shall be opened," Lewis ponders whether that means we must "hammer and kick the door like a maniac." And when God says, "Ask and you shall receive," why shouldn't we become discouraged when nothing happens? Perhaps, Lewis suggests, the problem is not with God but with us. "After all, you must have a capacity to receive, or even omnipotence can't give." He suggests our own panic or emotion may temporarily destroy our capacity to "let go and let God." Instead, we think we know how God should answer our prayers. Anything less than our desire is taken as a door slammed in our face.

Over time, Lewis gradually realized the bolted door was no longer bolted. He questions whether it was his own frantic need that had slammed it in his face. "The time when there is nothing at all in your soul except a cry for help may be just the time when God can't give it: you are like the drowning man who can't be helped because he clutches and grabs." For God to help us, we have to let go of our crisis and trust him to handle it in the way that is best for us in his eternal design. The answer may not be the one we want, but it is the right one.

I asked for strength that I might achieve; God made me weak that I might obey.
I asked for health that I might do greater things; he gave me
infirmity that I might do better things.
I asked for riches that I might be happy; I was given
poverty that I might be wise.
I asked for power that I might have the praise of man; I was
given weakness that I might feel the need of God.
I asked for all things that I might enjoy life; I was given life that
I might enjoy all things.
I received nothing that I asked for; all that I hoped for.
And my prayer was answered. I am most blessed.
~Poem left by a soldier on a Virginia battlefield in 1865

POST-IT MEDITATION FOR AUGUST 31
When I am overcome with trouble or tragedy, I will pray for the wisdom and capacity to turn my anxiety and distress over to God.

September 1

But the dove found no rest for the sole of her foot and returned unto [Noah]…And the dove came in to him in the evening, and, lo, in her mouth was an olive leaf.
~Genesis 8:9-11 (NKJV)

When Noah released a dove after the torrential rains stopped, she was unable to find a place to land because the waters still covered the earth. Seven days later, Noah released the bird again, and this time she came back to him with an olive leaf in her mouth, signifying that the waters were receding.

One wonders if Noah became discouraged and fearful the first time the dove returned. *We* might have doubted, but considering the faith Noah demonstrated by building an ark though no one had ever witnessed a flood or even seen rain, he likely held firm in his belief that he could trust God. And God proved him right. He had not forgotten Noah and the animals on the ark. He caused a wind to blow, and the waters were pushed back. The third time the dove was released, it did not return. Noah knew then it was safe for his family and the animals to disembark.

God knows when the time is right for everything that happens in our lives. He knows when to give encouragement and when to withhold it. Undoubtedly, he realizes we grow stronger when we have to wait. How wonderful faith is when we trust without a visible sign in the sky that all will be well. We can be assured God hears our prayers. He knows the concerns of our hearts, and when the time is right, "Through waves, and clouds, and storms he gently clears [the] way." As the timeless song continues, God sees our weakness. He knows how much we can endure as he perfects us for his kingdom.

A woman who was observing a silversmith noticed he held the silver in the middle of the fire where the flames were hottest. The silversmith explained this was necessary to burn away all of the impurities and that he had to watch the silver constantly to make sure it didn't get so hot it would be destroyed. The observer asked how he knew when to remove the silver from the fire; in other words, how could he tell when the silver was fully refined? With a smile, he responded, "Oh, that's easy—when I see my image in it."

So it is with the fires where God refines us. He holds us in the hottest part of the fire, but he keeps his eye on us and removes us when he can see his image in us.

POST-IT MEDITATION FOR SEPTEMBER 1
**When I feel the heat of the fire, I will remember
God is watching and will not let me be destroyed.**

September 2

Be wise in the way you act toward outsiders: make the most of every opportunity.
~Colossians 4:5 (NIV)

History is replete with famous people who had success despite numerous setbacks:

Abraham Lincoln ran for public office seven times—and was defeated every time—before running for president of the United States and winning.

Thomas Edison struggled through thousands of experiments before perfecting one invention—the light bulb—, later being awarded over one thousand patents.

Robert Kennedy flunked first grade but went on to become attorney general of the United States.

Albert Einstein didn't learn to talk until he was four years old but ultimately communicated complicated scientific theories throughout the world.

Clark Gable worked as a water boy in a mine, a lumberjack, a garage mechanic, and an actor in a tent show before attaining success on the big screen.

The key to realizing your life's goals is to refuse to give up. Many times the difference in results is simply a matter of perspective. The story of two salesmen supports this premise:

The two sales reps were sent from America to sell shoes to the aborigines. Each rep was sent to a different part of the Australian outback to see if they could drum up some business. Some time later, the company received telegrams from both agents.

The first one said, "No business here. Natives don't wear shoes."

The second one said, "Great opportunity here—none of the natives are wearing shoes."

God surrounds us with opportunities, but we are sometimes too blind to see them. Instead, we see potential failure and overwhelming obstacles. With God's help, we can reach goals we think are beyond us. He can give us the vision to see opportunities where alone we might see impossible hurdles. He can give us the ability and the persistence to accomplish great goals if we just ask for his help.

POST-IT MEDITATION FOR SEPTEMBER 2
The next time I see a situation as hopeless,
I will remember the sales reps and with
God's help, change my perspective—turning
the difficulty into a chance for success.

September 3

The God of heaven will give us success.
~Nehemiah 2:20 (GNT)

During World War II, a U.S. Marine was separated from his unit on a Pacific Island. The fighting had been intense, and in the smoke and the crossfire he lost touch with his comrades.

Alone in the jungle, he could hear enemy soldiers coming in his direction. Scrambling for cover, he found his way up a high ridge to several small caves in the rock. Quickly, he crawled inside one of the caves. Although safe for the moment, he realized once the enemy soldiers looking for him swept the ridge, they would soon search all the caves and he would be killed.

As he waited, he prayed, "Lord, if it be your will, please protect me. Whatever your will, though, I love you and trust you. Amen."

After praying, he lay quietly listening to the enemy begin to draw close. He thought, "Well, I guess the Lord isn't going to help me out of this one." Then he saw a spider begin to build a web over the front of his cave.

As he watched, listening to the enemy searching for him all the while, the spider layered strand after strand of web across the opening of the cave.

"Ha," he thought, "What I need is a brick wall, and the Lord sent me a spider web. God must have a sense of humor."

As the enemy drew closer, he watched from the darkness of his hideout and could see them searching one cave after another. As they came to his, he got ready to make his last stand. To his amazement, however, after glancing in the direction of his cave, they moved on. Suddenly, he realized that with the spider web over the entrance, his cave looked as if no one had entered for quite a while. "Lord, forgive me," prayed the young man. "I had forgotten that with you a spider's web is stronger than a brick wall."

When we face great crisis or difficulty, we forget God can use the most unlikely circumstances to give us victory. Just as Nehemiah reminded the Israelites when they had the daunting task of rebuilding Jerusalem, we should not forget that with God we will be successful.

POST-IT MEDITATION FOR SEPTEMBER 3
When I face fear, I will remember the spider web.

September 4

You will make me greater than ever.
~Psalm 71:21 (GNT)

A farmer planted two kinds of seeds side by side in a fertile field.

One species of seeds was excited, as a group declaring, "We want to see how far we can send our roots into the earth beneath us. Then we'll grow, thrusting our green sprouts up toward the sky, unfurling our tender tendrils to show the world we are alive. We'll be refreshed by the dew each morning. And thrill to feel the warmth of the sun." And so the plants grew, strong and well.

The second set of seeds seemed apprehensive. They wanted to allow their roots to dig deep into the earth and to experience the excitement of green leaves and buds, but worries held them back. "What if the earth swallows our roots and snuffs them out? What if breaking the crust of the earth damages our tender shoots of green? Worse still, what if a bug eats our leaves or a passing child jerks them from the ground?" Full of fear, the seeds decided to wait, maybe it would be safer later, or maybe life would be good just staying on top of the ground where the seeds could watch for danger. And so the seeds waited.

One morning, a red hen approached and began scratching the earth for food. Even though the seeds on the top of the ground saw what was about to happen, they were helpless against the huge monster. Unable to save themselves, they were eaten with enjoyment by the hen.

The above adaptation of a story originally written by Patty Hansen harbors a wakeup call for those who refuse to risk and grow: Beware— you may get swallowed up. If we want more out of life, we must take our deepest desires, fraught as they might be by dangers and risks, and turn our dreams into action.

Is there more to life than eating, drinking, working, and playing? The answer is an unequivocal "YES!" God wants us to live full lives, to use the abilities he gave us and go for our dreams. God-given dreams come with the strong faith to fulfill our desires.

POST-IT MEDITATION FOR SEPTEMBER 4
I will pray for strength to risk and grow because I trust God to be with me.

September 5

I am the Lord your God…who directs you in the way you should go.
~Isaiah 48:17 (GNT)

For a moment, go back in time—imagine yourself on the Western Frontier. It is 1810 and you've just crossed the Missouri River. You are headed west into new territory. All you have to go on is a rough, hand-sketched map, reports from mountain men and scouts, and a dream of a new life in a beautiful land of opportunity. You have mixed feelings about leaving behind the land and life you know. Danger and uncertainty lurk along the trail. On the other hand, you are filled with a sense of adventure. Every new bend in the wagon trail brings experiences and sights you've never witnessed before. You are thrilled about being one of the first to explore and settle the new land.

As Christians in the 21st century, we have begun a journey on a new frontier. Civilization has already gone through three frontiers, and we are heavily into the fourth. In the first frontier, nomadic herdsmen followed the animals and evolved into a society based on agriculture. It was a time of wandering tribes of hunters who moved onto farms and villages where life revolved around growing food from the soil. The second frontier was a society based on industry and manufacturing and was called the Industrial Age, a time when people left the farms and villages and established urban centers. The third frontier moved us away from the Industrial Age into a society based on technology and information. The shift has been dramatic and all-encompassing.

The fourth frontier, while expanding the Information Age, has rendered obsolete much of the technology that propelled the third frontier. From an expedited way to work and handle information, we have evolved into an age where technology dominates our lives. From smart phones to social media sites, it is a rare person who doesn't deal with technology daily, if not hourly. Internationally, we have seen technology explode, but we have also seen worldwide shifts in economic power, instability in money markets, skyrocketing health costs, and endless wars.

Do you ever wonder what God must think of the way humans have used the abilities and resources he gave us? Would he have preferred we stay in the western frontier and agricultural ages? Was the Industrial Age the beginning of our downfall? Is God sad because we will be leaving a legacy of problems and challenges to the next generation?

What would God have us do? America has lost its premier place in the industrial world; our economy threatens to collapse; our national debt is astronomical; and, the morality and values on which our nation was founded seem to have evaporated.

No one apparently has the answers. Politicians espouse solutions but play self-serving games. The only hope for America is for Christians to unite in prayer. We need to pray for leaders who are godly, leaders who still avow, "In God We Trust," and leaders who value the Ten Commandments and the Golden Rule. The territory ahead is uncharted; the new frontier promises crisis and disaster if we don't ask for God's help.

POST-IT MEDITATION FOR SEPTEMBER 5
I will join other Christians in praying for
God's guidance in the life of our nation.

September 6

Each man in his way is a treasure.
~Robert Falcon Scott, Royal Navy officer and explorer

As a man was exploring caves along the seashore, he discovered a canvas bag with a collection of hardened clay balls. It appeared someone had rolled the clay balls and left them out in the sun to bake. They didn't look like much, but they intrigued the man so he took the bag out of the cave with him.

As he strolled along the beach, he threw the balls one at a time out into the ocean as far as he could. He thought little about it, until he dropped one and it cracked open on a rock. Inside was a beautiful, precious stone! Someone had encrusted an exquisite gem inside the clay.

Excited, the man started breaking open the remaining clay balls. Each contained a similar treasure. In the 20 or so balls he had left, he found thousands of dollars in expensive jewels.

Then it struck him. He had been on the beach a long time. He had thrown maybe 50 or 60 of the balls of clay with their hidden treasure into the ocean waves. Instead of thousands of dollars in treasure, he could have taken home tens of thousands, but he had just thrown it away!

We never know where we will find hidden treasures. And, we should never forget that we ourselves, and indeed all human beings, are treasures God has baked into clay. How often do we treat others, and sometimes even ourselves, as though we are worthless balls of clay, when inside are precious souls. We may not look like much on the outside, but each of us is a unique jewel to be found as God reopens the clay from which he made us. None of us is worthless, and we should treat ourselves and each other as the priceless beings God created. We should take time to peel away the layers of those who may not appear to be lovely or of value. Who knows what we may find inside?

POST-IT MEDITATION FOR SEPTEMBER 6
I will try to find hidden treasures inside others—and inside myself—seeking to see what God sees.

September 7

Those who wait on the Lord shall renew their strength; they shall mount up with wings like eagles.
~Isaiah 40:31 (ESV)

Gilbert was eight years old and had been in Cub Scouts only a short time. During one of his meetings he was handed a sheet of paper, a block of wood, and four tires and told to return home and give it all to "dad."

That was not an easy task for Gilbert to do. His dad was not receptive to doing things with his son. But Gilbert tried. Dad read the paper and scoffed at the idea of making a pine wood derby car with his young, eager son. The block of wood remained untouched as the weeks passed. Finally, mom stepped in to see if she could figure this all out. The project began.

Within days Gilbert's block of wood was turning into a pinewood derby car. A little lopsided, but looking great (at least through the eyes of mom).

Gilbert had not seen any of the other kids' cars and was feeling pretty proud of his "Blue Lightning," the pride that comes with knowing you did something on your own. Then the big night came. With his blue pinewood derby in his hand and pride in his heart, he headed to the big race. Once there, the little guy's pride turned to embarrassment. Gilbert's car was obviously the only car made entirely on his own. All the other cars were a father-son partnership, with cool paint jobs and sleek body styles made for speed. A few of the boys giggled as they looked at Gilbert's, cock-eyed, wobbly, unattractive vehicle. To add to the shame, Gilbert was the only boy without a man at his side. A couple of the boys who were from single parent homes at least had an uncle or grandfather by their side; Gilbert had "mom."

As the race began, it was done in elimination fashion. You kept racing as long as you were the winner. One by one the cars raced down the finely sanded ramp. Finally, it was between Gilbert and the sleekest, fastest-looking car there. As the last race was about to begin, the wide-eyed, shy eight-year-old boy asked if the race could be stopped for a minute because he wanted to pray. The race paused. Gilbert hit his knees, clutching his funny looking block of wood between his hands. With a wrinkled brow, he set to converse with his Father. He prayed in earnest for a very long minute and a half. Then he stood, smiling, and announced, "Okay, I am ready."

As the crowd cheered, a boy named Tommy stood with his father as their car sped down the ramp. Gilbert stood with his Father within his heart and watched his block of wood wobble down the ramp with surprisingly great speed and rush over the finish line a fraction of a second before Tommy's car. Gilbert leaped into the air with a loud "Thank you" as the crowd roared in approval.

The Scout Master came up to Gilbert with microphone in hand and asked the obvious question, "So you prayed to win, huh, Gilbert?"

The young boy timidly responded, "Oh, no sir. That wouldn't be fair to ask God to help you beat someone else. I just asked him to make it so I don't cry when I lose."

Children seem to have wisdom far beyond adults. Gilbert didn't ask God to win the race; he didn't ask God to fix the outcome. Gilbert asked God to give him strength in the outcome—to supply grace to lose with dignity.

Perhaps we spend too much of our prayer time asking God to rig the race, make us number one, or remove us from the struggle, when we should be seeking God's strength to get through the race with dignity.

Gilbert, by stopping the race to speak to his Father, also showed the crowd he wasn't there without a "dad." His Father was most definitely there with him. Gilbert walked away a winner that night, with his Father at his side.

Occasionally, we get in races we cannot win. Along our journey on earth, we hit potholes and climb mountains that take their toll on our spiritual life. Even if we are walking with God, in the busyness of life we sometimes can't see beyond the end of the racetrack. When the competition of life seems unfair, we blame others, moan and complain, or ask, "Why me, Lord?"

Isaiah challenges such whining, pointing out when we object to what happens to us, we act as if God doesn't know about our troubles or even care about the injustices we suffer. He declares God never grows tired or weary, and we should follow his example, thus renewing our strength. We just have to claim the assurance from verse 31 that the Lord will enable us to mount up like eagles and trust him to give us the grace to accept the outcome.

POST-IT MEDITATION FOR SEPTEMBER 7
If I have a problem or trial that is weighing me down,
I will ask God to help me deal with the results, whatever they may be.

September 8

Dear friends, if this is how God loved us, then we should love one another.
~1 John 4:11 (GNT)

A farmer painted a sign advertising four puppies and set about nailing it to a post on the edge of his yard. As he was driving the last nail into the post, he felt a tug on his overalls and looked down into the eyes of a little boy.

"Mister," he said, "I want to buy one of your puppies."

"Well," said the farmer, as he rubbed the sweat off the back of his neck, "These puppies come from fine parents and cost a good deal of money."

The boy dropped his head for a moment. Then reaching deep into his pocket, he pulled out a handful of change and held it up to the farmer. "I've got thirty-nine cents. Is that enough to take a look?"

"Sure," said the farmer. And with that he let out a whistle. "Here, Dolly!" he called. Out from the doghouse and down the ramp ran Dolly, followed by four little balls of fur. The little boy pressed his face against the chain link fence. His eyes danced with delight.

As the dogs made their way closer to the fence, the little boy noticed something else stirring inside the doghouse. Slowly another little ball appeared— this one noticeably smaller. Down the ramp it slid. Then in a somewhat awkward manner, the little pup began hobbling toward the others, doing its best to catch up.

"I want that one," the little boy said, pointing to the runt. The farmer knelt down at the boy's side and said, "Son, you don't want that puppy. He will never be able to run and play with you like these other dogs would."

The little boy stepped back from the fence, reached down, and began rolling up one leg of his trousers, revealing a steel brace running down both sides of his leg, attached to a specially-made shoe. Looking back up at the farmer, he said, "You see, sir, I don't run too well myself, and he will need someone who understands."

With tears in his eyes, the farmer reached down and picked up the little pup. Holding it carefully, he handed it to the little boy.

"How much?" asked the little boy.

"No charge," answered the farmer. "There's no charge for love."

Sometimes it takes someone special to notice another special creation. And inevitably, the special one understands how another special being feels and what he needs.

POST-IT MEDITATION FOR SEPTEMBER 8
God, help me to see special people as gifts of love.

September 9

Let us love one another: for love is of God.
~1 John 4:7 (ASV)

Many years ago a teacher named Mrs. Thompson stood in front of her fifth grade class on the very first day of school and told the children a lie. Like most teachers, she said she loved them all the same. But she knew it wasn't true because a little boy named Teddy Stoddard was in her room. Mrs. Thompson had watched Teddy the year before and noticed he didn't play well with the other children; also, his clothes were dirty, and he always needed a bath. And Teddy could be unpleasant.

Mrs. Thompson was required to review each child's past records, and she put Teddy Stoddard's off until last, knowing it would be bad. She was in for a surprise. Teddy's first grade teacher wrote, "Teddy is a bright child with a ready laugh. He does his work neatly and has good manners...he is a joy to be around."

His second grade teacher wrote, "Teddy Stoddard is an excellent student, well-liked by his classmates, but he is troubled because his mother has a terminal illness and life at home must be a struggle."

His third grade teacher wrote, "His mother's death has been hard on him. He tries to do his best, but his father doesn't show much interest—his home life will soon affect him if some steps aren't taken."

Teddy's fourth grade teacher wrote, "Teddy Stoddard is withdrawn and doesn't show much interest in school. He has few friends and sometimes sleeps in class."

By now, Mrs. Thompson was ashamed of herself. She felt even worse when her students brought her Christmas presents, wrapped in beautiful ribbons and bright paper—except for Teddy's, which was clumsily wrapped in the heavy, brown paper from a grocery bag. Mrs. Thompson took pains to open it in the middle of the other presents. Some of the children started to laugh at the rhinestone bracelet with missing stones and a bottle one fourth full of perfume. But she stifled the children's laughter when she exclaimed how pretty the bracelet was. She put it on and dabbed some of the perfume on her wrist.

Teddy Stoddard stayed after school that day just long enough to say, "Mrs. Thompson, today you smelled just like my Mom used to." After the children left, she cried. On that very day, she quit teaching reading, writing, and arithmetic. Instead, she began to teach children.

As Mrs. Thompson began to pay particular attention to Teddy, working with him on his lessons, his mind seemed to come alive. The more she encouraged him, the faster he responded. Soon, Teddy had become one of the smartest children in the class and, despite her pledge that she would love all the children the same, Teddy Stoddard became her pet.

A year later, Teddy left a note under Mrs. Thompson's door, telling her she was still the best teacher he ever had in his whole life. Six years went by before she got another note from Teddy. He then wrote he had finished high school, third in his class, and she was still the best teacher ever.

Four years after that, she got another letter, saying while things had been tough at times, he stayed in school, had stuck with it, and would soon graduate from college with the highest of honors. He assured Mrs. Thompson she remained his best and favorite teacher.

Four years later another letter arrived. After he got his bachelor's degree, Teddy decided to go a little further. The letter was signed, Theodore F. Stoddard, M.D.

The story doesn't end there. Later that year, a letter informed Mrs. Thompson that Teddy had met this girl and was going to be married. He wondered if Mrs. Thompson would sit in his mother's place at the wedding.

Of course, Mrs. Thompson did. And guess what? She wore that bracelet, the one with missing rhinestones. And she made sure she was wearing the perfume Teddy remembered his mother wearing on their last Christmas together. As they hugged each other, Dr. Stoddard whispered in Mrs. Thompson's ear, "Thank you for believing in me. Thank you so much for making me feel important and showing me I could make a difference."

Mrs. Thompson, with tears in her eyes, whispered back. She said, "Teddy, you have it all wrong. You were the one who taught me I could make a difference. I didn't know how to teach until I met you."

POST-IT MEDITATION FOR SEPTEMBER 9
God, help me to love the unlovable—and help me
make a difference in the life of someone in need.

September 10

We love because he first loved us.
~1 John 4:19 (GNT)

There are days when life just isn't fair; everything seems to go wrong, and everyone around seems to dislike, maybe even hate, who we are. We feel put down, put upon, and put out. The actions, words, or looks from another person can cause our emotions to erupt. On those days, loving the unlovable seems more than we can tackle. After all, we feel unlovable ourselves.

At times like these, the little children's song can set us straight:

> *Jesus loves me – this I know, for the Bible tells me so.*
> *Little ones to Him belong; they are weak but He is strong.*
> *Yes, Jesus loves me. Yes, Jesus loves me.*
> *Yes, Jesus loves me – the Bible tells me so.*

Simple words that carry a powerful message. As children, we sang the words with confidence and assurance of love from above. That same love is complete and forever. No strings attached. The Bible tells us so.

Filled with God's love, we can then love the unlovable. The man on the street corner begging for food…the driver who cuts in front of us…the boss who doesn't treat us fairly…the preacher who commits adultery…the teenager in our classroom who refuses to listen…the co-worker who disparages others to look good himself…the brother who takes advantage of us…a mate who doesn't treat us with respect…a toddler who defies her parents. Add your own "unlovables" to the list. Because we can't see the heart or mind beneath the skin, we may need to alter how we usually pray…perhaps something like this:

Heavenly Father, help us remember that the jerk who cut us off in traffic tonight is a single mother who worked nine hours that day and was rushing home to cook dinner, help with homework, do the laundry, and spend a few precious moments with her children.

Help us remember that the pierced, tattooed, disinterested young man who can't make change correctly is a worried 19-year-old college student, balancing his apprehension over final exams with his fear of not getting his student loans for next semester.

Remind us, Lord, that the scary-looking bum, begging for money in the same spot every day (who really ought to get a job!), is a slave to addiction that we can only imagine in our worst nightmares.

Help us remember that the old couple walking annoyingly slow through the store aisles and blocking our shopping progress are savoring this moment, knowing that, based on the biopsy report she got back last week, this will be the last year they go shopping together.

Heavenly Father, remind us each day that, of all the gifts you give us, the greatest gift is love. It is not enough to share that love with those we hold dear. Open our hearts not just to those who are close to us, but to all humanity. Let us be slow to judge and quick to forgive, show patience, empathy, and love.

Loving the unlovable can be impossible if we rely on our own goodness, but if we rely on the love of God in our heart, we have his power within us, and we can love as he loves us. Granted, we cannot love perfectly and without exception as Christ loves us because we are imperfect humans. But with God's grace, we can practice Biblical love until it becomes a habit.

POST-IT MEDITATION FOR SEPTEMBER 10
I commit myself to loving others because God loves me unconditionally.

September 11

It is plain for anyone with eyes to see that at the present time all created life groans in a sort of universal travail. And it is plain, too, that we who have a foretaste of the Spirit are in a state of painful tension, while we wait for that redemption of our bodies which will mean that at last we have realized our full sonship in him.
~Romans 8:22-23 (PNT)

Like the day President Kennedy died, most of us who were around on September 11, 2001, will forever remember where we were when we first heard a plane had hit the World Trade Center in New York City. Many recall watching television or computer screens in disbelief as another plane struck the second tower and will never forget seeing the buildings come hurtling down with a deafening roar. Similar memories are indelibly lodged in our minds about the Pentagon strike and even more poignantly do we remember the cell phone calls from United Airlines Flight 93, where brave souls talked with family members before storming the cockpit, saving others while dying themselves.

Our world was forever changed the day terrorists took out 2,977 lives. More than twice that number have been killed in our military's response in Iraq and Afghanistan. How can those whose lives were personally touched by the tragedy on U.S. soil or by the subsequent wars lasting more than 10 years make sense of such tragedies? How can we find purpose behind the losses? If God loves us, why do we have so many troubles? If God is goodness and grace, why does he allow bad things to happen to good people?

It is not wrong to ask such questions, but it isn't helpful to dwell on them. Instead of accusing God of being unfair when tragedies invade our lives, we need to recognize that pain and suffering and loss will always be among us on earth. And, it is not reasonable to judge God and his plan for the universe based on the short snatch of time we occupy this planet. Likely, he is as grieved by trauma as we are. But he has promised that someday all will be set right. The tragic notes of the symphony are not the end. The mournful notes we hear now will change to glorious chords in eternity.

POST-IT MEDITATION FOR SEPTEMBER 11
*When I am hurting and confused, I will look beyond the
pain and seek healing and purpose.*

September 12

It gives me encouragement to know that even in my suffering, I can give Glory to God because He brought me through a tremendous storm and has never left me. God has truly comforted me, so I pray that I can bring His comfort to others.
~Elizabeth Ligon

On September 12, 2011, a column written by journalist David Cook was published in the *Chattanooga Times Free Press*:

Dr. Jeff Ligon has a brain tumor. A cruel one.

"It's the kind of tumor that usually wins," he said. "But that doesn't mean it always wins." About the size of a few bullet casings or a cracked walnut shell, the tumor is in his frontal lobe, the same part of his brain that also serves as a neurological trunk of memories:

Of nights reading bedtime stories and saying prayers with his yawning children, kissing the three of them goodnight as the white moon rose outside their Lookout Mountain home.

Of falling in love with his brown-haired wife, Elizabeth, at medical school in Memphis.

Of the first time he saw his newly adopted daughter, Abby, who three weeks ago was living in an orphanage in Ethiopia.

Ligon's tumor is a wrecking ball, for it has taken a family's normal life and broken it into pieces that may never be put back together. It feels not unlike a plane flying into a tall building: One day all is fine in the world, and the next moment, life is crashing down.

"It's your worst nightmare," Elizabeth said. "But I have filled pages of my journal describing ways that God has taken care of us throughout this. We are given new mercies each morning."

The Ligons want to tell their story only so you can read these words: God provides. Their story is one that belongs on September 11, a day of confusion, violence, and sorrow. But it also a story for September 12, the day of rebuilding, of response, of something stronger than fear.

"Hope," said Ligon.

"Definitely hope," said Elizabeth.

On April 5, Ligon, a dermatologist, and Elizabeth, an anesthesiologist, landed in Addis Ababa, the Ethiopian capital and home to the orphanage where Abby lived. Earlier in the day, Elizabeth had met the girl who would become their daughter, but Ligon had stayed behind, not feeling well.

That night, around midnight in their rented guesthouse, Ligon collapsed on his way to the bathroom. His body shook in a seizure. "There was no 9-1-1," Elizabeth said.

The next 24 hours were a tornado. Ethiopian doctors ran a CAT scan, found the tumor, and urged the Ligons to rush back to the United States. Landing a day later in Washington, D.C., Jeff underwent surgery in which doctors removed part of the tumor, then told Elizabeth her husband probably wouldn't be able to speak again.

"Two hours after surgery, he was talking to the nurses," she said. "It's a miracle."

After weeks of radiation and chemotherapy, an MRI showed the tumor had shrunk somewhat.

It wasn't the first time the family had faced disease. Six years previously, their son, Foster, developed leukemia. He's now healthy as a horse—or a normal sixth-grade boy—and is running cross-country (and biding his time until lacrosse season) at McCallie School, healed after three years of treatment and chemotherapy.

"I am a better father these days," Ligon said. "I used to come home, crash on the couch and fall asleep. Now, it's rare for me to miss bedtimes."

Eighteen days ago, Ligon watched his new daughter, Abby, walk inside their home for the first time. Most of her life had been spent in an orphanage, abandoned by her biological family who could no longer care for her.

On Labor Day, she turned 5 and ate birthday cake and opened presents—new tennis shoes, white with blue and pink glitter—with her new family.

When Foster kicked leukemia, the Ligons threw a party with lots of confetti. Curren, their daughter and a natural poet who turned 8 over the weekend, wrote about that day.

"It took a long time to clean up the confedy [sic]," she wrote. "Foster and I played with the confedy. We throw the confedy at each other."

This is the meaning of life for the Ligons: No matter what happens, throw confetti. Love each other. Believe the hand of God works for good, always and forever.

Even on days when planes fly into buildings, early-morning trains barrel down on the tracks, tumors strike in an Ethiopian guesthouse, and where nearby, a little girl stares at the night sky and wonders if she will ever have a mother or father again.

"I want our story to be a witness for what God has done in our lives," Elizabeth said. "We have to find goodness in every step."

In an epilogue to David Cook's story, Elizabeth wrote on the CaringBridge site on February 2, 2012:

Dear Family and Friends,

Thank you for all of your prayers and support of my family. The miracle we have all been praying for....the healing of Jeff's body... has come. Jeff is no longer with us, but he is present with his Lord who said, "Peace I leave with you; my peace I give you. I do not give to you as the world gives. Do not let your hearts be troubled and do not be afraid" (John 14:27).

Elizabeth

POST-IT MEDITATION FOR SEPTEMBER 12
I will believe God works for good even when he says, "No" because I also believe all will be made good in the next life.

September 13

In all these things we are more than conquerors, through him who loved us.
~Romans 8:37 (NIV)

"I don't think we're going to get out of this thing. I'm going to have to go out on faith."

It was the voice of Todd Beamer, the passenger who said, "Let's roll!" as he led the charge against the terrorists who had hijacked United Flight 93, the one that crashed in the Pennsylvania countryside.

The whole world knows how brave Beamer and his fellow passengers were on September 11, 2001. But what buttressed that bravery is not as well known: Faith in Jesus Christ. Todd died as he lived, a faithful evangelical believer.

In an article titled "The Real Story of Flight 93," *Newsweek* revealed gripping details from the actual transcripts of the recovered cockpit voice recorder, but those details were never widely circulated.

"*Todd had been afraid," Newsweek related. "More than once, he cried out for his Savior.*"

After passengers were herded to the back of the jet, Beamer called the GTE Customer Center in Oakbrook, Illinois, and told supervisor Lisa Jefferson about the hijacking. The passengers were planning to jump the terrorists, he said. And then he asked her to pray with him.

As Newsweek related, "Beamer had a Lord's Prayer bookmark in his Tom Clancy novel, but he didn't need any prompting. He began to recite the ancient litany, and Jefferson joined him: "Our Father who art in heaven, Hallowed be Thy name." As they finished, Beamer added, "Jesus, help me." And then, Beamer and his fellow passengers prayed a prayer that has comforted millions down through the centuries—the prayer David wrote in a time of great anguish:

"The Lord is my shepherd, I shall not want…Yea, though I walk through the valley of the shadow of death, I will fear no evil, for thou art with me…."

And then the famous last words: "Are you guys ready? Let's roll!"

We now know from the cockpit voice recorder that Beamer and other passengers wrestled with the hijackers and forced the plane to crash into the ground, killing themselves but foiling what was believed to have been the hijackers' plan to fly Flight 93 into the Capitol or the White House.

God can bring good from evil, and in Todd Beamer, the world witnessed a faith that held up in the direst of situations—a faith that still comforts his family.

Lisa Beamer later told NBC's Dateline, "…in the Lord's Prayer, it asks God to forgive our trespasses as we forgive those who trespass against us. As Todd prayed this prayer in the last moments of his life, in a way," Lisa said, "he was forgiving those people for what they were doing, the most horrible thing you could ever do to someone."

As Flight 93 hurtled towards destruction, Todd Beamer could not have known his quiet prayers would be heard over again and again in the years to come…that the story of his last acts on earth would be a witness to the Lord he loved and served—and a lasting example of true heroism.

POST-IT MEDITATION FOR SEPTEMBER 13
Thank you, God, for men like Todd Beamer and his fellow passengers, whose bravery and faith glorify your name.

September 14

I urge you, first of all, to pray for all people. Ask God to help them; intercede on their behalf, and give thanks for them.
~1 Timothy 2:1 (NLT)

An adventure ship was wrecked during a storm at sea, and only two of the men on it survived by swimming to a small, desert-like island.

Not knowing what else to do, the two survivors agreed to pray to God.

However, to determine whose prayers were effective, they agreed to divide the territory between them and stay on opposite sides of the island.

The first thing they prayed for was food.

The next morning, the first man saw a fruit-bearing tree on his side of the island, so he had fruit to eat. The other man's half of land remained barren.

After a week, the first man was lonely so he prayed for a wife. The next day, another ship wrecked nearby, and the only survivor was a woman who swam to his side of the land. On the other side of the island, there was nothing.

With confidence, the first man prayed for a house, clothes, more food. The next day, like magic, they all appeared. Sadly, the second man still had nothing.

Finally, the first man prayed for a ship, so that he and his wife could leave the island. In the morning, he found a ship docked at his side of the island and boarded the ship with his wife.

Looking across the island at his fellow survivor, the first man remembered none of the other man's prayers had been answered. He thus considered him unworthy to receive God's blessings, so he decided to leave the second man on the island.

As the ship was about to leave, the first man heard a loud voice from heaven, "Why are you leaving your companion on the island?"

"My blessings are a result of my faith and prayers, since I was the one who prayed for them," the first man answered. "His prayers were all unanswered, so I assumed God thought he did not deserve anything."

"You are sorely mistaken and are in great debt to him."

"How's that?" the first man asked.

"It was his great faith that invoked the blessings: He prayed that all your prayers might be answered."

POST-IT MEDITATION FOR SEPTEMBER 14
**I will be grateful for the prayers of others
that support my own.**

September 15

Sometimes I go about pitying myself, and all the while I am being carried across the sky by beautiful clouds.
~Ojibwe Proverb

Ryokan, a Zen master, lived the simplest kind of life in a little hut at the foot of a mountain. One evening a thief visited the hut only to discover there was nothing to steal.

Ryokan returned and caught him. "You have come a long way to visit me," he told the prowler, "and you should not return empty-handed. Please take my clothes as a gift."

The thief was bewildered. He took the clothes and slunk away.

Ryoken sat naked, watching the moon. "Poor fellow," he mused, "I wish I could have given him this beautiful moon."

In the ebb and flow of life, some suffer major losses—a job, a relationship, or a death. An act of nature—a fire, a tornado, a hurricane, or some other force—may take homes and possessions. Sometimes the situations that lead to self-pity are not as life-shattering: we lose something of value through a theft; we feel misunderstood or unappreciated; we are ashamed of our lives; others get all of the lucky breaks; we resent people who are overly judgmental; we feel we aren't needed; or numerous other circumstances mire our spirits in misery.

Life deals us all negative cards at times, but if we can put our self-pity on hold and examine our total being, most find the positives in our lives outweigh the negatives. A special place to find these positives is through our eyes and ears. Cumulous clouds, deafening claps of thunder, and fiery flashes of lightning all speak of God's creativity and power. A bright star in a dark sky or a full moon can carry our thoughts toward the heavens when earthly happenings threaten to drag us down. We can't always escape our surroundings and the incidents that distress us, but we can look to the sky for strength, allowing the clouds and other heavenly formations to carry our soul-sick spirits to God.

Pausing to thank God for the beauty of the sky, we can sing, as the psalmist David did, "The heavens declare the glory of God" (Psalm 19: 1, NIV).

How can we feel sorry for ourselves when God so richly blesses us with nature? "[The heavens] use no words…. Yet their voice goes out into all the earth…. [The sun] rises at one end of the heavens and makes its circuit to the other; nothing is deprived of its warmth" (Psalm 19: 3-4, 6, NIV).

POST-IT MEDITATION FOR SEPTEMBER 15
When I feel sorry for myself, I will lift my eyes toward the skies, watching and listening for God's message in the glory of the heavens.

September 16

God has filled him with his power and given him skill, ability, and understanding for every kind of artistic work.
~Exodus 35:31 (GNT)

In 1818 in France, a nine-year-old boy sat in his father's workshop, watching him make harnesses from leather.

"Someday, Father," said Louis, "I want to be a harness-maker just like you."

Smiling at his young son, the father responded, "Why not start now?" And he took a piece of leather and drew a design on it.

"Now, son, take the hole puncher and hammer and follow the design, but be careful not to hit your hand."

Eager and excited, the little boy began to work, but in just a few moments, when he hit the hole puncher, it flew out of his hand and pierced his eye. Immediately, he had no sight in that eye. Sadly, later he lost the sight in his other eye and became totally blind.

A few years passed, and one day Louis was sitting in the family garden when a friend handed him a pine cone. Rubbing his sensitive fingers over the cone, an idea emerged. He began to create an alphabet of raised dots on paper, and today the blind can feel and interpret what is written because Louis Braille saw beyond his sight and envisioned a way to read. The Braille alphabet has opened books to countless people.

Louis had a dream—he envisioned a solution to reading which none had thought possible. Possibility thinking opens doors where none exist. Just think: Not too many years ago no one had conceived it would be possible to take the heart out of a dead body and transplant it into another. No one had imagined computers would link the world through internet. It would have been unthinkable that man would ride through space, land on the moon, and return. Amputees who never expected to walk again hail the development of robotic legs. Who would have thought that smart phones could talk with us intelligently?

New discoveries occur daily. Some will transform our lives. Medical breakthroughs and technology innovations come from dreams and activity. But we should never forget our heavenly father created the brains that enable us to scan the horizon and create a better tomorrow.

POST-IT MEDITATION FOR SEPTEMBER 16
I will pray for faith to be a possibility thinker.

September 17

...our days on earth are as a shadow....
~1 Chronicles 29:15 (NIV)

Walker Percy, in a novel called <u>The Moviegoer</u>, *relates the story of a commuter whose daily train ride is a non-experience. Nothing exciting ever happens to interrupt the monotony of his life, an existence that is marked by boredom and even nameless despair, though he has no concrete reason for his malaise. But one day the commuter suffers a severe heart attack and is taken to an unfamiliar hospital in a town he has passed by many times but never paid much attention to—suddenly, he is in a strange town surrounded by strangers. As he looks about the sterile room, he glances down at his hand resting on the sheet in front of him. Almost as if he has never seen his hand before, he is taken aback at how his hand looks, at how it opens and closes. "My hand was open in front of my face. The fingers closed and opened. I felt like Rip Van Winkle waking up and testing his bones…."*

Percy describes the commuter's extraordinary response to his hand as an awakening, a revelation. Absorbed in the "everydayness" of his life, he had never before looked at himself and his life with such scrutiny. Now his immortality has shaken him from sluggishness into a desire to understand what life is and to savor it. His world had collapsed around him, but blessed with a mind and a spirit, he opened his eyes to learn who he was, grabbing his existence like a lost friend. From despair growing out of nothingness, he moved to a renewed life where even a hand could be a marvel. He heard the call from God to choose between stagnation and rebirth, between waiting around to die and living life to its fullest.

The answers to a fulfilling life lie within us, and if we will search, we can find who we are and discover a purpose for our lives through illness or adversity. What a wonder and blessing that God doesn't give up on us when we give up on ourselves and our lives!

POST-IT MEDITATION FOR SEPTEMBER 17
God, cleanse me of "everydayness" and renew me to the joy of your world.

September 18

At that time Jesus said, "I praise you, Father, Lord of heaven and earth, because you have hidden these things from the wise and learned and revealed them to little children.
~Matthew 11:25 (NIV)

In the days when an ice cream sundae cost much less, a 10-year-old boy entered a hotel coffee shop and sat at a table. A waitress put a glass of water in front of him. "How much is an ice cream sundae?" he asked.

"50¢," replied the waitress.

The little boy pulled his hand out of his pocket and studied the coins in it.

"Well, how much is a plain dish of ice cream?" he inquired. By now more people were waiting for a table, and the waitress was growing impatient.

"35¢!" the waitress brusquely replied.

The little boy again counted his coins. "I'll have the plain ice cream," he said. The waitress brought the ice cream, put the bill on the table, and walked away. When the boy finished the ice cream, he paid the cashier and left.

When the waitress came back, she began to cry as she wiped down the table. There, placed neatly beside the empty dish, were two nickels and five pennies. You see, the youth couldn't have the sundae because he had to have enough left to leave her a tip.

"Out of the mouth of babes," or in this case, "Out of the pocket of babes."

The story of the boy and his ice cream decision offer two lessons:

First, judging a person by how he looks is unfair and wrong. 1 Peter 2:17 tells us to honor all people—no exceptions. If God loves us in spite of our weaknesses and failures, we should show the same love and respect to strangers who may not look like us, may be dirty and unkempt, or may just be younger or older than we are.

Second, self-sacrifice is a virtue. It is the love of Christ shining through our smile and through our actions. Matthew 6:4 instructs us to give in secret—God will know and will reward us openly. Despite this assurance, sometimes we will give and nothing comes back. Doubtless, that was true of the little boy, but what he (and we) get is the satisfaction of giving with no expectation, of encouraging someone who is down, of showing appreciation even when it may not be deserved.

POST-IT MEDITATION FOR SEPTEMBER 18
God, give me the heart of an unselfish child.

September 19

For we are each responsible for our own conduct.
~Galatians 6:5 (NLT)

Compromise strengthens relationships; appeasement destroys them. Negotiating with friends and family shows a willingness to consider each other's opinions and desires, but there are limits. If two members of the family want to go to a movie and two want to go bowling, two individuals must cede to the wishes of the other two. But if two members want to go see an X-rated movie, then standing firm may be required. Compromising on our principles is not an option. Similarly, negotiating because someone yells loudly is wrong.

Bankei Zenji was born in the 17th century into a Samurai family. His father, a Confucian, died when Bankei was young. He disliked school so he often played truant. When the ferryman was instructed not to take him across the river on the way home until school ended, Bankei plunged in and swam across. He was unruly and a gang leader. Frequent quarrels with his elder brother caused him to be so frustrated and depressed that he attempted suicide. He swallowed a large number of spiders he thought were poisonous and sat in a shrine waiting for death. When nothing happened, he changed his mind about dying and began searching for truth. He studied Confucianism and later Buddhism before becoming a Japanese Rinzai Zen master and the abbot of the Ryomon-ji and Nyoho-ji. When Bankei held his weeks of seclusion and meditation, pupils from many parts of Japan came to attend. During one of these gatherings a pupil was caught stealing. The matter was reported to Bankei with the request that the culprit be expelled. Bankei ignored the case. No doubt part of his rationale came from his own experience as a rebellious youth, but there was more to it than that.

Later, the pupil was caught in a similar act, and again Bankei disregarded the matter. This angered the other pupils, who drew up a petition asking for the dismissal of the thief, stating that otherwise they would leave in a body.

When Bankei had read the petition he called everyone before him. "You are wise brothers," he told them. "You know what is right and what is not right. You may go somewhere else to study if you wish, but this poor brother does not even know right from wrong. Who will teach him if I do not? I am going to keep him here even if all the rest of you leave."

A torrent of tears cleansed the face of the brother who had stolen. All desire to steal had vanished. And those who would have left learned a powerful lesson.

While our religious beliefs may differ from those of Bankei, he offered a valuable lesson. Diverse negative opinions should be navigated carefully because we care about the other person. As John Kennedy once said, we should never negotiate out of fear, but we should never fear to negotiate.

In situations where what we do may have significant consequences or even create controversy, we need to be prepared to make difficult decisions. If we suspect a child is being abused, we should make the hard choice of reporting our suspicions to the authorities. (How many times have you read about a priest who abused youngsters while bishops stood idly by, fearing negative publicity would harm the church? And, of course, the sports world was appalled in 2012 when a Penn State coach was convicted of 45 counts of child molestation after reports of abuse were ignored or covered by high-level school officials over a decade-long period.) If we know a co-worker is stealing or drinking on the job, we have an obligation to confront the person or tell the boss. Martin Luther King avowed, "The ultimate measure of a man is not where he stands in moments of comfort and convenience, but where he stands at times of challenge and controversy."

At all times we should stand up for what is right and moral. Confrontation is never easy, but avoiding confrontation is not a caring action. The confrontation itself should be compassionate. The person we are confronting is a human being with feelings. We can be honest without being tactless and brutal; we can point out deficiencies without humiliating.

Tough love shows we care enough about others to do what is right for them and for us. Teenagers may get angry at their parents' actions and decisions. It's inevitable if parents want to keep sons and daughters going in the right direction. Parents shouldn't take the easy route, giving in to a teenager's demands. Supervisors shouldn't let employees get away with being slack. A spouse shouldn't ignore infidelity. Not making someone mad is a sure way to start them on the path to self-destruction. If we want others to act responsibly, we must act that way ourselves. And we must do it not with condemnation but with love and concern.

POST-IT MEDITATION FOR SEPTEMBER 19
I will seek to find the right relationship
between responsibility and compassion.

September 20

"Which of these…was neighbor to him who fell among the thieves?" The expert in the law replied: "He who showed mercy on him." Then Jesus said, "Go and do likewise."
~Luke 10:36-37 (NIV)

The story is told of a professor who routinely gave his students the same pop test about one-third of the way into the semester. Mary was a conscientious student and had breezed through the questions until she read the last one:
    "What is the first name of the woman who cleans the school?"
    "Surely this was some kind of joke," Mary thought. She had seen the cleaning woman several times. She was tall, dark-haired, and in her 50's. But Mary was puzzled: "How would I know her name?"
    Finally, Mary handed in her paper, leaving the last question blank. Just before class ended, one student asked if the last question would count toward the quiz grade.
    "Absolutely," said the professor. "In your careers, you will meet many people. All are significant. They deserve your attention and care, even if all you do is smile and say, 'Hello, Dorothy.'"
    Mary says she has never forgotten that lesson. And she'll never forget the cleaning lady's name was Dorothy.

God is not pleased when we look down on others or ignore them. Are we too pious or proud to speak to a cleaning lady? Or to the boy who sacks our groceries? The sales clerk in the shopping mall? The woman we pass going down the hall in the hospital? The unkempt man who sits too close to us on the church pew? Sometimes all it takes is a smile to brighten another person's life.

A smile costs nothing, but gives much.

It enriches those who receive, without making poorer those who give.

It takes a moment, but the memory of it sometimes lasts forever.

None is so rich or mighty that he can get along without it, and none is so poor, but that he can be made rich by it.

A smile creates happiness in the home, fosters good will in business, and is the countersign of friendship.

It brings rest to the weary, cheer to the discouraged, sunshine to the sad, and it is nature's best antidote for trouble.

Yet it cannot be bought, begged, borrowed, or stolen, for it is something that is of no value to anyone until it is given away.

Channel God's love wherever you go. As a Christian, see others through Christ's eyes, love them through a heart that loves Christ, and encourage them as Christ supports you. If you are the conduit for God's love, you will be blessed more than the person who receives the love. Just as an electrical wire conducts energy, let Christ's love flow through your words and actions. As the Good Samaritan stopped to show mercy to the man attacked by thieves, never pass by without touching somebody you don't know in some way, even if it is just with a smile.

POST-IT MEDITATION FOR SEPTEMBER 20
I will strive to let God's love flow through me to other people.

September 21

Which of you will listen to this or pay close attention in time to come?
~Isaiah 42:23 (NIV)

Memo from the desk of GOD

Effective Immediately:

Please be aware that there are changes you need to make in your life. These changes need to be completed so I may fulfill my promises to you to grant you peace, joy, and happiness in this life. I apologize for any inconvenience, but after all that I am doing, this seems very little to ask of you. I know, I already gave you the Ten Commandments. Keep them. But follow these guidelines as well...

1. *QUIT WORRYING: Life has dealt you a blow, and all you do is sit and worry. Have you forgotten I am here to take all your burdens and carry them for you? Or do you just enjoy fretting over every little thing that comes your way?*

2. *PUT IT ON THE LIST: Something needs done or taken care of. Put it on the list. No, not YOUR list. Put it on MY to-do-list. Let ME be the one to take care of the problem. I can't help you until you turn it over to me. And, although my to-do-list is long, I am, after all, God. I can take care of anything you put into my hands. In fact, if the truth were ever really known, I take care of a lot of things for you that you never even realize.*

3. *TRUST Me: Once you've given your burdens to me, quit trying to take them back. Trust in me. Have the faith that I will take care of all your needs, your problems, and your trials. Problems with the kids? Put them on my list. Problem with finances? Put it on my list. Problems with your emotional roller coaster? For my sake, put it on my list. I want to help you. All you have to do is ask.*

4. *LEAVE IT ALONE: Don't wake up one morning and say, "Well, I'm feeling much stronger now; I think I can handle it from here." Why do you think you are feeling stronger now? It's simple. You gave me your burdens, and I'm taking care of them. I also renew your strength and cover you with my peace. Don't you know that if I give you these problems back, you will be right back where you started? Leave them with me and forget about them. Just let me do my job.*

5. *TALK TO ME: I want you to forget a lot of things. Forget what was making you crazy. Forget the worry and the fretting because you know I'm in control. But there's one thing I pray you never forget. Please don't forget to talk to me—OFTEN! I love you. I want to hear your voice. I want you to include me in the things going on in your life. I want to hear you talk about your friends and family. Prayer is simply you having a conversation with me. I want to be your dearest friend.*

6. *HAVE FAITH: I see a lot of things from up here that you can't see from where you are. Have faith in me that I know what I'm doing. Trust me, you wouldn't want the view from my eyes. I will continue to care for you, watch over you, and meet your needs. You only have to trust me. Although I have a much bigger task than you, it seems as if you have so much trouble just doing your simple part. How hard can trust be?*

7. *SHARE: You were taught to share when you were only two years old. When did you forget? That rule still applies. Share with those who are less fortunate than you. Share your joy with those who need encouragement. Share your laughter with those who haven't heard any in such a long time. Share your tears with those who have forgotten how to cry. Share your faith with those who have none.*

8. *BE PATIENT: I managed to fix it so in just one lifetime you could have so many diverse experiences. You grow from a child to an adult, have children, change jobs many times, learn many trades, travel to so many places, meet thousands of people, and experience so much. How can you be so impatient then when it takes me a little longer than you expect to handle*

something on my to-do-list? Trust in my timing, for my timing is perfect. Just because I created the entire universe in only six days, everyone thinks I should always rush, rush, rush.

9. BE KIND: Be kind to others, for I love them just as much as I love you. They may not dress like you, or talk like you, or live the same way you do, but I still love you all. Please try to get along, for my sake. I created each of you different in some way. It would be too boring if you were all identical. Please know I love each of your differences.

10. LOVE YOURSELF: As much as I love you, how can you not love yourself? You were created by me for one reason only—to be loved, and to love in return. I am a God of Love. Love me. Love your neighbors. But also love yourself. It makes my heart ache when I see you so angry with yourself when things go wrong. You are very precious to me. Don't ever forget that!

With all my heart, I love you,
GOD

POST-IT MEDITATION FOR SEPTEMBER 21
I will listen for God's voice, knowing he cares for me and will help me.

September 22

So I recommend the enjoyment of life...
~Ecclesiastes 8:15 (GW)

An 83-year-old woman once wrote a letter to a good friend. She confessed she was reading more and dusting less, sitting in her yard and admiring the view without worrying about the weeds, and spending more time with friends and family instead of staying at home alone.

The elderly lady went on to say she believed, whenever possible, life should be a pattern of experiences to savor, not to endure. As she had aged, she was trying to recognize special moments and cherish them. She no longer saved her "good" china for special events or guests. She wore her good clothes everywhere, not just to church. Moreover, she had removed "someday" and "one of these days" from her vocabulary. "If it is worth seeing or hearing or doing, I want to see and hear and do it now," she declared.

With wisdom that comes from age, the lady wondered what others would have done if they had known they wouldn't be there for tomorrow. What would they have not wanted to leave undone, even little matters? Would they have called family and a few close friends to tell them they were loved? Would they have called former enemies to mend fences? Would they have enjoyed their favorite restaurants more? The questions are limitless—some mundane and some *heartrending. If we only knew when our time on earth is to end, we might make more of each day.*

As for the 83-year-old woman, she said, "I am trying very hard not to put off, hold back, or save anything that would add laughter and luster to my life and to the lives of others. And every morning when I open my eyes, I tell myself that it is special and say, "Good morning, God" instead of, "Good god, it's morning!"

We should all try telling God, "Good morning," and then relish the day he has given us with all its splendor and delight. Birds waking us with their melodious warbles, butterflies fanning us with their fragile wings, towering trees shadowing us from the sun, rain sparkling and shining the grass, wisps of wind brushing our faces like angels' wings... nature alone gives us a reason for joy. Add a newborn baby emerging from its mother's womb, children running on a seashore, a stranger stopping to help a homeless man, and we see love and delight embodied far and wide in God's gifts to humankind.

POST-IT MEDITATION FOR SEPTEMBER 22
Life may not be the party I hoped for,
but while I am here, I might as well dance.

September 23

"Tis a grey day."
"Ay, but dinna ye see the patch of blue?"
~Scottish shoemaker

Robert Collyer, English-born American Unitarian clergyman, once penned these words about Job:

"If Job could have known as he sat there in the ashes, bruising his heart on this problem of providence—that in the trouble that had come upon him, he was doing what one man may do to work out the problem for the world, he might again have taken courage." Job had no idea his response to tragedy and loss would be looked at by Christians of ages to come as the way to have faith even when we feel abandoned by God. "So, then," Collyer continues, "though we may not know what trials wait on any of us, we can believe that, as the days Job wrestled with his dark maladies are the only days that make him worth remembrance..., so the days through which we struggle, finding no way, but never losing the light, will be the most significant we are called to live."

When the sun hides behind the clouds, the depth of our souls is tested. Gloomy days can stretch long and can glaringly highlight our failures. Someone once said God has both the clouds and the sun at his disposal—and he knows when to show us a patch of blue and a ray of light behind the clouds. While the days remain grey, we need to take Collyer's words to heart, realizing the days without sunshine may be the most meaningful of our lives. They will test our strength and our conviction, and whether we pass or fail depends on our faith. Until we have lost our trust, we have not lost all. So it was with Job. As long as he had his faith, though his family and possessions were gone and he was afflicted with a terrible disease, he still had a future.

Had he listened to his friends, Job would have turned his back on God. Like Job, we should reject negative thoughts, remembering the psalmist's words, "Happy are those who reject the advice of evil people, who do not follow the example of sinners or join those who have no use for God (Psalm 1:1, GNT).

An old poem describes a woman walking through a meadow, meditating on nature. While strolling about, she came upon a field of golden pumpkins. In the corner of the field stood a majestic, huge oak tree.

She sat under the oak tree musing on the strange twists in nature which put tiny acorns on huge branches and huge pumpkins on tiny vines. She thought to herself, "God blundered with creation! He should have put the small acorns on the tiny vines and the large pumpkins on the huge branches."

Nodding off, the woman stretched out under the oak tree for a nap. A few minutes after falling asleep she was awakened by a tiny acorn bouncing off her nose. Chuckling to herself, she rubbed her nose and thought, "Maybe God was right after all!"

Job's friends couldn't see it, but God was right in allowing Job to endure hardship and heartache. Job wasn't perfect, but he knew his friends' advice was poisonous. Although he himself admittedly had doubts about the goodness of God at times, cursing the day he was born, in the end, he rejected the destructive thoughts that tried to control his mind, renewing his belief that God is good and great.

POST-IT MEDITATION FOR SEPTEMBER 23
I will not allow negative thoughts to destroy my faith.

September 24

For you are great, and do marvelous deeds; you alone are God.
~Psalm 86:10 (NIV)

We are innately programmed for a lifelong quest for meaning and purpose, but we often fail to recognize it even when it is pointed out to us.

After years of searching for truth and meaning, a man was told to go to a cave, in which he would find a well. He was advised to ask the well what truth was and was assured the well would reveal it to him. The man had no trouble finding the well and quickly asked his important question, knowing that finding the meaning of truth would give him purpose for his life.

From the deepness of the well came the answer, "Go to the village crossroads: there you shall find what you are seeking."

Eager and full of hope, the man ran to the crossroads, where he found three rather uninteresting shops. One shop was selling pieces of metal, another sold wood, and the last sold thin wires. Mystified, the seeker of truth couldn't discern how the three stores and their wares had anything to do with the revelation of truth.

Disappointed, the seeker returned to the well to demand an explanation, but the response was unsatisfactory: "You will understand in the future." Despite his loud protests, all he got in return were the echoes of his own shouts. Angry he had believed the voice from the well and embarrassed he had followed its instructions, the man went on his way, continuing his quest for truth. Over time, the memory hurt less and even gradually faded away—until a walk in the moonlight one night brought the three stores back into his consciousness when he heard some-one playing a sitar (a stringed instrument used in Indian classical music). The music was lovely and soothing, played with great mastery and inspiration.

Profoundly moved, the truth seeker felt drawn toward the player. He looked at the fingers dancing over the strings. He became aware of the sitar itself. And then suddenly he exploded in a cry of joyous recognition: The sitar was made out of wires and pieces of metal and wood just like those he had once seen in the three stores and had dismissed as having no significance.

As the epiphany unfolded, the man understood the message of the well: We have already been given everything we need; our task is to assemble and use it in creative ways. Nothing is meaningful so long as we perceive only separate fragments. But as soon as the fragments come together, a new entity emerges, whose nature we could not have foreseen by considering the fragments alone. That's what happens when we allow God to weave the pieces of our lives into a beautiful whole—we will find meaning, peace, and joy greater than we ever imagined would be possible.

POST-IT MEDITATION FOR SEPTEMBER 24
I will look for new meaning in simple objects.

September 25

Fathers, do not provoke your children to anger by the way you treat them. Rather, bring them up with the discipline and instruction that comes from the Lord.

~Ephesians 6:4 (NLT)

Life can be a rat race. We arise early, work late, and treasure any small moments of time we can find for ourselves. Anyone approaching us after a full day needs to be brave or crazy.

A man came home from work, late again, tired and irritated, to find his five-year-old son waiting for him at the door.

"Daddy, may I ask you a question?"

"Yeah, sure, what is it?" replied the man.

"Daddy, how much money do you make an hour?"

"That's none of your business! What makes you ask such a thing?" the man said angrily.

"I just want to know. Please tell me, how much do you make an hour?" pleaded the little boy.

"If you must know, I make $20.00 an hour."

"Oh," the little boy replied, head bowed. Looking up, he said, "Daddy, may I borrow $10.00 please?"

The father was furious. "If the only reason you wanted to know how much money I make is just so you can borrow some to buy a silly toy or some other nonsense, then you march yourself straight to your room and go to bed. Think about why you're being so selfish. I work long, hard hours every day and don't have time for such childish games."

The little boy quietly went to his room and shut the door.

The man sat down and started to get even madder about the little boy's questioning. How dare he ask such questions only to get some money.

After an hour or so, the man had calmed down and started to think he may have been a little hard on his son. Maybe there was something he really needed to buy with that $10.00, and he really didn't ask for money very often.

The man went to the door of the little boy's room and opened the door.

"Are you asleep son?" he asked.

"No daddy, I'm awake," replied the boy.

"I've been thinking, maybe I was too hard on you earlier," said the man. "It's been a long day and I took my aggravation out on you. Here's that $10.00 you asked for."

The little boy sat straight up, beaming. "Oh, thank you daddy!" he yelled. Then, reaching under his pillow, he pulled out some more crumpled up bills.

The man, seeing that the boy already had money, started to get angry again. The little boy slowly counted out his money, then looked up at the man.

"Why did you want more money if you already had some?" the father grumbled.

"Because I didn't have enough, but now I do,'" the little boy replied. "Daddy, I have $20.00 now. Can I buy an hour of your time?"

Are you ever so busy that you fail to spend time with the most important people in your life? We work for earthly gain so hard that we miss out on time with those we cherish. If we logged our time at home the way we schedule the rest of our day, what would it show about our priorities?

POST-IT MEDITATION FOR SEPTEMBER 25
*God, help me to never convey the message
that I don't have enough time for someone I love.*

September 26

And this world is fading away, along with everything that people crave. But anyone who does what pleases God will live forever.
~1 John 2:17 (NLT)

I love mystery stories, and I particularly like the part that occurs in some of them when the detective gathers all of the suspects in one place, points his accusing finger at one of them, and says, "You did it!"

At this point, of course, the case is solved, and all that remains is for the detective to tell us how he or she arrived at the guilty party.

Has someone ever proudly pointed at you and said, "You did it!" after some accomplishment? Did you puff up with pride? After all, you worked hard, you persevered, and you invested the time and energy that made it possible for you to get a degree, to get promoted, to have a strong marriage, to help young people or widows or the elderly or the ill, or some other noteworthy achievement. You may even have overcome tremendous obstacles or setbacks in your own life yet still persevered in your desire to lead a godly life serving others. Not only do you deserve to pat yourself on the back, you feel, you may even think you are better than others. If so, the story that follows may bring you back to earth with a better measure of your worth.

A man dies and goes to heaven. Of course, St. Peter meets him at the pearly gates. The good saint says, "Here's how it works. You need 100 points to make it into heaven. You tell me all the good things you've done, and I give you a certain number of points for each item, depending on how good it was. When you reach 100 points, you get in."

"Okay," the man says, "I was married to the same woman for 50 years and never cheated on her, even in my heart."

"That's wonderful," says St. Peter, "that's worth three points!"

"Three points?" he says. "Well, I attended church all my life and supported its ministry with my tithe and service."

"Terrific!" says St. Peter, "that's certainly worth a point."

"One point? Golly. How about this: I started a soup kitchen in my city and worked in a shelter for homeless veterans."

"Fantastic, that's good for two more points," he says.

"TWO POINTS!!" the man cries, "At this rate the only way I get into heaven is by the grace of God!"

"That's right! You got it right! You did it!" said St. Peter.

If we have ever been tempted to think too highly of ourselves or to be judgmental of others, we need to remember, as John Ruskin (English artist, poet, and author who lived from 1819 to 1900) wrote, that the highest reward for our toil is not what we get for it but what we become. When we become too proud or too critical, we have lost the true nature of self-sacrifice and thus tarnished our service. We may even slow down in our work for ourselves, for others, and for God.

The greatest successes are those with a long-lasting impact on the lives of others, and God didn't say we could stop when we feel we have done enough. The harvest is great, but the laborers are few (Luke 10:2), so we must not grow weary. We must pray for strength to work on behalf of those who need us. We must not grow so attentive to things that will pass away we fail to focus on those that build our future in the next world.

POST-IT MEDITATION FOR SEPTEMBER 26
Help me, God, not to avoid helping others while engaging in irrelevant pursuits.

September 27

Lord, how long will I call for help and you not listen?
~Habakkuk 1:2 (CEB)

An old Hindu poem by Ravindra Kumar Karnan tells the story of a child who whispered to God to speak to her. A meadow lark sang in response, but the child did not hear.

Frustrated, the child yelled, "God, speak to me!" This time, thunder rolled across the sky, but the child did not listen.

Desperate, the child looked toward the sky and begged, "God, let me see you." A bright star shone overhead, but the child failed to notice.

Pushing down her anger, the child cried out in despair, "Touch me, God, and let me know you are here!" Lovingly, God reached down and touched the child.

The desolate poem ends, "But the child brushed the butterfly away and walked away unknowingly."

How often does God speak when we ask but we never hear? Are we like the little girl in the Hindu poem, impatient to hear God's voice but deaf to his response? Most of us listen for a "still, small voice" like the one Elijah described in 1 Kings 19:12, and God does speak to us this way. But it is not the only way we hear from him. Sometimes his voice may come to us in spontaneous ways. For example, in the midst of other thought, a message may enter our mind to tell us to pray for someone. Could it be God's voice interrupting to give us a message?

God may also speak to us in visions or dreams. The night my sister Sylvia gave up drugs after 17 years of abuse, she had a dream that was so real she will never doubt God again. *She had been having the dream for months, but this time the end was different. Running down a dark road, she saw a mass of lights, and for an instant, she saw a figure in the middle of the lights. She woke herself up screaming, "Oh, my God; Oh, my God" and immediately knew God had given her that dream. She knew exactly what it meant. She had been on the dark road for too long, headed toward disaster without any hope, because God wasn't in her life. But after surrendering her addiction to him, God was showing her she was finally on the right road, and he was guiding her by his light.*

God speaks, but we have to be open to his voice in nature, in thoughts, in dreams, in visions, and in countless other ways.

SOURCE OF SYLVIA'S STORY: *HOOKED BUT NOT HOPELESS: Escaping the Lure of Addiction (Hoppe and Yates, 2011)*

POST-IT MEDITATION FOR SEPTEMBER 27
I will listen carefully, in noise and in silence, for God's voice.

September 28

Rejoice in hope, be patient in tribulation, be constant in prayer.
~Romans 12:12 (ESV)

Ray Kroc, the founder of McDonalds, was a not-too-successful 51-year-old Lily paper cup salesman when he stopped by the original McDonald's restaurant to try to sell the owners some paper cups. He was amazed to see a long line of people waiting to get their orders. Upon asking, he was told the restaurant had the best French fries in town. When he went inside to talk with the owners, Kroc asked them why they didn't franchise such a successful business. The McDonald brothers pointed to the top of a nearby hill and said, "When we leave here every day, we sit on the top of that hill and look out over this peaceful valley. Why would we want to have more? We would work harder and longer—it's not worth it."

Kroc thought about what they said—and about the long lines. He asked the brothers to sell HIM the franchise rights, and they did. Kroc borrowed the money and bought what he thought were the total rights. But, several years later, when the McDonald brothers saw how much Kroc was expanding and how much money he was making, they decided they deserved more than they had agreed to. They found a legal way to take such a large share of Kroc's success that he almost went under. But, despite heavy debt created to buy the McDonald brothers off, Kroc never gave up. Time and again, whenever he ran into obstacles, he persisted. And the rest of his success story is history.

Kroc's advice to others seeking success, in a book called *Grinding It Out*, is to "press on."

"Nothing in the world can take the place of persistence. Talent will not; nothing is more common than unsuccessful individuals with talent. Genius will not; education will not; the world is full of educated derelicts."

Persistence and determination come from purpose. For Christians, those attributes are amplified by faith. Often, it is at the point of failure that faith kicks in at its highest level. That's when we can turn to God for confidence to transform our disappointments and botched lives into victories. The old song "Victory in Jesus" rings truest when we hit the lowest valleys. And, if the success doesn't come in this life, we can still look forward to the mansion he has built for us in glory. We've "heard about the streets of gold beyond the crystal sea" and "about the angels singing"—and "some sweet day [we'll] sing up there the song of victory."

POST-IT MEDITATION FOR SEPTEMBER 28
When I am discouraged, I will sing, "Come and heal my broken spirit," because I know God will bring to me the victory.

September 29

Delight yourself also in the Lord, and he shall give you the desires of your heart. Commit your way to the Lord, trust also in him, and he shall bring it to pass.... Rest in the Lord, and wait patiently for him.
~Psalm 37:4,5,7 (NKIV)

Life presents choices to all of us, and we make decisions based on the values we hold.

In the Far East an emperor was growing old and knew it was time to choose his successor. Instead of choosing one of his assistants or his children, he decided to do something different. He called young people in the kingdom together one day. He said, "It is time for me to step down and choose the next emperor. I have decided to choose one of you." The children were shocked, but the emperor continued. "I am going to give each one of you a seed today—one very special seed. I want you to plant the seed, water it, and come back here one year from today with what you have grown from this one seed. I will then judge the plants that you bring, and the one I choose will be the next emperor."

One boy, named Ling, was there that day and he, like the others, received a seed. He went home and excitedly told his mother the story. She helped him get a pot and planting soil, and he planted the seed and watered it carefully. Every day, he watered it and watched to see if it had grown. After about three weeks, some of the other youths began to talk about their seeds and the plants that were beginning to grow. Ling kept checking his seed, but nothing ever grew. Three weeks, four weeks, five weeks went by, still nothing. By now, others were talking about their plants, but Ling didn't have a plant and he felt like a failure. Six months went by—still nothing in Ling's pot.

He just knew he had killed his seed. Everyone else had trees and tall plants, but he had nothing. Ling didn't say anything to his friends, however. He just kept waiting for his seed to grow. A year finally went by, and all the youths of the kingdom brought their plants to the emperor for inspection. Ling told his mother he wasn't going to take an empty pot. But his mother asked him to be honest about what happened.

Ling felt sick at his stomach, but he knew his mother was right. He took his empty pot to the palace. When Ling arrived, he was amazed at the variety of plants grown by the other youths. They were beautiful—in all shapes and sizes. Ling put his empty pot on the floor, and many of the other children laughed at him. A few felt sorry for him and just said, "Hey, nice try."

When the emperor arrived, he surveyed the room and greeted the young people. Ling tried to hide in the back. "My, what great plants, trees, and flowers you have grown," said the emperor. "Today one of you will be appointed the next emperor!"

All of a sudden, the emperor spotted Ling at the back of the room with his empty pot. He ordered his guards to bring him to the front. Ling was terrified. He thought, "The emperor knows I'm a failure! Maybe he will have me killed!"

When Ling got to the front, the Emperor asked his name. "My name is Ling," he replied. All the kids were laughing and making fun of him. The emperor asked everyone to quiet down. He looked at Ling, and then announced to the crowd, "Behold your new emperor! His name is Ling!"

Ling couldn't believe it. Ling couldn't even grow his seed. How could he be the new emperor?

Then the emperor said, "One year ago today, I gave everyone here a seed. I told you to take the seed, plant it, water it, and bring it back to me today. But I gave you all boiled seeds that would not grow. All of you, except Ling, have brought me trees and plants and flowers. When you found the seed would not grow, you substituted another seed for the one I gave you. Ling was the only one with the courage and honesty to bring me a pot with my seed in it. Therefore, he is the one who will be the new emperor!"

If you plant honesty, you will reap trust.
If you plant goodness, you will reap friends.

If you plant humility, you will reap greatness.
If you plant perseverance, you will reap victory.
If you plant consideration, you will reap harmony.
If you plant hard work, you will reap success.
If you plant forgiveness, you will reap reconciliation.
If you plant faith, you will reap miracles.
So, be careful what you plant now;
it will determine what you will reap tomorrow.

The seeds you now scatter will make life worse or better for you or for the ones who will come after you. Someday you will enjoy the fruits, or you will pay for the choices you make.

POST-IT MEDITATION FOR SEPTEMBER 29
Whatever I give to life, life will give me back.
I will rest in the Lord for the fruits of my labor.

September 30

There is one spectacle grander than the sea; that is the sky; there is one spectacle grander than the sky; that is the interior of the soul."
~Victor Hugo, French poet, novelist, and dramatist

The sky, with its continuously changing colors and designs, feeds our soul. And it is free—who among us cannot look up at the sky? Even most prisoners have a small window from which they can gaze into the heavens. And what a sight! Some days the sky is azure blue with not a speck of a cloud covering its pure color. At other times, the sky supplies the canvas for fat, cumulous clouds forming shapes that stir our imaginations and invite interpretations. Even days of grey skies hold a purpose—days when we want to hide from the world to regroup, to gather our thoughts and reshape them from despondent to hopeful.

At night, the sky may be black with just a sliver of the moon, or it may be dotted with stars, filling the dark night with glowing light. Stargazing has a certain charm, a mythical mystery that invites us to imagine what lies beyond the realm of the sky.

Night or day, dark or bright, the sky speaks to us, encouraging us, reminding us of our creator. The psalmist wrote, "When I consider your heavens, the work of your fingers, the moon and the stars, which you have set in place, what is mankind that you are mindful of them, human beings that you care for them? You have made them a little lower than the angels and crowned them with glory and honor" (Psalm 8:3-5 NIV).

God created the sky to hover above us, a crown of glory above the earth. And he made us to inhabit this planet, caring for us, providing the wonders of his magnificent design for us to look at each day. We can join American poet e.e. cummings in thanking God for the most amazing days, "...for the blue dream of sky and for everything which is natural, which is infinite...." God himself is the artist of the skies. He paints the clouds, dark or fair, the stars, large and small. His palette of colors is staggering as he applies strokes to heart-stirring sunrises and breathtaking sunsets. At times when we struggle to hear God, time alone gazing at the skies will surely bring his voice to our ears. As 11th century Persian poet and mystic Jalal ad-Din Rumi said, "Only from the heart can you touch the sky."

Mike Matenkosky remembers feeling close to God in the Sierra Nevada Mountains, "up there by the clear blue skies and the windswept passes." Raising his eyes to the heavens, he once described it as "holy ground." But, as he related in Guideposts, a joint disease left him unable to walk normally. He says he waddled like a penguin—an arduous way to move that made it impossible to hike the mountains he loved. Memories of nights in the Chain Lakes in Yosemite haunted him: "The world became dark and silent. Stars blanketed the sky." Citing the passage in the Bible about God moving over the face of the waters, Mike said hiking to a remote mountain lake gave that same sensation. But now he was confined to a wheelchair, and he was angry. He couldn't understand why "such a good and holy thing" had been taken away from him. He moved away from God, refusing to go to church with his wife and two daughters. Then, one day when he was sitting on his porch, a sparrow caught his eye as it darted down from the sky and paused at a bird feeder. When a finch joined the sparrow, he couldn't resist wheeling inside to get his camera. Pleased the birds were still feeding when he returned, he began to snap shots. The next day, he positioned himself near the bird feeder but far enough away not to frighten the birds. Soon, he discovered that the Central Valley of California where he lived was a major flight path for birds as they migrated from the Arctic to Mexico. Day after day, he took pictures of all kinds of exotic birds as they stopped for water and food in his backyard.

Although he could no longer hike to the top of a mountain to be close to the skies, Mike found another way to capture God's nature. His former depression obliterated, he went back to the mountains—not to the top but to the base of the Sierras, where he took pictures of beautiful landscapes from the road. Today, he is a professional nature photographer, selling his work online. He says he still walks like a penguin, but he now walks with a purpose. "The God who seemed so far away feels closer than ever." The feeling he had cherished on his hikes had returned: "A feeling of holiness in God's great outdoors. Only now that feeling had come in a parking lot, not beside a remote mountain lake. Was there a difference? Sure. I was in a car with my walker crammed into the trunk. But God was right where he'd always been. Where he'd always be."

SOURCE FOR MATENKOSKY STORY: http://www.guideposts.org/inspirational-stories/
inspiring-story-photographer-mike-matenkosky-taking-pictures-wheelchair

POST-IT MEDITATION FOR SEPTEMBER 30
*Wherever I am, beneath a cloud-filled sky or a starlit night,
I can be still and feel God's presence.*

October 1

The rich and the poor have a common bond; the Lord is maker of them all.
~Proverbs 22:2 (KJV)

Money isn't bad; we must have it to feed, house, and clothe ourselves
and our families. The problem is not with money or possessions—it is
how we feel about them and often, how we let them control our lives
and thinking.

Following the Great Depression, people began believing money
meant everything, and they wanted to be sure they put back enough
cash to see them through future bad times. Over the years, that attitude
changed as families dealt with the hardships accompanying World War
II. By the time the baby boom generation was born, finances began to
improve for many families; and, as the baby boomers grew into adulthood and had children of their own, they had an insatiable thirst for
their children to have more than they had. The result: a generation that
didn't have to work for what they were given; a generation that expected
others to take care of their needs. Some of these children, now adults,
accumulated wealth—from inheritances or through successful business
ventures. Then the deep recession of the 21st century hit, and rich and
poor alike came to realize money is never secure. Similar to the stock
market crash in the 1920s, though not as deep and devastating, stocks
fell to record lows in the middle of the first decade of the new century,
wiping out more than half of some families' entire savings. People lost
jobs, houses, and other valued possessions. Many suddenly found their
happiness and contentment with life had been tied to what they had
accumulated. They found, as Proverbs 11:28 (NLT) predicted, "Trust
in your money and down you will go."

Happiness should never be dependent on material possessions. It
shouldn't even be dependent on our jobs. Yes, we need career posi-
tions to pay the mortgage and buy food, but we don't need them to have
peace and happiness in spirit. At times, most of us have thought, "If I
had this or that, then I would be happy," only to find when we get what
we wanted, it doesn't bring the expected pleasure.

A beautiful, expensively-dressed lady complained to her psychiatrist that she felt her whole life was empty; it had no meaning. So the counselor called over the old lady who cleaned the office floors and then said to the rich lady, "I'm going to ask Mary to tell you how she found happiness. All I want you to do is listen."

So the old lady put down her broom, sat on a chair, and told her story: "Well, my husband died of malaria, and three months later my only son was killed by a car. I had nobody...I had nothing left. I couldn't sleep; I couldn't eat; I never smiled at anyone; I even thought of taking my own life. Then one evening a little kitten followed me home from work. Somehow I felt sorry for that kitten. It was cold outside, so I decided to let the kitten in. I got it some milk, and it licked the plate clean. Then it purred and rubbed against my leg, and for the first time in months, I smiled. Then I stopped to think; if helping a little kitten could make me smile, maybe doing something for people could make me happy. So the next day I baked some biscuits and took them to a neighbor who was sick in bed. Every day I tried to do something nice for someone. It made me happy to see them happy. Today, I don't know of anybody who sleeps and eats better than I do. I've found happiness by giving it to others."

When she heard that, the rich lady cried. She had everything wealth could buy, but she had lost the values which money cannot replace.

Money can buy beds but not sleep...food but not appetite...medicine but not health...books but not intelligence...luxury but not beauty...a house but not a home...intimacy but not love...diversions but not happiness...companionship but not fellowship.

As Proverbs 22:2 reminds us, the rich and poor have a common bond because God made us all. God also gives us a common bond in our spirituality. It is within our spirit we find contentment. Only God can fill our heart with joy and thanksgiving. He is the source of all we have—both worldly goods and peace within our inner being.

POST-IT MEDITATION FOR OCTOBER 1
*When I am tempted to complain about what
I don't have, I will look toward the heavens and
be thankful I have what God knows I need,
even if it is not what I want.*

October 2

God whispers to us in our pleasures, speaks in our conscience, but shouts in our pain. Pain is God's megaphone to rouse a deaf world.
~C. S. Lewis, Irish novelist and poet

Pain comes in all shapes and sizes, and it doesn't discriminate. In our lifetime, we will experience both physical and emotional agony. Our physical pain may range from sore throats and broken bones to devastating burns or cancer. Our emotional pain might come from verbal abuse, sorrow, loneliness, or rejection. The causes are endless, and they all hurt.

In his book *Where Is God When It Hurts?* Philip Yancey declares human beings have made great strides in insulating ourselves from pain. We have houses with air conditioning and heat to keep us comfortable, shoes to protect our feet, and medicine to heal our wounds. Most people in America never go hungry or thirsty. But there are some pains from which we can't escape. And in the presence of real pain—cruel and unrelenting—we feel helpless. It matters not whether it is our pain or the pain of someone we love.

Yancey tells about a newlywed who contracted Hodgkin's disease, with only a 50 percent chance of survival. After surgery and radiation, the young wife (Claudia) suffered intense physical pain and emotional despair. Though she and her husband were strong Christians, they couldn't hold back their anger against God. "Why us?" they questioned. And the guidance they received from Christian supporters didn't help. A deacon from their church advised them to reflect on what God was trying to teach them. One lady said the devil was at work and only when they mustered up enough faith to believe would the wife be healed. Another visitor came in like a cheerleader, telling Claudia she needed to come to the place where she could say, "God, I love you for making me suffer like this...You know what is best for me." Even the couple's pastor advised Claudia she had been appointed by Christ to suffer for him and would be rewarded. He added she had been chosen because of her great strength and integrity.

None of this helped. Claudia still cried out, "Why me, God? There are millions of Christians stronger and more honorable than I—couldn't you choose one of them?"

And so, Yancey asks, where is God when it hurts? Is he trying to tell us something through a megaphone? In the end, Yancey decides God designed a pain system to equip us for life on this planet. (After all, if we didn't feel pain, we could put our hand on a hot stove and not realize we were being burned.) In the process, he teaches us to turn to him. He is with us in our suffering. He may not take it from us, even as he did not take the cup from Christ when he was about to hang on the cross, but he never leaves us alone to bear our burdens. He simply shouts to get our attention.

POST-IT MEDITATION FOR OCTOBER 2
On this earth, I may never know why I have to suffer, but
I know I can depend on God to guide me through the dark days.

October 3

Then you shall see and become radiant. And your heart will throb and swell with joy.
~Isaiah 60:5 (NIV)

Once there was a little girl who lived in a small, simple house on a hill. As she grew, she became able to see over the dilapidated fence surrounding her yard. In the distance, her eyes beheld a wonderful house on a high hill across the valley. The windows of the house sparkled like gold, and the little girl dreamed of someday growing up and living in a house with golden windows. And although she loved her parents and her family, she yearned to move to such a glittering house and often thought how wonderful and exciting it would be to live there.

When the little girl grew older, she asked her mother if she could ride her bike outside the gate and down the lane. Reluctantly, the mother told her child to be careful and not to wander too far. As soon as she was outside the gate, the little girl headed for the golden house. Down the lane, across the valley, and up the hill she pedaled. At last she was at the gate post. Staring up at the path that led to the house, she was surprised it was so overgrown. And then—the house itself was rundown. Even the windows were plain and dirty, reflecting only neglect.

With a sad heart, the little girl went no further. She remounted her bike and turned toward home. As she glanced up, she saw an amazing sight: Across the way on her side of the valley was the little house she called home, and its windows glistened golden as the sun shone on it.

With wisdom beyond her age, the child realized she had been living in a golden house herself. It wasn't the size of the house that made a home shine—it was God's sunshine, and moreover, all the love and care within.

What we see in the distance may glitter, but it is not always gold. God's touch on our homes—and in our lives—transforms them into substances that not only shine like gold but *are* gold. Only then are our spirits satisfied. Only then do our wrongful desires dissolve into reality. Proverbs 23:5 (NLT) teaches that in the blink of an eye the illusion of wealth disappears, "for it will sprout wings and fly away like an eagle." Being content with what we have, counting our blessings rather than envying others, gives us true peace.

POST-IT MEDITATION FOR OCTOBER 3
I will revitalize my life and my faith by
adding up the assets God has given me.

October 4

How many times shall I forgive my brother when he sins against me? Up to seven times?
~Matthew 18:25 (NIV)

It was a year ago that nine-year-old Joshua Saffle got a bike for Christmas, and he rode it every day. That is, until recently, when the bike was gone from its usual place. Running to his front yard, Joshua saw a man loading it into his car. He shouted, but the man drove off. Joshua had strong faith and told his dad he forgave the thief. What's more, he wanted the thief to know he was forgiven. So the next day, Joshua dictated a message for his mother to write on a large poster board. He signed it, stapled it to a sawhorse, and put it in the front yard.

"To the person who stole my bike: You really hurt my feelings when you took my bike. But I am a Christian and because Jesus forgave me, I FORGIVE YOU!!"

When Joshua's father left for work the next day, the sign was face-down in the yard. But then, at the end of the driveway, the bike was back—with new handlebars, grips, and a new front fork assembly.

When Peter asked Jesus the question about how many times he should forgive his brother, the answer surprised him: "I do not say to you seven times, but seventy times seven." Most of us would probably have gasped. After all, patience has its limits. Jesus, knowing Peter and others listening would not comprehend why they should forgive over and over, shared a parable, comparing the kingdom of heaven to a king who wanted to settle his accounts with his servants.

In the parable, the first man owed the king 10,000 talents but couldn't pay. The king ordered him to be sold, along with his wife and children and all that they had. The poor servant fell on his knees, begging for patience, promising to pay all he owed in time. He seemed so pitiful the king released him and forgave the debt.

That same day, the forgiven servant came upon a fellow servant who owed him a small amount of money. Grabbing him by the throat, he demanded payment. In a scene reminiscent of the one in the king's castle, the second servant begged for time to repay the debt. But the first servant refused and had his fellow servant tossed into prison until the debt could be paid. Other servants were watching, just as they had watched when the king forgave him. Greatly distressed, they went to the king and told him what had happened. In anger, the king called the first servant back into his presence, calling him wicked. "I forgave you all that debt because you begged me; should not you have had mercy on your fellow servant, as I had mercy on you?" And then, he had him delivered to prison.

Jesus concluded, "So also my heavenly Father will do to every one of you, if you do not forgive your brother from your heart."

When we have been wronged by word or deed, our hearts hurt, and we sometimes want to injure the person who hurt us. Forgiveness is a two-way street, and we travel both ways, seeking forgiveness for ourselves and forgiving others. If we follow the footsteps of Jesus, who forgave the men who crucified him, we will be blessed. As St. Francis of Assisi avowed, "It is in pardoning that we are pardoned."

POST-IT MEDITATION FOR OCTOBER 4
I will remember to pray daily, "Lord, forgive me my sins,
as I forgive those who have sinned against me."

October 5

The fastest runner doesn't always win the race, and the strongest warrior doesn't always win the battle. The wise sometimes go hungry, and the skillful are not necessarily wealthy. And those who are educated don't always lead successful lives. It is all decided by chance, by being in the right place at the right time. People can never predict when hard times might come. Like fish in a net or birds in a trap, people are caught by sudden tragedy.
~Ecclesiastes 9:11-12 (NLT)

A Chinese story tells of an elderly farmer who had an old horse for tilling his fields. One day the horse escaped into the hills and, when all the farmer's neighbors sympathized with the old man over his bad luck, the farmer replied, "Bad luck? Good luck? Who knows?"

A week later the horse returned with a herd of wild horses from the hills, and this time the neighbors congratulated the farmer on his good luck. His reply was, "Good luck? Bad luck? Who knows?"

Then, when the farmer's son attempted to tame one of the wild horses, he fell off its back and broke his leg. Everyone thought this very bad luck. Not the farmer, whose only reaction was, "Bad luck? Good luck? Who knows?"

Some weeks later the army marched into the village and conscripted every able-bodied youth they found there. When they saw the farmer's son with his broken leg, they let him off. Now was that good luck? Bad luck?

Do you believe in good luck and bad luck? Are life's events chance happenings or God's direct intervention? A swift runner in the race may trip over the person in front of him who stumbles. Bad luck? Or did God make the first man fall to trip up the second one? In war, does God choose which soldier lives and which one dies, or does it happen by chance? If we believe Ecclesiastes 9:11-12, it seems a matter of luck, good or bad.

Ecclesiastes 2:14 (NLT) reinforces this notion: "For the wise can see where they are going, but fools walk in the dark. Yet I saw that the wise and the foolish share the same fate." As Christians, we are not protected from bad luck, and we are not promised good luck in every circumstance. But God knows what is happening to us, and if we walk in his will, we can be assured of his presence to comfort and support us regardless of fate.

POST-IT MEDITATION FOR OCTOBER 5
Unexpected and random events are not gifts or punishment from God,
but he will stand steadfastly beside me in good times and bad.

October 6

Autumn is a second spring when every leaf is a flower.
~Albert Camus, French author, journalist, and philosopher

The fall season is well underway. After scorching summer heat, mornings are crisp and cool, and the autumn array of vibrant reds, yellows, and oranges has created swaths of color in our yards, on the mountains, and along the roads we travel.

If you are a student of chemistry, you know that three chemicals lie behind the magnificent transformation: chlorophyll, carotenoids, and anthocyanins. Most of us are familiar with the first of these, the primary workhorse since it is responsible for the green leaves we enjoy in the spring and summer months. Hiding behind the green, though, carotenoids and anthocyanins lurk, waiting for shorter days and cooler temperatures, which cause less chlorophyll to be produced. When that happens, the other two chemicals burst forth because they require less light and heat. God's masterful design has carotenoids to produce yellow leaves, because they absorb light as blue and blue-green wavelengths. Similarly, as chlorophyll decomposes, anthocyanins absorb and reflect blue, blue-green, and green light, creating scarlet and purple hues.

Numerous other factors contribute to the changing colors of the leaves—temperature, humidity, acid or alkaline level, and soil conditions can influence the scenic range of colors we witness every fall. Whatever the process, the treasures of fall foliage it produces along rural byways, forested mountainsides, and city streetscapes never fail to amaze and thrill me.

As you watch the miraculous changing of leaf color this fall, as you witness the majesty of the glorious, stunning shades of gold to amber, orange to scarlet, and crimson to garnet, you probably won't think about the complex chemical changes undergirding the transformation. But few Christians can view fall foliage without thinking about the one who created the leaf—and it magnifies our amazement if we are mindful of the complex process that sets the stage for beauty heralded by the fall season.

Daniel 2:21 (GNT) tells us, "God controls the times and seasons...." God's intricate and resplendent creation is evidenced throughout the earth we occupy and the heavens we see above—fall carries its part of the seasons with grace and beauty.

POST-IT MEDITATION FOR OCTOBER 6
As I gaze at the brilliant fall color, I will remember
the hand that made the leaves and designed
the process that brings such a spectacular transformation.

October 7

That we find a crystal or a poppy beautiful means that we are less alone, that we are more deeply inserted into existence than the course of a single life would lead us to believe.
~John Berger, The Sense of Sight, 1980

A special teacher made a life-changing impact on her students a week after her husband died unexpectedly of a heart attack.

With late afternoon sun streaming through the windows, as the class was about to end, the teacher looked at her students with new-found wisdom and quietly said, "My thoughts this afternoon are unrelated to our lesson, but I want to share something that comes from my heart:

"Each of us is put here on earth to learn, share, love, appreciate, and give of ourselves. None of us knows when this fantastic experience will end. It can be taken away at any moment. Perhaps this is God's way of telling us we must make the most out of every single day."

Tears touching her eyelids, she went on. "So I would like you all to make me a promise. From now on, on your way to school, or on your way home, find something beautiful to notice. It doesn't have to be something you see—it could be a scent, perhaps of freshly baked bread wafting out of someone's house, or it could be the sound of a breeze slightly rustling the leaves in the trees, or the way the morning light catches one autumn leaf as it falls gently to the ground. Look for these things and cherish them. For, although it may sound trite to some, these things are the 'stuff' of life. The little things put on earth for us to enjoy. The things we often take for granted. Start noticing them...for at any time, it can all be taken away."

The class went completely quiet. The students all picked up their books and filed out of the room silently. Years later, one student related she noticed more things on her way home from school that day than she had that whole semester— and kept noticing them as she grew into adulthood.

Take notice of something special you see on your lunch hour today or as you walk your dog. Go barefoot and feel the fallen leaves. Walk down the street at sunset. Listen to the larks as you awaken tomorrow morning. Stop to gaze at a golden rose or a child running through a field of clover. Notice SOMETHING every day...many times a day. Appreciate all those things you often overlook. As English biologist and politician John Lubbock wrote, "Earth and sky, woods and fields, lakes and rivers, the mountain and the sea are excellent schoolmasters and teach some of us more than we can ever learn from books."

POST-IT MEDITATION FOR OCTOBER 7
I will pause each day to notice the world around me.

October 8

Anyone who listens to the word but does not do what it says is like someone who looks at his face in a mirror and, after looking at himself, goes away and immediately forgets what he looks like.
~James 1:23-24 (NIV)

Five frogs are sitting on a log in the swamp.
Four frogs decide to jump off the log and into the swamp.
How many frogs are left on the log?
Sound like a simple question? Not so—several possible answers are correct? Sure, one frog might be left. Or, two might be left...or three...or four...or even five. It all depends on how many frogs followed their decision with action. Deciding is not doing.

As French military leader Napoleon Bonaparte once advised, "Take time to deliberate, but when the time for action has arrived, stop thinking and go in."

We make decisions intellectually—and sometimes emotionally. But then the plunge has to be made, into unknown territory, into cold water, or into an impossible situation. If we make decisions and don't follow through with action, if we don't take risks, nothing will be accomplished. To get beyond fears of failure, faith is required. We must believe God will give us power to overcome obstacles and setbacks. We must believe we can succeed. In the end, we must believe God's will is perfect. Our job is to commit, perhaps to daring decisions, and leave the outcome to God.

Playing it safe results in boredom and stagnation. Jumping off the log into the swamp or running into the arena of life at least assures we will fill each day with excitement. Undoubtedly, every battle will not be won, and detractors on the sidelines may scoff at our efforts. It matters not. Theodore Roosevelt's "The Man in the Arena" reminds us that the honor and glory go to those "who spend themselves in a worthy cause."

It is not the critic who counts; not the man who points out how the strong man stumbles, or where the doer of deeds could have done them better. The credit belongs to the man who is actually in the arena, whose face is marred by dust and sweat and blood; who strives valiantly; who errs, who comes short again and again, because there is no effort without error and shortcoming; but who does actually strive to do the deeds; who knows great enthusiasms, the great devotions; who spends himself in a worthy cause; who at best knows in the end the triumph of high achievement, and who at worst, if he fails, at least fails while daring greatly, so that his place shall never be with those cold and timid souls who neither know victory nor defeat.

POST-IT MEDITATION FOR OCTOBER 8
I will seek God's power to enter the arena, working hard and being tenacious, turning my decisions into actions through faith and prayer.

October 9

Bless the Lord, O my soul, and all that is within me, bless his holy name! Bless the Lord, O my soul, and forget not all his benefits, who forgives all your iniquity, who heals all your diseases, who redeems your life from the pit, who crowns you with steadfast love and mercy, who satisfies you with good so that your youth is renewed like the eagle's.
~Psalm 103:1-5 (ASV)

In Proverbs 30:18-19 (CEV), Solomon points to eagles as one of God's creations he never gets tired of watching—they are so amazing he finds it difficult to explain how wonderful they are: "There are three of four things I cannot understand: How eagles fly so high or snakes crawl on rocks, how ships sail the ocean, or people fall in love." These intricacies and activities are beyond humanly explanation.

The eagle has the longest lifespan among birds. It can live for up to 70 years. But to reach this age, the eagle must make a difficult decision. In its 40s, its long and flexible talons can no longer grab the prey it needs for food. Its long, sharp beak becomes bent. Its old and heavy wings, with their thick feathers, stick to its chest and make it hard to fly. At that point, the majestic bird is left with two options: die or go through a painful process that will span up to 150 days.

The progression to new life begins with the eagle flying to its nest on the top of a mountain. There, it beats its peak against a rock until it plucks it out. The eagle then waits for a new beak to grow back, subsequently using it to pluck out its talons. When new claws replace the old ones, the eagle begins to pluck out its worn-out feathers, which are replaced with fresh ones. After five months, the eagle experiences its first flight of rebirth, beginning another 30 years of life.

Human beings, like eagles, must sometimes start a process of pain and change in order to survive. We sometimes need to get rid of old memories, habits, and past traditions. Only after we are freed of our old life can we begin the rest of our days with strength and hope.

God wants us to spread our wings and fly like eagles; and just as the eagle is innately endowed with the desire and ability for renewal, we have an inner drive and capacity to be reborn in the spirit.

POST-IT MEDITATION FOR OCTOBER 9
Like Solomon, I am amazed at the ways of the eagle. With God's guidance, I will use their renewal as a reminder of the rebirth he so freely gives.

October 10

He will cover you with his feathers, and under his wings you will find refuge....
~Psalm 91:4 (ESV)

After the earthquake had subsided, when the rescuers reached the ruins of a young woman's house, they saw her dead body through the cracks. But her pose was somehow strange—she knelt on her knees like a person worshiping; her body was leaning forward and her two hands were supporting an object. The collapsed house had crushed her back and her head.

With many difficulties, the leader of the rescuer team put his hand through a narrow gap on the wall to reach the woman's body. He was hoping this woman could still be alive. However, the cold and stiff body told him she had passed away. He and the rest of the team left this house and went to search the next collapsed building.

Later, without being able to explain why, the team leader was driven by a compelling force to go back to the house ruins where the dead woman still remained trapped. Again, he knelt down and this time used his hand through the narrow cracks to search the little space under the dead body.

Suddenly, he screamed, "A child! There is a child!"

The whole team worked feverishly, carefully removing the piles of ruined objects around the dead woman. There a three-month-old boy lay wrapped in a flowery blanket under his mother's dead body. The woman had made the ultimate sacrifice to save her son. When her house was falling, she used her body to make a cover to protect her son.

Human mothers aren't the only created beings who love their offspring so much they give up their own lives protecting them. An article in *National Geographic* several years ago provided a penetrating picture of another such mother:

After a forest fire in Yellowstone National Park, forest rangers began their trek up a mountain to assess the inferno's damage. One ranger found a bird literally petrified in ashes, perched statuesquely on the ground at the base of a tree.

Somewhat sickened by the eerie sight, he knocked over the bird with a stick. When he gently struck it, three tiny chicks scurried from under their dead mother's wings. The loving mother, keenly aware of impending disaster, had carried her offspring to the base of the tree and had gathered them under her wings, instinctively knowing the toxic smoke would rise. She could have flown to safety but refused to abandon her babies. When the blaze arrived and the heat scorched her small body, the mother had remained steadfast.

Just as the mother covered her baby with her body, the mother bird had been willing to die; and with her sacrifice, those under the cover of her wings lived to see another day. In the same way, but at a higher level, we have eternal life because Christ willingly gave his life for us. The baby birds and baby child didn't have to earn their mother's protection and saving grace; similarly, we have done nothing to warrant God's free gift of life.

Dottie Rambo's song "If That Isn't Love" captures the essence of God's grace. After reminding us Christ left the splendor of heaven despite knowing his destiny (just as the bird saved its chicks and the mother saved her baby, knowing what would happen to themselves), Rambo says, "If that isn't love, the ocean is dry. There's no star in the sky, and the sparrow can't fly. If that isn't love, then heaven's a myth, and there's no feeling like this"—the emotion we experience when our soul encounters grace.

POST-IT MEDITATION FOR OCTOBER 10
God's grace is great enough to cover all my sins and shortcomings.
In the safety of his wings, I will always find security.

October 11

So do not throw away your confidence; it will be richly rewarded. You need to persevere....
~Hebrews 10:35-36 (NIV)

How high is the bar you set for yourself? Do you dream big, even though failure is a possibility? Or do you dream small—perhaps not at all—to avoid not attaining your aspirations? Because they have been put down in their youth, been subjected to harsh criticism from family or co-workers, or been scarred from life's battles, many people choose to stay in the rut life has thrown them into instead of putting their hand to the wheel and making a jarring turn to change their lives.

God gave everyone potential, and he endowed us with the prospect of confidence necessary to achieve the maximum life can provide us. But some never claim that confidence, electing instead to stay where they are, even if they don't want to be there, not willing to ask for a helping hand.

During a hike in the woods, a troop of boy scouts came across an abandoned section of railroad track. Each, in turn, tried walking the rails but eventually lost his balance and tumbled off.

Suddenly, two of the boys, after considerable whispering, offered to bet they could both walk the entire length of the track without falling off. Challenged to make good on their boast, the two boys jumped up on opposite rails, extended a hand to balance each other, and walked the entire section of track with no difficulty whatever.

The lesson is simple: We do things better, we produce more, and we live more by helping each other. The person who lends a helping hand benefits himself at the same time he helps someone else.

If you could picture any life you want, what would it look like? Would you have a different job, live in another city, or have different friends? If you really want your life to be different, you must have a plan to get from where you are to where you want to be. Then, pray for confidence and guidance about the path you need to take. Will you get where you want to be in life? You won't ever know the answer to that question if you don't start the journey. And, like the two boy scouts, you may get there by joining together with others while looking for new ways to succeed.

POST-IT MEDITATION FOR OCTOBER 11
I will not stay stuck in a life if it's not where I want to be.
With confidence from God, I will begin a new path.

October 12

I believe in the incomprehensibility of God.
~Honore de Balzac, French novelist and playwright

An old farmer overheard a well-educated man declare he could never believe in anything he could not understand. Turning to the young intellectual, he said, "As I went into town today, I passed a field where some sheep were feeding. Do you believe that?"

"Yes," said the young man.

"Not far away from the sheep some cows were also grazing. Do you believe that?"

"Yes," was the reply.

"Not far from the cows were some pigs eating grass. Do you believe that?"

"Yes."

"What about the chickens pecking away at the grass—do you believe that?"

"Yes."

"All right, now you listen to this," said the farmer. "The grass the sheep ate turned into wool. The grass the cows ate turned into hair. The grass the pigs ate turned into bristles. The grass the chicken ate turned into feathers. Do you believe that?"

"Yes," the young man said.

"Do you understand it?"

"No," admitted the young man.

"Young man," said the farmer, "if you live long, you will find that there are a great many things which you believe without understanding. God is one of them."

Today, many might ask the same "do you understand" questions about cyberspace functions that are so prevalent in our lives. Most of us don't understand how they work—but we know they do. Why, then, is it so hard to believe in God?

Even with faith, sometimes God remains a mystery. It's not that most people don't believe in God—how can we not acknowledge him when the evidence of his existence is ever present in the master design of the universe? Still, our minds cannot possibly understand an eternal being whose beginning is unknown, whose physical presence is hidden, and whose plan for our lives is often unfathomable.

We struggle to understand a life form that cannot be described in human terms, whose power cannot be measured. We want to see God with our eyes as we see the sky, even if he is as ephemeral as a cloud. We want to put a human face on him, to attribute human thoughts and actions to him. Recognizing that is not possible, perhaps we can learn from a young student who, when asked what he thought of God, responded that God is not a thought; he's a feeling. And so it is that our hearts—not our minds—must experience God, not only in times of joy but also in times of great distress and sorrow.

Our hearts—our souls—know what our minds cannot possibly understand. They feel God's presence even when we cannot comprehend him. Yet, some want proof before they believe. In an age of science and technology, they find faith impossible. But that's what faith is—accepting the mystery and beauty of the unknown.

Martha Hickman compares a journey of faith to walking home in the dark. In the absence of light to guide our steps, "we grope our way in this familiar yet unfamiliar world…. Though we can't see ahead, the ground beneath our feet feels right…." It feels right because God put that ground in place. And, he can see in the dark even though we cannot. Psalm 139:11-12 (NKJV) tells us, "…Surely the darkness shall fall on me; even the night shall be light about me. Indeed, the darkness shall not hide from you, but the night shines as the day. The darkness and the light are both alike to you."

Our human mind cannot comprehend how darkness and light can be alike to God any easier than we can understand the other unknowns surrounding his origin and existence. Serious questions about the reality and complexities of God are not heresy—they simply reflect our sincere and desperate desire to believe. From those questions will come the feelings the young student described—in our hearts and souls we will sense our creator's being.

SOURCE OF FARMER STORY: Bruno Hagspiel, *The Millennium Stories by Frank Mihalic*

POST-IT MEDITATION FOR OCTOBER 12
In the midst of my restless seeking, I will let
God live in my heart,
grasping his mystery and accepting his presence.

October 13

For he shall give his angels charge over thee, to keep thee in all thy ways.
~Psalm 8:10 (KJ21)

Barefooted and dirty, the girl sat and watched the people go by. She never tried to speak, never said a word, but she had a sad look in her eyes. Many people passed, but no one stopped.

The next day, one regular park-goer noticed the little girl was in the same spot and decided to walk over to her. As she began moving toward the child, she could see the back of the little girl's dress indicated a deformity, a grotesquely shaped hump. As she got closer, the little girl slightly lowered her eyes. The lady smiled to let her know it was okay and sat down beside her with a simple, "Hello."

After a long stare into the woman's eyes, the shocked little girl stammered, "Hi," smiling shyly in response to the stranger's smile. Finally, the lady asked the girl why she was so sad. The little girl looked at her and with a sad face said, "Because I'm different."

"That you are!" the stranger said with a smile.

Even sadder, the little girl said, "I know."

"You remind me of an angel, sweet and innocent."

The child looked up and smiled, slowly standing to her feet, asking, "Really?"

"Yes, you are like a little guardian angel sent to watch over all those people walking by."

Brightening, the child nodded her head yes and smiled, and with that she literally spread her wings and with a twinkle in her eye, said, "I am. I'm your guardian angel."

Speechless, sure she was seeing things, the woman stared at the transformed child, who said, "Once you thought of someone other than yourself, my job here is done." Immediately the startled lady stood to her feet and said, "Wait, so why did no one stop to help an angel?"

The radiant angel child looked at her and smiled, "You're the only one who could see me, and you believe it in your heart." And she was gone.

Angels appear in the Bible from Genesis to Revelations. A number of the references indicate we have guardian angels. Angels are actually commanded by God to "encamp all around us" and keep us from falling or getting hurt... who have been with us and will be with us "...from this time forth and forever"...and even strengthen us, and minister to us (Psalm 34:7, 91:10-13, 121:8, ESV). Unfortunately, like the passers-by in the park, many of us can't see our guardian angels because we are too preoccupied and thus sometimes miss their wisdom, guidance, and protection.

POST-IT MEDITATION FOR OCTOBER 13
I will be on the alert for my guardian angel.

October 14

Be sensible and store up precious treasures—don't waste them like a fool.
~Proverbs 21:20 (CEV)

One day, a one dollar bill and a hundred dollar bill got folded together and began talking about their life experiences.

The hundred dollar bill began to brag:

"I've had a great life," he said. "I've been to all the big hotels; Donald Trump himself used me at his casino; I've been in the wallets of Fortune 500 board members; I've flown from one end of the country to the other! I've even been in the wallet of two Presidents of the United States, and once when Princess Diana visited the US, she used me to buy a packet of gum."

In awe, the dollar humbly responded, "Gee, nothing like that has ever happened to me...but I have been to church a lot!"

If we are blessed to have a job or other source of income, we have two choices: spend our money wisely or squander it on things that will not last. Unfortunately, many choose not only to spend on possessions they don't really need but also to become slaves to debt when they cannot tell themselves or their children, "No."

Jacques Lipchitz, a Lithuanian sculptor who fled the Nazi regime and resettled in New York, once remarked, "Real richness is how you spend your money."

Spending wisely means far more than putting shoes on your children's feet instead of pouring dollars into drinking or other vices. Although right and good, simply meeting basic needs of our families isn't sufficient. To be pleasing to God, we must plan and prioritize how we invest our resources. In an age when appearance has become increasingly important, Christians must ask if having manicures and pedicures, spending excessively on hair and make-up products, and buying expensive clothes have become a higher priority than paying down debt, ensuring their children get a Christian education, or helping family members in need. How we use our money is clear evidence of our priorities.

Until we analyze where our dollars go, it will be impossible to change. Critical to setting priorities is to know ourselves and what drives us to expend our income—for cars, homes, technology gadgets, fashionable clothes, etc. And, it is important to realize our minds play tricks on us—they convince us we need what we buy when we could easily live without it.

One more key to building a wise foundation for how we spend our money—don't hang around with people who have a lot more than you do. By comparison, you will always fall short, pushing you to buy what you don't need, even if you have to go in debt.

Lastly, giving back to God a portion of what he gives us is required. Gifts generate blessings. What we present to God—through our church or in other ways—helps today and stores up treasures for eternity.

POST-IT MEDITATION FOR OCTOBER 14
I will pray for God's guidance on how to spend
the money with which I am entrusted.

October 15

Every time you smile at someone, it is an action of love, a gift to that person, a beautiful thing.
~Mother Teresa

About ten years ago when she was an undergraduate in college, Laura was working as an intern at her university's Museum of Natural History. One day while working at the cash register in the gift shop, she saw an elderly couple come in with a little girl in a wheelchair.

As she looked closer at this girl, she saw that she was kind of perched on her chair. The student then realized the child had no arms or legs, just a head, neck and torso. She was wearing a little white dress with red polka dots.

As the couple wheeled her up to the register, Laura turned her head toward the girl and gave her a wink. As she took the money from the grandparents, she looked back at the girl, who was giving her the cutest, largest smile she had ever seen. All of a sudden her handicap was gone, and she was this beautiful girl, whose smile just melted Laura and almost instantly gave her a completely new sense of what life is all about. "She took me from a poor, unhappy college student and brought me into her world; a world of smiles, love, and warmth.

"A decade later, I'm a successful business person and whenever I get down and think about the troubles of the world, I remember that little girl and the remarkable lesson she taught me about life."

What if we smiled more? Have you ever turned to the car beside you at a stop light and smiled at the driver or passenger? Do you smile at the bank teller after standing in line for 15 minutes? How about that kid in the grocery cart who is giving his mother a hard time—would he pause for a moment if you smiled at him? The stranger standing sadly on a street corner—would a smile brighten his day?

Some people are too tired to give you a smile; give them one of yours, as none needs a smile so much as he who has no more to give. A smile is a small thing, but what a difference one can make.

A lady was having breakfast with her four grown children and her one grand-daughter when she noticed an older man at the next table enjoying the toddler as much as the family, smiling as he watched her capricious antics. After a while, though, he turned his head back toward his own breakfast, the look on his face suddenly somber.

As she watched the man at the next table, the lady pulled out a "smile card" from the stack she always carried with her and handed it to the waitress, telling her she wanted to pay the man's check anonymously and instead of the bill the waitress was to give him the smile card. Soon, the man left as the family continued its leisurely breakfast. Shortly, the waitress came over and said the man had passed the smile card on and paid for another table before he left. Then, a few moments later, the waitress came back and told them the people at the second table had paid for someone else and passed the smile card on, too.

Amazingly, by the time the family left, half the room had ended up paying for a different table—and the smile card wound up back with its original owner with complimentary breakfasts for the entire family.

As Zen monk Thich Nhat Nanh once said, "Sometimes your joy is the source of your smile, but sometimes your smile can be the source of your joy." Another writer, Joseph Addison, described smiles this way: "What sunshine is to flowers, smiles are to humanity. These are but trifles, to be sure; but scattered along life's pathway, the good they do is inconceivable."

POST-IT MEDITATION FOR OCTOBER 15
Today—and tomorrow—I will experiment with smiling at strangers.

October 16

Happiness is like a cloud; if you stare at it long enough, it evaporates.
~Sarah McLachlan, Canadian singer and songwriter
Mula came upon a frowning man walking along the road to town.

"What's wrong?" he asked.

The man held up a tattered bag and moaned, "All that I own in this wide world barely fills this miserable, wretched sack."

"Too bad," said Mula, and with that, he snatched the bag from the man's hands and ran down the road with it.

Having lost everything, the man burst into tears and, more miserable than before, continued walking.

Meanwhile, Mula quickly ran around the bend and placed the man's sack in the middle of the road where he would have to come upon it.

When the man saw his bag sitting in the road before him, he laughed with joy, and shouted, "My sack! I thought I'd lost you!"

Watching through the bushes, Mula chuckled. "Well, that's one way to make someone happy!"

When our lives glow with happiness, we feel blessed and thankful. But sometimes, even staring at it, like the frowning man on the roadway, we don't appreciate what we have. Or, we begin to fear the good times can't last. Free-floating anxiety—fretfulness not based on anything we can identify—invades our psyche, making us inexplicably concerned. It seems our cheerfulness disappears almost as soon as we begin to enjoy it.

Like American actress and singer Judy Garland, who regularly rose from depression only to sink back into its dark cave, we believe behind every cloud is another cloud. The brief moments of blue sky don't last; clouds form and then evaporate, only to reappear.

If multiple "bad" events push us down—if the man's bag had been stolen multiple times—it is easy to accept Garland's conviction about endless clouds as truth. But there is another alternative. We can believe a notion first expressed in a review of the novel *Marian*, by S. Hall, which appeared in *The Duplin Magazine* in 1840: "As Katty McCane has it, 'There's a silver lining in every cloud that sails about the heavens if we could only see it.'" Over the years, the last part of the sentence has been lost, but the lesson is still salient. Every bad situation has within it some good aspect *if we look deeply*. Even when we feel overwhelmed by what is happening to us, when we see no way out, somewhere in the dark cloud resides the potential for good. The theft and return of his bag caused the complaining man to find happiness in appreciating what he had, little though it might be.

In the quote by Sarah McLachlan, she predicts happiness will evaporate if we stare at it. Mula's victim stared at his bag and became convinced he had very little. He could have just as easily stared unhappiness down. If we have the courage to face the sad state of our lives when we feel overcome with trials, the gloomy cloud will evaporate, revealing God's vibrant blue skies and his silver lining for our lives.

POST-IT MEDITATION FOR OCTOBER 16
Life is a journey through white, fluffy clouds and dark, sinister ones. I will embrace the happy days and push through the dismal ones.

October 17

These troubles test your faith and prove that it is pure. And such faith is worth more than gold. Gold can be proved to be pure by fire, but gold will ruin. When your faith is proven to be pure, the result will be praise and glory and honor when Jesus Christ comes.
~I Peter 1:17 (ERV)

The Rev. Dr. John Vincent, in *Christ and Methodism*, described faith as "the willingness to act as if the completely improvable were true." Leslie Weatherhead, London minister and author of *The Christian Agnostic*, says this willingness requires "the committal of one's life with trustful hope to the person in whom one has faith." In 1964, a *London Times* writer called it "reason grown courageous," avowing, "Faith is not concerned with believing historical or other propositions on inadequate evidence."

How does healing fit into these definitions of faith?

Tommy had been a delight from the day he was born to his missionary parents. Full of life and fun, as a child he romped and played all day every day. But one day, he fell on the playground and was badly bruised. When the black and blue marks didn't disappear normally, Tommy's parents took him to his pediatrician. Routine blood tests revealed shocking results: Tommy had leukemia. For the next five years, he underwent chemotherapy as the family and their church friends prayed constantly for healing from the dread disease threatening to steal his life.

And, he became a young Christian, asking for God's saving grace. Although the leukemia refused to be beaten, the debilitating illness couldn't destroy Tommy's sweet spirit and cheerful nature. He inspired everyone with whom he came in contact—fellow patients, doctors and nurses, family, and friends. Scores of people prayed for a miracle. But Tommy died.

To the hundreds who petitioned God on Tommy's behalf, it was as if God shouted, "NO!"

So why wasn't Tommy healed? He had his whole life ahead of him and could have touched lives in special ways. Why didn't God say, "Yes," and leave Tommy to be a source of love and pleasure to family, friends, and strangers. Was the faith of Tommy, his family, and his friends not sufficient? Did they not pray hard enough or long enough? Why would God allow something so awful happen to parents who had dedicated their lives to bringing the lost into God's kingdom?

True faith requires we believe in God whether we get a miracle or not—in Tommy's case, whether he recovered or not. We assume the closer we are to God, the easier that will be, but a "no" when we so desperately want a "yes" can challenge even those of strong faith. As hard as it is to accept, there is truth in words Leslie Weatherhead wrote in a sermon, "It is essential to remember that one can have healing without faith. One can also have a grand faith without healing, because faith, like prayer, is certainly no cure-all."

If we don't receive the miracle for which we prayed, we may need to acknowledge, as writer William James did, "If the grace of God miraculously operates, it probably operates through the subliminal door." Or, perhaps God saves some of his miracles for unbelievers.

A young man who had been raised as an atheist was training to be an Olympic diver. The only religious influence in his life came from an outspoken Christian friend. The young diver never really paid much attention to his friend's sermons, but he heard them often.

One night the diver went to the indoor pool at the college he attended. The lights were all off, but as the pool had big skylights and the moon was bright, even though the area was dim, the young man thought there was enough light to practice.

The swimmer climbed up to the highest diving board, and as he turned his back to the pool on the edge of the board and extended his arms, he saw his shadow on the wall. The shadow of his body was in the shape of a cross. Instead of diving, he knelt down and asked God to come into his life. As the young man stood, a maintenance man walked in and turned the lights on. In the brightness, the diver was shocked to see the pool had been drained for cleaning.

POST-IT MEDITATION FOR OCTOBER 17
Even when God says, "No," I will believe he knows best.
He may be saving the miracle for an unbeliever.

October 18

Be strong and of good courage, do not fear nor be afraid of them; for the
LORD your God, he is the one who goes with you. He will not leave you nor
forsake you.
~Deuteronomy 31:6 (NKJV)
During World War II, Lieutenant Commander Butch O'Hare was a fighter pilot
assigned to the aircraft carrier Lexington in the South Pacific.

One day his squadron was sent on a mission. After he was airborne, he glanced at his fuel gauge and realized someone had forgotten to top off his fuel tank. He would not have enough fuel to complete his mission and get back to his ship. Ordered to return to the carrier by his flight leader, Butch reluctantly dropped out of formation and headed back to the fleet.

As he was returning to the ship, he saw something that turned his blood cold. Japanese bombers were headed toward the American fleet. The American fighters were gone on a sortie, and the fleet was all but defenseless. He couldn't reach his squadron and bring them back in time to save the fleet. Nor could he warn the fleet of the approaching danger.

There was only one thing to do. He must somehow divert the enemy from the fleet. Laying aside all thoughts of personal safety, he dove directly into the formation of the Japanese planes. Wing-mounted 50 caliber's blazed as Butch charged in, attacking one surprised enemy plane and then another. He weaved in and out of the now broken formation and fired at as many planes as possible until all his ammunition was spent.

Undeterred, he continued the assault, diving at the planes, trying to at least clip off a wing or tail, in hopes of damaging as many enemy planes as possible and leaving them unfit to fly. He was desperate to do anything he could to keep them from reaching the American ships. Finally, the weakened and disgraced Japanese squadron took off in another direction.

Deeply relieved, Butch O'Hare and his tattered fighter limped back to the carrier. Upon arrival he reported in and related the event surrounding his return. The film from the camera mounted on his plane told the tale. It showed the extent of Butch's daring attempt to protect his fleet. He had destroyed five enemy bombers. That was on February 20, 1942, and for that action he became the Navy's first Ace of WWII and the first Naval Aviator to win the Congressional Medal of Honor.

A year later Butch was killed in aerial combat at the age of 29. His home town would not allow the memory of his heroic action to die. And today, O'Hare Airport in Chicago is named in tribute to the courage of this great man.

A memorial statue is located between terminals one and two—visit it the next time you are in O'Hare to pay tribute to the brave young man who risked everything for love of country and his fellow service members.

POST-IT MEDITATION FOR OCTOBER 18
Thank you, God, for men and women who give their lives
for our freedom—and for your son, who gave his life for our eternity.

October 19

It is possible to give away and become richer! It is also possible to hold on too tightly and lose everything. Yes, the liberal man shall be rich! By watering others, he waters himself.
~Proverbs 11:24-25 (TLB)

There once was a farmer who grew award-winning corn. Each year he entered his corn in the state fair where it won a blue ribbon. One year a newspaper reporter interviewed him and learned something interesting—he discovered the farmer shared his seed corn with his neighbors.

"How can you afford to share your best seed corn with your neighbors when they are entering corn in competition with yours each year?" the reporter asked.

"Why sir," said the farmer, "didn't you know? The wind picks up pollen from the ripening corn and swirls it from field to field. If my neighbors grow inferior corn, cross-pollination will steadily degrade the quality of my corn. If I am to grow good corn, I must help my neighbors grow good corn."

The wise farmer was very much aware of the connectedness of life. His corn could not improve unless his neighbor's corn also improved. His corn could not stay pure unless his neighbor's corn did.

So it is with our lives. Those who choose to live in peace must help their neighbors live in peace, for one has no peace if his neighbor harbors anger and resentment. Those who choose to live well must help others live well, for the value of a life is measured by the lives it touches. And those who choose to be happy must help others find happiness, for the welfare of each is bound up with the welfare of all.

Horace Mann, American education reformer and 19th century congressman, reminded us, "Doing nothing for others is the undoing of ourselves." Some might be surprised this statement came from a Republican, but in the era in which it was made, helping others hadn't become part of partisan rhetoric. God doesn't look at our political party—he just looks at how we help our fellow man. But we should also note that the farmers receiving the seed corn planted and tilled it. Receiving from others carries an obligation to use wisely what you are given so that you may have a good harvest in the future.

The lesson for each of us is this: If we are to grow good corn, we must help our neighbors grow good corn. We need not worry about what we give away. As Anne Frank said, "No one has ever become poor by giving."

October 20

Religion that God our Father accepts as pure and faultless is this:...to keep oneself from being polluted by the world.
~James 1:27 (NIV)

Some people call them "different." Others refer to them as mentally challenged or retarded. God sees them as his special children.

I envy Kevin. My brother Kevin thinks God lives under his bed. At least that's what I heard him say one night. He was praying out loud in his dark bedroom, and I stopped to listen: "Are you there, God?" he said. "Where are you? Oh, I see. Under the bed...."

I giggled softly and tiptoed off to my own room. Kevin's unique perspectives are often a source of amusement. But that night something else lingered long after the humor. I realized for the first time the very different world Kevin lives in. He was born 30 years ago, mentally disabled as a result of difficulties during labor. Apart from his size (he's 6-foot-2), there are few ways in which he is an adult. He reasons and communicates with the capabilities of a 7-year-old, and he always will. He will probably always believe that God lives under his bed, that Santa Claus is the one who fills the space under our tree every Christmas, and that airplanes stay up in the sky because angels carry them.

I remember wondering if Kevin realizes he is different. Is he ever dissatisfied with his monotonous life?

Up before dawn each day, off to labor at a workshop for the disabled, home to walk our cocker spaniel, return to eat his favorite macaroni-and-cheese for dinner, and later to bed. The only variation in the entire week-day scheme is laundry, when he hovers excitedly over the washing machine like a mother with her newborn child. He does not seem dissatisfied.

He lopes out to the bus every morning at 7:05, eager for a day of simple work. He wrings his hands excitedly while the water boils on the stove before dinner, and he stays up late twice a week to gather our dirty laundry for his next day's laundry chores.

And Saturdays—oh, the bliss of Saturdays! That's the day my Dad takes Kevin to the airport to have a soft drink, watch the planes land, and speculate loudly on the destination of each passenger inside.

"That one's goin' to Chi-car-go!" Kevin shouts as he claps his hands. His anticipation is so great he can hardly sleep on Friday nights.

And so goes his world of daily rituals and weekend field trips. He doesn't know what it means to be discontented. His life is simple. He will never know the entanglements of wealth or power, and he does not care what brand of clothing he wears or what kind of food he eats. His needs have always been met, and he never worries that one day they may not be. His hands are diligent. Kevin is never so happy as when he is working. When he unloads the dishwasher or vacuums the carpet, his heart is completely in it. He does not shrink from a job when it is begun, and he does not leave a job until it is finished. But when his tasks are done, Kevin knows how to relax. He is not obsessed with his work or the work of others. His heart is pure.

He still believes everyone tells the truth, promises must be kept, and when you are wrong, you apologize instead of argue. Free from pride and unconcerned with appearances, Kevin is not afraid to cry when he is hurt, angry, or sorry. He is always transparent, always sincere. And he trusts God. Not confined by intellectual reasoning, when he comes to Christ, he comes as a child. Kevin seems to know God—to really be friends with him in a way that is difficult for an "educated" person to grasp. God seems like his closest companion.

In my moments of doubt and frustration with my Christianity, I envy the security Kevin has in his simple faith. It is then I am most willing to admit he has some divine knowledge that rises above my mortal questions. It is then I realize perhaps he is not the one with the handicap. I am. My obligations, my fear, my pride, my circumstance—they all become disabilities when I do not trust them to God's care.

Who knows if Kevin comprehends things I can never learn? After all, he has spent his whole life in that kind of innocence, praying after dark and soaking up the goodness and love of God. And one day, when the mysteries of heaven are opened, and we are all amazed at how close God really is to our hearts, I'll grasp and appreciate that God heard the simple prayers of a boy who believed God lived under his bed.

Kevin won't be surprised at all!

How wonderful it would be to have the child-like faith of Kevin and how blessed we might be to see the world through his eyes.

SOURCE FOR KEVIN'S STORY: http://www.inspirationpeak.com/cgi-bin/stories.cgi?record=64

POST-IT MEDITATION FOR OCTOBER 20
Help me never forget that God hears simple prayers.

October 21

Everyone who acknowledges me publicly here on earth, I will also acknowledge before my Father in heaven.
~Matthew 10:32 (NLT)

Football season sizzles with excitement at this time of year as competition heats up, championships and post-season play on the not-too-distant horizon. Nothing changes much in the annual rituals—different players put on different uniforms, but the goal stays consistent: win. Most players and coaches believe, as Vince Lombardi said, "Winning isn't everything; it is the *only* thing."

Lombardi was wrong. Winning is important, he believed, because "if not, why do they keep score?" But it is *not* the only thing. A principal at Roane County High School in Kingston, Tennessee knew what *is* important. At a football game in October 2003, he read the following statement over the public address system:

It has always been the custom at Roane County High School football games to say a prayer and play the National Anthem, to honor God and country. Due to a recent ruling by the Supreme Court, I am told that saying a prayer is a violation of Federal Case Law. As I understand the law at this time, I can use this public facility to approve of sexual perversion and call it "an alternate lifestyle," and if someone is offended, that's okay. I can use it to condone sexual promiscuity by dispensing condoms and calling it, "safe sex." If someone is offended, that's okay. I can even use this public facility to present the merits of killing an unborn baby as a "viable means of birth control." If someone is offended, no problem. I can designate a school day as "Earth Day" and involve students in activities to worship religiously and praise the goddess "Mother Earth" and call it "ecology." I can use literature, videos, and presentations in the classroom that depict people with strong, traditional Christian convictions as "simple minded" and "ignorant" and call it "enlightenment." However, if anyone uses this facility to honor God and to ask him to bless this event with safety and good sportsmanship, then Federal Case Law is violated.

This appears to be inconsistent at best, and at worst, diabolical. Apparently, we are to be tolerant of everything and anyone, except God and his commandments. Nevertheless, as a school principal, I frequently ask staff and students to abide by rules with which they do not necessarily agree. For me to do otherwise would be inconsistent at best, and at worst, hypocritical. I suffer from that affliction enough unintentionally. I certainly do not need to add an intentional transgression. For this reason, I shall "Render unto Caesar that which is Caesar's" and refrain from praying at this time. However, if you feel inspired to honor, praise, and thank God and ask him, in the name of Jesus, to bless this event, please feel free to do so. As far as I know, that's not against the law—yet."

One by one, the people in the stands bowed their heads, held hands with one another and began to pray. They prayed in the stands, they prayed in the team huddles. They prayed at the concession stand, and they prayed in the announcer's box. All because one principal had the character to stand for what he believed.

POST-IT MEDITATION FOR OCTOBER 21
*I will pray for our nation to re-open its hearts and
laws to the one on whom this great country was founded.*

October 22

The purpose of life is a life of purpose.
~Robert Byrne, author

*Once upon a time, a small bird named Tasoo lived in a vast jungle. One hot
summer day, a terrible wildfire erupted and the flames devoured many trees and
animals living in the rainforest. Other birds flew high into the sky and far away
to safety, but Tasoo couldn't bear to leave her precious jungle home to burn. Day
and night, she flew with all her might back and forth to the river, filling her tiny
beak with water to drop on the raging fires. Tasoo's rare heart of courage and
unshakable determination moved the heavenly God to shed tears, and a great
rain poured down upon the jungle, extinguishing the flames. And so it is that
even the smallest actions of a determined spirit can change the world.*

Rick Warren, author of *A Purpose-Driven Life*, tells us before beginning
the search for our purpose, we must recognize it's not about us. He
avows the purpose of our lives is not about our personal fulfillment, our
peace of mind, or even our own need for happiness and contentment.
He adds it goes far beyond our family, our jobs, and our aspirations for
the future. If we want to know why we were placed on this planet, he
declares, we must start with God. It is his purpose for our lives, not ours,
that we must seek before our true reason for being will evolve.

It was, perhaps, that sense of a purpose beyond himself that allowed
Victor Frankl to survive the horrors of the Auschwitz concentration
camp. As Frankl watched friends and family die daily, he despaired. But
eventually, he discovered that it was prisoners with no spiritual foundation who lost faith in their future, dooming themselves. Soon, mental and physical decay followed. In his book, *Man's Search for Meaning*,
Frankl reminds his readers of Nietzsche's words, "He who has a *why* to
live for can bear with almost any *how*." With an aim or purpose, prisoners could rise above the horrific "how" of their existence.

Frankl surmised a fundamental change in the prisoners' attitude
toward life was required—he needed to teach the despondent, hopeless men that "It did not really matter what we expected from life, but
rather what life expected from us." Instead of focusing on the nebu-
lous meaning of life, prisoners must respond in concrete ways to their
destiny. If a man's destiny was to suffer, he must make that his task and
purpose. And Frankl, again quoting Nietzsche, told fellow prisoners,

"That which does not kill me makes me stronger." The meaning of life, according to Frankl, includes "suffering and dying, deprivation and death." The hopelessness of the struggle, Frankl averred, "does not detract from its dignity and its meaning."

POST-IT MEDITATION FOR OCTOBER 22
If concentration camp prisoners could find meaning in the midst of depressing degradation and terrifying torture, then surely I can rise above my problems and find meaning in my own life.

October 23

Character is what you are in the dark.
~Dwight Moody, American evangelist and publisher

Writing in the *Minneapolis Star Tribune* in 1988, James P. Lenfestry told the story of a little boy who loved fishing from his family's cabin, which sat on an island in the middle of a lake in New Hampshire.

The day before bass season opened, the boy and his father went fishing that evening. With a new silver lure on his hook, the boy cast his line and watched as the lure rippled the water with colors reflecting the sunset. As the moon began to rise, something heavy pulled on the line, almost doubling the fishing pole over. With skill, the 11-year-old lad worked the huge fish—a bass—to the side of the dock and lifted it from the water.

As they stared at the largest bass they had ever seen, the father looked at his watch. "It's 10 p.m. You'll have to put it back, son."

Aghast, the boy cried, "Dad! I'll never catch a fish this big again."

Glancing around the lake and seeing no other boats or fishermen, the boy looked pitifully and hopefully toward his father. The stern look on his father's face didn't change, so the disappointed boy dislodged his hook and then lowered the giant fish back into the lake. Freed, the powerful fish disappeared into the dark waters.

More than three decades later, the boy, now a man, takes his own children fishing from the same dock where he caught the biggest fish of his life. He "still sees the fish—again and again—every time [he] comes up against a question of ethics." Lenkestry added, as his father taught him, "The questions we must ask are: Do we do right when no one is looking? Do we refuse to cut corners to get the job out on time? Or refuse to trade stocks based on information we know we aren't supposed to have? Do we admit mistakes or try to hide them?"

The man whose father taught him to put the fish back in the water when he was young can answer "yes" to these questions and more. He became a man of integrity and character because of his dad's insistence on doing what was right even though no one would have ever known had they kept the fish and had bragging rights to the biggest fish ever caught in the lake.

POST-IT MEDITATION FOR OCTOBER 23
God, help me teach the right lessons by doing the right things, even when it is hard.

October 24

The worth of a man must be measured by his life, not by his failure under a singular and peculiar trial.
~Richard Froude, Anglican priest

The Bible is full of examples of great men who made bad decisions and failed, suffering the consequences. When Abraham should have stayed still and trusted God, he fled to Egypt because he feared the drought. Moses, trying to help his people, struck the rock in anger because of a desperate need for water. David stayed home from the battlefield and committed adultery with Bathsheba and then plotted the murder of her husband. Peter denied the Lord three times in spite of boasting about his dependability and commitment. Yet, God used each of these men mightily.

What we see in Abraham, Moses, David, Peter, and other Biblical heroes, is that sometimes God must witness our sins and let us fail before he can bring about success in and for us. Religious writer J. Hamilton Keathley described it like a stepladder: "Our failures are often rungs on the ladder of growth—if we will learn from our mistakes rather than grovel in the dirt."

An unknown author penned the words of a simple poem reinforcing the truth of Keathley's words:

> *When things go wrong as they sometimes will,*
> *when the road you're trudging seems all uphill,*
> *when the funds are low and the debts are high,*
> *and you want to smile but you have to sigh,*
> *when care is pressing you down a bit,*
> *rest if you must, but don't you quit.*
> *Life is queer with its twists and turns,*
> *as everyone of us sometimes learns.*
> *And many a fellow turns about,*

when he might have won had he stuck it out.
Don't give up though the pace seems slow;
you may succeed with another blow.
Often the goal is nearer than
it seems to a faint and faltering man.
Often the struggler has given up,
when he might have captured the victor's cup.
And he learned too late when the night came down,
how close he was to the golden crown.
Success is failure turned inside out,
the silver tint of the clouds of doubt.
And you never can tell how close you are;
it may be near when it seems afar.
So stick to the fight when you're hardest hit.
It's when things seem worst that you mustn't quit.

POST-IT MEDITATION FOR OCTOBER 24
When I am down and discouraged, I will ask God for help to get up.

October 25

…Never will I leave you; never will I forsake you.
~Hebrews 13:5b (NIV)

Many years ago, an 8.2 earthquake struck Armenia, leading to thousands of deaths and many collapsed buildings. In the midst of this mess, a father hurried to his dear son's school but found only a shapeless pile of stones. Shocked, the father determinedly walked toward the place where his son's class used to be and started digging.

The other parents present at the time tried to get him out and convince him that it was too late. However, he listened to no one except his heart. Then the fire chief tried to pull him out, arguing explosions could occur that would endanger his life. Stubbornly, he maintained his work.

While the father continued digging and lifting heavy stones, 12, 18, 24, 30, 36 hours passed. At the 38th hour, he heard his son's voice. Instantly he screamed, "Armand!"

His son's voice came confidently, "Dad!" The son continued, "Dad, I was sure you would save me. I told my friends that if you were still alive, you would save me! You promised me you would always be here for me! You did it Dad!"

If this father, a human being, showed such limitless love, what can we expect from the God who created this loving father and who is the essence of love? God has promised to be near us whenever and wherever we call him. It may seem that he is not responding, not listening, and not sharing our sufferings. But the truth is that God is in the process of removing the heap of stones around us. He is always close by, and he is always helping us. Waiting patiently for his work in our lives is not easy because we are buried by earthly temptations and sins. But we will be pulled from the rubble and revived by God's grace if we believe he will save us.

POST-IT MEDITATION FOR OCTOBER 25
Thank you, God, for being faithful in fulfilling your promise to always be there for me.

October 26

The group of followers all felt the same way about everything. None of them claimed that their possessions were their own, and they shared everything they had with each other. In a powerful way the apostles told everyone that the Lord Jesus was now alive. God greatly blessed his followers, and no one went in need of anything. Everyone who owned land or houses would sell them and bring the money to the apostles. Then they would give the money to anyone who needed it.
~Acts 4:32-35 (CEV)

When you see geese heading south for the winter, flying in a "V" formation, you might consider what science has discovered about why they fly that way. As each bird flaps its wings, it creates an uplift for the bird immediately following. By flying in a "V" formation, the whole flock adds at least 71 percent greater flying range than if each bird flew on its own.

Similarly, people who share a common direction and sense of community can get where they are going more quickly and more easily because they are travelling on the thrust of one another.

When a goose falls out of formation, it suddenly feels the drag and resistance of trying to go it alone and quickly gets back into formation to take advantage of the lifting power of the bird in front.

If we have the sense of a goose, we will stay in formation with those people who are heading the same way we are.

When the head goose gets tired, it rotates back in the wing and another goose flies point.

It is sensible to take turns doing demanding jobs, whether with people or with geese flying south.

Geese honk from behind to encourage those up front to keep up their speed.

What message do we give when we honk from behind?

Finally—and this is important—when a goose gets sick or is wounded by gun-shot and falls out of the formation, two other geese fall out with that goose and follow it down to lend help and protection. They stay with the fallen goose until it is able to fly or until it dies; and only then do they launch out on their own or with another formation to catch up with their own group.

Before we go on with our lives, we should pause and help those who are injured or ill.

POST-IT MEDITATION FOR OCTOBER 26
Like the apostles, I will be of one heart and soul with others.

October 27

May the Lord make your love increase and overflow for each other and for everyone else….
~1 Thessalonians 3:12 (NIV)

The cheerful girl with bouncy golden curls was almost five, and times were tough. The great depression was just ending. Waiting with her mother at the checkout stand, she saw them: a circle of glistening white pearls in a pink foil box.

"Oh please, Mommy, can I have them? Please, Mommy, please?"

Quickly the mother checked the back of the little foil box and then looked back into the pleading blue eyes of her little girl's upturned face. "A dollar ninety-five. That's almost $2.00. If you really want them, I'll think of some extra chores for you—in no time you can save enough money to buy them for yourself. Your birthday's only a week away, and you might get another crisp dollar from Grandma."

As soon as Jenny got home, she emptied her piggy bank and counted out 17 pennies. After dinner, she did more than her share of chores and then went to the neighbor and asked if she could pick dandelions for ten cents. On her birthday, Grandma did give her another new dollar bill, and at last she had enough money to buy the necklace.

Jenny loved her pearls. They made her feel dressed up and grown up. She wore them everywhere—Sunday school, kindergarten, even to bed.

One night when her loving father tucked her in bed, he asked Jenny, "Do you love me?"

"Oh yes, Daddy. You know that I love you."

"Then give me your pearls."

"Oh, Daddy, not my pearls. But you can have Princess, the white horse from my collection. The one with the pink tail. Remember, Daddy? The one you gave me. She's my favorite."

"That's okay, Honey. Daddy loves you. Good night." And he brushed her cheek with a kiss. About a week later, after the story time, Jenny's Daddy asked again, "Do you love me?"

"Daddy, you know I love you."

"Then give me your pearls."

"Oh, Daddy, not my pearls. But you can have my new baby doll I got for my birthday."

"That's okay. Sleep well. God bless you, little one. Daddy loves you."

A few nights later when her daddy came in, Jenny was sitting on her bed with her legs crossed Indian-style; her chin was trembling and one silent tear rolled down her cheek.

"What is it, Jenny? What's the matter?"

Jenny didn't say anything but lifted her little hand up to her daddy. When she opened it, he saw her little pearl necklace. With a little quiver, she finally said, "Here, Daddy. It's for you."

With tears gathering in his own eyes, Jenny's daddy reached out with one hand to take the dime-store necklace, and with the other hand he reached into his pocket and pulled out a blue velvet case with a strand of genuine pearls and gave them to Jenny. He had them all the time. He was just waiting for her to give up the dime-store stuff so he could give her a genuine treasure.

Jenny's father is like our heavenly Father. He is waiting for us to give up our dime store stuff and seek him first so he can fling open the windows of heaven and pour out such a blessing that we will not have room enough to hold it.

What are you hanging on to? What is God waiting to give you when you surrender your most prized possession?

POST-IT MEDITATION FOR OCTOBER 27
Will I risk giving up something I love to see what God will give me?

October 28

I have told you these things, so that in me you may have peace. In this world you will have trouble. But take heart! I have overcome the world.
~John 16:33 (NIV)

There once was a King who offered a prize to the artist who would paint the best picture of peace. Many artists tried. The King looked at all the pictures, but he really liked only two. Even though he admired both, he had to choose between them.

One picture was of a calm lake. The lake was an ideal mirror for peaceful mountains towering all around it. Overhead was a blue sky with fluffy white clouds. All who saw this picture thought it was a perfect picture of peace.

The other picture had mountains, too. But these were rugged and bare. Above was an angry sky from which rain fell, in which lightning played. Down the side of the mountain tumbled a foaming waterfall. The scene did not look peaceful at all.

But the King, looking closely, spotted something others missed. Behind the waterfall, he glimpsed a tiny bush growing in a crack in the rock. In the bush a mother bird had built her nest. There, in the midst of the rush of angry water, sat the mother bird on her nest...perfect peace.

Which picture do you think won the prize? The King chose the second picture. Do you know why?

"Because," explained the King, "peace does not mean to be in a place where there is no noise, trouble, or hard work. Peace means to be in the midst of all those things and still be calm in your heart. That is the real meaning of peace."

As the song "Peace in the Midst of the Storm" assures us, when the world we are living in has crumbled at our feet, when our lives are all tattered and torn, when we've been windswept and battered, we can cling to the cross. Like the bird nestled beneath a bush, we can stay safe and secure hiding in the rock of Christ if we build our faith and our future on him. Angry skies and torrents of water will not touch us.

POST-IT MEDITATION FOR OCTOBER 28
When I am in the midst of trouble and turmoil, I can claim earthly safety from the one who gave his life for my eternal security.

October 29

You are the light of the world...let your light so shine before men that they will see your good works and glorify your Father in heaven.
~Matthew 5:14, 16 (KJ21)

R. L. Sharpe's poem "A Bag of Tools" declares that people of all walks of life—princes, kings, clowns, and common people like you and me—are builders for eternity. Each of us, Sharpe believes, is given "a bag of tools, a shapeless mass, [and] a book of rules." Before the end of our days, each of us will build, from the shapeless mass, a life that is "a stumbling block or a steppingstone" for others.

None of us want to be a stumbling block. In our hearts we want to help others, but we are human, and humans forget our desire to be stepping stones when we ourselves feel put upon and used, or downcast and depressed. Or, we feel we are so insignificant that we believe we are incapable of building up the lives of others. Granted, most of us will not feed as many hungry children as Mother Teresa did, but we can help one homeless person or one single mother or one orphaned child. And, we can applaud what others do, encouraging them in their quest to make a difference in our world, no matter how great or how small.

By doing little deeds or celebrating large ones, we become part of an inspiring force that helps light the earth with love. We may not be able to save the world, but, as Eleanor Roosevelt said, it is "better to light a candle than to curse the darkness." As we give love, love will return to us. The shapeless mass of our lives becomes formed as a stepping stone—not only for others but also for ourselves.

Taking the first step is sometimes difficult, because we fear commitment as much as we fear failure. But doing nothing is a choice itself. If we sit idly by while around us people need food or shelter or just encouragement and love, we become stumbling blocks. We can choose for the light we shine as Christians to be bright and cheerful or dim and depressing.

One day, as usually was the case, a young waif, a little girl, stood at the street corner begging for food, money, or whatever she could get. Dirty and disheveled, the child's thin body was covered by tattered clothes.

As it happens, a well-to-do young man passed that corner without giving the girl a second look. But when he returned to his expensive home, his happy and comfortable family, and his well-laden dinner table, his thoughts returned to the young waif, and he became very angry at God for allowing such conditions to exist.

He reproached God, saying, "How can you let this happen? Why don't you do something to help this girl?"

Then in the depths of his being, he heard God respond, "I did. I created You!"

When Christ lives in our hearts, our desire to help others should flow naturally. Unfortunately, many times we focus on selfish desires and pleasures rather than on the needs of others. Those without faith see our self-centeredness and want no part of our hypocrisy. But if we do good works, without expecting or wanting anything in return, God will be glorified and others will see that we live what we believe.

POST-IT MEDITATION FOR OCTOBER 29
***I want to be a shining light for others to illuminate
the stepping stones on the path to God.***

October 30

And the master said to the servant, "Go out to the highways and hedges and compel people to come in, that my house may be filled."
~Luke 14:23 (KJ21)

Putting close family members first requires little thought—we do it because we love them. But beyond those loved ones, what about our extended family members? Do we owe an obligation to serve them as selflessly as we do those in our immediate family? What about people who have done us wrong or have committed crimes? In the room where the Last Supper was served sat both loyalists to Christ and those who would deny and even betray him. Yet, Jesus arose from his meal, discarded his outer garment, and draped a towel around his waist. After that, he poured water into a basin and began to wash his disciples' feet, drying them with the towel that was wrapped around him (John 13:4-5). They weren't his family members. All of them didn't deserve his love or respect, yet he became their servant.

Should we help only those whose lives are closely intertwined with ours or only those who have earned our love? Does that gain God's respect? Robert Greenleaf, in *The Servant as Leader*, avows, "For a family to be a family, no one can ever be rejected." That means we accept and love family members regardless of how deserving or undeserving they are. But true servant discipleship goes beyond our closest family members—and even beyond blood relatives.

In Robert Frost's poem, "The Death of the Hired Man," we are introduced to Silas, a hired man who works for Mary and her husband Warren most of the year. But, when haying season comes and they need him, Silas sometimes is lured away to work for someone else for more money. Yet, he always comes back for the winter when there is little or no work. In the poem, we find he has come back one last time—to die. Warren doesn't want to take him in, saying he told Silas when he left the last time during haying, when he needed him most, that would end it. Mary tells Warren that Silas has no other place to go...theirs is the only home he has. Warren interjects, "Home is the place where, when you go there, they have to take you in." Mary sees it differently. She says a home is "something you somehow haven't to deserve."

JUSTICE is when you get what you deserve.
MERCY is when you don't get what you deserve.
GRACE is when you get what you don't deserve.

None of us deserve all we have, so should we be selfish in sharing it with others?

POST-IT MEDITATION FOR OCTOBER 30
Help me, God, to open my heart and my
home even to those who are undeserving.

October 31

God demonstrates his own love for us in this: While we were still sinners, Christ died for us.
~Romans 5:8 (NIV)

One rainy afternoon a mother was driving along one of the main streets of town. Suddenly, her son Matthew spoke up from his relaxed position in the rear seat.

"Mom, I'm thinking of something." This announcement usually meant he had been pondering some fact for a while and was now ready to expound all that his seven-year-old mind had discovered. His mother was eager to hear. *"What are you thinking?"* she asked.

"The rain is like sin, and the windshield wipers are like God, wiping our sins away."

"That's really good, Matthew," she replied. Then her curiosity broke in. How far would this little boy take this revelation? So she asked, *"Do you notice how the rain keeps on coming? What does that tell you?"*

Matthew didn't hesitate one moment with his answer: "We keep on sinning, and God just keeps on forgiving us."

The forces of good and evil run like waves of lightning through our lives. We want to do good, but our human nature strikes, pushing us toward evil. Isn't it great God loves us and is merciful regardless of our merit? How comforting it is to know God keeps forgiving us—that all we have to do is trust Jesus as our savior, and he will keep washing our sins away.

An anonymous author said with informality: God is crazy about us:

> *If God had a refrigerator, our picture would be on it.*
> *If he had a wallet, our photo would be in it.*
> *He sends us flowers every spring.*
> *He sends us a sunrise every morning.*
> *Whenever we want to talk, he listens.*
> *He can live anywhere in the universe, yet he chooses our heart.*
> *Face it, friend—he is crazy about us!*

What a gift! God is crazy enough about us to love and bless us despite our inadequacies. In turn, we should accept others and serve them… even if they do things we would never do…even if they make terrible mistakes. Acceptance of a person, regardless of actions or deed, obliges us to tolerate imperfection just as God bears the burden of our blemished human nature.

When we accept people as they are, they grow better and stronger, just as we develop deeper faith and conviction when God stands with us in our weakness. Before criticizing or condemning others, we should be mindful of Jesus' words to the mob who condemned the wicked woman: "Let the person among you who is without sin be the first to throw a stone at her."

POST-IT MEDITATION FOR OCTOBER 31
Help me, God, not to cast stones. Help me to be merciful, as you are.

November 1

…the one thing I do, however, is to forget what is behind me and do my best to reach what is ahead.
~Philippians 3:13 (GNT)

The story behind the Brooklyn Bridge is one of inspiration and determination.

John Roebling, an engineer, became inspired by a vision of a spectacular bridge connecting New York with Long Island. It was 1883, and experts throughout the world thought it was an impossible feat, but Roebling refused to give up. He convinced his son, also an engineer, to help him design the bridge and then hired a crew to build the dream. Sadly, only a few months later, a tragic accident on the site took Roebling's life and injured his son so badly he couldn't walk or talk or even move—except for one finger.

"Scrap the bridge." "It was a crazy idea." "The Roebling's were foolish to chase a wild vision." Comments like these resounded around the world. The younger Roebling (Washington), whose mind was still sharp though his body was helplessly disabled, never lost his inspiration. One day, with the single finger he could move, he tapped out a message to his wife, using a code he had developed. With the tap, tap, tapping of his fingers, he asked his wife to call a group of engineers to his side. Amazingly, the project was soon underway again after the meeting. Even more astounding, for 13 years the man tapped out instructions for building the bridge until it was finally completed. Today, the spectacular Brooklyn Bridge stands proudly, a tribute to the triumph of one man's vision and his son's indomitable spirit—his refusal to be defeated by his circumstances. Tribute also goes to the wife who patiently decoded the messages her husband tapped and then gave instructions to the engineers.

All of us face obstacles, sometimes on a daily basis, but in the light of the story of the younger Roebling—and in comparison to those around us who are sorely disabled, acutely ill, poor and destitute, or who endure thousands of other desperate conditions, our hurdles seem small and insignificant. At those times, legendary football coach Knute Rockne's words provide direction: "When the going gets tough, the tough get going."

POST-IT MEDITATION FOR NOVEMBER 1
**When I get discouraged or downhearted pursuing my dreams,
I will remember Washington Roebling.**

November 2

To keep a lamp burning, we have to keep putting oil in it.
~Mother Teresa, founder of the Missionaries of Charity

In Matthew 25, Jesus tells the story of ten bridesmaids who were waiting along-side a road to welcome the bridegroom, lighting his way with the brightly lit lamps they held. Five of the girls were wise and five were careless. The wise girls had brought plenty of extra oil in case they had to refill their lamps, but the fool-ish ones had brought only enough to fill their lamps once.

After waiting for hours, the girls finally fell asleep. But then there was a shout, "The bridegroom is coming!" Quickly, the bridesmaids arose, only to realize their lamps were burning low, almost out of oil. The wise bridesmaids refilled and lit their lamps, but the thoughtless ones had no more oil. They were destitute in the darkness.

"Can we borrow some of your oil?" they asked the wise girls, who promptly said, "No, indeed. There is not enough for you and for us. Go buy more oil for your-selves." So off the foolish girls went. While they were gone, the bridegroom arrived and the wedding party entered the wedding feast, closing the door behind them. When the other girls returned, they cried out to the bridegroom to be let in, but the answer from the bridegroom was unwelcoming. Jesus concluded his parable with a warning: "Watch out, then, because you do not know the day or the hour."

Importantly, all of the bridesmaids were in the same situation—their lamps were about to burn out; they faced deep darkness. From time to time, we all come close to running out of oil—when we travel the dark valleys in our lives—just as the girls did. It happens to all of us in times of anxiety and misfortune. From the parable, we learn the lesson to keep plenty of oil in reserve—in other words, we must keep our spiritual vessel full. We can do this by staying in close communion with God through prayer and reading his word. Unfortunately, many times we are so busy we neglect the most critical part of our lives. We let our spiritual well become depleted through thoughtless neglect. It is dangerous to wait until tomorrow to replenish the spiritual oil needed to refill our lamps. We risk not being able to light our lamps to see the coming challenges and crises on earth—and even more importantly, not being ready for Christ's return.

POST-IT MEDITATION FOR NOVEMBER 2
I will not get so busy with today that I let my oil
run low, knowing I will need it in the future.

November 3

You judge by human standards; I pass judgment on no one. But if I do judge, my decisions are right, because I am not alone. I stand with the Father, who sent me.
~John 8:15-16 (NIV)

How many times do you look the other way when you see a person with a sign asking for help on a street corner?

A businessman, who had just come from a car wash, parked in front of a mall and touched up his wet car while waiting on his wife. As he polished, he noticed a man who appeared to be a bum walking toward him. Not wanting to be bothered, the man turned his head the other way. He didn't want to get sucked into helping someone who, from his looks, had no car, no home, no clean clothes, and no money. Self-righteously, the man said to himself, "Bums are bums because they prefer that life to working."

But the unkempt man wouldn't get out of his line of vision. He sat down right in front of him on the curb, as if he were waiting for a bus, although he probably didn't have a dime in his pocket. Finally, the man couldn't ignore him any longer and responding to an inner voice telling him to ask the man if he needed any help, he did.

The bum responded with three simple and profound words: "Don't we all?" No outstretched hand, no request for money or food. Just words of wisdom one might expect from a person of learning and accomplishment.

The words hit the businessman like a twelve-gauge shotgun. Feeling high and mighty, successful and important, he suddenly realized he needed more help than the man he assumed was a bum. He needed to care more for his fellowman. He needed not to judge people by how they looked. He needed his heart of pride to be pricked by the reality that all people need help.

As he opened his wallet and gave the man a wad of money, he felt better. And he never forgot the man's words. He was helped more than he helped because maybe God looked down, called an angel, dressed him like a bum, then said, "Go minister to that man polishing his car; he needs help." Don't we all?

As Christians, the love in our heart should compel us to do what we can. If we don't have money, we can offer love and encouragement.

POST-IT MEDITATION FOR NOVEMBER 3
Touch my heart, God, and fill me with love and compassion for my fellow man.

November 4

Bless be the tie that binds our hearts in Christian love.
~John Fawcett, British theologian, pastor and hymn writer

The story is told about a village in Nigeria, West Africa, where the people made their living by farming in a rich valley fed by a deep river. Because the river overflowed sometimes, the villagers built a strong dam to hold back the water. One day a man named Modupe, who lived at the top of the mountain overlooking the valley, looked down and noticed the fall rains had swollen the river, which was now straining the dam. Knowing he had to warn his friends in the valley to escape the coming flood, Modupe struggled to find a way. Then, an idea came to him—he rushed to his small hut and set it afire.

When the people of the valley saw Modupe's house burning, they said, "Our friend is in trouble. Let's sound the alarm and go up to help him." As they reached the top of the mountain, a loud crashing noise behind them made them turn around, and they saw their houses, their temple, and their crops being destroyed by the river that had broken the dam. The people began to cry and moan at their loss, but Modupe comforted them. "Don't worry," he said, "my crops are still here. We can share them while we build a new village." Then all the people began to sing and give thanks because they realized that in coming to help a friend, they had saved themselves.

There is something special about Christian friends—the tie that binds us together cannot be torn apart by earthly events. We may occasionally disagree with those who worship the same creator differently than we do, but a bond based on God's amazing grace enables us to share mutual woes, to help each other bear burdens, and to embrace in sympathy when we lose a loved one. In recent years, we have had example after example of disasters across our nation when people have sacrificed themselves to help total strangers—from earthquakes to hurricanes to tornados, Americans have opened their hearts and wallets to aid the victims of terrible catastrophes. And, in helping others rebuild their physical community, we reaffirm our spiritual sense of community as well.

When we are troubled or in despair, we know our Christian friends are praying for us. The realization that others care for us and offer petitions to God on our behalf comforts and uplifts us. We know we are not alone. As someone once said, "I believe friends are quiet angels who lift us to our feet when our wings have trouble remembering how to fly."

Why is the Christian relationship so different? It is because our faith is founded on the same solid rock. We believe our God is a mighty fortress and that belief binds us on earth and beyond. The shared hope of meeting again seals us in love and in spirit.

Christian friends are a gift from God, and we have an obligation to provide a listening ear and to be there for support when fellow Christians are hurting. Through words or silence, we can offer assurance that we care and will be with them through good times and bad.

In sharing Christian love, we point to heaven and say, "God is like that." The hallmark of Christianity is action, not words. In that sense, others comprehend God fully in what we do rather than in what we say. As the old song asserts, "The fellowship of kindred minds is like to that above." And, if we also extend Christian love to non-believers, they may find their way to God and thus become kindred souls.

POST-IT MEDITATION FOR NOVEMBER 4
I am thankful for Christian friends who are there when I am in need. With God's help, I will likewise be there for them—and those who do not yet know Christ—in prayer and in person.

November 5

Satan, who is the god of this world, has blinded the minds of those who don't believe. They are unable to see the glorious light of the Good News. They don't understand this message about the glory of Christ, who is the exact likeness of God.
~2 Corinthians 4:4 (NLT)

An atheist was walking through the woods one day in Alaska, admiring all that evolution had created.

"What majestic trees! What a powerful river! What beautiful animals!" he declared to himself.

As he was walking alongside the river, he heard a rustling in the bushes behind him. Turning to look, he saw a 13-foot Kodiak brown bear beginning to charge toward him. He ran as fast as he could down the path, looking over his shoulder as the bear rapidly closed in on him. Somehow he ran even faster, so scared tears came to his eyes. He looked again and the bear was even closer. His heart pounding in his chest, he tried to run faster yet. But alas, he tripped and fell to the ground. As he rolled over to pick himself up, the bear was right over him, reaching for him with its left paw and raising its right paw to strike him.

In his fear, he yelled, "OH MY GOD!"

Time stopped. The bear froze. The forest was silent. Even the river stopped moving....

As a brilliant light shone upon the man, a thunderous voice came from all around.

"You deny my existence for all these years, teach others I don't exist, and even credit creation to some cosmic accident. Do you expect me to help you out of this predicament? Am I to count you as a believer?"

Difficult as it was, the atheist looked directly into the light and said, "I would be hypocritical to ask to be a Christian after all these years, but perhaps you could make the bear a Christian?"

"Very well," said God.

The light went out. The river ran. The sounds of the forest resumed, and the bear dropped down on his knees, brought both paws together, bowed his head and spoke:

"Lord, thank you for this food which I am about to receive."

The story of the man and the bear reminds me of W.C. Fields, also an avowed atheist, who was caught reading the Bible in the hospital just before his death. When asked what he was doing, he replied, "Looking for loopholes."

In the end, all of mankind will want the mercy Christians have been given—and it may be too late to look for loopholes.

POST-IT MEDITATION FOR NOVEMBER 5
I will pray for those who don't believe in God.

November 6

Far beneath the bitter snows lies the seed that, with the sun's love, in the spring becomes the rose.
~Amanda McBroom, American song writer

We are never too old to learn—and it is never too late to pursue a dream.

The first day of class the professor introduced himself and challenged his students to get to know someone they didn't already know. As one student stood up to look around, a gentle hand touched his shoulder. He turned around to find a wrinkled, little old lady beaming up at him with a smile that lit up her entire being.

"Hi, handsome," she said. "My name is Rose. I'm 87 years old. May I give you a hug?"

Laughingly, the 18-year-old responded, "Of course," and received a giant squeeze.

Intrigued, the young man asked the woman why she was in college. She jok-ingly replied she was there to meet a rich husband, get married, have a couple of children, and then retire and travel. Then, more seriously, she added, "I always dreamed of having a college education, and now I'm getting one!"

From that day forward, the young man and the old woman became buddies. He was mesmerized listening to a "time machine" as she shared her experience and wisdom. Over time, Rose became a campus icon. At the end of the semester, she was invited to speak at a large banquet.

After a little joke ("I'm jittery—I gave up beer for Lent and this whiskey is kill-ing me!"), she told the students there are only four secrets to staying young, being happy, and achieving success.

"You have to laugh and find humor every day.

"You've got to have a dream. When you lose your dreams, you die.

"Anybody can grow older. That doesn't take any talent or ability. The idea is to grow up by always finding the opportunity to change.

"Have no regrets. The elderly usually don't have regrets for what we did, but rather for things we did not do."

Rose concluded her speech by singing "The Rose," encouraging each student to study the lyrics and live them out in their daily lives.

The lyrics, written by Amanda McBroom and made famous by Bette Midner, declare love is a flower, and "you are its only seed." Rose knew, as the song reveals, "It's the dream, afraid of waking, that never takes a chance…And the soul, afraid of dying, that never learns to live." She wanted the young students to learn that, "far beneath the bitter snows" in the winter—the seasons in our lives when we think the clouds are dismal, dark, and dense, the times when we believe love and hope are for someone else—the seed we sow, "with the sun's love, in the spring becomes The Rose."

At the year's end, Rose finished the college degree she had begun many years ago. One week after graduation, she died peacefully in her sleep. Over 2,000 college students attended her funeral in tribute to the wonderful woman who taught by example that it's never too difficult, never too hopeless, and never too late to be all you can possibly be.

POST-IT MEDITATION FOR NOVEMBER 6
When I think it is too late to do something,
I will remember Rose.

November 7

Keep loving each other like family.
~*Hebrews 13:1 (CEB)*

In an uncertain world, often filled with turmoil, families should be more important than ever. Sadly, though, families have changed over the past few decades, often separated by distance and busy schedules. Even so, God wants us to keep solid bonds with family members, especially those who are growing older.

After 21 years of marriage, a man's wife wanted him to take another woman out to dinner and a movie. She said, "I love you, but I know this other woman loves you and would love to spend some time with you."

The other woman was the man's mother, who had been a widow for 19 years, but the demands of his work and his three children had made it possible to visit her only occasionally. That night he called to invite her to go out for dinner and a movie. "What's wrong, are you well?" she asked.

The man's mother was the type of woman who suspected that a late night call or a surprise invitation was a sign of bad news. "I thought it would be pleasant to spend some time with you," he responded. "Just the two of us." She thought about it for a moment, and then said, "I would like that very much."

That Friday evening, the man's mother waited in the door with her coat on. She had curled her hair and was wearing the dress she had worn to celebrate her last wedding anniversary. She smiled from a face as radiant as an angel's. "I told my friends I was going out with my son, and they were impressed," she said as she got into the car.

The two went to a restaurant that, although not elegant, was nice and cozy. The man's mother took his arm as if she were the First Lady. After they sat down, he had to read the menu. Her eyes could only read large print. Halfway through the entries, he lifted his eyes and saw his mom sitting there staring at him. A nostalgic smile caressed her lips. "It was I who used to have to read the menu when you were small," she said.

"Then it's time you relax and let me return the favor," he responded. During the dinner, they had an agreeable conversation—nothing extraordinary but catching up on recent events of each other's life. They talked so much they missed the movie. As they arrived at her house later, his mom said, "I'll go out with you again, but only if you let me invite you." He agreed.

"How was your dinner date?" asked his wife when he got home. "Very nice. Much more so than I could have imagined," he answered.

Within a few short days, the man's mother died of a massive heart attack. Some time later, he received an envelope with a copy of a restaurant receipt from the same place his mother and he had dined. An attached note said: "I paid this bill in advance. I wasn't sure I could be there; but nevertheless, I paid for two plates—one for you and the other for your wife. You will never know what that night meant for me. I love you, son."

At that moment, the man understood the importance of saying in time, "I love you," and the magnitude of giving loved ones the time they deserve.

Nothing in life is more important than your family. Share time with them—some moments should not be put off until "some other time."

November 8

Your beauty should not come from outward adornment…. Rather, it should be that of your inner self, the unfading beauty of a gentle and quiet spirit, which is of great worth in God's sight.
~1 Peter 3:3-4 (NIV)

The old saying, "Beauty is in the eye of the beholder" becomes a double entendre in the following story:

The park bench was deserted as the woman sat down to read beneath the long, straggly branches of an old willow tree, disillusioned by life.

And if her frustration with the cards life had dealt her weren't enough to ruin her day, a young boy, clearly out of breath, approached her. He stood right before her with his head tilted down and said with great excitement, "Look what I found!"

In his hand was a flower, and what a pitiful sight, with its petals all worn and dry. Wanting him to take his dead flower and go off to play, the weary woman faked a small smile and then shifted in the other direction.

Instead of retreating, the young boy sat down with her, placing the flower to his nose, and declared with surprise, "It sure smells pretty and it's beautiful, too. That's why I picked it; here, it's for you."

The weed was dying or dead. Not vibrant of colors, orange, yellow, or red. But the lady knew she must take it, or he might never leave. So she reached for the flower, and replied, "Just what I need." But instead of placing the flower in her hand, the child held it mid-air. It was then she noticed the weed-toting boy could not see—he was blind.

Her voice quivering, tears shining like the sun, the lady thanked the boy for picking such a beautiful flower. "You're welcome," he smiled, and then ran away, unaware of the impact he'd had on her day.

The woman sat there and wondered how the little boy managed to see a self-pitying woman beneath an old willow tree. How did he know of her self-indulged plight? Perhaps from his heart, he'd been blessed with true sight.

Through the eyes of a blind child, at last the woman could see the problem was not with the world; the problem was her. And for all of those times she herself had been blind, she vowed to see beauty and appreciate every God-given second.

And with a contented sigh she held that wilted flower and breathed in the fragrance of a beautiful rose. Then she smiled as that young boy, another weed in his hand, went to change the life of an unsuspecting old man.

November 9

But you, take courage! Do not let your hands be weak, for your work shall be rewarded.
~2 Chronicles 15:7 (ESV)

Years ago in Illinois, a young man with six months schooling to his credit ran for an office in the legislature. As might have been expected, he was beaten. Next he entered business but failed in that too, and he spent the next seventeen years paying the debts of his worthless partner. He fell in love with a charming lady and became engaged—and she died. He had a nervous breakdown. He ran for Congress and was defeated. He then tried to obtain an appointment to the U.S. Land Office but didn't succeed. He became a candidate for the Vice-Presidency and lost. Two years later he was defeated for Senator. He ran for office once more and was elected. That man was Abraham Lincoln. What if he had quit after one of his setbacks?

If you are tempted to be a quitter, Lincoln's story and the following imaginary conversation with God might give you strength to try again.

One day I decided to quit...I quit my job, my relationship, my spirituality...I wanted to quit my life. I went to the woods to have one last talk with God.

"God," I said. "Can you give me one good reason not to quit?"

His answer surprised me. "Look around," he said. "Do you see the fern and the bamboo?"

"Yes," I replied.

God continued, "When I planted the fern and the bamboo seeds, I took very good care of them. I gave them light. I gave them water. The fern quickly grew from the earth. Its brilliant green covered the floor. Yet nothing came from the bamboo seed. But I did not quit on the bamboo.

"In the second year the fern grew more vibrant and plentiful. And again, nothing came from the bamboo seed. But I did not quit on the bamboo.

"In year three there was still nothing from the bamboo seed. But I would not quit.

"The same in year four. Then in the fifth year, a tiny sprout emerged from the earth. Compared to the fern, it was seemingly small and insignificant. But just six months later, the bamboo rose to over 100 feet tall. It had spent the five years growing roots. Those roots made it strong and gave it what it needed to survive.

"I would not give any of my creations a challenge it could not handle. Did you know, my child, that all this time you have been struggling, you have actually been growing roots? I would not quit on the bamboo. I will never quit on you.

"Don't compare yourself to others," God said. "The bamboo had a different purpose than the fern. Yet they both make the forest beautiful.

"Your time will come," God said to me. "You will rise high."

"How high should I rise?" I asked.

"How high will the bamboo rise?" he asked in return.

"As high as it can?" I questioned.

"Yes." God added, "Give me glory by rising as high as you can."

I left the forest, realizing God will never give up on me.

And he will never give up on you.

Never regret a day in your life. Good days give you happiness; bad days give you experiences from which to learn; both are essential to growth and life.

POST-IT MEDITATION FOR NOVEMBER 9
On tough days, I will remember the bamboo.

November 10

…I have come that they may have life and that they may have it more abundantly.
~John 10:10 (KJ21)

God wants us to have a full life—an abundant life—but instead of the full dinner with dessert he offers, we often opt only to accept the appetizer.

We go to church on Sunday morning, maybe Sunday night, and the unlikely event of a mid-week service. But that's just an appetizer. He offers us so much more. The main course is where we find the abundant life, but we just nibble around the edges. We do like to have God around during sickness and, of course, at funerals. However, we don't have time, or room, for him during work or play because that's the part of our lives we think we can, and should, handle on our own. We sample his dessert at confirmations, weddings, and other special occasions, but we leave so much good food on the plate—food that will help us grow as Christians.

The main course, which we sometimes skip, sustains our soul. St. Augustine avowed, "Our souls are restless till they rest in Thee." We stay restless because we are constantly looking for something more, and sadly, we are usually looking in the wrong places. When we search within, when we seek God in our innermost being, we find peace and rest.

Psalm 18:36 tells us God enlarges our path. And he thinks BIG. When he created the universe, his vision was so large we still don't know all about his divine plan for the galaxies. God created *us* with incalculable brain capacity, so we need to dream big about his plan for our lives. To open our minds for God's vision to flow through, we simply need to focus on him—not just on Sunday morning or on special occasions but on every day of our lives.

Most of us never really focus because we don't know the power of focus. We constantly feel a kind of irritating psychic chaos because we keep trying to think of too many things at once. There's always too much up there on the screen. And sometimes what we see on the screen is scary.

There was an interesting motivational talk on this subject given by former Dallas Cowboys coach Jimmy Johnson to his football players before a tough game:

"I told them that if I laid a two-by four plank across the room, everybody there would walk across it and not fall, because our focus would be that we were going to walk that two-by-four. But if I put that same two-by-four plank 10 stories high between two buildings, only a few would make it, because the focus would be on failing. Focus is everything. The team that is more focused today is the team that will win this game."

Johnson told his team not to be distracted by the crowd, the media, or the possibility of losing, but to focus on each play of the game itself just as if it were a good practice session.

The Cowboys won the game 52-17.

When we make God first in our lives, we tap his unfathomable power and imagination. Then we will be filled with dreams of the impossible—that he can make possible. He is the source of an abundant life.

POST-IT MEDITATION FOR NOVEMBER 10
By spending time in prayer, Bible reading, and contemplation,
I will discern God's wonderful plan for my life.

November 11

...If you obey my teaching, you are really my disciples; you will know the truth, and the truth will set you free.
~John 8:31-32 (GNT)

We live in an age where right is no longer right, and wrong is no longer wrong. Black and white have melded into gray. Our country, founded on Christian principles, a strong work ethic, and an unequivocal commitment to equality for all, has distorted or lost much of what our founding fathers believed in.

Today we mourn the passing of a beloved old friend by the name of Common Sense, who has been with us for many years. No one knows for sure how old he was since his birth records were long ago lost in bureaucratic red tape. He will be remembered as having cultivated such valued lessons as knowing when to come in out of the rain, why the early bird gets the worm, and that life isn't always fair. Common Sense lived by simple, sound financial policies (don't spend more than you earn) and reliable parenting strategies (adults, not kids, are in charge).

His health began to rapidly deteriorate when well-intentioned but overbearing regulations were set in place. Reports of a six-year-old boy charged with sexual harassment for kissing a classmate, teens suspended from school for using mouthwash after lunch, and a teacher fired for reprimanding an unruly student all worsened his condition.

It declined even further when schools were required to get parental consent to administer aspirin to a student but could not inform the parents when a student became pregnant and wanted to have an abortion.

Finally, Common Sense lost the will to live as the Ten Commandments became contraband; churches became businesses; prayer was banished from our schools; and criminals received better treatment than their victims.

Common Sense finally gave up the ghost after a woman who failed to realize that a steaming cup of coffee was hot spilled a bit in her lap and was awarded a huge settlement. Common Sense was preceded in death by his parents, Truth and Trust; his wife, Discretion; his daughter, Responsibility; and his son, Reason. He is survived by two stepbrothers: My Rights and Ima Whiner. Not many attended his funeral because so few realized he was gone.

All this happened while Christians sat idly by. We elect officials but don't hold them accountable. Will God hold *us* accountable for our inaction?

POST-IT MEDITATION FOR NOVEMBER 11
Before it is too late, before America totally abandons its Christian principles, I will get involved and stand for God.

November 12

Jesus said to him, "I am the way, and the truth, and the life. No one comes to the Father except through me."
~John 14:6 (ESV)

The fear of death is perhaps the greatest fear of all—a psychiatrist once said it was the mother of all fears. Only with faith can we conquer such a deep-seated, classic fear. Faith begins with believing the God who made the world, who created us, is still alive today. Moreover, it is the belief that out of his great love for us, he sent his only son to die so we might live again after our earthly body turns back to dust. Through Christ, we have the assurance not only that our sins are forgiven but also that eternal life awaits us after death.

Even with these firmly rooted beliefs, the unknown can frighten us.

One day a doctor brought his Labrador Retriever to work with him so that he could take him to the vet during his lunch break. He put a dog bed in a small room, gave the dog a big bone, and then went to his office to begin seeing patients. About an hour later, a sick man turned to his doctor as he was leaving the room following an examination, and said, "Doctor, I am afraid to die. Tell me what lies on the other side."

Very quietly the doctor said, "I don't know."

"You don't know? You, a Christian man, do not know what is on the other side?"

The doctor was holding the handle of the door. On the other side of the door there came the sound of scratching and whining. As he opened the door, the doctor's dog sprang into the room and leaped on him with an eager show of gladness.

Turning to the patient, the doctor said, "Did you notice that dog? He had never been in this room before. He did not know what was inside. He knew nothing except that his master was here, and when the door opened, he sprang in without fear. I know little of what is on the other side of death, but I do know one thing: I know my master is there, and that is enough. And when the door opens, I shall pass through with no fear, but with gladness."

And so it is—as long as we trust that God is still alive and awaits us, the unknowns won't engulf us, won't rob us of the peace and assurance that comes through Christ's death and resurrection. We may not know exactly what happens at the moment of death—what the transition from this life to the next is like—and we may not know exactly how our souls operate without our bodies until the two are reunited, but God knows. Witnessing his magnificent creation and its intricate complexities, we should have no doubt his master design for life after death will be greater than anything we could ever envision with our human minds.

POST-IT MEDITATION FOR NOVEMBER 12
With faith, I can conquer fears of the unknown.

November 13

The Lord will command his angels to take good care of you.
~Psalm 91:11 (NIRV)

Loved ones who have crossed the great divide sometimes speak to us in ways only we recognize.

A sad-looking lady walked into the grocery store, not particularly interested in buying groceries. She wasn't hungry. The pain of losing her husband of 37 years was still too raw. And this grocery store held so many sweet memories. Rudy often came with her and almost every time he'd pretend to go off and look for something special. She knew what he was up to. She'd always spot him walking down the aisle with the three yellow roses in his hands. Rudy knew she loved yellow roses.

With a heart filled with grief, the woman only wanted to buy a few items and leave, but even grocery shopping was different since Rudy had passed on. Shopping for one took time, a little more thought than it had for two. Standing by the meat, she searched for the perfect small steak and remembered how Rudy had loved his steak.

Suddenly a woman came beside her. She was blond, slim, and lovely in a soft green pantsuit. The new widow watched as the younger woman picked up a large pack of T-bones, dropped them in her basket, hesitated, and then put them back. She turned to go and once again reached for the pack of steaks. She saw the older lady watching her and smiled. "My husband loves T-bones, but honestly, at these prices, I don't know."

The sorrowing woman swallowed the emotion in her throat and met the younger woman's pale blue eyes. "My husband passed away eight days ago," she said. Glancing at the package in the other woman's hands, she fought to control the tremble in her voice. "Buy him the steaks. And cherish every moment you have together."

The young woman had tears in her eyes as she placed the package in her basket and wheeled away.

A few moments later, the older lady saw first the green suit, then recognized the pretty lady coming towards her. In her arms she carried a package. On her face she wore a bright smile, and it was almost as if a soft halo encircled her blond hair as she kept walking. As she came closer, the woman of sorrow saw what she held and tears began misting in her eyes. "These are for you," the young woman said and placed three beautiful long-stemmed yellow roses in her arms. "When you go through the line, they will know these are paid for." She leaned over and placed a gentle kiss on the older woman's cheek, then smiled again.

The widow wanted to tell the young lady what she'd done, what the roses meant, but still unable to speak, she watched as the young wife walked away, tears clouding her vision. Looking down at the beautiful roses nestled in the green tissue wrapping, the woman found it surreal. How did she know? Suddenly the answer seemed so clear. She wasn't alone. "Oh, Rudy, you haven't forgotten me, have you?" she whispered, with tears in her eyes. He was still with her, and the young woman was his angel.

POST-IT MEDITATION FOR NOVEMBER 13
Thank you, God, for angels and signs.

November 14

To forgive oneself? No, that doesn't work; we have to be forgiven. But we can only believe this is possible if we ourselves can forgive.
~Dag Hammarskjold, Swedish diplomat and Secretary General of the United Nations

This letter was written to a man on death row by the father of the man whom the man on death row had killed:

You are probably surprised that I, of all people, am writing a letter to you, but I ask you to read it in its entirety and consider its request seriously. As the father of the man whom you took part in murdering, I have something very important to say to you.

I forgive you. With all my heart, I forgive you. I realize it may be hard for you to believe, but I really do. At your trial, when you confessed to your part in the events that cost my son his life and asked for my forgiveness, I immediately granted you that forgiving love from my heart. I can only hope you believe me and will accept my forgiveness.

But this is not all I have to say to you. I want to make you an offer—I want you to become my adopted child. You see, my son who died was my only child, and I now want to share my life with you and leave my riches to you. This may not make sense to you or anyone else, but I believe you are worth the offer. I have arranged matters so that if you will receive my offer of forgiveness, not only will you be pardoned for your crime, but you also will be set free from your imprisonment, and your sentence of death will be dismissed. At that point, you will become my adopted child and heir to all my riches.

I realize this is a risky offer for me to make to you—you might be tempted to reject my offer completely—but I make it to you without reservation.

Also, I realize it may seem foolish to make such an offer to one who cost my son his life, but I now have a great love and an unchangeable forgiveness in my heart for you.

Finally, you may be concerned that once you accept my offer you may do something to cause you to be denied your rights as an heir to my wealth. Nothing could be further from the truth. If I can forgive you for your part in my son's death, I can forgive you for anything. I know you will never be perfect, but you do not have to be perfect to receive my offer. Besides, I believe once you accept my offer and begin to experience the riches that will come to you from me, your primary response (though not always) will be gratitude and loyalty.

Some would call me foolish for my offer to you, but I wish for you to call me your father.

Sincerely,
The Father of Jesus

We all commit wrongs—against ourselves, against God, and against our family and friends, or even against strangers. In words found in the Episcopal Confession of Prayer, we sin "in thought, word, and deed, by what we have done and what we have left undone."

God's forgiveness comes from the death of his son on a wooden cross, a sacrifice that paid the price for our sins. "Paid" is the key. Forgiveness is ours simply by asking. It is a gift of grace.

Forgiving ourselves doesn't come as easily, but I think Hammarskjold was wrong. We can remove the burden of remorse from our heart. Granted, the price seems so high we sometimes don't discern what it is. We just know our heart hurts from terrible guilt. We rail against a loved one in anger. We fail to tell someone we love her, and then it is too late—she is taken from our lives with one heartbeat. We talk about someone behind his back. Or, we cheat on our spouse. We hit someone while driving drunk. We kill a person who invades our home. For my husband, it was killing a person in self-defense on a dark, winding road in the wee hours of the morning, launching a life-long struggle with self-forgiveness.

The acts do not have to be big, like taking the life of another person; even small actions that injure others mount up to fill us with shame. Large or small, they hang over our heads like dark clouds. We ask God for forgiveness, and it is readily given. But regrets still smother us. How, then, can we let go of our guilt and forgive ourselves?

The first step is to acknowledge we are sinful creatures, The next step is to realize we cannot change most of what has happened in the past. Lastly, we should believe there is goodness in us and with God's help, we can be the person he wants us to become.

POST-IT MEDITATION FOR NOVEMBER 14
When besieged by regret and remorse, I will accept the miracle of God's forgiveness and follow his example, forgiving myself.

November 15

Don't be careless. Instead, be very careful. Don't forget the things your eyes have seen. As long as you live, don't let them slip from your mind. Teach them to your children and their children after them.
~Deuteronomy 4:9 (NIRV)

A Sunday school teacher was discussing the Ten Commandments with her five and six-year-olds. After explaining the commandment to "honor" thy father and thy mother, she asked, "Is there a commandment that teaches us how to treat our brothers and sisters?"

One little boy, the oldest child in his family, looked up and said in all serious-ness: "Thou shalt not kill."

~~~

One day a little girl was watching her mother do dishes and suddenly noticed her mother had several strands of white hair among her brunette ones. She looked at her mother inquisitively and asked, "Why are some of your hairs white, Mom?"

Her mother replied, "Well, every time you make me cry or unhappy, one of my hairs turns white."

The little girl thought about this revelation for a while and then queried, "Momma, how come ALL of grandma's hairs are white?"

~~~

The children were lined up in the cafeteria of a Catholic elementary school for lunch. At the head of the table sat a large pile of apples, where a nun had posted a note:

Take only ONE. God is watching.

Moving further along the lunch line, at the other end of the table was a large pile of chocolate chip cookies. A child had attached a note:

Take all you want. God is watching the apples.

~~~

Out of the mouth of babes.... They surprise us, they dismay us, and they charm us. They are God's gifts, and he expects us to teach them from his word and our hearts, even as we enjoy their delightful ways.

POST-IT MEDITATION FOR NOVEMBER 15
Thank you, God, for precious children to teach and love.

November 16

Man looks at the outward appearance, but the Lord looks at the heart."
~1 Samuel 16:7b (ESV)

Our house sat across the street from the entrance to John Hopkins Hospital in Baltimore. We lived downstairs and rented the upstairs rooms to outpatients at the clinic. One summer evening as I was fixing supper, a knock sounded at the door. I opened it to see a truly awful looking man. "Why, he's hardly taller than my eight-year-old," I thought, staring at the stooped, shriveled body. But the appalling aspect was his raw, red face—lopsided from swelling. Yet, his voice was pleasant as he said, "Good evening. I've come to see if you've a room for just one night. I came for a treatment this morning from the eastern shore, and there's no bus 'til morning."

The misshapen man told me he'd been hunting for a room since noon but with no success; no one seemed to have a vacancy. "I guess it's my face...I know it looks terrible, but my doctor says with a few more treatments...." For a moment I hesitated, but his next words convinced me: "I could sleep in this rocking chair on the porch. My bus leaves early in the morning." I told him we would find him a bed, but to rest on the porch. I went inside and finished getting supper. When we were ready, I asked the old man if he would join us. "No thank you. I have plenty." And he held up a brown paper bag.

When I had finished the dishes, I went out on the porch to talk with him a few minutes. It didn't take a long time to see this old man had an oversized heart crowded into that tiny body. He told me he fished for a living to support his daughter, her five children, and her husband, who was hopelessly crippled from a back injury. He didn't tell it by way of complaint; in fact, every other sentence was prefaced with thanks to God for a blessing. He was grateful no pain accompanied his disease, which was apparently a form of skin cancer. He thanked God for giving him the strength to keep going.

At bedtime, we put a camp cot in the spare room for him. When I got up in the morning, the bed linens were neatly folded and the little man was out on the porch. He refused breakfast, but just before he left for his bus, haltingly, as if asking a great favor, he said, "Could I please come back and stay the next time I have a treatment? I won't put you out a bit. I can sleep fine in a chair." Pausing a moment, he added, "Your children made me feel at home. Grownups are bothered by my face, but children don't seem to mind." I told him he was welcome to come again.

On his next trip he arrived a little after seven in the morning. As a gift, he brought a big fish and a quart of the largest oysters I had ever seen. He said he had shucked them that morning before he left so that they'd be nice and fresh. I knew his bus left at 4:00 a.m., and I wondered what time he had to get up in order to do this for us.

In the years he came to stay overnight with us there was never a time that he did not bring us fish or oysters or vegetables from his garden. Other times we received packages in the mail, always by special delivery; fish and oysters packed in a box of fresh young spinach or kale, every leaf carefully washed. Knowing that he must walk three miles to mail these, and knowing how little money he had made the gifts doubly precious. When I received these little remembrances, I often thought of a comment our next-door neighbor made after he left that first morning. "Did you keep that awful looking man last night? I turned him away! You can lose roomers by putting up such people!" Maybe we did lose roomers once or twice. But oh! If only they could have known him, perhaps their illness would have been easier to bear. I know our family always will be grateful to have known him; from him we learned what it was to accept the bad without complaint and the good with gratitude to God.

Recently I was visiting a friend who has a greenhouse. As she showed me her flowers, we came to the most beautiful one of all, a golden chrysanthemum, bursting with blooms. But to my great surprise, it was growing in an old dented, rusty bucket. I thought to myself, "If this were my plant, I'd put it in the *loveliest container I had!" My friend changed my mind. "I ran short of pots," she explained, "and knowing how beautiful this one would be, I thought it wouldn't mind starting out in this old pail. It's just for a little while, 'til I can put it out in the garden." She must have wondered why I laughed so delightedly, but I was imagining just such a scene in heaven.*

"Here's an especially beautiful one," God might have said when he came to the soul of the sweet old fisherman. "He won't mind starting in this small body." All this happened long ago and now, in God's garden, how tall this lovely soul must stand. The Lord does not look at the things man looks at.

POST-IT MEDITATION FOR NOVEMBER 16
**I will try harder to see beyond how a person looks,
seeking to perceive what God grasps within the person as beautiful.**

November 17

Be very careful, then, how you live—not as unwise but as wise, making the most of every opportunity….therefore do not be foolish, but understand what the Lord's will is.
~Ephesians 5:15-17 (NIV)

How would we spend our days if we sat down and calculated the number we might have left based on the average life span? Would we use our time differently, more wisely? What if we knew we had 10 years left (3650 days)? What if we only had one year (365 days) or perhaps just 30 days? If we have 40 years (14,600 days), do we have plenty to waste?

We learn from Peter that one day to God is as a thousand years and a thousand years are as a day…what does this mean? Are the 2000-plus years since Christ walked on earth no more than two days to God? Or are they like two million days to him? How can we possibly comprehend God's perspective on time?

Kenneth Boa, president of Reflection Ministries, concluded, "An infinitesimal moment is like eternity, and eternity is like an infinitesimal moment." He extends this to explain how God is able to communicate with all of his children and hear all of our prayers at the same time: "It is part of his ability to be omnipresent. God, being everywhere at once, views all things as part of an eternal here and now. And, in each moment, he has all the 'time' he needs to provide for each of us the care he has promised. For him, there is no beginning and no end, no before and no after, save in the way he chooses to communicate with us."

If time is so flexible for God and if he cares for each of us, then Boa asserts that he gives each of his children the time needed to accomplish

God's purpose for each life. In a way that is unfathomable to us, God's plan has been unfolding beyond the concept we know as time. American poet and philosopher Henry David Thoreau wisely stated, "We cannot kill time without injuring eternity."

We are told in Psalm 90:12 to consider our mortality, so that we might live wisely. The psalmist meditates on God's greatness and his eternal nature in contrast to the brevity of man's life. The prayer that follows in Psalm 90 is for the ability to take the life God has given him and make it meaningful. Similarly, we want our lives to count for God so that our mortality may lead us to eternity. The difficulty is that we are prone to live for today rather than for tomorrow, concentrating on the present time instead of eternity. When we focus on the life after this one, we may find more value and purpose on earth.

These lines, written by an unknown author, lead us in the right direction:

Take time to think; it is the source of power.
Take time to read; it is the foundation of wisdom.
Take time to play; it is the secret of staying young.
Take time to be quiet; it is the opportunity to seek God.
Take time to be aware; it is the opportunity to help others.
Take time to love and be loved; it is God's greatest gift.
Take time to laugh; it is the music of the soul.
Take time to be friendly; it is the road to happiness.
Take time to dream; it is what the future is made of.
Take time to pray; it is the greatest power on earth.

Adapted from two sources: Ken Boa's Time Management retrieved from http://bible.org/seriespage/time-management and http://www.inspirationalarchive.com/2848/take-time/#ixzz1wUz2yTcS

POST-IT MEDITATION FOR NOVEMBER 17
As I live today on Planet Earth, I will keep my eyes on eternity, wisely using the time God has given me.

November 18

I do not understand what I do. For what I want to do I do not do, but what I hate I do.
~Romans 7:15 (NIV)

According to tradition, this is how an Eskimo hunter kills a wolf:

First, the Eskimo coats his knife blade with animal blood and allows it to freeze. He then adds layer after layer of blood until the blade is completely concealed by the frozen blood.

Next, the hunter fixes his knife in the ground with the blade up. When a wolf follows his sensitive nose to the source of the scent and discovers the bait, he licks it, tasting the fresh frozen blood. He begins to lick faster, more and more vigorously, lapping the blade until the keen edge is bare. Feverishly now, harder and harder, the wolf licks the blade in the cold Arctic night. His craving for blood becomes so great that the wolf does not notice the razor-sharp sting of the naked blade on his own cold tongue. Nor does he recognize the instant when his insatiable thirst is being satisfied by his own warm blood. His carnivorous appetite continues to crave more until, in the morning light, the wolf is found dead on the snow.

Many begin using drugs, drinking alcohol, smoking cigarettes, or engaging in unsafe sexual behavior for the same reasons the wolf begins licking the knife blade. It seems safe and delicious at first, but it doesn't satisfy. More and more is desired, leading to a crisis or death. Once we start down a sinful path, turning back can be difficult.

How many times do we surrender our bad habits to God and within days (or even hours), we find ourselves doing the opposite of what we want to do? We are not alone. Even the apostle Paul struggled, as evidenced in Romans 7:15.

We may never be totally free in controlling our bad actions even if we have given our lives to Christ. This is a result of "how" we gave our lives. Did we just give God our sins and ask him to forgive us and help us not to sin anymore? If we don't give him total control, if we still hang on to the power to decide what we will do, our human nature will cause us to sin. We are slaves to sin, and the only way we can escape is to give it all to our creator.

In an earlier devotion, my sister's struggle with addiction was discussed. For almost 17 years, she repeatedly tried to break out of the prison of prescription drug abuse. It was only when she admitted to herself and to God she couldn't control her "gotta have it" feelings that she was given the power to overcome the cravings destroying her life. Like Paul, she couldn't do what she wanted to do; she continued to do what she hated until she gave it all to God.

Do you have a bad habit or sin you can't overcome? Do you worry and fret too much? Do you ask God to contain your temper yet blow your top when someone offends you or tries to control you? Do you pray to spend your money wisely but give in to temptation when you see someone else with what you would like to have? Do you try not to lust but your thoughts go crazy at the sight of a beautiful woman (or handsome man)?

Temptation haunts all of us in one form or another, and we condemn ourselves when our willpower fails. One way to say no when we want to say yes is to imagine whatever we are doing or thinking flashed across a giant screen in the sky—few of us would want our sinful thoughts and actions visible to the world, and certainly not to God. Another way, when anger, lust, temptation, or other sins threaten, is to replace those thoughts with a scripture like Psalm 51:10 (NIV): "Create in me a pure heart, and renew a steadfast spirit within me." God's word can help us overcome any desire or reaction.

Wolf story adapted from Hot Illustrations for Youth Talks by Wayne Rice, Youth Specialties, Inc.

POST-IT MEDITATION FOR NOVEMBER 18
I will keep an arsenal of scripture ready to replace sinful thoughts.

November 19

So let us run the race that is before us and never give up. We should remove from our lives anything that would get in the way.
~Hebrews 12:1 (NCV)

Dante Gabriel Rossetti, the famous 19th-century poet and artist, was once approached by an elderly man. The old fellow had some sketches and drawings he wanted Rossetti to look at and tell him if they were any good, or if they at least showed potential talent.

Rossetti looked over them carefully. After the first few, he knew they were worthless. Although Rossetti was a kind man, he was sorry, but he could not lie to the man. He told the elderly man as gently as possible the pictures were without much value and showed little talent. The man was disappointed but seemed to expect Rossetti's judgment.

The old man then apologized for taking up Rossetti's time but asked him to look at a few more drawings.

Rossetti looked over the second batch of sketches and immediately became enthusiastic over the talent they revealed. "These," he said, "oh, these are good. This young student has a great talent. He should be given every help and encouragement. He has a great future."

Rossetti could see that the old fellow was deeply moved.

"Who is this fine young artist?" he asked. "Your son?"

"No," said the old man sadly.

"It is me…40 years ago. If only I had heard your praise then! For you see, I got discouraged and gave up–too soon."

How many times do we give up too quickly? Do you have a dream you never pursued? Why not shoot for the moon? God didn't think small when he created the universe, and he doesn't want us limited by our lack of self-confidence. We all have God-given talents. If we have good and godly dreams, if we go for these dreams and give them our all, God will encourage and support us.

POST-IT MEDITATION FOR NOVEMBER 19
I will not wait until it is too late to pursue my dreams.

November 20

Who among the gods is like you, Oh Lord? Who is like you—majestic in holiness, awesome in glory, working wonders?
~Exodus 15:11 (NASB)

In a book called *The Kneeling Christian*, we are urged to be bold in asking God to answer prayer. "It is natural for God to answer prayer…he wants us to pray…."

A little girl went to her bedroom and pulled a glass jelly jar from its hiding place in the closet. She poured the change out on the floor and counted it carefully. Three times, even. The total had to be exactly perfect. No chance here for mistakes. Carefully placing the coins back in the jar and twisting on the cap, she slipped out the back door and made her way six blocks to Rexall's Drug Store with the big red Indian Chief sign above the door. She waited patiently for the pharmacist to notice her, but he was too busy at that moment. Tess twisted her feet to make a scuffing noise. Nothing. She cleared her throat with the most disgusting sound she could muster. No good. Finally she took a quarter from her jar and banged it on the glass counter. That did it!

"And what do you want?" the pharmacist asked in an annoyed tone of voice. "I'm talking to my brother from Chicago, whom I haven't seen in ages," he said without waiting for a reply to his question.

"Well, I want to talk to you about <u>my</u> brother," Tess answered back in the same annoyed tone. "He's really, really sick…and I want to buy a miracle. I prayed and God told me I would find one here."

"I beg your pardon?" said the pharmacist.

"His name is Andrew and he has something bad growing inside his head, and my daddy says only a miracle can save him now. So how much does a miracle cost?"

"We don't sell miracles here, little girl. I'm sorry, but I can't help you," the pharmacist said, softening a little.

"Listen, I have the money to pay for it. If it isn't enough, I will get the rest. Just tell me how much it costs."

The pharmacist's brother, a well-dressed man, stooped down and asked the little girl, "What kind of a miracle does your brother need?"

"I don't know," Tess replied with her eyes welling up. I just know he's really sick, and Mommy says he needs an operation. But my Daddy can't pay for it, so I want to use my money."

"How much do you have?" asked the pharmacist's brother.

"One dollar and eleven cents," Tess answered barely audibly. "And it's all the money I have, but I can get some more if I need to."

"Well, what a coincidence," smiled the man. "A dollar and eleven cents—the exact price of a miracle for little brothers."

He took her money in one hand and with the other hand he grasped her mitten and said, "Take me to where you live. I want to see your brother and meet your parents."

That well-dressed man was Dr. Carlton Armstrong, a surgeon, specializing in neurosurgery. The operation was completed free of charge, and soon Andrew was home again and doing well.

Mom and Dad were happily talking about the chain of events that had led them to this place. "That surgery," her Mom whispered, "was a real miracle from God. I wonder how much it would have cost?"

Tess smiled. She knew exactly how much a miracle cost...one dollar and eleven cents....plus the faith and determination of a little child.

POST-IT MEDITATION FOR NOVEMBER 20
**I will trust God with all my problems and
needs and be thankful for his miracles.**

November 21

...Let every man be quick to listen but slow to use his tongue, and slow to lose his temper. For man's temper is never the means of achieving God's true goodness.
~James 1:19-20 (PNT)

A man and woman had been married for more than 60 years. They had shared everything. They had talked about everything. They had kept no secrets from each other, except the woman had a shoe box in the top of her closet that she had cautioned her husband never to open or ask her about.

For all of those years, he had never thought about the box; but one day his wife got very sick, and the doctor said she would not recover.

In trying to sort out their affairs, the old man took down the shoe box and took it to his wife's bedside. She agreed it was time he should know what was in the box. When he opened it, he found two crocheted dolls and a stack of money totaling $95,000. He asked her about the contents. "When we were to be married," she said, "my grandmother told me the secret of a happy marriage was to *never argue. She told me if I ever got angry with you, I should just keep quiet and crochet a doll."*

The husband was so moved he had to fight back tears. Only two precious dolls were in the box! She had only been angry with him two times in all those years of living and loving. He almost burst with happiness. "Honey," he said, "that explains the dolls, but what about all of this money? Where did it come from?"

"Oh," she said, "that's the money I made from selling the dolls."

This oft-repeated story has meaning behind its humor. How much more peaceful the marriage had been because the woman didn't spew her anger on her husband. Instead of attacking him or harboring her feelings inside, she simply redirected it in a positive way.

Anger is understandable—it is a human emotion and can be used constructively. But, it can also be destructive, leading to hostilities and hurts that take a long time to heal. The best way to avoid the negative consequences of anger is to take our wrath to God, asking him to heal us. And, as the crocheting wife did, if we can find a way to divert the rage where it can't hurt anyone, that's good, too.

POST-IT MEDITATION FOR NOVEMBER 21
Help me, God, to find ways to soften rather than harden my anger.

November 22

...the word of God cuts all the way through, to where soul and spirit meet....
~Hebrews 4:12 (GNT)

I first saw Tommy 14 years ago in the opening session of the university class I taught on the theology of faith. He was combing his hair, which hung six inches below his shoulders. My quick judgment wrote him off as strange. He turned out to be my biggest challenge, constantly objecting to or smirking at the possibility of an unconditionally loving God. When he turned in his final exam, he asked in a slightly cynical tone, "Do you think I'll ever find God?"

"No," I said emphatically.

"Oh," he responded. "I thought that was the product you were pushing."

I let him get five steps from the door and then called out. "I don't think you'll ever find him, but I am certain he will find you." Tommy shrugged and left.

Later I heard Tommy had graduated, and I was grateful for that. Then came a sad report: Tommy, only 24, had terminal cancer. Before I could search him out, he came to me. When he walked into my office, his body was badly wasted, and his long hair had fallen out because of chemotherapy. But his eyes were bright and his voice, for the first time, was firm.

"Tommy! I've thought about you so often. I heard you were very sick," I blurted out.

"Oh, yes, very sick. I have cancer. It's a matter of weeks."

Then he told me why he had come.

"It was what you said to me on the last day of class when I asked if you thought I would ever find God. I thought about your response a lot, even though my search for God was hardly intense at that time. But when the doctors removed a lump from my groin and told me that it was malignant, I got serious about locating God. And when the malignancy spread into my vital organs, I really began banging against the bronze doors of heaven. But nothing happened. Well, one day I woke up, and instead of my desperate attempts to get some kind of message, I just quit. I decided I didn't really care about God, an afterlife, or anything like that. I decided to spend what time I had left doing something more important. I thought about you and something else you had said: 'The essential sadness is to go through life without loving. But it would be almost equally sad to leave this world without ever telling those you loved that you loved them.' So I began with the hardest one: my dad."

Tommy's father had been reading the newspaper when his son approached him.

"Dad, I would like to talk with you."

"Well, talk."

"I mean, it's really important."

The newspaper came down three slow inches.

"What is it?"

"Dad, I love you. I just wanted you to know that."

Tommy smiled at me as he recounted the moment. "The newspaper fluttered to the floor. Then my father did two things I couldn't remember him doing before. He cried and he hugged me. And we talked all night, even though he had to go to work the next morning.

"It was easier with my mother and little brother," Tommy continued. "They cried with me, and we hugged one another and shared the things we had been keeping secret for so long. Here I was, in the shadow of death, and I was just beginning to open up to all the people I had actually been close to.

"Then one day I turned around, and God was there. He didn't come to me when I pleaded with him. Apparently he does things in his own way and at his own hour. The important thing is that you were right. He found me even after I stopped looking for him."

"Tommy," I added, "could I ask you a favor? Would you come to my theology-of-faith course and tell my students what you told me?"

Though we scheduled a date, he never made it. Of course, his life was not really ended by his death, only changed. He made the great step from faith into vision. He found a life far more beautiful than the eye of humanity has ever seen or the mind ever imagined.

Before he died, we talked one last time. "I'm not going to make it to your class," he said.

"I know, Tommy."

"Will you tell them for me? Will you...tell the whole world for me?"

"I will, Tommy. I'll tell them."

Poet Edna St. Vincent Millay wrote, "The soul can split the sky in two and let the face of God shine through." Within each of us resides a desire to know God—an unquenchable thirst drives us on our quest. Psalm 42:1 (GNT) suggests, "As a dear longs for clear water, so I long for you, oh God." Literally, when a deer is being chased by a predator, it longs for a body of water where it can immerse itself, covering its scent. When the predator loses the deer's scent, it can no longer detect the presence of its prey. The deer is now safe.

David wrote the passage in Psalm 42 when he was heartsick, outcast from public worship, weary from persecution. Even so, his most urgent need was communion with God. Like water to the deer, his soul, his very life, insatiably sought the sense of the divine presence.

Our souls will never be satisfied or safe without God. When we immerse ourselves in the streams of living water of God's word and prayer, like the deer cleanses himself in a cool brook, we are transformed into sweet spirits, making us less vulnerable to foes.

POST-IT MEDITATION FOR NOVEMBER 22
I will be glad when my heart longs for God,
knowing he will quench the thirst of my soul.

November 23

Hypocrisy and distortion are passing currents under the name of religion.
~*Mahatma Gandhi, Indian leader*

A man was being tailgated by a stressed-out woman on a busy boulevard. Suddenly, the light turned yellow, just in front of him.

He did the right thing, stopping at the crosswalk, even though he could have beaten the red light by accelerating through the intersection.

The tailgating woman hit the roof—hitting the horn, screaming in frustration as she missed her chance to get through the intersection with him. As she was still in mid-rant, she heard a tap on her window and looked up into the face of a very serious police officer. The officer ordered her to exit her car with her hands up, then took her to the police station where she was searched, fingerprinted, photographed, and placed in a cell.

After a couple of hours, a policeman approached the woman's cell and opened the door. She was escorted back to the booking desk, where the arresting officer was waiting with her personal effects.

"I'm very sorry for this mistake. You see, I pulled up behind your car while you were blowing your horn, flipping the guy off in front of you, and cussing a blue streak at him. I noticed the 'Choose Life' license plate holder, the 'What Would Jesus Do' bumper sticker, the 'Follow Me to Sunday School' bumper sticker, and the chrome-plated Christian fish emblem on the trunk. Naturally, I assumed you had stolen the car."

Was the lady with road rage a hypocrite masquerading as a Christian? Was she doing more harm than good for God's kingdom? She left something behind—and it wasn't a good impression of a Christ-like life. If she had followed the admonition in 1 Corinthians 16:14, ASV ("Let all that you do be done with love") not only would she not have ended up in jail, but she also would not have denigrated the name of Jesus. And, as the poet Longfellow wrote, her life would have left the right kind of footprints on the sands of time.

POST-IT MEDITATION FOR NOVEMBER 23
Help me to act in ways that inspire others to want to be Christians.

November 24

The Lord works everything out for his own purposes.
~Proverbs 16:4 (NIRV)

A carpenter was building crates for the clothes his church was sending to an orphanage in China. On his way home, he reached into his shirt pocket to find his glasses, but they were gone. Mentally replaying his earlier actions, he realized what happened; the glasses had slipped out of his pocket unnoticed and fallen into one of the crates, which he had nailed shut. His brand new glasses were heading for China!

The Great Depression was at its height, and this man had six children. He had spent $20 for those glasses that very morning. He was upset by the thought of having to buy another pair. "It's not fair," he told God as he drove home in frustration. "I've been very faithful in giving of my time and money to your work, and now this."

Several months later, the director of the orphanage was on furlough in the United States. He wanted to visit all the churches that supported him in China, so he came to speak one Sunday at the man's small church in Chicago. The missionary began by thanking the people for their faithfulness in supporting the orphanage. "But most of all," he said, "I must thank you for the glasses you sent last year. You see, the Communists had just swept through the orphanage, destroying everything, including my glasses. I was desperate. Even if I had the money, there was simply no way of replacing those glasses. Along with not being able to see well, I experienced headaches every day, so my coworkers and I were much in prayer about this. Then your crates arrived. When my staff removed the covers, they found a pair of glasses lying on top."

The missionary paused long enough to let his words sink in. Then, still gripped with the wonder of it all, he continued: "Folks, when I tried on the glasses, it was as though they had been custom-made just for me! I want to thank you for being a part of that."

The people listened, happy for the miraculous glasses. But the missionary surely must have confused their church with another, they thought. There were no glasses on their list of items to be sent overseas. But sitting quietly in the back, with tears streaming down his face, an ordinary carpenter realized the Master Carpenter had used him in an extraordinary way.

Before we complain about misfortune, we might pause and wonder if God is using our trouble for a higher purpose. We can use our faith to rise above problems—or at least maneuver around them or through them. Maintaining spiritual equilibrium, balancing the bad that happens to us with the possibility of good that might come from it, takes trust beyond what we can see.

POST-IT MEDITATION FOR NOVEMBER 24
When bad things happen, I will believe God is using them for his purpose.

November 25

Then Jesus looked up and said, "Father, I thank you that you have heard me."
~John 11:41 (NIV)

Judy Braddy, author, minister, and inspirational speaker, shared an email she received around Thanksgiving from a man she'd met at a local writer's conference:

The email opened with Psalm 75:1 (NLT): "We give thanks, O God. We give thanks because you are near. People everywhere tell of your wonderful deeds." The man then proceeded to share a number of wonderful deeds God had done in his own family and personal life. He ended, "I can give thanks for the many friendships that I have, that our family are all walking with the Lord, and that Mom and Dad are doing great. In everything we do let us give thanks."

Braddy notes the man's story would just be another nice email about gratitude except the writer had battled cerebral palsy for most of his life.

At 50 years of age, the man had to use a walker and had difficulty communicating. Short of a God-given miracle, his circumstances would not change. Yet, he saw beyond his disability and struggles, praising God for his blessings.

Dr. Henry W. Frost, a missionary to China from 1893 to 1929, once told about a blessing he received after hearing bad and sad news from home while he was in China. He said deep shadows darkened his soul, and even after praying, he couldn't find peace. Although he tried to find strength and faith over the next few days, the darkness deepened. But then, on the wall of a mission home he saw the words, "Try Thanksgiving." Dr. Frost says, "I did, and in a moment every shadow was gone, not to return." He adds it is good to give thanks unto the Lord.

Giving thanks when we are going through tough times can be hard. How can someone who has lost his job, his home, his health, or his family give thanks? How can parents be thankful after their children die? How can a person thank God when a spouse cheats and then leaves? How can a paraplegic thank God for life? How can we be thankful for cancer that causes pain and suffering? How can we be thankful for a tornado, a hurricane, or an earthquake that devastates lives? It may help to think of Job, who had everything God had given him taken away. Or, consider that Jesus did not complain when he was arrested, brutally beaten, and crucified. He even asked for forgiveness for his tormentors.

In everything give thanks?

It is not impossible. If we can summon faith from our innermost being and offer thanks, God will give us peace. It pleases God when we express appreciation to him not only in good times but also in bad. And no doubt he smiles when we thank him in the *midst* of trials—before he has seen us through to the other side of the situation.

Jesus thanked God before Lazarus was raised from the dead. He had wept at the news of Lazarus' death and had quickly walked to the tomb where the body had been laid, thanking God for what he was about to do. And then he called for Lazarus to rise and come out. The dead man came out, still bound and covered in grave trappings.

How many of us give thanks to God before he answers our prayers? Praise is preparation for a miracle. We open the door for God's blessing when we thank him even before it is received.

POST-IT MEDITATION FOR NOVEMBER 25
In the midst of trials and blessings alike, I will praise God, knowing every gift comes from him and is perfect.

November 26

In everyone's life, at some time, the inner fire goes out. It is then burst into flame by an encounter with another human being. We should all be thankful for those people who rekindle the inner spirit.
~Albert Schweitzer, German/French theologian, philosopher, and medical missionary

Sandra felt as low as the heels of her Birkenstocks when she pushed against a November gust and the florist shop door. Her life had been easy, like spring breeze. Then in the fourth month of her second pregnancy, a minor automobile accident stole her ease.

During this Thanksgiving week she would have delivered a son. She grieved over her loss. As if that weren't enough, her husband's company threatened a transfer. Then her sister, whose holiday visit she coveted, called saying she could not come. What's worse, Sandra's friend infuriated her by suggesting her grief was a God-given path to maturity that would allow her to empathize with others who suffer.

"She has no idea what I'm feeling," thought Sandra with a shudder.

"Thanksgiving? Thankful for what?" she wondered. "For a careless driver whose truck was hardly scratched when he rear-ended me? For an air bag that saved my life but took that of my child?

"Good afternoon, may I help you?" The shop clerk's approach startled her.

"I....I need an arrangement," stammered Sandra.

"Are you looking for something that conveys gratitude this Thanksgiving?" asked the clerk.

"Not exactly!" Sandra blurted out. "In the last five months, everything that could go wrong has gone wrong."

Sandra regretted her outburst and was surprised when the shop clerk said, "I have the perfect arrangement for you."

Then the door's small bell rang, and the shop clerk said, "Hi, Barbara...let me get your order."

She politely excused herself and walked toward a small workroom, then quickly reappeared, carrying an arrangement of greenery, bows, and long-stemmed thorny roses. The ends of the rose stems were neatly snipped: there were no flowers.

Sandra watched for the customer's response. Was this a joke? Who would want rose stems with thorns but no flowers! She waited for laughter, but neither woman laughed.

"Uh," stammered Sandra, "that lady just left with, uh....she just left with no flowers!"

"Right, said the clerk, "I cut off the flowers. That's the Special. I call it the 'Thanksgiving Thorns Bouquet'."

"Oh, come on, you can't tell me someone is willing to pay for that!" exclaimed Sandra.

"Barbara came into the shop three years ago feeling much like you feel today," explained the clerk. "She thought she had very little to be thankful for. She had lost her father to cancer, the family business was failing, her son was into drugs, and she was facing major surgery."

"That same year I had lost my husband," continued the clerk, "and for the first time in my life, I was facing the holidays alone. I had no children, no husband, no family nearby, and too great a debt to allow any travel."

"So what did you do?" asked Sandra.

"I learned to be thankful for thorns," answered the clerk quietly. "I've always thanked God for good things in life and never asked him why those good things happened to me; but when bad stuff hit, did I ever ask! It took time for me to learn that dark times are important. I have always enjoyed the 'flowers' of life, but it took thorns to show me the beauty of God's comfort. You know, the Bible says God comforts us when we're afflicted, and from his consolation we learn to comfort others."

Sandra sucked in her breath as she thought about the very thing her friend had tried to tell her. "I guess the truth is I don't want comfort. I've lost a baby and I'm angry with God."

Just then someone else walked in the shop. The same scenario ensued—a man named Phil picked up an arrangement of thorns. In response to Sandra's query, he explained that four years previously he and his wife nearly divorced after forty years of marriage. He happened to be in the flower shop when someone picked up one of the "special" Thanksgiving arrangements. Learning their significance, he took one home to his wife—together they labeled each one for a specific problem and gave thanks for what the problem taught them.

"Hey, Phil!" shouted the clerk to the balding, rotund man.

As Phil paid the clerk, he said to Sandra, "I highly recommend the 'Special'."

I don't know if I can be thankful for the thorns in my life," Sandra said to the clerk. "It's all too...fresh."

"Well," the clerk replied carefully, "my experience has shown me thorns make roses more precious. We treasure God's providential care more during trouble than at any other time. Remember, it was a crown of thorns that Jesus wore so we might know his love. Don't resent the thorns."

Tears rolled down Sandra's cheeks. For the first time since the accident, she loosened her grip on resentment.

"I'll take those twelve long-stemmed thorns, please," she managed to choke out.

"I hoped you would," said the clerk gently. "I'll have them ready in a minute."

"Thank you. What do I owe you?" Sarah asked.

"Nothing; nothing but a promise to allow God to heal your heart. The first year's arrangement is always on me." The clerk smiled and handed a card to Sandra. "I'll attach this card to your arrangement, but maybe you would like to read it first."

It read:

"My God, I have never thanked you for my thorns. I have thanked you a thousand times for my roses, but never once for my thorns. Teach me the glory of the life I bear; teach me the value of my thorns. Show me that I have climbed closer to you along the path of pain. Show me that, through my tears, the colors of your rainbow look much more brilliant."

POST-IT MEDITATION FOR NOVEMBER 26
God, I praise you for my roses and thank you for my thorns.

November 27

Give thanks to the Lord; for he is good; for his mercy endures forever.
~1 Chronicles 16:34 (NIV)

One of the simplest and fastest ways to change your mood or mental outlook is to remind yourself of all the good things in your life. Appreciating faithful friends, close family members, and your precious pets can bring a smile to your face.

David had a very nice family, and he lived in a very nice house. He had a fun little sister named Sally and a wonderful dog named Rusty. He had nice toys to play with, and he went to the very best school. There was just one thing David did not have—he did know how to be happy. Nothing seemed to make David smile, no matter what his mother, father, sister, and even Rusty did, David was always frowning.

One day when David was sitting on his swing in the backyard feeling sad, a little girl walked right into his yard and said, "Hi, my name is Sandy, have you seen the Thankful Coat around here?" David thought for a moment and said, "I never heard of anything called a Thankful Coat. No, I haven't seen one around here. What exactly does one look like anyway?"

"Well," said the little girl. "It is the most wonderful coat in the whole world. It makes you feel happy when you wear it."

David asked, "What color is it?"

"Oh, it is the color of the rainbow," said Sandy. "Come on, let's look together to see if we can find it and then you'll know what one looks like!"

So Sandy and David looked everywhere. They looked behind the house. They looked behind the bushes. They looked all over the backyard. They looked and looked and looked.

Suddenly, they heard a commotion. All the birds, bees, bunnies, squirrels, butterflies, chipmunks, and even David's dog Rusty were gathered around a large oak tree. There, hung on one single branch of the oak tree: a beautiful coat. It was the color of a rainbow, just like Sandy had told him. The animals made beautiful sounds that reverberated like lovely music.

"See David, here is the Thankful Coat," said Sandy. "Come on, let me put it on you, and you'll see it will make you feel happy." So, David held out his arms while Sandy slid the coat over his shoulders as he put one arm in one sleeve and then the other.

David said, "Gee, this coat feels nice, and I feel better, Sandy." David felt very thankful all of a sudden. David was thankful for the beautiful blue sky. David was thankful for his new friend Sandy. David was thankful for his fun dog Rusty. David was thankful for his family. The more thankful David became, the happier he felt. David was especially thankful to Sandy. "Sandy, thank you so much for this coat, I feel happy for the very first time in a very long time."

Sandy looked at David and said, "I must leave now David, so that I can bring this coat to other unhappy children."

"What?" David said in disbelief. "How can you take this coat away, Sandy? I don't want to go back to being unhappy."

Sandy smiled and said, "David, now that you know the secret to happiness is being thankful, you can make your own Thankful Coat to wear every day. Your Thankful Coat can be an imaginary one, and you can make it any color you would like it to be. Every day when you get up, put on your imaginary coat and start to think of all the things you are thankful for and you will be happy.

The next morning David got out of bed and put on his imaginary Thankful Coat. The more thankful he became, the happier he felt and his smile got bigger and bigger. He remained thankful for the rest of his days.

What color will you make your Thankful Coat?" Why not make it bright and colorful, put it on tomorrow, and be grateful you have lived another year to enjoy the special holiday called Thanksgiving? As we prepare our hearts and minds to observe a day of gratitude, these words from an unknown writer offer good advice:

> *Count your blessings instead of your crosses;*
> *Count your gains instead of your losses.*
> *Count your joys instead of your woes;*
> *Count your friends instead of your foes.*
> *Count your smiles instead of your tears;*
> *Count your courage instead of your fears.*
> *Count your full years instead of your lean;*
> *Count your kind deeds instead of your mean.*
> *Count your health instead of your wealth;*
> *Count on God instead of yourself.*

Tomorrow will likely be a busy day with meal preparation and fellowship with friends and family. Before the rush begins, make this evening a time of retrospection and spiritual inventory. A time to be grateful for good blessings—and for hard times that teach us clouds lift and the sun returns in our lives.

SOURCE OF THE THANKFUL COAT STORY: *http://karenharveycox.wordpress.com/2008/04/04/the-thankful-coat/*

POST-IT MEDITATION FOR NOVEMBER 27
*On this Thanksgiving eve, I will put on my Thankful
Coat and praise God, "from whom all blessings flow."*

November 28

Now, our God, we give you thanks, and praise your glorious name.
~1 Chronicles 29:13 (NIV)

Today I am grateful for the crisp coolness of a late fall day, for leafless trees, for cloud-filled skies, and for barren fields.

I am blessed by joy in God's creation, by sustenance from his fruitful earth and seas, and by hands that prepare the food that makes our hearts glad.

I am thankful for rain that refreshes the earth and stormy skies giving way to rainbows.

I am thankful for the human family, who despite differences and struggles, can be bound by God's love.

I am grateful for the vastness of the universe, for the sun that lights the day and the stars that sparkle the night, for the incredible order that keeps the earth in orbit.

I am filled with gratitude for the infinite complexity of human life—for hearts that beat, brains that think, and bodies that link together in the most marvelous way to create new life.

I am appreciative of family and friends who touch my life, enriching it with joy and love.

I am thankful for children, for their wisdom and for their innocence.

I am grateful for answered prayers, knowing they are granted in accordance with God's will.

I am blessed to live in a country founded on Christian principles.

I am grateful for the men and women of our armed forces at home and abroad who defend our freedoms.

I am eternally blessed by a God who cares, a God who sustains and strengthens, and a God who loves me despite my weaknesses and sins.

I am thankful for disappointments, heartaches, and failures that lead me to know God is always there to help.

And in words from *The Book of Common Prayer*, I am thankful for God's "inestimable love in the redemption of the world by our Lord Jesus Christ, for the means of grace, and for the hope of glory." In gratitude, "we show forth praise not only with our lips, but in our lives...."

POST-IT MEDITATION FOR NOVEMBER 28
*God is worthy of glory and praise; his
works reveal his wisdom and love.*

November 29

LORD, remind me how brief my time on earth will be. Remind me that my days are numbered—how fleeting my life is.
~Psalm 39:4 (NLT)

Life goes by so quickly that few of us pause to ponder how long we will live. This story illustrates one way to increase awareness of the time we have left.

As a man was shuffling toward his basement with a steaming cup of coffee in one hand and the morning paper in the other, he turned the dial up on his ham radio and came across an older-sounding chap, with a tremendous signal and a golden voice. He was talking about "a thousand marbles." Intrigued, the man stopped to listen.

"Well, Tom, it sure sounds like you're busy with your job. I'm sure they pay you well, but it's a shame you have to be away from home and your family so much. Hard to believe a young fellow should have to work sixty or seventy hours a week to make ends meet. Too bad you missed your daughter's dance recital." He continued, "Let me tell you something, Tom, something that has helped me keep a good perspective on my own priorities." And then he explained his theory of a thousand marbles.

"You see, I sat down one day and did a little arithmetic. The average person lives about seventy-five years. I know, some live more and some live less, but on average, folks live about seventy-five years. I multiplied 75 times 52 and I came up with 3900, which is the number of Saturdays the average person has in an entire lifetime. It took me until I was fifty-five years old to think about all this in any detail," he went on, "and by that time I had lived through over twenty-eight hundred Saturdays. I got to thinking that if I lived to be seventy-five, I only had about a thousand of them left to enjoy. So I went to a toy store and bought every single marble they had. I ended up having to visit three toy stores to round up 1000 marbles. I took them home and put them inside of a large, clear plastic container right here in the sack next to my gear. Every Saturday since then, I have taken one marble out and thrown it away.

"I found, by watching the marbles diminish, I focused more on the really important parts of life. There is nothing like watching your time here on this earth run out to help get your priorities straight. And, let me tell you one last thing before I sign off with you and take my lovely wife out for breakfast: This morning, I took the very last marble out of the container. I figure if I make it until next Saturday then I have been given a little extra time. And the one thing we can all use is a little more time.

"It was nice to meet you, Tom, I hope you spend more time with your family. 75-year-old man, this is K9NZQ, clear and going QRT, good morning!"

You could have heard a pin drop on the radio band when this fellow signed off. I guess he gave all listening a lot to think about. The man who tuned in by serendipity had planned to work on his antenna that morning, and then he was going to meet up with a few hams to work on the next club newsletter. Instead, he went upstairs and woke his wife with a kiss. "C'mon honey, I'm taking you and the kids to breakfast."

"What brought this on?" she asked with a smile.

"Oh, nothing special, it's just been a long time since we spent a Saturday together with the kids. Hey, can we stop at a toy store while we're out? I need to buy some marbles."

POST-IT MEDITATION FOR NOVEMBER 29
I'm going to do a little math, and then I'm going to buy some marbles!

November 30

God is coming to us. But in order for that to truly happen, we must go as well to God. The highway runs in two directions. The invitation is for the divine and human to meet halfway.
~Wendy Wright, American singer, author, and actress

When we are immobilized by fear, indecision, sorrow, or other trouble, we may feel God has abandoned us. We wonder, does he not care? Does he not even know we are suffering?

If we believe God knows when a sparrow falls and the very hairs on our head are numbered (Luke 12:7), why can we not fathom that he understands what we are going through and how we feel? Perhaps because it is easier to sigh, groaning, "Why me?"

We read scripture and accept it as truth, citing it to others in need; but when we ourselves suffer, we may not be able to feel God's presence. We suspect he is angry or has given up on us. Why else would he let bad things happen to us, over and over? Instead of asking, "Why me?" maybe we should ask, "Why not me?" None of us is good enough to earn a trouble-free life, to be spared suffering and sorrow, difficulty and despair. Our sinful natures began in the Garden of Eden. Yet, God still loves us and can use the foul pieces of our lives for his glory.

A little boy was telling his grandma how everything was going wrong—school, family arguments, and an upset stomach. As he talked, his grandmother pulled items from the refrigerator and pantry and began making a cake.

"Would you like a snack?" she asked. When her grandson responded with a hearty, "Yes," she said, "Here, have some cooking oil."

"Yuck!" the boy said.

"How about a couple of raw eggs?"

"Gross, Grandma!"

"Would you like some flour, then, or maybe baking soda?"

"Grandma, all of those would taste yucky."

With a smile, the grandmother replied, "Yes, all those things seem bad all by themselves; but when they are put together in the right way, they make a delightfully delicious cake."

God works the same way. We wonder why he lets us go through yucky times, but he knows he can put them together to make something superb.

Despite our human weaknesses, we are precious in God's sight. He never gives up on us. But he also expects us to help ourselves. Just as the grandmother had to put the ingredients together, stir them, and bake them, God expects us to do some work. If we meet him halfway, or even a quarter of the way, he will lead us the rest of the journey.

POST-IT MEDITATION FOR NOVEMBER 30
When faced with issues that seem terrible, I will find faith, knowing God cares and will help.

December 1

Reach out to Jesus; he's reaching out to you.
~Ralph Carmichael, composer

Carmichael's song asks if your burden is heavy…and if you are bearing it all alone. He questions whether the road you are traveling harbors dangers yet unknown. And finally, he queries whether you are growing weary in the struggle.

If you are in the midst of life's troubles, the answer to the song's questions can be a resounding, "Yes!" Life stresses you, and you think no one cares. Weighed down by worry, tired and friendless, you feel you have lost your way. But the song doesn't leave you in despair. It reminds you Jesus will help you if you will call his name. He's always there, even when you feel alone, and he hears every prayer. He walks by your side— you just have to reach out to him.

Amy Wilson Carmichael, a missionary to India in the late 1800's and the first half of the next century, tells how she proved God over and over. One story in Nor Scrip, *the book recounting her life as a missionary, relates her desperate need for a hundred rupees to rescue a Hindu child from a life of shame. It was a lot of money, but she felt led to pray that God would send her the round sum of a hundred rupees—no more, no less—if it was his will the money should be spent for the child. And the money arrived in the mail! The sender explained she had sat down to write a different amount to send to the missionary, but as she wrote, she felt compelled to make it for exactly one hundred rupees.*

Carmichael says the story of the Hindu child was one of countless times she put God to the test—and not once did he fail her. "Never once in fifteen years has a bill been left unpaid; never once has a man or woman been told no when in need of help, never once have we lacked any good thing.… Once 25 pounds came by telegram. Sometimes a man would emerge from a clamoring crowd at a railway station, slip some gift of money into my hand, and be lost in the crowd before he could be identified." God worked behind the scenes, but he fulfilled every need.

Could it be that God wants to make us aware of our dependence on him? When our lives are free of trials and hardship, we may have a tendency to think we can handle our daily existence without any help. His power and strength may become hidden when we don't feel a need to seek it.

How many of us pray as much when our lives are trouble free as when they are filled with adversity? Does the length of our prayers vary with the state of our lives? A close walk with God will not protect us from misfortune, but it may shape how we respond.

God's strength and power are most evident when we are being tested by fire. It is then we take his hand and lean on him. How much better our lives would be if we walked by the same faith daily. When we walk continuously and consistently with God through days of contentment and days of turmoil, as Amy Carmichael did, we build a deep and resilient foundation of faith. With such steadfast faith, if we are tested in tragedy or hardship, we can wait with a sense of peace that may not come if we only turn to God in dire need. Philippians 4:6-7 (NLT) assures us, "Don't worry about anything; instead, pray about everything. Tell God what you need, and thank him for all he has done. Then you will experience God's peace, which exceeds anything we can understand."

J. Hudson Taylor, a missionary to the Chinese in the late 1800s and early 1900s, once said, "The Lord is my shepherd; is on Sunday, is on Monday, and is through every day of the week; is in January, is in December, and every month of the year. Is at home and is in China; is in peace and is in war; is in abundance and is in penury!" The Lord is our shepherd all day, every day; anyplace and everyplace. We shall not want.

POST-IT MEDITATION FOR DECEMBER 1
I will not only believe God can answer prayer;
I will believe he does answer them.

December 2

Then God said, "Let the earth produce every sort of animal, each produc-
ing offspring of the same kind—livestock, small animals that scurry along
the ground, and wild animals...." And God saw that it was good.
~Genesis 1:24-25 (NLT)

Chief Seattle of the Dwanish Tribes authored this thoughtful question
and a profound response:

What is man without the beasts?
If all the beasts were gone,
Man would die from a great loneliness of spirit.
For whatever happens to the beasts soon happens to the man.
All things are connected.
Man did not weave the web of life.
He is merely a strand in it.
Whatever he does to the web,
He does to himself.

Have you ever felt the comfort of a beloved dog or cat? Or stood
in awe at the majesty of a mighty beast of prey? Those who love and
admire animals know God created them to inspire, protect, and uplift
man. They are as much a part of the web of life as we are.

I once watched a dove mourn its mate, standing over it for hours, and
was touched by its depth of feeling. When I read *When Elephants Weep,* I
was astounded by the hundreds of anecdotes, published by such noted
behaviorists as Jane Goodall, Dian Fossey, and Cynthia Moss, supporting
the theory that animals possess an emotional sensibility not unlike that
of humans. Dancing squirrels and shy gorillas are among the array of
animals who display emotions in intriguing stories in the book. Authors
Masson and McCarthy's chapters on love, joy, anger, fear, shame, compassion, and loneliness of four-legged creatures serve as a powerful reminder
that we have a deep obligation to treat animals with respect and dignity.
Like we humans, they were created by God. We should not only find
pleasure in them but protect and love them as part of God's universe.

The front page story of the <u>San Francisco Chronicle</u> on Thursday, December
15, 2005, told about a female humpback whale who had become entangled in a
spider web of crab traps and lines:

The fifty-foot whale was weighted down by hundreds of pounds of traps that
caused her to struggle to stay afloat. In addition, hundreds of yards of line rope
wrapped around her tail and her torso, with one line pulling on her mouth.

A fisherman spotted the whale just east beyond the Golden Gate, near the Farallone Islands, and radioed an environmental group for help. Within a few hours, the rescue team arrived and determined the only way to save the humpback was to dive in and untangle her—a very dangerous plan because one wallop of the tail could kill a rescuer.

The rescuers worked for hours with curved knives and eventually freed the trapped whale. When she was free, the divers say she swam in what seemed like joyous circles, then came back to each and every diver, one at a time, and nudged them, pushed them gently around, obviously thanking them. Some said it was the most incredibly beautiful experience of their lives.

POST-IT MEDITATION FOR DECEMBER 2
**Thank you, God, for your creatures who touch and
enrich my life—and for those
who help untangle the ropes binding me.**

December 3

I believe that I shall look upon the goodness of the Lord in the land of the living!
~Psalm 27:13 (ESV)

A little girl walked daily to and from school. Though the weather one morning was questionable and clouds were forming, she made her daily trek to the elementary school.

As the day progressed, the winds whipped up, accompanied by thunder and lightning. The mother of the little girl worried her daughter would be frightened as she walked home from school, and she herself feared the electrical storm might harm her child.

As roar after roar of thunder preceded lightning cutting through the sky like a flaming sword, the mother's worries increased. Concerned, she got into her car and drove along the route to her child's school. Soon she saw her daughter walking along, but at each flash of lightning, the child would stop, look up, and smile. One bolt of electricity followed another, each with the little girl stopping, looking at the streak of light and smiling.

Fiinally, the mother called her over to the car and asked, "What are you doing?"
The child answered, "Smiling while God takes pictures of me."

While the mother's fears and worries turned into anxiety, her daughter saw God's loving hand in the lightning. Isn't it amazing how positive thinking can affect our perspective?

Norman Cousins' book, *The Anatomy of an Illness: As Perceived by the Patient*, became a best-seller because people saw that optimism could do more than doctors and medicine. Like the little girl walking in the storm, Cousins didn't accept the typical perspective. Hospitalized in 1964 with an extremely rare, crippling disease diagnosed as incurable, he did a reverse take on the theory that negative emotions are harmful to the body. He decided he would focus on happy thoughts, good outcomes, and joy. Almost immediately, he found that two hours of belly laughter at old Marx Brothers' films and *Candid Camera* reruns gave him an equal amount of sleep without pain—without any pills. He continued to ply his brain with upbeat, laugher-filled films; and in time, his disease began to reverse itself, and he almost completely recovered.

How we deal with what happens to us is a matter of "mind over body." Realistically, we know everyone will not escape lightning strikes and everyone will not be cured, but in whatever time we have, living joyously will contribute to a good life.

POST-IT MEDITATION FOR DECEMBER 3
I believe in the goodness of God.

December 4

He plants trees to benefit another generation.
~Caecilius Statius, Roman comic poet

Will Allen Dromgoole (1860-1934) was the last of several children born to Rebecca Mildred (Blanche) and John Easter Dromgoole in Murfreesboro, Tennessee. She attended the Clarksville Female Academy, where she graduated in 1876. Later she studied law with her father; but women were not allowed to become lawyers, so she took a position as a staff member in the state legislature in 1883.

A prolific writer, Dromgoole published both prose and poetry. She was also a journalist for the *Nashville American*, a newspaper based in the Middle Tennessee city. It is thought she adopted the pseudonym "Will Allen" to make her writings more widely acceptable.

Among Dromgoole's 7500+ poems was "The Bridge-Builder," which has not only moral but also religious connotations:

The poem tells of an old man going down a lone highway. In the evening, he came to a chasm, vast, wide, and steep. Waters rolled in front of him in the twilight, but the old man crossed with no problem. When he reached the other side, he turned and built a bridge to span the tide.

A fellow sojourner, passing nearby, stopped and stared. "Old man," he said, "you are wasting your strength with building here." He added that the old man's journey would end with the closing of the day, and thus he would never pass

Enraged by the old man's response, the farmer was tempted to fire him on the spot. Instead, he hurried outside to prepare for the storm. To his amazement, he discovered all of the haystacks had been covered with tarpaulins. The cows were in the barn, the chickens were in the coops, and the doors were barred. The shutters were tightly secured. Everything was tied down. Nothing could blow away. The farmer then understood what his hired hand meant, and he returned to bed to also sleep while the wind blew.

When we're prepared, we have nothing to fear. Can you sleep when the wind blows through your life? The hired hand in the story was able to sleep because he had secured the farm against any storm that might come. We secure ourselves against the gales of life by grounding ourselves firmly in the word of God.

POST-IT MEDITATION FOR DECEMBER 6
I am secure in God's word, protected against the gales of life.

December 7

Has not God chosen those who are poor in the eyes of the world to be rich in faith and to inherit the kingdom he promised those who love him?
~James 2:5 (NIV)

Fellow sojourners on this journey called life may not know the extent of our needs, but God does. And occasionally he puts his hand on the scales and tips it for our benefit.

A poorly dressed lady with a look of defeat on her face walked into a grocery store. Humbly, she approached the owner and explained her husband was very ill and unable to work; they had seven children and needed food. "Would you please let me charge some groceries until I can pay?" she asked hopefully.

The grocery owner refused, and despite the desperate lady's begging, he rebuffed her, asking her to leave his store. About that time, another customer walked up and told the grocer he would stand good for whatever she needed for her family. Reluctantly, the storekeeper told the woman to put her grocery list on the scales and whatever the list weighed, he would give her that amount in groceries. Even though the grocer wasn't the one donating the food, he had come up with a ridiculous, contrived way to keep the amount of donated groceries very small.

The woman hesitated a moment with a bowed head, then she reached into her purse and took out a piece of paper, scribbling something on it before laying it on the scale carefully. The eyes of the grocer and the customer showed amazement when the scales went down and stayed down. Staring at the scales, the grocer muttered, "I can't believe it." But the customer just smiled as the grocer started putting the groceries on the other side of the scales. The scale did not balance, so he continued to put more and more groceries on them until the scales would hold no more.

Disgusted, the grocer grabbed the piece of paper from the scales and looked at it with greater amazement. It was not a grocery list; it was a prayer: "Dear Lord, you know my needs, and I am leaving this in your hands." The grocer gave her the groceries he had gathered and stood in stunned silence.

The woman expressed her appreciation and left the store. The customer handed a fifty-dollar bill to the grocer and said, "It was worth every penny of it."

Only God knows how much a prayer weighs.

POST-IT MEDITATION FOR DECEMBER 7
If I have little, I will pray for God's abundance;
if I have much, I will share with others.

December 8

I can never escape from your Spirit! I can never get away from your presence! If I go up to heaven, you are there; if I go down to the grave, you are there. If I ride the wings of the morning, if I dwell by the farthest oceans, even there your hand will guide me, and your strength will support me.
~Psalm 139:7-10 (NLT)

A little boy wanted to meet God. He knew it was a long trip to where God lived, so he packed his suitcase with Twinkies and a six-pack of Root Beer and started his journey.

When the child had gone about three blocks, he met an old man sitting in the park just staring at some pigeons. The boy sat down next to him and opened his suitcase. He was about to take a drink from a Root Beer when he noticed the old man looked hungry, so he offered him a Twinkie.

The stranger gratefully accepted it and smiled at the little boy. His smile was so pleasant the boy wanted to see it again, so he offered him a Root Beer.

Again, the man smiled at him. The boy was delighted! They sat there all afternoon eating and smiling, but they never said a word.

As it grew dark, the boy realized how tired he was and he got up to leave; but before he had gone more than a few steps, he turned around, ran back to the old man, and gave him a hug. The elderly soul gave him his biggest smile ever.

When the boy opened the door to his own house a short time later, his mother was surprised by the look of joy on his face. She asked him, "What did you do today that made you so happy?"

He replied, "I had lunch with God." But before his mother could respond, he added, "You know what? He's got the most beautiful smile I've ever seen!"

Meanwhile, the old man, also radiant with joy, returned to his home. His son, stunned by the look of peace on his face, asked, "Dad, what did you do today that made you so happy?"

He replied, "I ate Twinkies in the park with God." Before his son responded, he added, "You know, he's much younger than I expected."

Too often we underestimate the power of a touch, a smile, a kind word, a listening ear, an honest compliment, or the smallest act of caring, all of which have the potential to brighten a life. People come into our lives for a reason, a season, or a lifetime. Embrace all equally!

POST-IT MEDITATION FOR DECEMBER 8
I will look for God in strangers I meet today.

December 9

What are the angels, then? They are spirits who serve God and are sent by him to help those who are to receive salvation.
~Hebrews 1:14 (GNT)

One afternoon in December 2000, a couple was traveling when suddenly at a far distance they saw a woman in the middle of the road waving at them to stop. The wife told her husband to keep on driving because it might be dangerous, but the husband decided to pass by slowly to check out the lady. As they got closer, they noticed the woman had cuts and bruises on her face and arms.

Because of her condition, they decided to stop and see if they could be of any help. The injured lady began begging for help, telling them she had been in a car accident and her husband and son, a newborn baby, were still inside the car, which was in a deep ditch. Her husband was already dead, she said, but her baby seemed to still be alive.

The husband immediately climbed down the ditch to rescue the baby, asking the hurt woman to stay with his wife inside their car. When he got down, he noticed two dead people in the front seat of the car. Seeing they were beyond help, he quickly picked up the baby. When he made it up to the road, he didn't see the mother anywhere so he asked his wife where she had gone. She told him the woman had followed him back to the crashed car. Concerned, the man went to look for the woman. Back at the car, when he looked closely at the two dead people, he saw that one of them was the exact same woman who had begged them for help in the beginning.

Do you think it was a miracle of God, a mother who took the form of an angel to save her baby? That infant now lives with family members, according to the unknown author who posted this story to a website.

God sent an angel when Daniel was in the lions' den to shut the mouths of the ferocious creatures that could rip him apart

(Daniel 6:22). An angel rolled away the stone from Christ's tomb and told Mary Magdalene and the other Mary that he was not there, but risen (Matthew 28:1-20). In Acts 8:26, an angel gave Philip instructions to a road in the desert. Hundreds of other Biblical passages speak of angels. Why should we not believe angels are among us now?

POST-IT MEDITATION FOR DECEMBER 9
I believe in angels, and I believe in miracles, because I believe in God.

December 10

People say true friends must always hold hands, but true friends don't need to hold hands because they know the other hand will always be there.
~Unknown

On Christmas night, 1970, I sat in a movie theatre with my soon-to-be husband watching *Love Story*, which had just been released.

The film tells of Oliver Barrett IV, who comes from a family of wealthy and highly respected Harvard University graduates, and Jennifer Cavilleri, a working-class, quick-witted, and beautiful Radcliffe College student. After graduation, the two marry despite the strong objection of Oliver's father, who severs ties with his son. Without the financial support of Oliver's father, the young couple struggles to pay Oliver's law school tuition on Jenny's salary as a private school teacher; but by living frugally, they survive. Graduating third in his class at Harvard Law, Oliver snags a position at a New York law firm. With Oliver's new income, the pair of 24-year-olds decide to have a baby. After unsuccessful attempts, they consult a medical specialist. Following extensive tests, the doctor informs Oliver that Jenny is ill with what appears to be leukemia and doesn't have long to live.

With their days together numbered, Jenny begins costly cancer treatment, and soon Oliver finds he is unable to afford the mounting medical expenses. Desperate, he goes to his father for help but when asked if he needs the money because he got some girl "in trouble," Oliver says yes instead of sharing the truth about Jenny's raging illness.

From her hospital bed, Jenny tells Oliver to avoid blaming himself and asks him to embrace her tightly before she dies. In a heart-breaking scene, Oliver climbs in the hospital bed with Jenny, holding her as she takes her last breath.

One short but powerful line in the movie, spoken twice, has forever since been indelibly etched in my mind: "Love means never having to say you're sorry." The first time Jenny speaks the words to Oliver, who has expressed remorse for his anger. The second time, as a grief-stricken Oliver leaves the hospital, he is met by his father who now wants to apologize for the way he treated his son. Oliver repeats the words Jenny said, "Love means never having to say you're sorry," and cries.

Regardless of who said the words, their message remains the same: The love that binds two people together creates a connection that cannot be severed by anger or any other negative emotion. And, with love pure and true, when we offend the other person, saying we are sorry isn't necessary—the other person knows love still resides behind the moment of frustration, disappointment, or rejection.

After Jenny's death, Oliver is left to struggle for words: "What can you say about a twenty-five-year-old girl who died? That she was beautiful and brilliant. That she loved Mozart and Bach. The Beatles. And me." The last two words hold the answer—Jenny loved him. And he knew that love would be there even though he could no longer hold hands with her. Jenny's hand was still there, not physically, but in his heart and in his spirit. And, Oliver knew his father loved him despite the way he had treated him. His father's hand, extended in love, came too late for Jenny, but it was there for Oliver.

There's another hand, not physical, that holds our hand through every trial and tribulation in life. Christmas Day celebrates his birth and reminds us of his undying love and constant care in our lives. This year, as the holiday season approaches, why not focus on the hand that holds ours in love? Put love at the forefront of our celebration, remembering the real reason for the season, instead of centering our thoughts on how much we will give or receive.

POST-IT MEDITATION FOR DECEMBER 10
I will treasure the gift of love that never dies.

December 11

Set your heart, then, on the most important gifts.
~1 Corinthians 12:31 (GNT)

Christmas was approaching, and a three-year-old girl lovingly wrapped a present in expensive gold paper. When her father arrived home that night and saw what she had done, he scolded her for being wasteful—money was tight, he said with resentment before sending her to her room.

When Christmas morning dawned, the little girl slowly approached her father, handing him the gift wrapped in the fine gold paper. "This is for you, Daddy," she said with love.

The man was embarrassed by his earlier overreaction, but his temper flared again when he discovered the box was empty. "Why would you waste good paper on an empty box?"

"Oh, Daddy," the little girl said through tears. "It's not empty at all. I blew kisses into the box. The kisses are for you to tell you how much I love you."

Crushed, the man pulled the little girl into his lap, hugging her and kissing away her tears. With his own eyes overflowing, he asked for her forgiveness.

A short time later, the child died in a tragic accident. For many years, the father kept the gold box, often taking out an imaginary kiss as he remembered the special love his daughter had put there.

Over a lifetime, each of us receives many gold-wrapped boxes filled with precious love and kisses—from God, from family members, and from friends. Such gifts are to be treasured as life's greatest gifts. Why is it that we feel compelled to give mountains of expensive gifts at Christmas, birthdays, or other special occasions when unconditional love is the most cherished present we can bestow on anyone we love. Technological wonders, stylish clothes, and tons of toys last for a limited time, but love is carried in the heart forever. Children—and adults— may not remember what you gave them, but they will always treasure the love you share in their hearts and souls. There is nothing wrong with giving lavish gifts if you can afford to, but they will never be as special as kisses in a box.

POST-IT MEDITATION FOR DECEMBER 11
*As I plan for gifts in the future, I will be
mindful of unique ways I can express my love.*

December 12

Dear children, let us not love with words or speech but with actions and in truth.
~1 John 3:18 (NIV)

An eyewitness tells the story of a young boy peering into a New York City shoe store on a blustery, cold day in December, less than two weeks before Christmas:

As the barefooted boy of about 10 years of age shivered in the cold, a lady walked by and saw him. Pausing, she asked, "My little fellow, why are you looking so earnestly in that window?"

"I was asking God to give me a pair of shoes," the boy responded hopefully.

Taking the little boy by the hand, the lady led him into the store and asked the clerk to give the boy a half dozen pairs of socks. She then asked for a basin of water and a towel, which he quickly brought. She walked the child to the back of the store, and removing her gloves, knelt down and washed and dried his feet. By the time the two returned to the front of the store, the clerk was back with the socks. After putting a pair on the little boy's feet, the lady bought him a pair of shoes. When the purchase was complete, she gave the boy the socks, patted him on the head, and bid him goodbye.

As the lady turned to go, the dumbfounded little boy caught her by the hand. Looking up with tears in his eyes, he asked, "Are you God's wife?"

Any of us can be "God's wife." We can help a child in need, a homeless person, a lonely teenager, or an elderly man or woman.

The lady walking down the wintry street in New York City could have turned her head and walked on by, much like we do when we pass a destitute person on a street corner. Looking away, we try to shut the person out of our mind, focusing instead on more pleasant scenes.

How many times do we turn away rather than help? We read about the number of homeless people depending on a local food kitchen, but do we volunteer to serve meals or even write a check to buy food? We see the widower sitting on his front porch as we drive by, and we wave, but do we stop and brighten his day for a few moments?

The Bible reminds us in Matthew 25:35-40 (ESV) that in helping others, we help God: "For I was hungry and you gave me food, I was thirsty and you gave me drink, I was a stranger and you welcomed me, I was naked and you clothed me, I was sick and you visited me, I was in prison and you came to me....Truly I will tell you, whatever you did for one of the least of these brothers and sisters of mine, you did for me."

Christmas is approaching. What better way to share the spirit of the season than to help those who are less fortunate than we are and to touch the lives of those who are lonely?

"I always thought of Christmas time," Charles Dickens wrote, "when it has come round, as a good time; a kind, forgiving, charitable time; the only time I know of, in the long calendar of the year, when men and women seem by one consent to open their shut-up hearts freely, and to think of people below them as if they really were fellow passengers to the grave, and not another race of creatures bound on other journeys."

POST-IT MEDITATION FOR DECEMBER 12
When I see a person in need, I will see the face of God.

December 13

He who is generous will be blessed, for he gives some of his food to the poor.
~Proverbs 22:9 (NASB)

A seven-year-old child showed her grandmother the list of all she wanted for Christmas. After reading it, the grandmother exclaimed, "My goodness, that really is a long list!" Then she picked the little girl up and set her on her lap in the big rocking chair and told this story:

Once there was a little girl named Katy who came to live in an orphanage in Denmark. When Christmas time grew near, all of the other children began telling Katy about the beautiful Christmas tree that would appear in the huge downstairs hall on Christmas morning.

Now the headmaster of the orphanage was very stern, and he thought Christmas was too hyped and meaningless. In his mind, the girls were lucky to get anything. So, after their usual, very plain breakfast, each child would be given their one and only Christmas gift: a small, single orange.

On Christmas Eve, the headmaster caught Katy creeping down the stairs to catch a peek at the much-heard-of Christmas tree. Coldly, with sharp words he declared the little girl would not receive her Christmas orange because she had been so curious as to disobey the rules. Katy ran back to her room brokenhearted and crying at her terrible fate.

The next morning as the other children were going down to breakfast, Katy stayed in her bed. She couldn't stand the thought of seeing the others receive their gifts when there would be none for her.

Later, as the children came back upstairs, Katy was surprised to be handed a napkin. As she carefully opened it, there to her disbelief was an orange all peeled and sectioned.

"How could this be?" she asked.

It was then Katy found how each child had taken one section from her own orange and given it to her so that she, too, would have a Christmas orange.

It is human nature to be selfish—to put our own needs and desires before others. We typically think this is truer of children than adults. We expect them to fuss about sharing toys, to want the first ice cream cone handed out, or to squeal loudly when we tell them to take turns, but some children surprise us. The little orphans had hearts greater than most of us. They knew the real meaning of Christmas joy.

Are you helping others in need? Christmas is an especially good time to share what God has given us. Let us not be selfish, thinking only of ourselves and those we love. We should look beyond our families and friends and brighten the Christmas morning of someone whose day may be dismal without our gifts.

POST-IT MEDITATION FOR DECEMBER 13
When I stuff stockings this year, I will remember the shared sections of an orange and do my part in spreading Christmas joy.

December 14

Christmas time was approaching; snow was starting to fall...People filling the mall.

Children waiting for Santa with excitement and glee.
A little boy tugged my sweater, looked up and asked me,
Where's the line to see Jesus? Is He here at the store?
If Christmas time is His birthday, Why don't we see Him more?
~Lyrics by Becky Kelly

One December, a mother vowed to make Christmas a calm and peaceful experience. She cut back on nonessential obligations—extensive card writing, endless baking, lavish decorating, and even overspending. Yet, she still found herself exhausted, unable to appreciate precious family moments, and of course, the true meaning of Christmas. A child's mistake reopened her eyes:

My son, Nicholas, was in kindergarten that year. It was an exciting season for a six-year-old. For weeks, he'd been memorizing songs for his school's "Winter Pageant."

I didn't have the heart to tell him I'd be working the night of the production. Unwilling to miss his shining moment, I spoke with his teacher. She assured me there would be a dress rehearsal the morning of the presentation. All parents unable to attend that evening were welcome to come then. Fortunately, Nicholas seemed happy with the compromise.

So, the morning of the dress rehearsal, I filed in ten minutes early, found a spot on the cafeteria floor and sat down. Around the room, I saw several other parents quietly scampering to their seats.

As I waited, the students were led into the room. Each class, accompanied by their teacher, sat cross-legged on the floor. Then, each group, one by one, rose to perform their song.

Because the public school system had long stopped referring to the holiday as "Christmas," I didn't expect anything other than fun, commercial entertainment songs of reindeer, Santa Claus, snowflakes, and good cheer. So, when my son's class rose to sing "Christmas Love," I was slightly taken aback by its bold title.

Nicholas was aglow, as were all of his classmates, adorned in fuzzy mittens, red sweaters, and bright snowcaps upon their heads. Those in the front row— center stage—held up large letters, one by one, to spell out the title of the song.

As the class would sing "C is for Christmas," a child would hold up the letter C. Then, "H is for Happy," and on and on, until each child holding up his portion had presented the complete message, "Christmas Love."

The performance was going smoothly, until suddenly, we noticed her; a small, quiet, girl in the front row holding the letter "M" upside down, totally unaware her letter "M" appeared as a "W."

The children in the audience of first through sixth graders snickered at this little one's mistake. But she had no idea they were laughing at her, so she stood tall, proudly holding her "W."

Although many teachers tried to shush the children, the laughter continued until the last letter was raised, and we all saw it together. A hush came over the audience and eyes began to widen.

In that instant, we understood the reason we were there, why we celebrated the holiday in the first place, why even in the chaos, there was a purpose for our festivities.

For when the last letter was held high, the message read loud and clear:

C H R I S T W A S L O V E

And, I believe, he still is.

POST-IT MEDITATION FOR DECEMBER 14
Christmas began in the heart of God.
Christians keep it in their hearts when they remember the Christ child.

December 15

But when you give to the needy, do not let your left hand know what your right hand is doing, so that your giving may be in secret. Then your Father, who sees what is done in secret, will reward you.
~Matthew 6:3-4 (NIV)

A man says his grandma taught him everything about Christmas:

As a kid, I remember tearing across town on my bike to visit her on the day my big sister dropped the bomb: "There is no Santa Claus," jeered my sister. "Even dummies know that!"

My grandma was not the gushy kind, never had been. I fled to her that day because I knew she would be straight with me. I knew Grandma always told the truth, and I knew the truth always went down a whole lot easier when swallowed with one of her world-famous cinnamon buns.

Grandma was home, and the buns were still warm. Between bites, I told her everything. She was ready for me.

"No Santa Claus!" she snorted. "Ridiculous! Don't believe it. That rumor has been going around for years, and it makes me mad, plain mad. Now, put on your coat, and let's go."

"Go? Go where, Grandma?" I asked. I hadn't even finished my second cinnamon bun.

"Where" turned out to be Kerby's General Store, the one store in town that had a little bit of just about everything. As we walked through its doors, Grandma handed me ten dollars. That was a bundle in those days.

"Take this money," she said, "and buy something for someone who needs it. I'll wait for you in the car." Then she turned and walked out of Kerby's.

I was only eight years old. I'd often gone shopping with my mother, but never had I shopped for anything all by myself. The store seemed big and crowded, full of people scrambling to finish their Christmas shopping. For a few moments I just stood there, confused, clutching that ten-dollar bill, wondering what to buy, and who on earth to buy it for. I thought of everybody I knew: my family, my friends, my neighbors, the kids at school, the people who went to my church.

I was just about thought out, when I suddenly thought of Bobbie Decker. He was a kid with bad breath and messy hair, and he sat right behind me in Mrs. Pollock's grade-two class. Bobbie Decker didn't have a coat. I knew that because he never went out for recess during the winter. His mother always wrote a note, telling the teacher he had a cough; but all we kids knew Bobbie Decker didn't have a cough, and he didn't have a coat.

I fingered the ten-dollar bill with growing excitement. I would buy Bobbie Decker a coat. I settled on a red corduroy one with a hood. It looked real warm, and he would like that. I didn't see a price tag, but ten dollars ought to buy anything. I put the coat and my ten-dollar bill on the counter and pushed them toward the lady behind it.

She looked at the coat, the money, and me. "Is this a Christmas present for someone?" she asked kindly. "Yes," I replied shyly. "It's...for Bobbie. He's in my class, and he doesn't have a coat." The nice lady smiled at me. I didn't get any change, but she put the coat in a bag and wished me a Merry Christmas.

That evening, Grandma helped me wrap the coat in Christmas paper and ribbons, and write, "To Bobbie, From Santa Claus" on it—Grandma said Santa always insisted on secrecy.

Then she drove me over to Bobbie Decker's house, explaining as we went that I was now and forever officially one of Santa's helpers. Grandma parked down the street from Bobbie's house, and she and I crept noiselessly and hid in the bushes by his front walk.

Suddenly, Grandma gave me a nudge. "All right, Santa Claus," she whispered, "get going."

I took a deep breath, dashed for his front door, threw the present down on Bobbie's step, pounded his doorbell twice, and flew back to the safety of the bushes and Grandma. Together we waited breathlessly in the darkness for the front door to open. Finally it did, and there stood Bobbie. He looked down, looked around, picked up his present, took it inside, and closed the door.

Forty years haven't dimmed the thrill of those moments spent shivering, beside my grandma, in Bobbie Decker's bushes. That night, I realized those awful rumors about Santa Claus were just what Grandma said they were: Ridiculous! Santa was alive and well ... AND WE WERE ON HIS TEAM!

POST-IT MEDITATION FOR DECEMBER 15
Help me, God, to display a child-like, Christ-like concern for others, not just at Christmas, but all year long.

December 16

The best remedy, for those who are afraid, lonely, or unhappy, is to go outside, somewhere where they can be quite alone with the heavens, nature, and God. Because only then does one feel that all is as it should be and that God wishes to see people happy, amidst the simple beauty of nature. As long as this exists, and it certainly always will, I know that then there will always be comfort for every sorrow, whatever the circumstances may be. And I firmly believe that nature brings solace in all troubles.
~Anne Frank, Holocaust survivor

This is a story of a star and a cross.

My mother, Helen Howard, sang the song "Star of the East" every Christmas for many years at Chattanooga Valley Baptist Church. Many people said it wasn't Christmas until Mother sang it. As a child, I must confess I was embarrassed by it. Mother wore a long, angel-like robe with tinsel adorning it and her hair. A lighted star hung on the wall, and at the end of the song, she extended her arm to point to it and then knelt.

At the age of 43, Mother suffered a stroke; and although she mostly recovered, she was no longer able to play the piano at church services (which she had done every Sunday for more than 15 years) or sing solos. But one year, the person in charge of the Christmas program insisted Mother sing "Star of the East" again. She did, and as I played the piano for her, the true meaning of the song hit me for the first time, and I could barely see the music through my tears. (Unstable because of the stroke, Mother fell as she knelt at the end of the song. In true "Helen" style, she was lying on the floor laughing as people rushed to help her!)

My sister Sylvia also has a story about a star—with the addition of a cross. From the time she was a child until she was grown, Sylvia remembered Mother pointing to the star as she sang and believed there was something special about it. So...whenever Sylvia faced problems or situations she didn't feel she could handle, she would always look for a star in the sky. A star always reassured her that God cared for her and would be with her during dark days of uncertainty.

In 1984, Mother was taken to the hospital just before Christmas; and, as her condition worsened, Sylvia nervously sat beside her bed. She walked to the window and looked for a star to reassure her God was in control, but there was not one star in the cloudy sky outside. On the way home that night, she searched the skies for a star again, but they all remained hidden behind the clouds.

On Christmas Eve, after many patients had been sent home for the holidays, the remaining ones were consolidated on one wing of each floor so some of the staff could be home with their families. After mother was moved to the opposite side of the hospital, still desperate to find a star in the sky, Sylvia opened the blinds and looked out. Directly in front of her was a huge, lighted star on top of a Christmas tree in the hospital courtyard. Even on a dark, cloud-filled light, God was continuing to assure her he was there and would comfort her as mother's life faded.

A day or two later as Sylvia was rushing to get to the hospital, her five-year-old daughter Stacie gave her something she had made for "Nanny" Helen. Sylvia didn't take time to look at it until she stopped at a red light. Tears flowed as she realized Stacie had cut a star and a cross out of construction paper. She had taped the star at an angle above the cross.

Is it not amazing that God would use a five-year-old child, who knew nothing of the Star of the East story, to illustrate her mother could have confidence in the star because of what Christ did on that cross? But there's more...at the bottom of the cut-out cross, Stacie had cut out a brown piece of construction paper and taped it to the foot of the cross. Sylvia didn't know what the brown piece was, so after Mother's death a few days later, when Sylvia took the cut-out artwork home, she asked Stacie about it. Stacie said the round object was a rock. Instantly, Sylvia knew God was her rock—he would give her the strength and grace to get through the loss of her mother. Christ had died on the cross so her mother could live forever in heaven with him, among the stars.

Mother believed in that star and in the cross it led to. She not only sang and played about them—she lived by them. "Star of the East" lyrics (written by New York lyricist George Cooper in 1890) represented the "hope of her soul." Its rays brought her "peace, joy, and love" through her husband's five-year battle with cancer and her own struggles with cancer and then Parkinson's disease. She had a strong, optimistic faith and was an inspiration to others in countless ways. She knew "sorrow and grief were lulled by [its] light... While round [her] here, the dark billows roll[ed]..." undimmed by each cloud, the star helped her follow where God led. "Fearless and tranquil," she looked to God on earth, "knowing thou beam'st through eternity," and was guided "onward to that blessed shore after earth's toil was o'er."

I'm sure, during this Christmas season, her prayer for you would be that you will have the same kind of faith she had in Jesus Christ and that you will allow God, through a star and the cross, to guide and strengthen you in life's darkest and most dismal problems and situations.

AUTHOR'S NOTE: The above letter was written by my sister, Flavia Fleming, and was sent to a number of Mother's friends in December 2008.

POST-IT MEDITATION FOR DECEMBER 16
Thank you, God, for signs like a star, a cross, and a rock that give us hope and joy.

December 17

Having gifts that differ according to the grace given to us, let us use them: if prophecy, in proportion to our faith.
~Romans 12:6 (ESV)

A man named Bob May, depressed and brokenhearted, stared out his drafty apartment window into the chilly December night.

His four-year-old daughter Barbara sat on his lap quietly sobbing. Bob's wife, Evelyn, was dying of cancer. Little Barbara couldn't understand why her mommy could never come home. Barbara looked up into her dad's eyes and asked, "Why isn't Mommy like everybody else's Mommy?" Bob's jaw tightened and his eyes welled with tears. Her question brought waves of grief, but also of anger. It had been the story of Bob's life. Life always had to be different for Bob.

Small when he was a kid, Bob was often bullied by other boys. He was too little at the time to compete in sports. He was often called names he'd rather not remember. From childhood, Bob was different and never seemed to fit in. Bob did complete college, married his loving wife, and was grateful to get his job as a copywriter at Montgomery Ward during the Great Depression.

Then he was blessed with his little girl. But it was all short-lived. Evelyn's bout with cancer stripped them of all their savings, and now Bob and his daughter were forced to live in a two-room apartment in the Chicago slums. Evelyn died just days before Christmas in 1938.

Bob struggled to give hope to his child, for whom he couldn't even afford to buy a Christmas gift. But if he couldn't buy a gift, he was determined to make one—a storybook! Bob created an animal character in his own mind and told the animal's story to little Barbara to give her comfort and hope.

Again and again Bob told the story, embellishing it more with each telling. Who was the character? What was the story all about?

The story Bob May created was his own autobiography in fable form. The character he created was a misfit outcast like he was. The name of the character? A little reindeer named Rudolph, with a big shiny nose. Bob finished the book just in time to give it to his little girl on Christmas Day.

But the story doesn't end there.

The general manager of Montgomery Ward heard about the little storybook and offered Bob May a nominal fee to purchase the rights to print the book. Ward's went on to print *Rudolph, the Red-Nosed Reindeer* and distribute it to children visiting Santa Claus in their stores.

By 1946 Ward's had printed and distributed more than six million copies of *Rudolph*. That same year, a major publisher wanted to purchase the rights from Ward's to print an updated version of the book.

In an unprecedented gesture of kindness, the chief executive officer of Ward's returned all rights back to Bob May. The book became a best seller. Many toy and marketing deals followed and Bob May, now remarried with a growing family, became wealthy from the story he created to comfort his grieving daughter.

But the story doesn't end there either.

Bob's brother-in-law, Johnny Marks, made a song adaptation of *Rudolph*. Though the song was turned down by such popular vocalists as Bing Crosby and Dinah Shore, it was recorded by the singing cowboy, Gene Autry. "Rudolph, the Red-Nosed Reindeer" was released in 1949 and became a phenomenal success, selling more records than any other Christmas song with the exception of "White Christmas."

The gift of love Bob May created for his daughter so long ago kept coming back to bless him again and again. And Bob May learned the lesson, just like his dear friend Rudolph, that being different isn't so bad. In fact, being different can be a blessing.

POST-IT MEDITATION FOR DECEMBER 17
Thank you, God, for creating human beings who are unique and precious in your sight.

December 18

Be sure your love is true love....
~Romans 12:9 (NLV)

Christmas is for love. It is for joy, for giving and sharing, for laughter, for reuniting with family and friends, for tinsel and brightly decorated packages. But mostly, Christmas is for love.

A number of years ago a teacher said she had not believed this until a small elf-like student with wide-eyed innocence and soft rosy cheeks gave her a wondrous gift one Christmas.

Mark was an 11-year-old orphan who lived with his aunt, a bitter, middle-aged woman greatly annoyed with the burden of caring for her dead sister's son. She never failed to remind young Mark, if it hadn't been for her generosity, he would be a vagrant, homeless waif. Still, with all the scolding and hardheartedness at home, he was a sweet and gentle child.

The teacher had not noticed Mark particularly until he began staying after class each day to help straighten up the room. They did this quietly and comfortably, not speaking much, but enjoying the solitude of that hour of the day. When they did talk, Mark spoke mostly of his mother. Though he was quite small when she died, he remembered a kind, gentle, loving woman, who always spent much time with him.

As Christmas drew near, Mark failed to stay after school each day. His teacher looked forward to his coming, and when the days passed and he continued to scamper hurriedly from the room after class, she stopped him one afternoon and asked why he no longer helped her in the room. She told him how she had missed him, and his large gray eyes lit up eagerly as he replied, "Did you really miss me? I've been making you a surprise," he whispered confidentially. "It's for Christmas." With that, he became embarrassed and dashed from the room.

Finally came the last school day before Christmas. Mark crept slowly into the room late that afternoon with his hands concealing something behind his back. "I have your present," he said timidly when his teacher looked up. "I hope you like it." He held out his hands, and there lying in his small palms was a tiny wooden box.

"It's beautiful, Mark. Is there something in it?" she asked, opening the top to look inside.

"Oh, you can't see what's in it," he replied, "and you can't touch it, or taste it or feel it, but mother always said it makes you feel good all the time, warm on cold nights, and safe when you're all alone."

Gazing into the empty box. "What is it, Mark," the teacher asked gently, "that will make me feel so good?"

"It's love," he whispered softly, "and mother always said it's best when you give it away." And he turned and quietly left the room.

For years, the teacher kept the small box, crudely made of scraps of wood, on the piano in her living room and only smiled as inquiring friends raised quizzical eyebrows when she explained to them that it was filled with love.

Yes, Christmas is for gaiety, mirth, and song, for good and wondrous gifts. But mostly, Christmas is for love.

POST-IT MEDITATION FOR DECEMBER 18
Simple gifts are the best gifts.

December 19

We do not want you to be uninformed about those who sleep in death, so that you do not grieve like the rest of mankind, who have no hope. For we believe Jesus died and rose again, and so we believe God will bring with Jesus those who have fallen asleep in him.
~1 Thessalonians 4:13-14 (NIV)

The brand new pastor and his wife, newly assigned to their first ministry (reopening a church in suburban Brooklyn), arrived in early October, excited about their opportunities. When they saw their church, it was very run down and needed much work, but they set a goal to have everything done in time to have their first service on Christmas Eve. They worked hard, repairing pews, plastering and painting walls, and were ahead of schedule by the middle of December. But, on December 19, a driving rainstorm hit the area and lasted two days.

On the 21st, the pastor went over to the church. His heart sank when he saw that the roof had leaked, causing a large area of plaster about 12 feet by 8 feet to fall off the front wall of the sanctuary just behind the pulpit. The pastor cleaned up the mess on the floor, and not knowing what else to do but postpone the Christmas Eve service, headed home. On the way he noticed a local business was having a flea market sale for charity so he stopped in. One of the items was a beautiful, handmade, ivory-colored, crocheted tablecloth with exquisite work, fine colors, and a cross embroidered right in the center. It was just the right size to cover up the hole in the front wall. He bought it and headed back to the church.

By this time it had started to snow. An older woman running from the opposite direction was trying to catch the bus. When she missed it, the pastor invited her to wait in the warm church for the next bus, which ran 45 minutes later. She sat in a pew and paid no attention to the pastor while he got a ladder to put up the tablecloth as a wall tapestry. The pastor could hardly believe how beautiful it looked as it covered up the entire problem area. Then he noticed the woman walking down the center aisle, her face pale. "Pastor," she asked, "where did you get that tablecloth?"

The pastor explained. The woman asked him to check the lower right corner to see if the initials EBG were crocheted into it there. They were. These were the initials of the woman, and she had made this tablecloth 35 years before, in Austria. The woman explained that before the war she and her husband were well-to-do people in Austria, but when the Nazis came, she was forced to leave. Her husband was going to follow her the next week. Sadly, she was captured, sent to prison, and never saw her husband or her home again.

The pastor wanted to give her the tablecloth; but she made the pastor keep it for the church. The pastor insisted on driving her home; it was the least he could do. She lived on the other side of Staten Island and was only in Brooklyn for the day for a housecleaning job.

What a wonderful service they had on Christmas Eve. The church was almost full. The music and the spirit were great. At the end of the service, the pastor and his wife greeted everyone at the door and many said they would return. One older man, whom the pastor recognized from the neighborhood, continued to sit in one of the pews and stare, and the pastor wondered why he wasn't leaving. The man asked him where he got the tablecloth on the front wall because it was identical to one his wife had made years ago when they lived in Austria before the war. How could there be two tablecloths so much alike?

He told the pastor how the Nazis came, how he forced his wife to flee for her safety. Before he could follow her, he was arrested and put in a prison. He never saw his wife or his home again in the next 35 years. The pastor asked him if he would allow him to take him for a little ride. They drove to Staten Island to the same house where the pastor had taken the woman just days earlier. He helped the man climb the three flights of stairs to the woman's apartment and knocked on the door. Then, he witnessed the greatest Christmas reunion he could ever imagine.

December 20

Whoever gives to the poor will not want....
~Proverbs 28:27 (ESV)

The commercialism of Christmas has entangled most of us. Even when we recognize that we spend too much money and place too much emphasis on worldly goods, it is difficult to withdraw from the rhythms of Christmas.

The small, white envelope nestled among the branches of a family's Christmas tree bore no name, no identification, no inscription. Yet, that same envelope had peeked through the branches at this time of the year for the past 10 years or so.

It all began because a man named Mike hated Christmas. It wasn't that he disliked the true meaning of Christmas, but he detested the commercial aspects of it—the overspending, the frantic running around at the last minute to get a tie for grandpa and the dusting powder for grandma, gifts given in desperation because the giver couldn't think of anything else.

Aware of her husband's feelings, Mike's wife made a decision one year to forego the usual shirts, sweaters, ties, and so forth. This year, all that would be replaced with something special for her beloved. Searching, she came up dry, and then the inspiration emerged in an unusual way.

The couple's 12-year-old son was wrestling at the junior level at the school he attended. Shortly before Christmas, a non-league match against a team sponsored by an inner city church produced an idea for Mike's gift. The inner city kids were mostly minorities, dressed in sneakers so ragged that only shoestrings seemed to hold them together. The opponents presented a sharp contrast to their son's team in spiffy blue and gold uniforms, sparkling new wrestling shoes, and fancy headgear. The other team wrestled hard, but the home team ended up walloping them—in every weight class.

Seated beside his wife, Mike shook his head sadly. "I wish just one of them could have won," he exclaimed. "They have a lot of potential, but losing like this could take the heart right out of them." Mike loved kids—all kids. He understood kids in competitive situations, having coached little league football, baseball, and lacrosse. That's when the idea for his present came.

That afternoon, Mike's wife took off to a local sporting goods store and bought an assortment of wrestling headgear and shoes and sent them anonymously to the inner city church. On Christmas Eve, she placed a white envelope on the tree. Inside, she included a note telling Mike what she had done as his gift from her.

She said his smile was a mile-wide that year—and in subsequent years when the tradition was followed each Christmas. One year a group of mentally challenged youngsters got to go to a hockey game. Another year a check was hand-delivered to a pair of elderly brothers whose home had burned to the ground the week before Christmas, and on and on. The envelope became the much-awaited climax of the family's Christmas. Always the final gift opened on Christmas morning, it surpassed new toys and other gifts set aside as the children waited for their dad to take the envelope from the tree and open it. Even as the children grew, the envelope never lost its magic.

Still, the story doesn't end there.

The year Mike died from cancer, when Christmas dawned, the envelope placed on the tree by the grieving widow was joined by three more. Each of the couple's children, unknown to the others, had placed an envelope on the tree for their dad.

What a wonderful tradition to pass down to children and then grandchildren, and maybe great-grandchildren. Perhaps for generations to come, children will watch as their fathers take down their envelopes, understanding the real meaning of Christmas.

AUTHOR'S NOTE: The envelope story first appeared in <u>Woman's Day</u> magazine in 1982. The author, Nancy Gavin, died two years after the story was published, but her family continues the tradition of the white envelopes.

POST-IT MEDITATION FOR DECEMBER 20
This year, I will begin the tradition of the white envelope, spreading the true spirit of Christmas.

December 21

Christmas is more than trees and twinkling lights, more than toys and gifts and baubles of a hundred varieties. It is love. It is the love of the Son of God for all mankind. It is magnificent and beautiful.
~Gordon B. Hinckley, American religious leader and writer

In September 1960, I woke up one morning with six hungry babies and just 75 cents in my pocket. Their father was gone.

The boys ranged from three months to seven years; their sister was two. Their Dad had never been much more than a presence they feared. Whenever they heard his tires crunch on the gravel driveway, they would scramble to hide under their beds.

He did manage to leave $15 a week to buy groceries. Now that he had decided to depart permanently, there would be no more beatings, but no food either. If there was a welfare system in effect in southern Indiana at that time, I certainly *knew nothing about it. I scrubbed the kids until they looked spotless and then put on my best homemade dress, loaded them into the rusty old '51 Chevy and drove off to find a job.*

The seven of us went to every factory, store, and restaurant in our small town. No luck. The kids stayed crammed into the car and tried to be quiet while I attempted to convince whoever would listen that I was willing to learn or do anything. I had to have a job. The last place we went to, just a few miles out of town, was an old Root Beer Barrel drive-in that had been converted to a truck stop. It was called the Big Wheel.

An old lady named Granny owned the place, and she peeked out the window from time to time at all those kids. She needed someone on the graveyard shift, 11 at night until 7 in the morning. She paid 65 cents an hour, and I could start that night. I raced home and called the teenager down the street who babysat for people.

I bargained with her to come and sleep on my sofa for a dollar a night. She could arrive with her pajamas on, and the kids would already be asleep. This seemed like a good arrangement to her, so we made a deal. That night when the little ones and I knelt to say our prayers, we all thanked God for finding Mommy a job. And so I started at the Big Wheel.

When I got home in the mornings I woke the babysitter up and sent her home with one dollar of my tip money—fully half of what my tips averaged every night. As the weeks went by, heating bills added a strain to my meager wage. The tires on the old Chevy had the consistency of penny balloons and began to leak. I had to fill them with air on the way to work and again every morning before I could go home.

One bleak fall morning, I dragged myself to the car to go home and found four tires in the back seat. New tires! There was no note, no nothing, just those beautiful brand new tires. Had angels taken up residence in Indiana I wondered? I made a deal with the local service station. In exchange for his mounting the new tires, I would clean up his office. I remember it took me a lot longer to scrub his floor than it did for him to put on the tires.

I was now working six nights instead of five, and it still wasn't enough. Christmas was coming and I knew there would be no money for toys for the kids. I found a can of red paint and started repairing and painting some old toys— then hid them in the basement so there would be something for Santa to deliver on Christmas morning. Clothes were a worry too. I was sewing patches on top of patches on the boy's pants, and soon they would be too far gone to repair.

On Christmas Eve the usual customers were drinking coffee in the Big Wheel. There were the truckers, Les, Frank, and Jim, and a state trooper named Joe. A few musicians were hanging around after a gig at the Legion and were dropping nickels in the pinball machine. The regulars all just sat around and talked through the wee hours of the morning and then left to get home before the sun came up.

When it was time for me to go home at seven o'clock on Christmas morning, to my amazement, my old battered Chevy was filled full to the top with boxes of all shapes and sizes. I quickly opened the driver's side door, crawled inside and kneeled in the front facing the back seat. Reaching back, I pulled off the lid of the top box. Inside was a whole case of little blue jeans, sizes 2-10! I looked inside another box: It was full of shirts to go with the jeans.

Then I peeked inside some of the other boxes—candy, nuts, bananas, and bags of groceries. An enormous ham for baking, along with canned vegetables and potatoes, was tucked inside. There was pudding and Jell-O and cookies, pie filling and flour. There was a whole bag of laundry supplies and cleaning items. And there were five toy trucks and one beautiful little doll. As I drove back through empty streets as the sun slowly rose on the most amazing Christmas Day of my life, I was sobbing with gratitude. And I will never forget the joy on the faces of my little ones that precious morning.

Yes, there were angels in Indiana that long-ago December. And they all hung out at the Big Wheel truck stop.

POST-IT MEDITATION FOR DECEMBER 21
I will do my part to help someone in need have a joyous Christmas. I will put Christ back in CHRISTmas because without him, there is no reason for the season.

December 22

Think how much the Father loves us. He loves us so much that he lets us be called his children, as we truly are.
~1 John 3:1 (CEV)

In 1994, two Americans answered an invitation from the Russian Department of Education to teach morals and ethics based on biblical principles in the public schools. They were invited to teach at prisons, businesses, fire and police departments, and a large orphanage. About 100 boys and girls who had been abandoned, abused, and left in the care of a government-run program were in the orphanage. One of the Americans relates the following story in his own words:

It was nearing the holiday season, 1994, time for our orphans to hear, for the first time, the traditional story of Christmas. We told them about Mary and Joseph arriving in Bethlehem. Finding no room in the inn, the couple went to a stable, where the baby Jesus was born and placed in a manger.

Throughout the story, the children and orphanage staff sat in amazement as they listened. Some sat on the edges of their stools, trying to grasp every word. Completing the story, we gave the children three small pieces of cardboard to make a crude manger. Each child was given a small paper square, cut from yellow napkins I had brought with me. No colored paper was available in the city.

Following instructions, the children tore the paper and carefully laid strips in the manger for straw. Small squares of flannel, cut from a worn-out nightgown an American lady was throwing away as she left Russia, were used for the baby's blanket. A doll-like baby was cut from tan felt we had brought from the United States.

The orphans were busy assembling their mangers as I walked among them to see if they needed any help. All went well until I got to one table where little Misha sat. He looked to be about six years old and had finished his project. As I glanced at the little boy's manger, I was startled to see not one, but two babies in the manger. Quickly, I called for the translator to ask the lad why there were two babies in the manger.

Crossing his arms in front of him and looking at this completed manger scene, the child began to repeat the story very seriously. For such a young boy, who had only heard the Christmas story once, he related the happenings accurately until he came to the part where Mary put the baby Jesus in the manger. Then Misha started to ad-lib. He made up his own ending to the story as he said, "And when Mary laid the baby in the manger, Jesus looked at me and asked me if I had a place to stay. I told him I have no mamma and I have no papa, so I don't have any place to stay. Then, Jesus told me I could stay with him. But I told him I couldn't, because I didn't have a gift to give him like everybody else did. I wanted to stay with Jesus so much, so I thought about what I had that maybe I could use for a gift. I thought maybe if I kept him warm, that would be a good gift. So I asked Jesus, 'If I keep you warm, will that be a good enough gift?'

"And Jesus told me, 'If you keep me warm, that will be the best gift anybody ever gave me.'

"So I got into the manger, and then Jesus looked at me and he told me I could stay with him...for always."

As little Misha finished his story, his eyes brimmed full of tears that splashed down his little cheeks. Putting his hand over his face, his head dropped to the table, and his shoulders shook as he sobbed and sobbed. The little orphan had found someone who would never abandon or abuse him, someone who would stay with him forever.

POST-IT MEDITATION FOR DECEMBER 22
It's not what you have in your life, but the savior you have in your life that counts.

December 23

Contribute to the needs of the saints and seek to show hospitality.
~Romans 12:13 (ESV)

In the hustle and bustle of holidays, pausing to help someone in need will warm our hearts and turn our thoughts to the real meaning of Christmas.

A lady hurried into the local department store to grab some last minute Christmas gifts. Looking at the horde of people, she grumbled to herself: "I'll be in here forever, and I have so much to do." Christmas was beginning to become such a drag she wanted to just sleep through the season. But she hurried through all the people to the toy department, mumbling at the prices of all the toys, wondering if the grandkids would even play with them.

When she reached the doll aisle, out of the corner of her eye she saw a little boy, about five, holding a lovely doll, touching her hair and holding her gently. Drawn to the child, the lady kept looking over at him and wondered who the doll was for. She watched him turn to a woman, and he called his aunt by name and said, "Are you sure I don't have enough money?"

The woman replied a bit impatiently, "You know you don't have enough money for it." The aunt told the little boy not to go anywhere while she went to get some other things—she would be back in a few minutes. And then she left the aisle.

The boy continued to hold the doll. After a bit the lady asked the boy who the doll was for. He said, "It is the doll my sister wanted so badly for Christmas. She just knew Santa would bring it." With a smile, the lady told him maybe Santa was going to bring it.

He said, "No, Santa can't go where my sister is...I have to give the doll to my Mama to take to her."

When she asked him where his sister was, he looked up with the saddest eyes and said, "She has gone to be with Jesus. My Daddy says Mama is going to have to go be with her. I told my Daddy to tell Mama not to go yet. I told him to tell her to wait till I got back from the store."

Her heart overflowing with love, the lady handed the child the money for the doll. He softly said, "Thank you, Jesus, for giving me enough money." Then he said, "I asked Jesus to give me enough money to buy this doll, so Mama can take it with her to give to my sister. And he heard my prayer. I wanted to ask him for enough to buy my Mama a white rose, but I didn't ask him. Now I have enough to buy the doll and a rose for my Mama. She loves white roses."

Two days later, the lady read in the paper about a drunk driver hitting a car, killing a little girl and leaving the mother in serious condition. Now the family had disconnected life support, and the young woman had died. The lady could not forget the little boy and kept wondering if the two were somehow connected. Later that day, she could not help herself and bought some white roses, taking them to the funeral home where the young woman was. And there she lay in a casket, holding a lovely white rose and the beautiful doll.

The lady left in tears, her life changed forever. The love the boy had for his little sister and his mother was overwhelming. And in a split second a drunk driver had ripped the life of that little boy to pieces. But he still trusted Jesus, and Jesus had answered his prayer.

POST-IT MEDITATION FOR DECEMBER 23
Thank you, God, for answered prayers, for little boys, and for angels of mercy.

December 24

...He loved his son, but he decided to send him.
~Mark 12:6 (ERV)

There was once a man who didn't believe in God, and he didn't hesitate to let others know how he felt about religion and religious holidays like Christmas. His wife, however, did believe, and she raised their children to have faith in God and Jesus, despite her husband's disparaging comments.

One snowy Christmas Eve, the wife was taking their children to a Christmas Eve service in the farm community in which they lived. She asked her spouse to come, but he refused. "That story is nonsense!" he said. "Why would God lower himself to come to earth as a man? That's ridiculous!" So she and the children left, and he stayed home.

A while later, the winds grew stronger, and the snow turned into a blizzard. As the man looked out the window, all he saw was a blinding snowstorm. He sat down to relax before the fire for the evening. Then he heard a loud thump. Something had hit the window. Then another thump. He looked out but couldn't see more than a few feet. When the snow let up a little, he ventured outside to see what could have been beating on his window. In the field near his house he saw a flock of wild geese. Apparently they had been flying south for the winter when they got caught in the snowstorm and could not go on. They were lost and stranded on his farm, with no food or shelter. They just flapped their wings and flew around the field in low circles, blindly and aimlessly. A couple of them had flown into his window, it seemed.

The man felt sorry for the geese and wanted to help them. The barn would be a great place for them to stay, he thought. It was warm and safe; surely they could spend the night and wait out the storm. So he walked over to the barn and opened the doors wide, then watched and waited, hoping they would notice the open barn and go inside. But the geese just fluttered around aimlessly and did not seem to notice the barn or realize what it could mean for them. The man tried to get their attention, but that just seemed to scare them and they moved further away. He went into the house and came back out with some bread, broke it up, and made a breadcrumb trail leading to the barn. They still didn't catch on. Now he was getting frustrated. He got behind them and tried to shoo them toward the barn, but they only got more scared and scattered in every direction except toward the barn. Nothing he did could get them to go into the barn where they would be warm and safe.

"Why don't they follow me?!" he exclaimed. "Can't they see this is the only place where they can survive the storm?" He thought for a moment and realized that they wouldn't follow a human. "If only I were a goose, then I could save them," he said out loud. Then he had an idea. He went into the barn, got one of his own geese, and carried it in his arms as he circled around behind the flock of wild geese. He then released it. His goose flew through the flock and straight into the barn—and one by one the other geese followed it to safety.

He stood silently for a moment as the words he had spoken a few minutes earlier replayed in his mind: "If only I were a goose, then I could save them!" Then he thought about what he had said to his wife earlier. "Why would God want to be like us? That's ridiculous!" Suddenly it all made sense. That is what God had done. We were like the geese— blind, lost, perishing. God had his son become like us so he could show us the way and save us. That was the meaning of Christmas, he realized. As the winds and blinding snow died down, his soul became quiet and pondered this wonderful thought. Suddenly he understood what Christmas was all about, why Christ had come. Years of doubt and disbelief vanished like the passing storm. He fell to his knees in the snow and prayed his first prayer: "Thank You, Jesus, for coming in human form to show me the way out of the storm!"

SOURCE OF GOOSE STORY: http://www.inspirationalarchive.com

POST-IT MEDITATION FOR DECEMBER 24
Help me to follow Christ wherever he leads.

December 25

And the Lord God made all kinds of trees grow out of the ground—trees that were pleasing to the eye and good for food.
~Genesis 2:9 (NIV)

Deciduous trees are barren now, stripped of their amber and crimson leaves by winter's harsh winds and frigid nights. But even exposed and unprotected, disrobed of their glory, the trees display a different kind of beauty. Like the jack pine described by author Douglas Wood, "in the calligraphy of [their] shape against the sky is written strength of character and perseverance, survival of wind, drought, cold, heat, disease." It is a design created by God, and as French writer Francois-Rene de Chateaubriand wrote, "Forests were the first temples of the

Divinity, and it is in the forests that men have grasped the first idea of architecture."

But trees give us more than noteworthy designs. In the late 1800s, Lucy Larcom penned a poem about the meaning of trees, telling us that when we plant a tree, we plant hope. Even bared and naked, trees remind us rebirth will come with the spring rains. And, as we learn in Job 14: 7-9 (NIV): "If it is cut down, it will sprout again, and its new shoots will not fail. Its roots may grow old in the ground and its stump die in the soil, yet at the scent of water it will bud and put forth shoots like a plant."

Spiritually, trees play a unique role in the Jewish and Christian scriptures, from the Garden of Eden to the wooden manger to Christ's cross. They represent the best and worst of mankind. Since the beginning of time, they have been there to serve us in many ways. Perhaps the most meaningful of all trees are those used to celebrate Christmas.

It was December 25, 1914, only five months into World War I. German, British, and French soldiers, already sick and tired of the senseless killing, disobeyed their superiors and fraternized with "the enemy" along two-thirds of the Western Front (a crime punishable by death in times of war). German troops held Christmas trees up out of the trenches with signs that read, "Merry Christmas."

"You no shoot, we no shoot." Thousands of troops streamed across a no-man's land strewn with rotting corpses. They sang Christmas carols, exchanged photographs of loved ones back home, shared rations, played football, even roasted some pigs. Soldiers embraced men they had been trying to kill a few short hours before. They agreed to warn each other if the top brass forced them to fire their weapons—and to aim high.

A shudder ran through the high command on both sides. Here was disaster in the making: soldiers declaring their brotherhood with each other and refusing to fight. Opposing generals declared this spontaneous peacemaking to be treasonous and subject to court martial. By March 1915 the fraternization movement had been eradicated, and the killing machine put back in full operation. By the time of the armistice in 1918, fifteen million would be slaughtered. But for that one day, Christmas trees became a gesture of good will and peace on earth.

"Trees can reduce the heat of a summer's day, quiet a highway's noise, feed the hungry, provide shelter from the wind and warmth in the winter. You see, the forests are the sanctuaries not only of wildlife, but also of the human spirit. And every tree is a compact between generations" (George Bush, 41st U.S. President). Moreover, for many, when the spirit returns to God, the body will be buried "at the foot of a friendly tree… That this dust may rise and rejoice among the branches." As we await our second birth, how comforting it is that we may be part of "a tree that looks at God all day and lifts her leafy arms to pray" (Joyce Kilmer, "Trees," 1914).

Today, we celebrate the birth of the one who gives us that second birth. Christmas trees glitter and shine, casting light on all the packages beneath their branches. But the true celebration of Christmas is not found in those gifts—it is found in the hearts of men like those who shared peace and good will on December 25, 1914.

POST-IT MEDITATION FOR DECEMBER 25
Thank you, God, for trees...that provide relief from summer heat,
turn from green to amber and crimson and back again,
wear nests of sparrows in their branches, and look heavenward every day
as we await our rebirth.
But most of all, God, thank you for the true spirit of Christmas, even in a
war-torn world.

December 26

They will know we are Christians by our love.
~Peter Scholtes and Carolyn Arends, song writers

Christmas is over. We have been reminded of the love of God, the gift of his son, and the deep love for us that led him to the cross to die for our sins. But on the day after celebrating his birth, will that love live in our hearts?

His name is Bill. He has wild hair, wears a T-shirt with holes in it, jeans, and no shoes. This was literally his wardrobe for his entire four years of college. He is brilliant. Kind of esoteric and very, very bright. He became a Christian recently while attending college.

Across the street from the campus is a well-dressed, very conservative church. One day just after Christmas, Bill decided to go there. He walked in with no shoes, jeans, his T-shirt, and wild hair. The service had already started, but Bill started down the aisle looking for a seat. The church was completely packed, and he couldn't find a place to sit. By now people were really looking a bit uncomfortable, but no one said anything. Bill got closer and closer and closer to the pulpit and, when he realized there were no seats, he just squatted down right on the carpet. (Although perfectly acceptable behavior at a college fellowship, this had never happened in this church before!)

By now the people were really uptight, and the tension in the air was thick. About this time, the minister realized, from way at the back of the church, an elder was slowly making his way toward Bill. The elder was in his eighties, had silver-gray hair, and wore a three-piece suit. A godly man, very elegant, very dignified, very courtly. He walked with a cane and, as he started walking toward this boy, everyone was saying to themselves that you couldn't blame him for what he was going to do. How could you expect a man of his age and background to understand some college kid on the floor? It took a long time for the man to reach the boy. The church was utterly silent except for the clicking of the man's cane. All eyes were focused on him. You couldn't even hear anyone breathing. The minister couldn't preach the sermon until the elder did what he had to do. And now they saw this elderly man drop his cane on the floor. With great difficulty he lowered himself and sat down next to Bill and worshiped with him so he wouldn't be alone.

Everyone choked up with emotion. When the minister gained control, he said, "What I'm about to preach, you will never remember. What you have just seen, you will never forget. Be careful how you live. You may be the only Bible some people will ever read."

When we live and act with love in our hearts, we will be known as Christians. As the old hymn says, "We are one in the spirit; we are one in the Lord...We will work with each other, we will work side by side... And we'll guard each one's dignity and save each one's pride."

POST-IT MEDITATION FOR DECEMBER 26
I pray that others will know I am a Christian by my love.

December 27

God, you answer our prayers and do what is right. You do amazing things to save us. People all over the world know they can trust in you, even those who live across the sea.
~Psalm 65:5 (ERV)

Most of us don't think about General George Patton at Christmas, likely because his name conjures up pictures of war, not thoughts of "peace on earth, good will toward men." So began an article in the *Nashville Banner* on December 8, 1993. Ruth Ann Leach, the columnist, was reporting on a Christmas story called "Old Blood and Guts" to be presented by Larry Gates, a man who performs inspirational one-man shows on biblical and patriotic topics. I had the pleasure of seeing "Old Blood and Guts" many years later, and I was reminded of the story recently as I thought of our troops who are in harm's way to protect our freedom during this Christmas season.

Larry's research was impeccable—he had talked with people who had actually been with Patton, he says. "I talked with them about what he was like and what happened during the Christmas of 1944." As he talks about his monologue, his face brightens with the delight of a true story-teller.

"In late December, Patton's patience had, they say, long since boiled over. The German general was beating the hell out of the Allied armies, specifically the 101st Airborne division holding out in Bastogne," Larry explains, setting the scene.

"The weather was terrible, which prevented air support from coming to help the Allied troops. The prediction was for more cold, snow, rain, and rotten weather." He adds, "Patton was a deeply devout, religious man whose faith was a very important part of his normal workday. He frequently had talks with God. He had one of those talks on December 23, 1944, when he was very angry with God about the weather."

It so happens this particular conversation between Patton and God was overheard by a chaplain. When Patton concluded his ranting and railing against God, the chaplain sat down to talk with the General. Humbly, Patton asked the man of God to write a prayer to be printed on the other side of Patton's Christmas message to his troops. At noon on December 24, it was printed and distributed to the soldiers:

"Almighty and most merciful Father, we humbly beseech Thee, of Thy great goodness, to restrain these immoderate rains with which we have to contend. Grant us fair weather for battle. Graciously harken to us as soldiers who call upon Thee that armed with Thy power, we may advance from victory to victory, and crush the oppression and wickedness of our enemies, and establish Thy justice among men and nations. Amen."

Astonishingly, Larry declares, "In a matter of four hours, the weather changed dramatically for the first time in two weeks. The sun broke out. The airplanes, the fighters, the bombers, all came out and trapped the German army. On Christmas Day, the 4th Armored Division was in sight of Bastogne, and by December 27, the Germans were in rapid retreat."

POST-IT MEDITATION FOR DECEMBER 27
God, help me to believe in the power of prayer.

December 28

That out of his glorious, unlimited resources he will empower you with inner strength through his spirit.
~Ephesians 3:16 (NLT)

Norman Vincent Peale, in The Power of Positive Thinking*, tells about a golfing day when he bemoaned hitting his ball into the rough, saying he would never get it out of the high grass. A fellow golfer brought Peale up short when he asked, "Didn't I read something about positive thinking in your book?" He then challenged Peale to use that kind of thinking on the golf course.*

447

"The rough is only mental. In other words, it is rough because you think it is. In your mind you have decided that here is an obstacle which will cause you difficulty. The power to overcome this obstacle is in your mind. If you visualize lifting the ball out of the rough, believing you can do it, your mind will transfer flexibility, rhythm, and power to your muscles, and you will handle the club in such a manner that the ball will rise right out of there in a beautiful shot. All you need to do is to keep your eye on that ball and tell yourself you are going to lift it out of the grass with a lovely stroke." And that's exactly what Peale did—and he says with the shot he gained a gem of wisdom for which he was forever grateful.

The rough is only mental. Obstacles and problems are real, but if we think we can overcome them, we can. Peale encourages us to remember this formula: "I think victory" equals "I get victory." He suggests we write the words down on a piece of paper and stick it on our mirror, on our desk, or in our wallet, reading the words aloud over and over until "the truth drives into the depths of your consciousness, until it permeates your whole mental attitude, until it becomes a positive obsession."

With God's help, no obstacle is too large, no problem too serious, no trial too great to overcome. What happens, though, is that we speak "defeat speech." We tell ourselves over and over, sometimes for days and even weeks or months, there is nothing we can do to get past an issue. Our heads become filled with negative thoughts, and we give up before we even make an effort. Peale, who declared, "I believe God will always make a way where there is no way," offers the solution to the vicious cycle of negativity. It's worth trying.

POST-IT MEDITATION FOR DECEMBER 28
I THINK VICTORY = I GET VICTORY

December 29

Then the angel showed me the river of the water of life, bright as crystal, flowing from the throne of God and of the Lamb through the middle of the street of the city; also, on either side of the river, the tree of life with its twelve kinds of fruit, yielding its fruit each month. The leaves of the tree were for the healing of the nations. No longer will there be anything accursed, but the throne of God and of the Lamb will be in it, and his servants will worship him. They will see his face, and his name will be on their foreheads. And night will be no more. They will need no light of lamp or sun, for the Lord God will be their light, and they will reign forever and ever.
~Revelation 22:1-5 (ESV)

There was a young woman who had been diagnosed with a terminal illness and had been given three months to live. As she was getting her things "in order," she contacted her pastor and had him come to her house to discuss certain aspects of her final wishes. She told him which songs she wanted sung at the service, what scriptures she would like read, and the outfit she wanted to be buried in. With her wishes carefully written, the pastor was preparing to leave when the young woman suddenly remembered something very important to her.

"There's one more thing," she said excitedly.

"What's that?" the pastor asked.

"This is very important," the young woman continued. "I want to be buried with a fork in my right hand."

The minister stood looking at the young woman, not knowing quite what to say.

The young woman explained. "My grandmother once told me this story, and from that time on I have always tried to pass along its message to those I love and those who are in need of encouragement.

"In all my years of attending socials and dinners, I always remember when the dishes of the main course were being cleared, someone would inevitably lean over and say, 'Keep your fork.' It was my favorite part because I knew something better was coming...like velvety chocolate cake or deep-dish apple pie. Something wonderful, and with substance!

"So, when people see me in that casket with a fork in my hand, I want them to wonder, 'What's with the fork?' Then I want you to tell them: 'Keep your fork, the best is yet to come.'"

The eyes of the man of God welled up with tears of joy as he hugged the young woman good-bye. He knew this would be one of the last times he would see her before her death. But he also knew the young woman had a better grasp of heaven than he did. She had a deeper awareness of what heaven would be like than many people twice her age, with twice as much experience and knowledge.

She KNEW something better was coming.

At the funeral, as people walked by the young woman's casket, they saw the cloak she was wearing and the fork placed in her right hand. Over and over, the pastor heard the question, "What's with the fork?" And over and over, he smiled.

During his message, the pastor told the people of the conversation he had with the young woman shortly before she died. He also told them about the fork and what it symbolized to her. He told the people how he could not stop thinking about the fork and told them they probably would not be able to stop thinking about it either.

He was right. So the next time you reach down for your fork let it remind you, ever so gently, that the best is yet to come.

POST-IT MEDITATION FOR DECEMBER 29
I am keeping my fork....

449

December 30

If you abide in me, and my words abide in you, ask whatever you wish, and it will be done for you.
~John 15:7 (ESV)

Have you ever wished you had the faith to move a mountain—or even had a desire to witness such an awesome answer to prayer? One small group of believers proved to their entire congregation that miracles do happen.

A small congregation in the foothills of the Great Smoky Mountains built a new sanctuary on a piece of land willed to them by a church member. Ten days before the new church was to open, the local building inspector informed the pastor the parking lot was inadequate for the size of the building. Until the church doubled the size of the parking lot, they would not be able to use the new sanctuary.

Unfortunately, the church with its undersized parking lot had used every inch of their land except for the mountain against which it had been built. In order to build more parking spaces, they would have to move the mountain out of the back yard.

Undaunted, the pastor announced the next Sunday morning he would meet that evening with all members who had "mountain-moving faith." They would hold a prayer session asking God to remove the mountain from the back yard and to somehow provide enough money to have it paved and painted before the scheduled opening dedication service the following week.

At the appointed time, 24 of the congregation's 300 members assembled for prayer. They prayed for nearly three hours. At ten o'clock the pastor said the final "Amen."

"We'll open next Sunday as scheduled," he assured everyone. "God has never let us down before, and I believe he will be faithful this time too."

The next morning as he was working in his study there came a loud knock at his door. When he called, "Come in," a rough-looking construction foreman appeared, removing his hard hat as he entered.

"Excuse me, Reverend. I'm from Acme Construction Company over in the next county. We're building a huge new shopping mall over there, and we need some fill dirt. Would you be willing to sell us a chunk of that mountain behind the church? We'll pay you for the dirt we remove and pave all the exposed area free of charge, if we can have it right away. We can't do anything else until we get the dirt in and allow it to settle properly."

The little church was dedicated the next Sunday as originally planned, and there were far more members with "mountain-moving faith" on opening Sunday than there had been the previous week!

POST-IT MEDITATION FOR DECEMBER 30
Help me, God, to have faith large enough to
accept your miracles.

December 31

The saying is trustworthy and deserving of full acceptance, that Christ Jesus came into the world to save sinners.
~1 Timothy 1:15 (ESV)

As the old year draws to a close and we look to the future, most of us will be setting goals. The following suggestions might help:

Do not set your goals by what other people deem important. Only God knows what is best for you.

Do not take for granted the things closest to your heart. Cling to them as you would your life, for without them, life is meaningless.

Do not let your life slip through your fingers by living in the past nor for the future. By living your life one day at a time, you live all the days of your life.

Do not give up when you have something to give. Nothing is really over until the moment you stop trying. It is a fragile thread that binds us to each other.

Do not be afraid to encounter risks. It is by taking chances we learn how to be brave.

Do not shut love out of your life by saying it is impossible to find. The quickest way to receive love is to give love. The fastest way to lose love is to hold it too tightly.

Do not dismiss your dreams. To be without dreams is to be without hope. To be without hope is to be without purpose.

Do not run through life so fast that you forget, not only where you have been, but also where you are going. Life is not a race, but a journey to be savored each step of the way as you walk with God.

And, if you are wondering why God would want you, these words from an unknown writer might convince you:

"I'm not perfect. I have all kinds of problems. I have no ability. I have no gifts. I'm just not worthy. Why would God want me?"

The writer offered an answer: "Well, did you know that Moses stuttered; Timothy had ulcers; Hosea's wife was a prostitute; Amos' only training was in the school of fig-tree pruning; Jacob was a liar; David had an affair; Abraham was too old; David was too young; Peter was afraid of death; Lazarus was dead; John was self-righteous; Naomi was a widow; Paul was a persecutor of the church; Moses was a murderer; Jonah ran from God's will; Miriam was a gossip; Gideon and Thomas both doubted; Jeremiah was depressed and suicidal; Elijah was burned out; John the Baptist was a loudmouth; Martha was a worry-wart; Noah got drunk."

One can almost imagine the smile on the writer's face as she added, "Did I mention that Moses had a short fuse? So did Peter, Paul…well, lots of folks did."

God doesn't require a job interview for salvation. He's our Heavenly Father. He doesn't look at financial gain or loss. He's not prejudiced or partial, not judging, grudging, sassy, or brassy, not deaf to our cry, not blind to our need. He knows who we are and what we are and loves us in spite of ourselves.

Satan says to you, "You're not worthy."

Jesus says to Satan, "So what? I am."

Satan looks back and sees your mistakes.

God looks back and sees the cross.

God doesn't calculate where you messed up in the year now ending. It's not even on the record.

Unquestionably, there are lots of reasons why God shouldn't call us. But if we love him, if we hunger for him, he'll use us in spite of who we are, where we've been, what we have done, or the fact that we are not perfect! Remember, God doesn't call the equipped; he equips the called. He'll always be there to love and guide you on to great days in the new year that begins tomorrow.

POST-IT MEDITATION FOR DECEMBER 31
Thank you, God, for being willing to use me despite my weaknesses.

452

AN INDIAN PRAYER

O GREAT SPIRIT,

Whose voice I hear in the winds, And whose breath gives life to all the world, hear me! I am small and weak. I need your strength and wisdom.

Let me walk in beauty, and make my eyes ever behold the red and purple sunset.

Make my hands respect the things you have made and my ears sharp to hear your voice.

Make me wise so that I may understand the things you have taught your people.

Let me learn the lessons you have hidden in every leaf and rock and cloud.

I seek strength, not to be greater than my brother, but to fight my greatest enemy—myself.

Make me always ready to come to you with clean hands and straight eyes.

So when my life fades, as the fading sunset, my spirit may come to you without shame.

--St. Ignatius Mission, Montana

Translations Used

AKJV	American King James Version
AMP	Amplified Bible
ASV	American Standard Version
CEB	Common English Bible
CEV	Contemporary English Version
DRV	Douay-Rheims 1899 American Edition
ERV	Easy to Read Version
ESV	English Standard Version
ESVUK	English Standard Version Anglicized
GNB	Good News Bible
GNT	Good News Translation
GW	God's Word Translation
KJV	King James Version
KJ21	21st Century King James Version
NASB	New American Standard Bible
NCV	New Century Version
NIRV	New International Reader's Version
NKJV	New King James Version
NIV	New International Version
NLV	New Life Version
NLT	New Living Translation
PNT	J. B. Phillips New Testament
TLB	The Living Bible
WE	Worldwide English

Clouds come floating into my life, no longer to carry
rain or usher storm, but to add color to my sunset sky.
—Rabindranath Tagore, Indian poet

Made in the USA
Middletown, DE
23 May 2016